SOLON AND THESPIS

SOLON AND THESPIS

Law and Theater in the English Renaissance

---

edited by

DENNIS KEZAR

UNIVERSITY OF NOTRE DAME PRESS
NOTRE DAME, INDIANA

Copyright © 2007 by University of Notre Dame
Notre Dame, Indiana 46556
www.undpress.nd.edu
All Rights Reserved

Published in the United States of America

Library of Congress Cataloging-in-Publication Data

Solon and Thespis : law and theater in the English Renaissance /
   edited by Dennis Kezar.
      p. cm.
   Includes bibliographical references and index.
   ISBN-13: 978-0-268-03313-2 (pbk. : alk. paper)
   ISBN-10: 0-268-03313-7 (pbk. : alk. paper)
      1. English drama—Early modern and Elizabethan, 1500–1600—History and criticism.
2. English drama—17th century—History and criticism.   3. Law and literature—England—
History—16th century.   4. Law and literature—England—History—17th century.
5. Law in literature.   I. Kezar, Dennis, 1968– .
   PR658.L38S66   2006
   822'.309—dc22

                                                                                           2006023896

∞ *The paper in this book meets the guidelines for permanence and durability of
the Committee on Production Guidelines for Book Longevity of the Council on Library Resources.*

For Heather, with love and gratitude

Contents

Introduction   1
  – *Dennis Kezar*

JONSON AND THE TRIBE OF LAW

ONE
Trial by Theater: Jonson, Marston, and Dekker in the Court of Parnassus   19
  – *Matthew Greenfield*

TWO
The Law versus the Marketplace in Jonson's *Bartholomew Fair*   40
  – *Paul Cantor*

THREE
Ben Jonson and London Courtrooms   64
  – *Frances Teague*

LEGAL RHETORIC AND THEATRICAL PRESSURE

FOUR
"They took from me the use of mine own house": Land Law in Shakespeare's *Lear* and Shakespeare's Culture   81
  – *Heather Dubrow*

Contents

viii

FIVE
Sycorax's "Thing"   99
— *Ernest B. Gilman*

SIX
The Witch of Edmonton and the Guilt of Possession   124
— *Dennis Kezar*

LAW STAGED AND THEORY TROUBLED

SEVEN
"Paper Bullets": Texts, Lies, and Censorship in Early Modern England   163
— *Debora Shuger*

EIGHT
"So Many Books, So Many Rolls of Ancient Time":
The Inns of Court and *Gorboduc*   197
— *Karen J. Cunningham*

NINE
The Rich Cabinet: Bacon, Chapman, and the Culture of Corruption   218
— *Luke Wilson*

Epilogue: The True Image of Authority   264
— *Deak Nabers*

Contributors   289

Index   291

Introduction

Dennis Kezar

In the archetypal confrontation from which our volume takes its title, the Athenian lawmaker blames the first man of the theater for a professional deceit that threatens to pervade society:

> Thespis, at this time, beginning to act tragedies, and the thing, because it was new, taking very much with the multitude, though it was not yet made a matter of competition, Solon, being by nature fond of hearing and learning something new, and now, in his old age, living idly, and enjoying himself, indeed, with music and with wine, went to see Thespis himself, as the ancient custom was, act; and after the play was done, he addressed him, and asked him if he was not ashamed to tell so many lies before such a number of people; and Thespis replying that it was no harm to say or do so in a play, Solon vehemently struck his staff against the ground: "Ay," said he, "if we honor and commend such play as this, we shall find it some day in our business."[1]

By responding anxiously to the hypocrisy of acting, Solon gives voice to what Jonas Barish has termed the "antitheatrical prejudice." Central to this prejudice is the belief that theater confuses pointless *play* with purposeful *business*, just as an "ontologically subversive" stage debases privileged truth.[2] Allegorically, Solon's criticism of Thespis directs us to a fundamental motivation of this volume: exchanges between theater and law frequently take shape as an institutional antagonism over the tenuous distinction between theater's inconsequential fiction and the real world's socially consequential fact. While this antagonism has often had the effect of separating theater and law as objects of study, it can itself be revelatory of their important institutional connections and interdependences. Even as they are each in their own way influenced by such antagonism, the essays collected here investigate the transactions between theater and law that Solon's hostility seeks to prevent.

By focusing on the connections between law and theater, this volume foregrounds a disciplinary relation just beginning to emerge from Solon's pronouncement. And by focusing on the professional theater of the English Renaissance, this volume engages a historical period when Solon's distinction between "play" and "our business" had become markedly and importantly untenable, when a culture's claim that "all the world's a stage" had stretched metaphor to tautology. Organizing our study is an emphasis both generic and historical that responds to a crucial moment in England's cultural and legal formation when both theater and law were emerging as increasingly secular and increasingly powerful institutions. If Solon feared the future relevance of drama to the real world of commerce and law, the Renaissance experienced this relevance as reciprocal. Its legal processes were subject to dramatic representation and appropriation. Its commercial theater was not simply subversive of the law but also subject to the law and often populated by law students and practitioners. Indeed theater and law were not simply relevant to each other in the early modern period; they participated with each other and defined an institutional co-presence. In the following essays, we demonstrate some of the important consequences of this fact by presenting the connections between Renaissance theater and law not simply as thematic but as conceptual and substantive.

The "law and literature movement" describes a space in which institutional momentum and interdisciplinary inquiry meet with often intriguing but frequently short-lived and theoretically inarticulate results. Few can define this "field" compellingly or lastingly enough to describe what would amount to an orthodoxy, let alone an intervention.[3]

The intervention intended by this volume is relatively modest in scope, but that scope is aimed at a moving target. We hope, in a sustained and unified way, to bring Renaissance law and Renaissance theater into the same interpretive realm and to insist upon the neglected scholarly importance of this nexus. But there is a double-barreled, much less modest claim subtending this first. We believe that theater and law (not only in the slice of historicity we cut but also transhistorically) *require* the other for themselves to be fully understood; and we believe that in the amorphous movement to which this volume appeals (the movement of "law and literature") connections between theater and law have constituted a perennial blind spot. A case for this grander claim need not be made with contemporary bibliography.[4] It could begin with Solon versus Thespis, then course through some of the entrenched positions graphed by Professor Barish, then dwell upon the vexed relations between nineteenth-century British law and that period's drama,[5] and conclude with Alan Dershowitz's contemporary reenactment of Solon's encounter with Thespis.

Dershowitz vehemently calls for the exclusion of literary (and specifically dramatic) forms from the courtroom. Confusing generic and literary epistemologies with "real" forensics can only corrupt the latter. He specifically objects to the importation of drama into the legal process—claiming that this "art form" is essentially scripted and prejudicial, failing accurately to imitate the chaos of the real: "[The] critical dichotomy between teleological rules of drama and interpretation, on the one hand, and mostly random rules of real life, on the other, has profoundly important implications for our legal system. When we import the narrative form of storytelling into our legal system, we confuse fiction with fact and endanger the truth-finding function of the adjudicative process."[6] Consider the timelessness of this complaint. Like Solon's desire to exclude "play" from "our business," Dershowitz's insistence on a "critical dichotomy" between the form of drama and the "real life" of the law attempts to drive a disciplinary wedge between theater's corrupting fictions and the law's endangered fact.[7] Dershowitz's articulation of this dichotomy offers an explicit example of the way Solon's antitheatrical legacy structures much current thinking about the proper relation between law and literature.

The danger Dershowitz identifies lies in a formal or generic contagion that threatens to invade the legal system, converting its human beings into characters. His "real life" is best judged without the lens of genre, his law most effective when kept discrete from the forms of literature. While some recent studies of law and literature—including several of the essays in this volume—admit and even celebrate genre's function in the judicial process, law and literature have generally been conceived as divided by the fact that one is more generic than the other. For law and literature figures such as Martha Nussbaum, to give just one example, Dershowitz's dichotomy is simply reversed, with literature's humanism offering an important corrective to the law's formalism.

Genre, in other words, is itself a contagion in the law and literature movement. As I wrote this introduction, I had several readers' reports in front of me, one of which claims that the majority of the essays that follow treat Renaissance theater as "superfluous" to their interest in law, and one of which claims that these same essays are strong readings of Renaissance plays that regrettably treat law and legal history in a "subordinate" and sometimes "tangential" manner. We believe that an important value of this volume lies in its diversity, but it would be wrong for us to present that diversity as a challenge to current disciplinary divisions without also admitting its status as a symptom of such divisions.[8]

It would also be wrong for us to overstate our case. In today's law schools and English departments there is, of course, a vital and diverse interest in law and literature that attests to a general blurring of the boundaries that Solon and Dershowitz seek to preserve.[9] Moreover, both literary critics and legal historians have begun to consider theater more specifically in the law and literature field. A growing body of scholarship on Shakespeare and the common law, for instance, recognizes important connections between developing legal ideas and methods of dramatic representation.[10] And historians such as Theodore Ziolkowski have traced the origins of and important transitions in Greek drama to Greek law and the development of jury trial.[11] In this analysis, early Greek drama frequently engages precisely the kinds of questions a trial might pose and resolves those questions in part (through a chorus) as a jury might. When he applies this approach (briefly) to *The Merchant of Venice*, Ziolkowski avoids the narrativizing tendencies of most legal readings of drama to ask questions such as those we wish to ask in this volume: "What if it were Shakespeare's intention not to advocate either the need for strict liability or the appeal of equity but to expose the unpredictability of the legal system in which Shylock and Portia encounter each other? What if it were his aim not to contrast Venice and Belmont but to reveal the anomy governing the society that embraces them both? If we read the play in this way, in the legal and social context of the 1590s, we lose a romantic comedy, but we gain a remarkable commentary on Elizabethan England."[12] Ziolkowski's study of an emergent drama and emergent law in Greece has offered an important precedent for our own volume, which focuses on a similar moment of legal and theatrical emergence in Renaissance England.

Drama has more typically been elided, however, from investigations of law and literature that concern genre. Broadly speaking, the study of law and literature has tended to focus on literary genres other than the more inclusive dramatic mode. The literary kinds most frequently associated with law have been lyric and narrative. Lyric has gained prominence when scholars have conceived as structural the legal issues in which "law and literature" is invested. In such approaches, literature is deployed to challenge or call attention to those structures on which the law allegedly relies. In the hands of Nussbaum, for instance, lyric comes to stand for the entire enterprise of self-conscious reflection—which, she claims, good judges perform by imaginatively placing themselves in the subject position of an other.[13] In some of Barbara Johnson's more recent work a similar claim emerges, though in her case the lyric is less a normative structure to which judges should be accountable than a form of subjectivity that the law should acknowledge as an essential part of the very category of the human. Hence the law's normative accounts of persons should be replaced with those of poets.[14]

Dershowitz's silent conflation of "drama" with "the narrative form of storytelling" points to another general tendency to subordinate drama in generic investigations of law and literature. When "law and literature" has been less concerned with the differing ways in which law and literature conceive of persons, and with finding solutions to these conflicts, it has tended to focus upon the methods by which the law generates and sanctions accounts of these conflicts. Here the generic emphasis seems decidedly narrative. But we might say that the emphasis is actually more epistemological than generic. Wai Chee Dimock praises literature for its principled refusal to honor the claims of narrative truth required by the law. Reversing Dershowitz's argument, she holds that "literature" requires skepticism and that the conventions of "law" involve epistemological errors that literature's skepticism exposes. Consequently, Dimock is interested in essentially narrative generic forms like the novel, especially the realist novel.[15] Some scholars have developed a similar analysis of the narrative content of dramatic works by treating them as narrative forms. While I shall suggest below the virtues of resisting the narrativizing of drama in analysis interested in the law, conceiving the relation between literature and law as one of skepticism versus fideism offers a limited but useful approach to investigating the law-theater connection. An important aspect of the law-theater dynamic explored by several essays in this volume, in fact, lies not only in the stage's ontological subversiveness but in its *epistemological* subversiveness—its challenge to legal ways of seeing, its destabilization of "representation," "exhibit," and "proof."

There are compelling reasons for thinking about the law in the generically specific terms of drama and for subordinating lyric and narrative emphases to the complex dynamics of the stage. Both court cases and drama are essentially and explicitly[16] polyvocal and agonistic. Both present less a unified authorship and authority than multiple performative agencies participating in the constitution of a reality that is on some level representational and juridical.[17] And if plays (even Ben Jonson's) should not be conceived as devoted to constructing from all their diverse voices a definitive verdict, they nonetheless pose questions of narrative authority strikingly similar to those that emerge in the courtroom. Indeed, the fractious "War of the Theaters" that contested the terms of dramatic authority on England's public stage at the end of the sixteenth century was termed by its participants a series of "Law cases in Verse." As an ever-present if frequently resisted analogy to the courtroom, drama presents us with an especially appropriate literary genre for reformulating the disciplinary relation between law and literature, generally but fairly characterized by Shoshana Felman:

> The dialogue between the disciplines of law and literature has so far been primarily thematic (that is, essentially conservative of the integrity and of the stable epistemological boundaries of the two fields): when not borrowing the tools of literature to analyze (rhetorically) legal opinions, scholars in the field of law and literature most often deal with the explicit, thematized reflection (or "representation") of the institutions of the law in works of the imagination, focusing on the analysis of fictional trials in a literary plot and/or on the psychology or the sociology of literary characters whose fate or whose profession ties them to the law (lawyers, judges, or accused).[18]

Simply put, there are no "stable epistemological boundaries" between theatrical and legal performance, between dramatic and legal representation, between audiences and juries. And while several essays in this volume certainly concern thematic dialogue between law and theater, this dialogue does not leave law and theater in discrete parallel or in a relation of simple analogy.

An exemplary case appears in Matthew Greenfield's essay, which argues that Jonson's *Poetaster* explores generic instabilities and anxieties shared by the legal apparatus of the state. The "critical dichotomy" between literary form and real life—asserted by Solon and Dershowitz, inverted by Nussbaum—collapses in an argument for the generic and social intersection of theater and law. Though pursued through the habits of literary criticism, our shared interest in such intersection can best be described not as "law *in* theater" but as the near-appositive "law *and* theater." Each institution invokes the other; neither appears without the other.

Such a strong connective claim is not supported, however, by nominally dramatic representations of law and literature in which drama is often a subordinate or fugitive analytic term. The neglect of drama in law and literature analysis misses an excellent opportunity to coordinate literary criticism with legal theory. While the idea of polyvocality has been central to some of the most important recent developments in modern legal theory, legal theorists rarely establish structural connections with the polyvocality of the dramatic mode. The legal theorist who has been most interested in thinking about the way in which different voices interact in the law, for instance, has thought about the interaction largely in terms of the history of the law. And this theorist, Ronald Dworkin, has tended to think about these interactions in largely nondramatic terms. Indeed, in *Law's Empire*, he conceives the interaction as serial authorship (several hands writing the same story) rather than as a paradigm more specifically dramatic.[19] Law and literature studies that focus upon rhetoric, such as Lorna Hutson and Victoria Kahn's fascinating volume *Rhetoric and Law in Early Modern Europe*, tend to emphasize nondramatic and indeed extraliterary texts; and when dramatic texts are concerned in such studies, they are divided into their constituent rhetorical parts.[20] Some influential law and literature figures, such as James Boyd White, have studied dramatic works to emphasize their local rhetorical constructs and to contrast them with the rhetorical constructs of legal works. For White, however, the terms of drama itself would seem to place it beyond the pale of any straightforward rhetorical analysis; he performs analyses of speeches within plays but rarely considers the complex and mediated speech acts of plays themselves.

A partial but important exception appears, however, in White's reading of Shakespeare's *Richard II*,[21] which recognizes that the drama "works on the principle that the truth cannot be said in any single speech or language, but lies in the recognition that against one speech or claim or language is always another one. In this sense its [*Richard II*'s] life is that of voice speaking against voice; this life is what it ultimately holds out as authoritative: not the crown or the usurper, but its own performances."[22] For White these claims are not entirely exclusive to drama. Indeed, he introduces the passage above with the phrase "like his sonnets, like his other plays"; his template for reading *Richard II* is often the *Crito*, not a drama but instead a rather teleological dialectic; and he frequently has Shakespeare's play tell the "story" or "the narrative"[23] of a fall into the modern crisis of authority. The legal-historical story White wishes to tell ends in "incoherence" and "inconclusion,"[24] so in a sense we should not be surprised by his strategic attention to these aspects of the play. But by paying this attention he finds in drama what our volume presents as an important generic "capacity to hold in the mind at once, or in rapid sequence, a variety of incompatible ways of talking, none of which can be a master language."[25]

White comes close to acknowledging the specifically generic nature of this capacity, in fact, when for once the lyric is dramatized rather than the drama lyricized: "To use the sonnet for a moment as an example of a general tendency I mean to describe, one might say that this form, for Shakespeare, is like a little drama, in which he starts with a moment, a phrase, a situation, and then explores by contrast and transformation the possibilities for human speech that it occasions."[26] We contend that on an important level the dynamic White describes here is not "a general tendency" but a revelatory generic connection between theater and law. White's description of Shakespeare's play as a kind of moot court, as Karen Cunningham's essay in this volume will explore quite explicitly, points as well to an interest defining the collection more generally.

— A consequence of approaching Solon through Thespis is that "the law" does not resolve into any simple focus, instead refracting into economic, judicial, legislative, ethical, and religious applications. Such diversity and specificity result from attending to the resonance of the law in Renaissance culture. "The law" is also inherently mobile when invoked on the Renaissance stage, which looks in on sixteenth- and seventeenth-century London but also out to different economies, countries, and historical periods. Our collection of essays therefore has several axes of organization.

A majority of the essays concern the plays of Shakespeare or Jonson, and these two playwrights produce very different accounts of the relation between theater and law. A distinctive Ben Jonson emerges in this volume. Just as he seeks the innovative economic and literary metamorphosis of plays into works, so does Jonson seek to substantiate the economic and ethical claims of his drama with appeals to the material relevance of law. Readers of this volume will notice an interesting difference between Jonson and Shakespeare on this point.[27] The two playwrights would seem to have very different readings of Hamlet's famous deployment of theater to assess guilt and provide for justice: "The play's the thing / Wherein I'll catch the conscience of the king." For Shakespeare, Hamlet's is a statement of metaphoric opportunity: the theater of revenge clearly is *not* an efficacious courtroom, but resemblance opens the door to selective appropriation, adaptation, and ambiguity. By contrast, Jonson's interest lies in the reification of theater as an actual instrument of social justice.

Investigations of law and literature, including those collected here, also define themselves by choosing to seek Jonson's level of legal specificity or Shakespeare's literary transmutations. The evolving field of law and literature, in fact, might be understood as replicating the imaginative tension between Jonson and

Shakespeare as an analytical tension. When the law is privileged as a source of rigor and substance, terms such as *literary quality* identify a potential for irresponsible wordplay that must be remanded to the legally real if the critic is not to be guilty by arbitrary association. For those reading the law through "imaginative literature," however, legal specificity can appear less appealing precisely because its interpretive positivism restricts association, replacing literary criticism with a kind of case law. The original tension between Solon and Thespis survives in the creative tension between Jonson and Shakespeare and is reproduced in criticism of law and literature. In fact one important function of the title of this volume is to indicate that each essay participates in an ongoing dialogue and that such participation can involve taking preestablished sides.

Here is where another well-known distinction between Jonson and Shakespeare can be particularly helpful in illuminating a disciplinary tension between law and literature. In prologue after prologue, Jonson instructs his audience how to watch and read his plays, legislating interpretation by specifying authorial intention. By contrast Shakespeare often effaces his own dramatic author-function while at the same time inviting his audiences to respond to his plays as they like it, to make of his plays what they will. This divergence, an important development in the history of the stage, prefigures Richard Posner's characterization of the difference between legal and literary interpretation: "I do think a judge should pay more attention to legislators' conscious intentions than a literary critic should pay to the author's conscious intentions.... I see no inconsistency between being a pragmatist judge who emphasizes legislative intention and practical consequences and a formalist literary critic in the style of the New Criticism. This just illustrates my opening point in this chapter about the field-dependence of interpretation."[28] Posner's "field-dependence of interpretation," while presenting obstacles to the disciplinary claims of "law and literature," appears *within* the dramatic works considered in this volume. Like Jonson, Posner's pragmatist judge conceives authority as legible authorship. Like Shakespeare, the formalist critic conceives interpretation as an associative activity conducted in the absence of an author. Posner's formalist literary criticism may seem irrelevant to the readings presented in this volume, which could be described as new historicist in orientation. But the formalist aspect of new historicism—by which juxtapositions of text and context are justified by a chiastic paradigm[29]—has for some time now been recognized by its practitioners and critics.

In readings of law and drama, does one follow Jonson and use the law as a model by which literary criticism becomes a kind of finding of fact? In her essay on *Volpone*, Frances Teague argues that Jonson revisits a notorious law case to dramatize a nearly ideal legal system; in his essay on *Bartholomew Fair,* Paul Cantor argues that Jonson enacts in his play a specifically legal endorsement of the free market. Or does one take Shakespeare's cue and imagine the work of criticism as predicated upon associative opportunity? In her essay on *King Lear,* Heather Dubrow reads in Shakespeare's indirect and unspecific references to land law a more pervasive interest in categories of the alien; in his essay on *The Tempest,* Ernest Gilman finds in Shakespeare's mention of an offstage witch a symbolic representation of the legal apparatus of colonialism. Does *law* mean "text," privileged with intended signification, or "context," designating all evidence as subject to further proof?

Perhaps the most polarizing question to ask of each essay is how it negotiates Solon's antitheatricalism—whether or not it calls Renaissance theater as a friend of the court. In each essay, the answer to this question involves not only epistemological concerns but ethical ones. To conceive drama as a degradation of important legal principles, for instance, is in some sense to take the antitheatrical position of Stephen Gosson, for whom the Renaissance stage travesties the courtroom, leaving the defendant with no voice and replacing a single judge with an injudicious jury: "At stage plays it is ridiculous, for the parties accused to reply, no indifference of judgment can be had, because the worst sort of people have the hearing of it, which in respect of their ignorance, of their fickleness, and of their fury, are not to be admitted in place of judgment. A judge must be grave, sober, discreet, wise, well exercised in cases of government, which qualities are never found in the baser sort."[30] In his sympathy with "the parties accused" by the stage, and in his anxious sense of a "baser sort" given to slander, Gosson adapts an early modern concern with defamation that interests Debora Shuger. Radically revising the standard account of Tudor-Stuart censorship, Shuger asserts that early modern censorship laws sought to control not the dissemination of subversive political ideas but the possibility of libelous misrepresentation—not dangerous truths but dangerous lies. While her essay demonstrates that Renaissance dramatic characterization often accommodated this ethical legislation, the dynamic between law and theater that emerges in her argument is one of justified policing and dangerous license; for Shuger censorship laws protect real persons from representations that can cause real harm. Her theater, where the potential and consequence of misrepresentation are high, is not necessarily a friend of a court presented as civic and protective.

Matthew Greenfield investigates this ethically charged notion of representation as acted out in the generic innovations of the War of the Poets, in which Jonson, Marston, and Dekker transformed the theater into a courtroom and arraigned each other for slander. In these dramatic exchanges, satirist figures serve as trial lawyers and judges; the stakes in these cases include not only the reputations of the playwrights but also the source and nature of artistic authority. Jonson distrusts his audiences and instructs them to defer to the judgment of the learned; Marston and Dekker submit themselves humbly to the judgment of the public. Jonson therefore imagines theater as governed by a kind of Roman law, in which cases are decided by an elite, appointed judiciary, while Marston and Dekker use the language of English common law and imagine the audience as a jury of peers. We might describe Greenfield's litigious theater as a friend of the court, in that the satires he considers employ legally conventionalized forms of justice, punishment, and rehabilitation. In his essay, comical satire emerges as a central repository of values, and the satirist collaborates in the state's regulation of behavior—a regulation, when applied in theater, of writers and indeed genres. But the divide between Jonson's Roman law adjudicator and Marston and Dekker's common-law audience suggests more than a simple theatrical appropriation of legal practice. The divide suggests, in fact, a mutually informed development in theatrical and legal institutions that would have profound consequences in the seventeenth century—coming to a head in 1649, when the law closed the theaters and killed a theatrical king.

To refine still further the poles represented by the essays of Greenfield and Shuger, we might say that on one side, theater and law assume collaborative positions; on the other side, theater and law may exploit each other's resources, but the process is presented as competitive and exhausting of one or both. Under such rubrics, the first group would include the essays of Frances Teague, Karen Cunningham, and Luke Wilson. In "Ben Jonson and London Courtrooms," Teague reads Jonson's *Volpone* as a carefully distanced response to the Privy Council's investigation of Guy Fawkes and the Gunpowder Plot conspirators. Jonson's Scrutineo may reveal intractable juridical problems, such as perjury, but in many respects Venice represents a model of legal judgment; and in Teague's reading, the very fact that the play is set in Venice, rather than London, suggests Jonson's increasingly uncritical accommodation of England's legal system. Cunningham's essay concerns the collaborative energy between London's stage and the Inns of Court, where court-centered authority was often contested and the pedagogical practice of mooting encouraged improvised performance. Cunningham's argument does not posit a general and conservative harmony between law and theater, then, but a mutual interest in one of the more destabilizing aspects of legal education: in mooting, the law was taught not as a uniform code, nor as a reaction to *real* events, but as an act of imagination. Wilson also investigates a connection between law and theater that lies in imaginative exercise. His essay considers the legal category of bribery, which, like dramatic representation, makes agency visible. Making agency visible is arguably a representational desire of theater, but, like the antitheatrical account of the stage, bribery is understood to consist in a covert and illegitimate means of exerting influence or force over the behavior of others in the pursuit of selfish ends. In Wilson's reading, then, bribery functions as a theatrically and dramaturgically useful metaphor for human agency. But the concept of bribery, like witchcraft, also articulates rather abstract anxieties about human experience—anxieties that interest the stage even as they call its function into question.

As the essays in this collection move from the collaborationist law-theater model represented by Greenfield to the contestatory law-theater model represented by Shuger, gender, sexuality, and "otherness" are correspondingly foregrounded as objects of investigation. Occupying an important middle ground in this respect, Heather Dubrow, Ernest Gilman, and I consider theatrical interventions in legal and political instabilities. Where Cunningham's essay considers an aspect of the law that itself challenges institutional unity and coherence, Dubrow's concerns a historical moment of instability when land law and property rights are being reconceived. In her reading of *King Lear*, Dubrow shows that recognizing the legal complexities and perils associated with land law and burglary can offer a further perspective on fears of invasive Others, typically studied primarily in terms of national politics. By extension, acknowledging the instability of land ownership complicates the commonplace associations between real estate and women; in *King Lear*, the text that opens on the division of property pivots on its alienation and gendering. Gilman similarly presents *The Tempest*, a play that thematizes problems of land ownership and ethnic anxieties, as hinged upon a woman's body and the law to which it is subject. Sycorax's status as a pregnant witch—condemned, reprieved, and banished by the law—offers an index into the cultural double vision by which the European imagination constructs a "new" world as a re-encounter with the old. Presenting Sycorax as the symbol of that re-encounter, Gilman argues that the play's complex vision of the past produces, and is re-produced in, the protocolonial future. To remember Sycorax is to admit cultural implications and responsibilities that the play, and the exclusionary legal code it practices, are otherwise invested in abjuring. Gilman's essay demonstrates that theatrical critiques of law frequently involve critiques of theater itself. This correspondence defines the method of my reading of *The Witch of Edmonton*, a play in which a critique of the legal fictions necessary to convict and execute a witch coextends with a metatheatrical critique of the credulous audience necessary to witness the play itself. I argue that *The Witch of Edmonton* constitutes an anatomy of courtroom drama—directed not toward entertaining the audience with a spectacular sanctioning of the judicial process in early modern witchcraft trials but toward inviting the audience metatheatrically to question the theater in which it participates as a jury. That the play also encourages this participation and continues to benefit from the kind of credibility established in the courtroom, however, suggests that the dramatists and spectators are not simply a jury but under indictment themselves.

The stage appears much more clearly an agent rather than an object of indictment in the essays in this collection that present theater as an important ethical or social corrective to law. But Shakespeare's characterization of misjudging men and innocent women limits responsibility to the expectations we bring to theater, and to the world into which we exit the theater. Focusing on a radically de-troped "economy," Paul Cantor reads Jonson's theater as a praiseworthy challenge to legal restriction; the liberation and enrichment he celebrates are material, not metaphorical, and they are fearless of anachronism. In an essay that complements the collection's several considerations of Ben Jonson and the law, Cantor presents *Bartholomew Fair* as the first literary portrait of how a free market operates. Recognizing that the play's enthusiasm for proto-capitalism is tempered by the recognition of its liability to abuse, Cantor observes that *Bartholomew Fair* reserves its sharpest criticism for those forces that want to use the power of the law to regulate economic activity. Though Jonson's stage contests the law's restrictive misapplication, his fair's free market identifies the terms by which theater can operate legally and profitably.

There are several rubrics under which our title might be pursued, and it is tempting to follow the vectors sketched above, to perpetuate the divisions that motivated this volume in the first place: *Solon v. Thespis* and *Thespis v. Solon*. Such an organization might yield the following categorization:

Thespis v. Solon: Dubrow, Gilman, Kezar
Solon v. Thespis: Cunningham, Shuger, Wilson

But such an organization would fail entirely to capture the authorial intent in each of the following essays. And such an organization would require a parenthetical category bridging the transactions of theater and law. That bridge would certainly include essays by Cantor, Greenfield, Shuger, Teague, and Wilson. Most importantly, such an organization would not accurately advertise the reader's experience of the collection—unified (we hope) by pontification in the best sense, by each author's commitment to blurring institutional boundaries. We hope that the reader will experience the scheme of organization that we chose as devoted to intersection rather than exclusion and that the reader will feel invited to violate it:

Jonson and the Tribe of Law: Greenfield, Cantor, Teague
Legal Rhetoric and Theatrical Pressure: Dubrow, Gilman, Kezar
Law Staged and Theory Troubled: Shuger, Cunningham, Wilson
Epilogue: Nabers

NOTES

1. *Plutarch's Lives, the Translation Called Dryden's,* ed. A. H. Clough, 5 vols. (New York: Bigelow, Brown, 1911), 1:209.

2. Jonas Barish, *The Antitheatrical Prejudice* (Berkeley: University of California Press, 1981), 37.

3. For an excellent elegy on some versions of the law and literature movement, see Julie Stone Peters, "Law, Literature, and the Vanishing Real: On the Future of an Interdisciplinary Illusion," *PMLA* (Summer 2005): 442–53.

4. Though we will gesture toward that bibliography in the following pages and can narrowly exemplify here with Theodor Meron's *Bloody Constraint: War and Chivalry in Shakespeare* (New York: Oxford University Press, 1998) and Paul Kahn's *Law and Love: The Trials of King Lear* (New Haven: Yale University Press, 2000). Both books are excellent examples, in the field specified by our own volume, of what "law and literature" often looks like from the perspective of legal scholars. They are important, but with a few exceptions their importance has failed to register in the discipline of Renaissance literary studies — registering instead in elective seminars at schools of law or political science and in "law and literature" as it is conceived by legal scholars for whom literature is an interesting but subordinate coordinate of interdisciplinarity. There are reasons both books have not registered with equal impact in departments of English, and I suggest those reasons not to justify them but to describe the divide that our own volume also negotiates. Meron sensitively reads Shakespeare, especially *Henry V,* from the point of view of international humanitarian law; the analytical results are fascinating (and in my view frequently illuminating of the playtexts) but frequently at the expense of what many scholars of Shakespeare would call "the literary" and "the historical." To a slightly lesser extent, Kahn also is comfortable with anachronism, with reading Shakespeare through a universalizing and timeless lens of legal and ethical tradition. Such analytical moves can sound, to contemporary literary critics, reminiscent of a moralizing and hypostatizing brand of criticism that the last three decades have been devoted to destroying.

5. Deak Nabers's epilogue will do some of this dwelling.

6. Alan M. Dershowitz, "Life Is Not a Dramatic Narrative," in *Law's Stories: Narrative and Rhetoric in the Law*, ed. Peter Brooks and Paul Gewirtz (New Haven: Yale University Press, 1996), 101.

7. Dershowitz's essay curiously admits the importation of literary forms into the courtroom and into the human experience of "real life" while insisting at the same time that such importation should be resisted where the law is concerned. The weakness of this argument would seem to lie in the fact that experiential constructs resist such prophylaxis and that the law itself, narrativized or not, might be read as such a construct. Truth also becomes a problematic category when experiential constructs are introduced as its opposite. Dershowitz suggests ("Life," 100), for instance, that religion can be read as a construct, an imaginative response to our need for order and teleology. Why should the law, directed toward justice and social order, not be read in this way?

8. In note 4, the reader will find a disciplinary inversion of the account of our own readers' reports just presented.

9. For a useful introduction to, survey of, and intervention in the law and literature field, see Guyora Binder and Robert Weisberg, *Literary Criticisms of the Law* (Princeton: Princeton University Press, 2000).

10. See especially William M. Hawley, *Shakespearean Tragedy and the Common Law: The Art of Punishment* (New York: Peter Lang, 1998). See also Lorna Hutson, *The Usurer's Daughter: Male Friendship and Fictions of Women in Sixteenth-Century England* (London: Routledge, 1994); R. S. White, *Natural Law in English Renaissance Literature* (Cambridge: Cambridge University Press, 1996); and Lindsay Kaplan, *The Culture of Slander in Early Modern England* (Cambridge: Cambridge University Press, 1997).

11. See Theodore Ziolkowski, *The Mirror of Justice: Literary Reflections of Political Crises* (Princeton: Princeton University Press, 1997), chaps. 2 and 8. Important predecessors of Ziolkowski's work include George Thomson, *Aeschylus and Athens: A Study in the Social Origins of Drama* (1940; reprint, New York: Haskell House, 1967), and J. Peter Euben, ed., *Greek Tragedy and Political Theory* (Berkeley: University of California Press).

12. Ziolkowski, *Mirror of Justice*, 174.

13. See Martha C. Nussbaum, *Poetic Justice: The Literary Imagination and Public Life* (Boston: Beacon Press, 1995), esp. 82.

14. See Barbara Johnson, "Anthropomorphism in Lyric and Law," *Yale Journal of Law and Humanities* 10 (Summer 1998): 549–74.

15. See Wai Chee Dimock, *Residues of Justice: Literature, Law, Philosophy* (Berkeley: University of California Press, 1996), esp. 9.

16. By *explicitly* I mean to distinguish drama from a Bakhtinian conception of narrative. For the audience of drama, polyvocality is not an interpretive discovery but merely the sentient response to what is advertised by the playtext as performed. Most, though not all, of the novels under Bakhtin's lens do not explicitly place the reader in the position of juror—if by *juror* we mean the announced auditor and arbiter of competing voices of legitimacy. Every Renaissance play does (unless the reader of this volume wishes to except Jonson).

17. This claim for the law becomes more obvious when we consider, for instance, the narratives and characterizations necessary to convince jurors of categories of culpability such as negligence.

18. Shoshana Felman, "Forms of Judicial Blindness, or the Evidence of What Cannot Be Seen: Traumatic Narratives and Legal Repetitions in the O. J. Simpson Case and in Tolstoy's *The Kreutzer Sonata,*" *Critical Inquiry* 23 (1997): 739.

19. Ronald Dworkin, *Law's Empire* (Cambridge, MA: Harvard University Press, 1986), esp. 228–54.

20. Lorna Hutson and Victoria Kahn, *Rhetoric and Law in Early Modern Europe* (New Haven: Yale University Press, 2000). In general, this volume does not focus on literary texts, although some of the essays do treat literature substantially. Two essays (Luke Wilson's and Lorna Hutson's), moreover, treat specifically dramatic texts. Hutson's essay, "Not the King's Two Bodies," challenges the tendency of historians old and new to read Edmund Plowden through the lens of Ernst Kantorowicz. Hutson's new reading of Plowden—whose fame and importance in his own time lay in his enabling of lawyers to apply the interpretive principles of equity to a burgeoning mass of statutory legislation—leads to a new reading of Hal's reformation in *1 and 2 Henry IV*. In Hutson's reading, Hal's coming to power is distinguished from the triumph of the absolute monarch; rather, it demonstrates the triumph of the common lawyers as interpreters of legislative intention.

21. James Boyd White, *Acts of Hope: Creating Authority in Literature, Law, and Politics* (Chicago: University of Chicago Press, 1994), 47–81.

22. Ibid., 50.

23. See, for instance, ibid., 47, 71.

24. See ibid., 71–76.

25. Ibid., 76.

26. Ibid., 78.

27. Though I should note that at least one of the volume's contributors (Luke Wilson) does not agree with some aspects of the following claim.

28. Richard A. Posner, *Law and Literature*, rev. ed. (Cambridge, MA: Harvard University Press, 1998), 245. Posner carefully qualifies this statement elsewhere in the chapter in which it appears, and of course the line between legal and literary interpretation blurs considerably when one reads the law as an activist or constructivist and when one reads literature biographically or as intentional signification.

29. This paradigm is presented by Louis Montrose as "the textuality of history and the historicity of the text." See his "'The Place of a Brother' in *As You Like It*: Social Process and Comic Form," *Shakespeare Quarterly* 32:1 (1981): 28–54, and the introduction to his *The Purpose of Playing: Shakespeare and the Cultural Politics of the Elizabethan Theatre* (Chicago: University of Chicago Press, 1996). See also Alan Liu, "The Power of Formalism: The New Historicism," *ELH* 56 (Winter 1989): 721–71.

30. Stephen Gosson, *Playes Confuted in Five Actions* (London, 1582), C8^v.

JONSON AND
THE TRIBE OF LAW

ONE

Trial by Theater
Jonson, Marston, and Dekker in the Court of Parnassus

Matthew Greenfield

RUFUS LABERIUS CRISPINUS, and DEMETRIUS FANNIUS, hold up your hands. You are, before this time, ioyntly and severally indited, and here presently to be arraigned, upon the Statute of Calumny, or Lex Remmia (The one by the name of RUFUS LABERIUS CRISPINUS, alias CRISPINAS, Poetaster, and plagiary: the other, by the name of DEMETRIUS FANNIUS, play-dresser, and plagiary) That you (not having the feare of PHOEBUS, or his shafts, before your eyes) contrary to the peace of our liege lord, AUGUSTUS CAESAR, his crowne and dignitie, and against the forme of a Statute, in that case made, and provided; have most ignorantly, foolishly, and (more like your selves) maliciously, gone about to deprave, and calumniate the person and writings of QUINTUS HORATIUS FLACCUS, here present, poet and priest to the muses: and to that end have mutually conspir'd, and plotted, at sundry times, as by severall meanes, and in sundry places, for the better accomplishing your base and envious purpose; taxing him, falsly, of self-love, arrogancy, impudence, rayling, filching by translation, &c. Of all which calumnies, and every of them, in manner and forme aforesaid, what answere you? Are you guiltie, or not guiltie?[1]

At the end of the sixteenth century John Marston and Thomas Dekker exchanged insults with Ben Jonson in the controversy we now know as the War of the Poets.[2] The passage cited above comes from Jonson's *Poetaster, or His Arraignement*: "Crispinus" and "Demetrius" are Jonson's versions of Marston and Dekker, and "Horace" represents Jonson himself. Although Jonson claimed in his conversations with Drummond that he "beate Marston and took his pistoll from him," we no longer know how the quarrel began or how it ended.[3] What survives are a group of plays staged between 1598 and 1601 in which the playwrights present idealized versions of themselves and caricatures of their enemies: Marston's *Histrio-mastix* (1599), *Jack Drum's Entertainment* (1600), and *What You Will* (1601); Jonson's *Every Man Out of His Humor* (1599), *Cynthia's Revels* (1600), and *Poetaster, or His Arraignement* (1601); and Dekker's *Satiromastix* (1601).[4] Like the Marprelate Controversy, the War of the Poets served as a laboratory within which generic experimentation proceeded at a rapid pace, with writers on both sides appropriating the innovations of the enemy and extending them. Together, the quarreling poets developed a new hybrid species of drama, the comical satire.

Jonson called his final salvo in the War of the Poets *Poetaster, or His Arraignement*. In the folio, he added as a subscript the label *A Comicall Satyre*. Discussions of the play's generic self-definition have focused on this label and ignored the curious word *arraignment* in the title. In the argument that follows, I suggest that this word is also a generic label, one that refers to a genre of legal narrative with conventions quite different from those of comical satire. This legal genre includes both the representations made in court by prosecutors and a variety of pamphlets that describe trials or justify their verdicts. These pamphlets typically have names like "A True Report of the inditement, Arraignment, conviction, condemnation, and execution of John Weldon, William Hartley, and Roger Sutton" (London, 1588) or "The Censure of a Loyal Subject: Upon Certaine Noted Speach and Behaviors, of those fourteene notable Traitors, at the place of their executions, the xx and xxi of September last past."[5] Jonson uses the word *arraignment* to acknowledge the play's internalization of this legal genre, with its plot structure and its theory of human agency. *Poetaster* takes the shape of a prosecutor's reconstruction of a crime. In this case, the crime is the alleged slandering of Jonson by John Marston and his accomplice Thomas Dekker. Like any legal representation, the play attempts to establish not only the actions but the intentions of its defendants: without a felonious intent, no act, no matter how destructive, constitutes a crime. Prosecutors need to represent defendants as agents who have chosen to commit a crime and are responsible for their actions. Conversely, defendants often represent themselves as having acted under compulsion, crippled by some pathology of the will that left them incapable of moral choice. I am not being entirely frivolous when I suggest that it might be difficult to prove that an allegorical figure had formed a felonious intention. Similarly, a Jonsonian humorous character might successfully plead not guilty by reason of insanity. Driven by a compulsion, such characters are incapable of making moral choices or visualizing the consequences of their actions. A prosecutor has to resist arguments of this kind, and prosecutorial narratives tend to represent a kind of agent antithetical to the flat or damaged agents of comical satire or satire more generally. Where satire attacks people by representing their degeneration into beasts, automata, or allegorical figures, prosecutors attack defendants by representing them as fully human and responsible for their actions. As one might expect, then, Jonson's "arraignment" of Marston and Dekker is a highly unstable generic hybrid, one that must negotiate between two representational modes and two definitions of the human. Ultimately, I argue, Jonson allows legal narrative to qualify, frame, and displace the conventions of verse satire.

Poetaster follows the fortunes of three groups of poets in Augustan Rome. One group, which includes Ovid, Gallus, Tibullus, and Propertius, passes its time in hedonistic revelry. A second group that includes Horace and Virgil engages in higher-minded pursuits. A third group, the play's villains, includes the mediocre poets Crispinus and Demetrius. Crispinus and Demetrius stand for Marston and Dekker, and Horace is an idealized version of Jonson himself. The fortunes of the three groups of poets reflect differences in their authorial projects. Ovid's group is aristocratic and resolutely anticommercial: when Ovid's father accuses him of preparing a play for the theater, he responds, "They wrong mee, sir, and doe abuse you more, / That blow your eares with these untrue reports. / I am not knowne unto the open stage, / Nor do I traffique in their theaters. / Indeed, I doe acknowledge, at request / Of some neere friends . . . I have begunne a poeme of that nature" (1.2.61–67). Ovid and his friends resemble the poets Richard Helgerson calls amateurs, who wrote for members of their own coteries rather than for publication or the stage.[6] For them, poetry is a mark of social distinction, a pleasurable indulgence, and the medium of transactions with lovers, friends, and patrons. For Horace and Virgil, poets of the type Helgerson calls "laureates," poetry is an ethical instrument: when they read to the emperor, they offer him instruction as well as entertainment. Crispinus and Demetrius, on the other hand, are professionals. They write to earn money and to attack rivals. One of the play's functions is to sort these three groups into a hierarchy. By placing Virgil and Horace at the top, above the aristocratic amateurs, the play envisions the rearrangement rather than merely the preservation of the social order. Despite this revisionary project, though, the play has a deeply conservative view of the role of the laureate poet: Virgil and Horace collaborate with the state in the production of a particular kind of subject: rational, ethical, and self-disciplined. The work of the laureate poet is to articulate values and to develop techniques for the regulation of conduct.

Poetaster begins with allegory: the "infected bulke" (21) of Envy takes the stage and encourages the audience to misconstrue the play, to find slanderous topical meanings in it. Although the play's central task is to malign Marston and Dekker, the prologue denies any reference to living persons, claiming that the play is purely historical: "What should I doe?" Envy complains. "ROME? ROME? O my vext soule, / How might I force this to the present state?"[7] Envy then asks if there are any actors or playwrights in the house with a gift for misinterpretation. She offers them some of the snakes iconographically associated with her:[8]

> . . . or else choose
> One of my longest vipers, to sticke downe
> In your deep throats; and let the heads come forth
> At your ranke mouthes; that he may see you arm'd
> With triple malice, to hisse, sting, and teare
> His work, and him . . .
> (48–53)

Envy is female, but her snakes give her a peculiar masculinity. This gender ambiguity threatens to contaminate her male allies. Swallowing the snake involves being penetrated, but having it protrude from one's mouth gives one a frightening phallic aggressiveness. The vivid, sexualized figure of the snake functions as an emblem of the obsessive behavior characteristic of the objects of satire: it imagines the impulse to slander as a foreign body, an alien implantation in the psyche. The snake-swallowing detractors whom Envy envisions would possess a sort of partial agency, enough to choose to swallow the snakes. Once the snakes begin to speak for them, though, they would no longer have any choice about how to behave. This ambiguity situates Envy's allies on the border between two types of subjectivity and two narrative modes. The first type of subject acts compulsively and the second has a capacity for moral choice. The first is an allegorical figure, and the second inhabits a narrative mode with stronger mimetic pretensions. This second mode is juridical: it involves an attempt to establish responsibility.[9]

Legal conceptions of intention have always been most heavily contested, and hence most clearly articulated, in cases involving insanity and negligence. Anglo-Saxon law relied on the principle of "absolute liability," of responsibility for the effects of one's actions regardless of one's intentions. If one killed a man, whether through negligence, in self defense, while insane, or on a whim, one owed the victim's kin a fixed blood-price. One might also be liable for damage or death caused by one's possessions, one's animals, or one's servants. After the Norman Conquest, as an increasing number of ecclesiastics became jurists, theological ideas about moral states softened the principle of absolute liability. The new standard of guilt required the presence of *voluntas nocendi*, the desire to cause harm. The thirteenth-century compendium *De legibus et consuetudinibus Angliae* gave this standard an influential formulation: "For crime is not committed unless the will to harm be present.... [I]n misdeeds we look to the will and not the outcome." In 1603 Edward Coke reiterated the principle: "The punishment of a man who is deprived of reason and understanding cannot be an example to others. No felony or murder can be committed without a felonious intent and purpose."[10] Coke lists four species of defects of the will: "1. Ideot or fool natural: 2. He who was of good and sound mind and by the visitation of god has lost it: 3. *Lunaticus, qui gaudet lucidis intervallis* [a lunatic, who is lucky enough to have lucid intervals] and sometimes is of sound memory, and sometimes *non compos mentis* [not of sound mind] 4. By his own act, as a drunkard."[11]

Although Coke's formulation sounds relatively clear, attempts to define the idea of felonious intent have grown steadily more complex, and jurists have been forced to think philosophically about what it means to form an intention. Their definitions and their debates have not always followed those of the philosophers and the theologians. Most legal theorists agree that forming an intention requires an ability to visualize the consequences of one's actions, but this ability has proven difficult to define. Another site of legal debate is the concept of the overwhelming compulsion: it remains an open question how one treats criminals who understand the difference between good and evil, understand that their actions will have evil consequences, and suffer from a mental disorder that impels them to perform those actions anyway. Some legal theorists refuse to recognize compulsions of this kind—they insist that "possession of knowledge of consequences is a sufficient and necessary condition of the capacity for self-control."[12] In practice, though, all of these definitions are renegotiated each time a trial raises the question of intention. Prosecutors from the sixteenth century onward have attempted to construct narratives about a particular kind of intention. The accused must have the capacity to form an intention: they should be able to tell good from bad, know that they are committing a crime, and be capable of visualizing the effects of that crime. A strong emotion that overwhelms the reason and the will can partially exonerate a defendant, so the prosecution must attempt to show the absence of such emotion. The defendant's guilt is deeper if the prosecutor can show that the crime was premeditated—that the intent to commit the crime existed as a steady glow and not just a brief flash of mental activity. Since forming an intention is a mental act that leaves no material traces, legal narratives attempt to reconstruct intentions through the examination of circumstantial evidence. This reliance on inference from circumstantial evidence makes legal narratives epistemologically anxious in a way that satire, for example, is not.[13] Comical satire leaves little room for debate about intention: the mental state of a humorous character is continuously visible and available for inspection.

In trials for capital crimes in early modern England, defendants frequently contested the prosecution's description of their intentions rather than denying the facts of the case. The Catholic William Parry, for example, argued that he had contemplated and discussed assassinating the queen but had not fully formed an intention to do so. He had never actually attempted to kill her. Two of the Babington conspirators, John Savage and John Ballard, used the same argument: they had discussed killing the queen but never formed a strong enough intention to act. Thomas Lee, a captain who had served Elizabeth in Ireland, also used this argument: he had discussed a hypothetical scenario but had not actually plotted treason. Conversely, defendants in other cases attempted to exonerate themselves by claiming that they had acted in a sudden rage or under compulsion, driven by an emotion that overpowered their self-control. Robert Creighton, Lord Sanquire, used such a defense in 1615. He had lost an eye in a match with a fencing teacher named Turner and two years later arranged for Turner to be shot by two hired murderers. Sanquire argued that his will and reason had been overpowered by an uncontrollable resentment. Francis Bacon, speaking for the prosecution, retorted, "All passions are assuaged with time; love, hatred, grief, &c. all burns out with time, if no fewel be put to it: for you to have been in the gall of bitterness so long, and to have been in so restless a case of his blood, is a strange example."[14] The prosecution in these trials needed to demonstrate that the defendant possessed a capacity to form intentions, to make moral choices. Jonson's "Arraignment" of Marston and Dekker also attempts to reconstruct the intentions of its defendants: *Poetaster* conducts a profound and sustained meditation on responsibility and compulsive action.

In *Poetaster*, it is not the real villains who resemble the humorous characters of the previous plays. The ones whose capacity for moral choice has been overwhelmed by an irresistible impulse are the amateurs, with whom Jonson feels genuine sympathy, and not the professionals, who stand for Marston and Dekker. The compulsiveness of the amateurs partially exonerates them for their irresponsible behavior. Poetry comes to them as a daimon, drawing them irresistibly away from prudence, responsibility, and the law. This antagonism is particularly painful for Ovid. Ovid is a law student who is drawn to literature, like many of the Inns of Court students of Jonson's time. In the play's first scene, we discover Ovid writing verses instead of studying his casebooks. In a reminder of the play's allegorical opening, the poem is addressed to Envy.[15] Although speaking to an allegorical figure is a thoroughly conventional poetic fiction, it has an eerie resonance here, since the embodied figure of Envy has just descended below the stage. An audience seeing the play for the first time could not be sure that Envy would not answer Ovid or perhaps even return to the stage, entering the main plot of the play as the ghost in Senecan tragedy sometimes did. When he recites the poem, Ovid enters a liminal space between representational modes, a space within which a person might encounter an allegorical personification.

Ovid Senior, an eminent lawyer, enters while his son recites the poem. Enraged, the father threatens to disinherit the son if he continues to neglect his law books: "[I]s this the scope and aime of thy studies? are these the hopeful courses, wherewith I have so long flattered my expectation from thee? verses? *poetrie?* Ovid, whom I thought to see the pleader, become Ovid the play-maker?" (1.2.5–9). Ovid Senior alludes to the censorship of satires and plays: "If nothing else, yet this alone, the very reading of the publike edicts should fright thee from commerce with them; and give thee distaste enough of their actions. But this betrayes what a student you are: this argues your proficiency in the law" (1.2.56–60). Both Ovid and his father insistently oppose poetry to the law. They think of law as a practical, lucrative, and civic-minded occupation, and they agree that poetry is an irresponsible and private indulgence. Propertius, another of the amateurs, provides a striking demonstration of the erotic poet's rejection of the community when he walls himself up in the tomb of his dead lover. Law and erotic poetry each have their own ethos, their mode of conduct. The rhetorical powers they draw on are intimately related, but the two disciplines move toward different ends. Ovid highlights the difference in his promise to reform: "Sir, let me crave you will, forgoe these moodes; / I will be any thing; or studie any thing: / I'le prove the unfashion'd body of the *law* / Pure elegance, and make her ruggedst straines / Runne smoothly, as PROPERTIUS elegies" (1.2.103–7). Ovid ignores the pragmatic goal of legal rhetoric and focuses on its potential for elegance. Ovid compulsively aestheticizes moral and practical questions, as his angry father observes: "Why, he cannot speake, he cannot thinke out of *poetrie*, he is bewitcht with it" (1.2.110–11). Ovid and his father speak different languages, a fact that Jonson underlines by putting the father's words in prose and the son's in blank verse.

In the next scene, Tibullus enters to find the younger Ovid absorbed in his studies. Curious about what Ovid is working on, Tibullus snatches a sheet of paper from Ovid and discovers a couplet: "*If thrice in field, a man vanquish his foe, / 'Tis after in his choice to serve, or no*" (1.3.5–6). Tibullus asks, "How now Ovid! *Law*-cases in verse?" (7). Ovid answers, "In troth, I know not: they runne from my pen unwittingly, if they be verse" (8–9). Ovid cannot speak his father's language no matter how hard he tries.[16] Tibullus has come bearing an invitation from Ovid's lover Julia, the daughter of Augustus. When Tibullus presents the invitation, Ovid abandons his efforts to reconcile poetry and the law: "Oh, in no labyrinth, can I safelier erre, / Then when I lose myself in praysing her. / Hence *Law*, and welcome, *Muses* .... Iulia's love / Shall be a law, and that sweet law I'll studie" (1.3.47–56). When Ovid commits himself to the ethos of erotic poetry, he becomes irrational and compulsive, incapable of choosing how to behave. Poetic inspiration does to him what Envy does to her followers: like the snake-eating slanderers, Ovid has been contaminated by the single-mindedness of an allegorical figure. Satire normally attacks its victims by representing them as machines. In *Poetaster*, though, compulsiveness is characteristic of the less serious crimes.[17]

It is only the poetic inspiration of the amateurs that leads away from social responsibility. Virgil and Horace, by contrast, have an ethos that involves reason, self-discipline, and obedience to precept, and their poetry functions as part of a discursive system that includes the law. Both Virgil's epic and Horace's satire participate in the definition of values required for the administration of justice. In *Poetaster*, public servants and laureate poets speak the same language: when Horace converses with the eminent lawyer Trebatius, both men speak in verse.

The moral agency of the play's villains falls somewhere in between that of the rational, self-disciplined laureate poets and the compulsive amateurs. Where Ovid and his friends are driven by obsessions, Crispinus and Demetrius have only weak motives for their crimes. When Virgil asks "what cause they had to maligne HORACE," Demetrius answers, "In troth, no great cause, not I; I must confesse: but that he kept better company (for the most part) then I: and that better men lov'd him, then lov'd me: and that his writings thriv'd better then mine, and were better lik't, and grac't: nothing else" (5.3.447–53). The qualifications—"no great cause," "for the most part"—may be calculated to hide the magnitude of Demetrius's envy. The effect, though, is to suggest that Demetrius does not slander Horace out of an overwhelming compulsion. Unlike the humorous characters of Jonson's first two comical satires, Demetrius chose to commit a crime. He did not slander Horace because it was his nature to do so. In an earlier scene, Histrio the player explains that his acting company has hired Demetrius to write a play abusing Horace because "it will get us a huge deale of money . . . and wee have need on't; for this winter has made us all poorer than so many starv'd snakes" (3.4.327–29). Crispinus also becomes a coauthor out of a combination of cupidity and injured pride: when he first encounters Horace, Crispinus attempts to form a partnership with the older poet. Just after Horace has snubbed him, Crispinus contracts with a theatrical company to collaborate with Demetrius in order to pay off his debts. Crispinus also has another, unrelated project, the seduction of a citizen's wife. This multiplication of motives gives Crispinus and Demetrius a thickness or complexity that makes them quite unlike humorous characters or allegorical figures. Where a humor makes characters rigid and unresponsive to their environment, the poetasters have an equally dangerous flexibility and instability of character. They respond all too well to cues from their environment. Although their ability to visualize the consequences of their actions is weak, Crispinus and Demetrius are capable of rational choice and competent to stand trial. Moreover, as the first four acts of the play establish, their criminal acts are premeditated, their intentions are sustained, and they have entered a criminal conspiracy, which within the legal taxonomy of intentions results in the highest level of culpability. In the words of the arraignment, Crispinus and Demetrius have acted "*most ignorantly, foolishly, and (more like your selves) maliciously,*" and have "*mutually conspir'd, and plotted, at sundry times, as by severall meanes, and in sundry places, for the better accomplishing your base and envious purpose*" (5.3.224–25, 228–30). The question of the intentions of Crispinus and Demetrius seems to arouse the kind of epistemological anxiety characteristic of legal narrative: when the defendants plead not guilty, the prosecutors feel compelled to produce material evidence in the form of slanderous writings.

Although Crispinus and Demetrius are not allegorical agents, a pattern of references links them to the figure of Envy. First, as we have seen, Histrio compares his company to "starv'd snakes." Then, just before the trial of Crispinus and Demetrius, Virgil recites a randomly selected passage from the *Aeneid* that proves to be the description of Rumor from book 4.[18] Like Jonson's Envy, Rumor is a female figure with a grotesque body that contains too many moving parts: she is covered with eyes, ears, and tongues. During his first encounter with Crispinus, Horace asks Apollo to "naile to the earth / This PYTHON . . . this HYDRA of discourse, here" (3.1.281–85). Later, during the trial, Horace makes the connection more direct: "Now thou curl'st up, thou poore, and nasty snake, / And shrink'st thy poys'nous head into thy bosome: / Out viper, thou that eat'st thy parents, hence" (5.3.325–27). This parent-devouring snake is reminiscent of another of Envy's relatives, Spenser's Errour, whose spawn gorge on her blood, burst, and die.[19] Horace imagines Crispinus as a static emblem or allegorical personification of slander. In *Poetaster*, though, this is not an accurate description of the villains but a premonition of their punishment. Augustus's punishment makes the hypocritical Captain Tucca into an emblem of his vice: "*Lictors*, gag him: doe. / And put a case of vizards o're his head, / That he may looke *bi-fronted*, as he speakes" (5.3.433–35). Similarly, Virgil commutes Demetrius's sentence from being branded on the forehead to wearing a fool's costume: "Demetrius Fannius, thou shalt here put on / That coate, and cap; and henceforth thinke thy selfe / No other, then they make thee" (5.3.576–78). Like Tucca, Demetrius is reduced by his punishment to an emblem.[20]

The punishment of Crispinus is more complex, perhaps because Crispinus has committed aesthetic as well as moral crimes. Where Demetrius is merely a poorly educated mediocrity, Crispinus possesses a genuine erudition that he has used in perverse ways. Crispinus's slander is, as Virgil notes, "strangely worded" (297):

> What, shall thy lubricall and glibberie Muse
> Live, as she were defunct, like punke in stewes?
> . . . .
> No; teach thy incubus to poetize;
> And throwe abroad thy spurious snotteries,
> Upon that puft-up lumpe of barmy froth . . .
> (277–78, 282–84)

These ink-horn terms advertise Crispinus's learning in a heavy-handed way. Like Nashe and Harvey, Marston was fond of neologisms. He too coined numerous words which have remained in circulation. After *Poetaster* was staged, though, Marston's diction became less elaborate: he seems to have taken Jonson's criticism to heart.[21] Within the play, the punishment of Crispinus is a satiric tour de force. With the consent of Augustus, Horace administers an emetic to Crispinus that "should purge / His braine, and stomach of those tumorous heates" (393–94). A few minutes later, Crispinus begins to vomit words:

> HORACE. A bason, a bason, quickly; our physick works. Faint not man.
> CRISPINUS. O—*retrograde—reciprocall—incubus.*
> CAESAR. What's that HORACE?
> HORACE. *Retrograde, reciprocall,* and *Incubus* are come up.
> GALLUS. Thankes be to *IUPITER.*
> CRISPINUS. O—*glibbery—lubricall—defunct*—o—
>
> (466–72)

The treatment mixes moral and aesthetic correction: it purges Crispinus of pride and refines his diction. It is a literalizing punishment: like the costumes imposed on Tucca and Demetrius, it gives a material presence to an abstract judgment. The words become objects that possess the properties they name: "clumsie" sticks in Crispinus's throat and "prorumped" makes a loud noise that interrupts the conversation, while "glibberie" and "lubricall" come up smoothly. At the end of the process, Crispinus professes to feel "Pretty, and well" (530). Horace warns that the purge has only a temporary efficacy. To achieve lasting health, Crispinus must change his diet, replacing "Gallo-belgick" literary delicacies with a more wholesome menu of classical authors. This menu includes Cato, Homer, and Hesiod but not Plautus or Lycophron, who is "too darke, and dangerous a dish" for Crispinus to digest (548). Like swallowing one of Envy's snakes, Horace's dietary suggestions present a paradox. The authors one consumes will override or shape one's will, but one can choose to read particular authors, to become a particular kind of person. In *Poetaster*, character is no longer destiny: through a sustained exercise of literary self-discipline, one can reshape one's own character. In the culture imagined by this play, the state depends on its laureate poets to supervise this internalization of the disciplinary mechanism. Conversely, the state has taken over many of the functions that satirists conventionally claimed for themselves: Augustus orders that one character be whipped and three others made into emblems of their crimes.

— *Satiromastix* is Dekker's reply to *Poetaster*. Like Marston's *Jack Drum's Entertainment* and *What You Will, Satiromastix* is an awkward hybrid that combines a satirical plot with a romantic comedy.[22] The satiric plot of *Satiromastix* responds to *Poetaster* with a point-by-point rebuttal, revising Jonson's account of events and motivations. Dekker incorporates many of the central characters of Jonson's play, including Crispinus/Marston, Demetrius/Dekker, Horace/Jonson, and Jonson's comic creation Captain Tucca. Dekker adds a fawning acolyte of Horace's named Asinius Bubo.[23] Like Jonson's play, *Satiromastix* analyzes the origin of the quarrel. In *Satiromastix*, though, it is Jonson who is found guilty and punished by a tribunal of poets. Dekker presents himself and Marston as reasonable and amiable. They forgive Horace repeatedly but are eventually forced to bring him to the bar of the "court of Parnassus." As the preface to the play makes clear, Dekker followed Jonson in imagining the theater as a courtroom and the play as a trial: "Horace *hal'd his* Poetasters *to the Barre, the* Poetasters *untruss'd* Horace: *how worthily eyther, or how wrongfully,* (World) *leave it to the Iurie.*"[24] Both *Poetaster* and *Satiromastix* are in effect lawyer's summations—each gives the prosecution's recapitulation of the crimes, rebuts the arguments advanced by the other side, and concludes with a recommendation concerning the sentence, a vision of the punishment of the defendants. The first four acts of *Satiromastix* supply evidence to the audience, and the fifth act imagines an extravagant punishment, a public humiliation like the one the play itself is intended to inflict on Jonson. Like *Poetaster*, *Satiromastix* attempts to locate the weak but definite intention associated with maximum culpability: Horace's slanders are conscious, deliberate, and premeditated, and neither compulsive nor involuntary. There are no humorous characters in *Satiromastix*, no compulsive satirical agents. Horace and Asinius are eccentric but capable of rational choice.

Like Jonson's comical satires, *Satiromastix* reflects continuously on the cultural and political work performed by literature and especially by satire, but Dekker arrives at different conclusions. The similarity in the backgrounds of the two men makes the difference in their self-presentation especially interesting. Dekker and Jonson both came of humble backgrounds, both lacked university degrees, and both began their careers in public theater. These similarities made Jonson especially aggressive in distinguishing their authorial projects. Jonson placed Dekker and other theatrical professionals at the bottom of the literary hierarchy, just above the skilled craftsmen Dekker represented in *The Shoemakers' Holiday*. For himself Jonson invented a role as laureate modeled on the careers of Virgil and Spenser.[25] He distanced himself from the literary marketplace and identified his interests with those of the aristocracy. Where the professional practiced a craft, Jonson represented himself as deriving his authority from wisdom, moral gravity, and even divine inspiration.[26] Dekker's response involves skepticism about the laureate role: *Satiromastix* reexamines the "evidence" presented in *Poetaster*. The first time we encounter Horace in *Satiromastix* he is in his study, working on a poem about celestial inspiration but struggling with questions of craft, with the stubborn and intractable raw material of poetry, the sound of words:

> . . . O me thy Priest inspire.
> For I to thee and thy immortall name,
> In—in—golden tunes,
> For I to thee and thine immortal name—
> In—sacred raptures flowing, flowing, swimming, swimming:
> In sacred raptures swimming,
> Immortal name, game, dame, tame, lame, lame, lame,
> Pux, ha it, shame, proclaime, oh—
> In sacred raptures flowing, will proclaime, not—
> O me thy Priest inspyre!
> For I to thee and thy immortall name,
> In flowing numbers fild with spright and flame,
> Good, good, in flowing numbers fild with spright and flame.
> (1.2.8–20)

In *Poetaster*, Jonson's Horace is composing this poem when he encounters Crispinus for the first time (3.1.8–12).[27] Before Crispinus interrupts him, he composes five perfect lines without any apparent effort. Although Jonson wrote the poem himself, it sounds like a Horatian ode. An ode invoking a god was an ambitious poem, one that aspired to the highest level of decorum and was closely related to the epic invocation.[28] When Dekker recontextualizes the writing of the poem, he undercuts the ode's claim to poetic inspiration. Behind the appearance of "flowing numbers filled with spright and flame," Dekker shows, is the humble exercise of a craftsman's skill. In Horace's search for the right rhyme, the meaning of words remains a secondary concern. No central core of ethical knowledge determines the outward shape of the poem, and no god or daimon inhabits Dekker's Horace; even in the heat of poetic composition, he maintains perfect control of himself. The passage reflects a genuine respect for Jonson's skill and even a certain affection, making the accusation of vanity that much more piercing.

Dekker displays a clear understanding of Jonson's laureate self-presentation and dismantles it point by point. In an effort to suggest that Jonson practices a craft rather than an art, Dekker repeatedly mentions Jonson's careers as bricklayer and actor. Captain Tucca gives a particularly vivid account of the beginnings of

Jonson's career: "thou call'st Demetrius Iorneyman Poet, but thou putst up a Supplication to be a poore Iorneyman Player, and hadst beene still so, but that thou couldst not set a good face upon't: thou hast forgot how thou amblest (in leather pilch) by a play-wagon, in the high way, and took'st mad Ieronimoes part, to get service among the Mimickes" (4.1.127–32). This is a keen thrust, since Jonson frequently used Kyd's *Spanish Tragedy* as an example of the lower reaches of theater from which he was trying to distance himself.[29] The play also disputes Jonson's claim of a privileged relation to the court. When a disgruntled patron mentions Horace to the king, the king responds, "Horace, what's he sir *Vaughan?*" (2.1.114). When Crispinus and Demetrius describe Horace's laureate ambitions, the king says,

> "If a cleare merit stand upon his praise,
> Reach him a Poets Crowne (the honour'd Bayes)
> But if he claime it, wanting right thereto,
> (As many bastard Sonnes of Poesie doe)
> Race down his usurpation to the ground.
> *True Poets are with Arte and Nature Crown'd*
> (5.2.119–24)

When Crispinus refers to his rival as "*selfe-creating Horace*" (5.2.138), the term is a disparagement—Dekker sees Jonson's self-presentation as theatrical and inauthentic. This inauthenticity is linked to Jonson's dependence on patronage. In *Satiromastix*, writing for the public theater is a dignified occupation that makes one independent and disinterested in one's social relations; seeking out patrons, on the other hand, results in a degrading confusion of the social and the commercial. It forces one to distort and falsify one's emotions. The play shows Horace executing a humiliating commission to write a poem disparaging baldness. The gallant who pays for the poem is competing with a bald man for the favor of a bourgeois widow. Horace also has a stock of flattering letters that he reuses with each new gallant whose acquaintance he makes. Jonson represented his verse epistles for patrons as motivated by friendship and a disinterested respect for virtue, but Dekker's Horace writes encomia for money.[30]

Horace also has ignoble motives for writing satire. Where Jonson claimed to write to correct vice, Horace invents slanders to vex the innocent. His attacks are covert. When discovered, he attempts to conciliate his victim, swearing eternal friendship and repudiating the intentions behind the slander. When Crispinus and Demetrius visit him, Horace dismisses their suspicions of him: "Deliver me your hands, I love you both, / As deare as my owne soule, proove me, and when / I shall traduce you, make me the scorne of men" (1.3.267–69). When Captain Tucca confronts him, Horace blames his decision to distribute slanderous epigrams on a temporary loss of self-control:

> Captaine, I'm sorry that you lay this wrong,
> So close unto your heart: deare Captaine thinke
> I writ out of hot bloud, which (now) being colde,
> I could be please'd (to please you) to quaffe downe,
> The poyson'd Inke, in which I dipt your name.
> (4.2.64–68)

Hot blood and *continuing fury* were the key terms, in the judicial opinion of *Salisbury's Case* (1553), that "distinguished deliberate but sudden homicide from homicide through something approaching true premeditation."[31] Horace makes a similar distinction, claiming that his slanders against Tucca were deliberate but not premeditated. The play systematically undermines Horace's account of his actions, making it clear that they are premeditated, habitual, and based on pragmatic calculations about their consequences. Horace slanders not in a momentary flash of anger but out of a sustained intention based on a rational calculation of his interests. The moment Tucca leaves, Horace begins to compose further slanders against him. Horace's behavioral flexibility and his sensitivity to his social environment make him the antithesis of a humorous character.

In the play's last act the entire community decides to punish Horace and Asinius: they costume the two offenders as satyrs and place a crown of thorns on Horace's head. The poetasters use the costume to accuse Horace of writing a regressive, archaic species of satire, the satire of a prelegal revenge culture. Through an etymological mistake, Renaissance writers and critics associated satires with satyrs. The satyr was frequently invoked in discussions that placed verse satire at the bottom of the hierarchy of genres: his shaggy, sylvan figure served to authorize a low level of decorum and rough writing. In *Satiromastix*, it is not Horace but Crispinus and Demetrius who practice a higher form of satire and deserve to be citizens of a state with a fully developed legal culture. The crown of thorns also has a complex symbolic function. The stinging of the thorns punishes the presumption of what Richard Helgerson calls the "self-crowned laureate."[32] It is difficult to know what to make of the allusion to that other crown of thorns, the one placed on Christ's head. Dekker certainly does not intend to represent Jonson's punishment as a martyrdom, so the allusion probably represents a dangerously blasphemous joke.

The arraignment of Horace, like the arraignment in the previous play, makes some careful discriminations concerning the intentions of the criminal:

> Under controule of my dread Soveraigne,
> We are thy Iudges; thou that didst *Arraigne*,
> Are now prepar'd for condemnation;
> Should I but bid thy *Muse stand to the Barre*,
> Thy selfe against her wouldst give evidence:
> For flat rebellion gainst the Sacred lawes
> Of divine Poesie: heerein most she mist,
> *Thy pride and scorne made her turne Saterist,*
> *And not her love to vertue* (as thou Preachest).
> (5.2.209–17)

The indictment addresses not only the nature of the act but its motivations. Horace had claimed to be compelled to write satire by his muse, a power outside the periphery of the self. Crispinus not only redefines Horace's motivation as "pride and scorne" rather than "love to vertue" but also locates the intention to slander within Horace rather than in his muse, making him fully accountable for his actions. Unlike the Ovid of *Poetaster*, Dekker's Horace does not take dictation from a daimon.

The punishment concludes with what looks like a serious effort at behavior modification: guided by Crispinus and Demetrius, Sir Vaughan forces Horace to swear to renounce a long list of habits, all reflecting vanity: "*Imprimis,* you shall sweare by *Phoebus* and the halfe score muses lacking one: not to sweare to hang your selfe, if you thought any Man, Ooman, or Silde, could write Playes and Rimes, as well-favour'd ones as yourself" (5.2.290–93). Like *Poetaster*, *Satiromastix* represents a penal system whose end is rehabilitation rather than punishment. The idea of rehabilitation is intimately linked to the representational mode of legal narrative, a mode in which characters possess the capacity to reflect on their actions, to change, and to discipline themselves. The conclusions of *Poetaster* and *Satiromastix* ask their defendants to internalize the regulatory apparatus that has been brought to bear on them.

The epilogue of *Satiromastix* expresses a willingness to continue the conflict: "if you set your hands and Seales to this, Horace will write against it, and you may have more sport: he shall not loose his labour, he shall not turne his blanke verses into wast paper: No, my Poetasters will not laugh at him, but will untrusse him agen, and agen, and agen" (20–25). *Satiromastix*, though, was the last frontal assault in the War of the Poets. By 1604, Jonson and Dekker were friendly enough to collaborate on the coronation celebration for James I, and Marston dedicated *The Malcontent* to Jonson.[33] If the War of the Poets had a larger significance, it may rest in a feature of the controversy that I have not yet discussed: Jonson's play invokes Roman law, while Dekker's trial, which involves a jury, seems to be governed by English common law. The ideological differences between the two legal systems became more starkly apparent in the seventeenth century: Roman law infamously favored monarchical prerogative, while common law allowed citizens to resist the claims of the monarch and insist on their customary rights. The War of the Poets maps these antagonistic legal systems onto different conceptions of authorship. Jonson frequently described his theatrical audiences as juries, and his prologues attempt to instruct those juries in the fundamentals of taste and criticism: Jonson did not trust the common auditor. Dekker more gracefully accepts the judgment of audiences, and he binds juries and theatergoers, popular sovereignty and the entertainment market, into a single ideological complex—one that remains with us today.

NOTES

The writing of this article was supported by grants from the Whiting Foundation and the Professional Staff Congress of the City University of New York.

1. Ben Jonson, *Poetaster, or His Arraignement* (5.3.213–34), in *Ben Jonson*, ed. C. H. Herford and Percy Simpson, vol. 4 (Oxford: Oxford University Press, 1932). All subsequent citations are given parenthetically in the text. Unless otherwise noted, all italics are those of the folio.

2. There have been two recent books on the poetomachia: Matthew Steggle, *Wars of the Theaters: The Poetics of Personation in the Age of Jonson* (Victoria, BC: University of Victoria, 1998); and James Bednarz, *Shakespeare and the Poets' War* (New York: Columbia University Press, 2001). Steggle's book is particularly strong on the imitation of Roman literature, and he does a careful, meticulous job of dating and contextualizing the plays. Bednarz focuses on the way that the conflict influenced the artistic development of both Shakespeare and Jonson. The only sustained discussion of the use of legal discourse in *Poetaster* is Lindsay Kaplan, *The Culture of Slander in Early Modern England* (Cambridge: Cambridge University Press, 1997), 64–91. Ann Barton has written a magisterial account of the poetomachia in *Ben Jonson, Dramatist* (Cambridge: Cambridge University Press, 1984), 58–91. Other helpful discussions include Rosalind Miles, *Ben Jonson: His Craft and*

Art (New York: Routledge, 1990), 38–68; Lawrence Danson, "Jonsonian Comedy and the Discovery of the Social Self," *PMLA* 99 (March 1984): 179–93; Richard Dutton, *Ben Jonson: To the First Folio* (Cambridge: Cambridge University Press, 1983), 34–53; A. L. Beaurline, *Jonson and Elizabethan Comedy: Essays in Dramatic Rhetoric* (San Marino, CA: Huntington Library, 1978); J. B. Bamborough, *Ben Jonson* (London: Hutchinson, 1970), 22–49; Anthony Caputi, *John Marston, Satirist* (Ithaca: Cornell University Press, 1961), 80–116; and M. C. Bradbrook, *The Growth and Structure of Elizabethan Comedy* (London: Chatto and Windus, 1955), 94–103. For analyses of Jonson's career and his strategies of self-presentation I am also indebted to Richard Helgerson, *Self-Crowned Laureates: Spenser, Jonson, Milton, and the Literary System* (Berkeley: University of California Press, 1983), 122–44; George E. Rowe, *Distinguishing Jonson: Imitation, Rivalry, and the Direction of a Dramatic Career* (Lincoln: University of Nebraska Press, 1988); and Joseph Loewenstein, "The Script in the Marketplace," *Representations* 12 (Fall 1985): 101–14.

3. Herford and Simpson, *Ben Jonson*, 1:136.

4. There is another comical satire, written by an anonymous playwright, that has no connection to the War of the Poets; see *Every Woman in Her Humour: A Critical Edition*, ed. Archie Mervin Tyson (New York: Garland, 1980). It appears to have been written between 1600 and 1608. Like the comical satires of Marston and Dekker, this play combines a marriage plot with a satirical plot. Like *Poetaster* and *Satiromastix*, it is set in Rome: the love plot features Cicero.

5. The latter pamphlet (London, 1587) is by George Whetstone. In dialogue form, it justifies the decision to condemn the Babington conspirators by describing their failure to repent.

6. Helgerson, *Self-Crowned Laureates*, esp. 25–35.

7. Lines 33–34. This denial of a perfectly obvious topicality is characteristic of what Annabel Patterson has described as the hermeneutics of censorship; see her *Censorship and Interpretation: The Conditions of Writing and Reading in Early Modern England* (Madison: University of Wisconsin Press, 1984). Here, of course, Jonson is concerned not just with state censorship but with the possibility of a civil suit.

8. Jonson is drawing on Ovid's description of Envy in the *Metamorphoses*: "Videt intus edentem / vipereas carnes, vitiorum alimenta suorum, / Invidiam" (He saw Envy eating vipers as her meat, the nourishment of her vices). Cited in Herford and Simpson, *Ben Jonson*, 9:537, note to line 44; my translation.

9. Luke Wilson fascinatingly suggests that the "governing legal metaphor" in tragedy tends to be the law of homicide, while in comedy it tends to be the law of contract. Wilson goes on to remark that there are comedies in which the law of homicide is also important, including *The Merchant of Venice* and *Measure for Measure*. See Luke Wilson, *Theaters of Intention: Drama and the Law in Early Modern England* (Stanford: Stanford University Press, 2000), 5. Given the barely latent violence characteristic of satire, it makes sense that comical satire would also be a borderline case, relying on criminal as well as civil law.

10. The passages from *De legibus et consuetudinibus Angliae* (attributed to Henry de Bracton) and Coke are both cited in Joel Peter Eigen, *Witnessing Insanity: Madness and Mad-Doctors in the English Court* (New Haven: Yale University Press, 1995), 35. My summary of legal debates over the concept of intention draws on Eigen's book; on Anthony Duff's *Intention, Agency, and Criminal Liability: Philosophy of Action and the Criminal Law* (Cambridge: Basil Blackwell, 1990); on James Marshall's *Intention in Law and Society* (New York: Funk and Wagnalls, 1968); and on Robert Dreher's "Origin, Development, and Present Status of Insanity as a Defense to Criminal Responsibility in the Common Law," *Journal of the History of the Behavioral Sciences* 3 (1967): 47–55.

11. *The Reports of Sir Edward Coke Knight* (London, 1698), 335. The translations in brackets are mine. Like Envy's snake-swallowing agents, drunkards voluntarily enter a state of defective agency, although their actions become unpredictable rather than compulsive. In Coke's view, drunkenness aggravates rather than reduces culpability.

12. H. L. A. Hart, "Negligence, Mens Rea, and Criminal Responsibility," in *Philosophy of Law*, ed. Joel Feinberg and Hyman Gross (Encino, CA: Dickinson, 1975), 401. Hart is skeptical about this rather Platonic position.

13. Katharine Eisaman Maus discusses the law's epistemological anxiety concerning the intentions of the defendant; see *Inwardness and Theater in the English Renaissance* (Chicago: University of Chicago Press, 1995), esp. 104–27. John Langbein discusses the evolution of laws concerning testimony and evidence in *Torture and the Law of Proof* (Chicago: University of Chicago Press, 1977). Only gradually did the law relinquish its dependence on the confession of the accused.

14. All of these examples come from *A Complete Collection of State Trials*, ed. T. B. Howell, 21 vols. (London: Longman, Hurst, Rees, and Browne, 1816). For Parry's trial in 1584, see 1:1095–11. For the trials of the Babington conspirators in 1586, see 1:1127–41 and 1141–60. For Thomas Lee, see 1:1403–09. For Sanquire, see 2:743–64; for Bacon's words, 2:751.

15. The poem is based on Marlowe's translation of Ovid's *Amores*, 1.15, cited in Herford and Simpson, *Ben Jonson*, 9:538 n.

16. In the apologetical dialogue that follows the play, Jonson quotes Ovid's remark about his father's hostility to poetry: "Saepe pater dixit, studium quid inutile tentas? / Maeonides nullas ipse reliquit opes" [Often father asked, "Why do you pursue useless studies? Homer himself left no wealth behind"] (*Tristia*, 4.10.21–22). Discussed in Herford and Simpson, *Ben Jonson*, 9:540 n.; my translation.

17. In the *Tristia*, Ovid makes a related use of the idea of poetic inspiration. He represents his poetry as the product of a sort of illness, an external force that overcame him and worked against his own interests: "at nunc—tanta meo comes est insania morbo— / saxa malum refero rursus ad icta pedem." (But as it is—such madness accompanies my disease—I am once more returning my luckless foot to the stone it has struck.) *Tristia, ex Ponto* (Cambridge, MA: Harvard University Press, 1988), vol. 6 of *Ovid*, 2nd ed., trans. Arthur P. Wheeler, rev. G. P. Goold (2.1.15–16). See also 3.3.74, 3.7.9–10, and 4.1.19–36.

18. As Kaplan notes, this is an anachronistic example of the medieval fortune-telling practice known as the *sortes Vergilianae*; see *Culture of Slander*, 76.

19. For a genealogy of allegorical emblems of slander and envy, see Jane Aptekar, *Icons of Justice: Iconography and Thematic Imagery in Book V of "The Faerie Queene"* (New York: Columbia University Press, 1969), 202–11.

20. For the idea that the Elizabethan courts assigned punishments that functioned as metaphors for the particular crimes of the defendant, see Kaplan, *Culture of Slander*.

21. See Herford and Simpson, *Ben Jonson*, 11:578–79, note to lines 453–529.

22. In the romantic comedy, Sir Walter Terrill is about to marry Celestine when the king decides to exercise his droit de seigneur to deflower the bride. When the bride attempts suicide, the king relents and allows the couple to marry. The two plots seem completely unrelated, leading at least one critic to suggest that Dekker had been writing a romantic comedy and then grafted the satirical plot onto it in order to get a response to *Cynthia's Revels* to the stage more quickly (Barton, *Ben Jonson*, 87). But Marston's *Jack Drum's Entertainment* and *What You Will* both have a similar structure.

23. E. A. J. Honigman identifies Asinius with John Weever in *John Weever: A Biography of a Literary Associate of Shakespeare and Jonson, Together with a Photographic Facsimile of Weever's "Epigrammes" (1599)* (Manchester: Manchester University Press, 1987), 39–41, 47–51. *The Whipping of the Satyre* (1601), which was probably written by Weever, slanders both Marston and Jonson. For the question of the authorship of this pamphlet, see Arnold Davenport's introduction to *The Whipper Pamphlets* (Liverpool: University Press of Liverpool, 1951), vii–xi.

24. Thomas Dekker, *Satiromastix. OR The untrussing of the Humourous Poet*, in *The Dramatic Works of Thomas Dekker*, ed. Fredson Bowers (Cambridge: Cambridge University Press, 1953), preface, lines 12–14. All subsequent citations are given parenthetically in the text.

25. My account of Jonson's presentation of his laureate ambitions in his comical satires draws on the work of Helgerson, *Self-Crowned Laureates*, 122–44, and Rowe, *Distinguishing Jonson*, 68–90.

26. Jonson was ambivalent about the concept of poetic inspiration. Usually he tended to privilege craft and learning over inspiration, but see "Ode. To Sir William Sidney, on His Birthday," "The Vision of Ben Jonson, on the Muses of His Friend M. Drayton," "Ode Allegoric," and especially "Proludium": "A further fury my raised spirit controls, / Which raps me up to the true heaven of love; / And conjures all my faculties to approve / The glories of it. Now our muse takes wing, / And now an epode, to deep ears, we sing" (12–16), all in Herford and Simpson, *Ben Jonson*, vol. 8.

27. Although the final line remains the same, there are differences between Jonson's version and Dekker's. Even as he undercuts the conventions of the ode, Dekker shows that he too can write in this lofty vein.

28. For a typology of the diverse kinds assembled under the label *ode*, see Paul Fry, *The Poet's Calling in the English Ode* (New Haven: Yale University Press, 1980), 1–13.

29. See, for example, the prologue to *Cynthia's Revels*, lines 209–11.

30. For discussions of Jonson's patronage strategies, which attempted to preserve his own dignity, see Richard S. Peterson, *Imitation and Praise in the Poems of Ben Jonson* (New Haven: Yale University Press, 1981).

31. Thomas Andrew Green, *Verdict According to Conscience: Perspectives on the English Criminal Jury Trial 1200–1800* (Chicago: University of Chicago Press, 1985), 121–22. For *Salisbury's Case* (1553), see Edmund Plowden, *The Commentaries or Reports of Edmund Plowden* (Dublin: H. Watts, 1792, trans. from *Les Commentaries*, 1558), fol. 100. Before *Salisbury*, the law did not distinguish murder from manslaughter. Jonson's ability to claim benefit of clergy for his killing of Gabriel Spencer in 1598 depended on this distinction.

32. Helgerson, *Self-Crowned Laureates*.

33. Bednarz, *Shakespeare and the Poets' War*, 257–64, detects further sniping in the work of all participants, including Shakespeare. Loewenstein, in his examination of the coronation celebration, finds Jonson and Dekker subtly disparaging each other in the published versions of their respective contributions; see Joseph Loewenstein, Ben Jonson and Possessive Authorship (New York: Cambridge University Press, 2002), 170–72.

TWO

The Law versus the Marketplace in Jonson's *Bartholomew Fair*

Paul Cantor

I

Compared to Jonson's earlier comic masterpieces, *Volpone* and *The Alchemist*, *Bartholomew Fair* seems unfocused and diffuse.[1] It lacks a pair of central characters around whom the play is organized and who appear to direct its action, such as Volpone and Mosca in *Volpone* or Face and Subtle in *The Alchemist*.[2] The play is constantly threatening to veer off into irrelevance, incoherence, and even absurdity. But its apparent formlessness and lack of a center reflect a deeper order and sense of form. By liberating the dialogue from the normal constraints of dramatic action, Jonson freed himself to put an unparalleled slice of Renaissance life on the stage. What seems at first to be a weakness of *Bartholomew Fair*—its lack of focus—turns out to be its great strength—its ability to embrace a wide variety of human types and develop them in their full diversity, without imposing any narrowing artistic or moral conceptions upon them.

Bartholomew Fair is thus deeply paradoxical. Though a highly artful play, it succeeds in concealing its artifice and may at first seem to be just thrown together on the stage like an improvisation.[3] Though seemingly the most formless of Jonson's plays, it actually obeys the unities of time and place as strictly as any of his other works.[4] In fact, it comes as close to unfolding in real time on stage as any

Renaissance drama. Remarkably, in *Bartholomew Fair* Jonson found a way to remain within the bounds of his neoclassical conception of dramatic form, while still imparting a feeling of spontaneity to the play. In short, the play obeys Jonson's cherished law of the unities, while appearing to be wholly free and above or beyond any formal law.[5]

The tension between law and spontaneity evident in the form of *Bartholomew Fair* turns out to be at work in the content as well. In recreating Bartholomew Fair on the stage, the play offers a remarkable portrait of one of the great marketplaces of Renaissance London.[6] Throughout his career, Jonson was fascinated by the emerging market economy in Renaissance Europe. He was intrigued by the new categories of human identity the market was creating (the roles of merchants, bankers, financiers, and entrepreneurs), and he was evidently troubled by the new forms of corruption and vice endemic to protocapitalist life. *Bartholomew Fair* gave Jonson a chance to anatomize the lawlessness of the marketplace. Through the comments of his Puritan characters, Jonson shows how the fair violates religious law, and he uses Adam Overdo, a justice of the peace, to rail against the ways the merchants continually violate the criminal law as well. As Jonson presents it, Bartholomew Fair is the original home and headquarters of all the charlatans, cheaters, and thieves in London.

Yet for all his criticism of the marketplace in *Bartholomew Fair*, Jonson ends up being more critical of its critics.[7] From the standpoint of traditional religion and politics, the market may look lawless, but Jonson explores the possibility that it may obey laws of its own. In a remarkable anticipation of free-market economics, he appears to sense that the market may be a self-regulating mechanism, capable of bringing peace to a society that seems otherwise to be tearing itself apart in religious and political conflicts.[8] The characters who stand up for religious and political principles in *Bartholomew Fair* turn out to be the divisive forces in the play, while the seemingly lawless participants in the fair work to bring about a kind of civil harmony, based on the satisfaction of fundamental economic needs and natural human desires. Jonson exposes all the faults of an unregulated marketplace, but he more profoundly subjects its would-be regulators to a withering critique. He reveals their self-interested motives for wanting to regulate the fair and, more importantly, lays bare their sheer incompetence to manage the marketplace successfully.

In contrast to what happens in Jonson's earlier masterpieces, *Volpone* and *The Alchemist*, in *Bartholomew Fair* the apparent forces of disorder triumph at the end and frustrate the efforts of those who try to impose order on their economic activities.[9] As grave as Jonson's doubts about an unregulated market may be, in the end he seems to suggest that a regulated market would be a good deal worse, if only because the regulators are no better than the regulated. For all its faults, the market in Jonson's portrayal answers to deep-seated needs in human nature, and he ultimately seems to recognize the value of the freedom it offers, as well as the fact that freedom is compatible with its own kind of order. In short, Jonson seems to have an inkling of the idea of spontaneous order as it was to be developed in the twentieth century by the Austrian economist Friedrich Hayek.[10] *Bartholomew Fair* offers an example in miniature of a community that is ordered, not by regulations imposed from above by an outside authority, but by self-regulating principles generated from within, a system of checks and balances that relies on the common material interests of its participants to bring about their harmony. *Bartholomew Fair* may be the first portrait in literary history of how a free market operates.

If Jonson displays unusual sympathy for the nascent free markets of the Renaissance in *Bartholomew Fair*, the reason may be that he recognized that as a professional dramatist and actor he was a participant in a marketplace himself. Bartholomew Fair is the headquarters of charlatans and thieves, but it is also the home of playwrights and actors. Jonson seems to have come to realize that if marketplaces are regulated, the theater will always be among the first to come under government control and the results will not always be beneficial to the theater and its public.[11] As he shows particularly in his Puritan characters, Jonson understood that critics of the marketplace inevitably become critics of the theater as an especially conspicuous example of market principles. In *Bartholomew Fair* Jonson seems to allow his professional commitment to the theater to overcome the contempt for the world of commerce he shared with many of his aristocratic patrons. He even seems to have tried to shape a new dramatic form in *Bartholomew Fair* that would mirror the freedom and spontaneity of the marketplace it represents. The apparent formlessness of the play actually answers to an inner law—the spontaneous order of the free market—and its artful artlessness suggests in aesthetic terms how the principles of order and freedom can be reconciled.[12] *Bartholomew Fair* thus explores the issue of law on several levels at once—religious law, political law, economic law, and aesthetic law—and charts the complex interaction of these various legal domains.

II

At first sight, *Bartholomew Fair* seems to carry on the critique of the nascent market economy of the Renaissance Jonson had developed in earlier plays such as *Volpone* and *The Alchemist*. Like many of his contemporaries, Jonson was particularly disturbed by the way his society was moving from a conception of wealth based on land to one based on money. In *Volpone*, he satirizes the way money begets money in the devious schemes of Volpone and Mosca, who appear to be utterly unproductive and living like parasites off the wealth of others. In *The Alchemist*, Jonson images the world of trade and finance as a giant con game, in which greedy and ambitious men on the make are seduced into a variety of get-rich-quick schemes by the charlatans Face and Subtle. To Jonson, the act of market exchange looks like alchemy, the fraudulent promise to create value out of nothing, to change something worthless into something precious, as the alchemist claims to transmute base metals into gold.

Jonson is thus a good illustration of Hayek's claim that the market economy looks like magic to people who do not understand the complexities of economic transactions. Many fail to recognize the genuine contributions entrepreneurs make to economic life by their ability to ferret out knowledge of market conditions and their willingness to take risks; these people thus picture the businessman as a kind of sorcerer. As Hayek writes:

> Such distrust and fear have, since antiquity and in many parts of the world, led ordinary people as well as socialist thinkers to regard trade not only as distinct from material production, not only as chaotic and superfluous in itself, . . . but also as suspicious, inferior, dishonest, and contemptible. . . . Activities that appear to add to available wealth, "out of nothing," without physical creation and by merely rearranging what already exists, stink of sorcery. . . . That a mere change of hands should lead to a gain in value to all participants, that it need not mean gain to one at the expense of the others (or what has come to be called exploitation), was and is nonetheless intuitively difficult to grasp. . . . As a consequence of all these circumstances, many people continue to find the mental feats associated with trade easy to discount even when they do not attribute them to sorcery, or see them as depending on trick or fraud or cunning deceit.[13]

As Hayek points out, this kind of distrust of the businessman is particularly acute early in economic history. For example, during the Renaissance, when capitalist principles were beginning to dissolve feudalist ways of doing business, many people were confused and alienated by the initial results.[14]

Jonson seems to have spent much of his career in reaction to and rebellion against what can be described as his lower-middle-class origins.[15] His stepfather was a bricklayer, and by following in his footsteps Jonson was exposed early in his life to the world of trade. Fortunately he received an excellent education at the famous Westminster School in London and pursued the typical middle-class path of rising in society by using his wits and learning.[16] Probably in 1594 he entered the world of the professional theater, first as an actor and then as a playwright. The theater was one of the more advanced segments of the Elizabethan economy, employing financial and marketing techniques that were sophisticated for the time (for example, the theaters were early examples of joint-stock companies and were heavily capitalized by Renaissance standards). As the cases of Marlowe and Shakespeare had already shown, the Elizabethan theater offered a marvelous opportunity for a talented young man to make money and a name for himself.[17]

Although Jonson prospered in the theater world, he seems to have resented the source of his income and success. He repeatedly shows signs of believing that the conditions of the commercial theaters forced him to compromise his art to please the debased taste of the public. He made fun of the way other playwrights (including Shakespeare) catered to their audience, and he often got embroiled in controversy as a result. He sought to purge the theater of what he perceived to be its vulgarity, conceiving of himself as the playwright who would restore classical dignity to drama, in part by consciously imitating Roman models in many of his plays. Jonson was the first English playwright to bring out a published edition of his plays (in 1616), no doubt with a view to proving that his works were not the mere ephemeral products of the entertainment marketplace but literature of lasting value.[18]

Throughout his literary career, Jonson did everything he could to escape the commercial theater world, above all turning to aristocratic and royal patronage as an alternative to his bourgeois source of income in the entertainment business. He wrote poetry in quest of aristocratic patrons, and even in his dramatic career he alternated between writing for the public theaters and writing for the royal court.[19] He was the great master of the court masque and was richly rewarded over the years by James I for his contribution to royal entertainments. Aside from the financial advantages of writing for the court, Jonson seems to have been attracted by the prospect of composing with aristocratic taste in mind, rather than the lower- and middle-class taste that prevailed in the commercial theaters. The stage history of *Bartholomew Fair* encapsulates Jonson's theatrical career in miniature. The play was first staged on October 31, 1614, at one of the public theaters, the Hope, and the following evening it was performed at court before James I.[20] In the published version of the play, both the prologue and the epilogue are addressed to James, and Jonson shamelessly flatters the king for having taste superior to the mob's. In this one play, Jonson for once seems to have it both ways.[21] He gives his popular audience the kind of vulgar spectacle it craves and then repackages the same material for a court audience, presenting it in a condescending fashion and implying that he and his aristocratic patrons are above this sort of foolery.[22]

In that sense, *Bartholomew Fair* seems to embody everything that was conservative and backward-looking in Jonson's drama. He seems to side with the aristocracy and its world of feudal privilege against the rising middle class and its world of money and commerce.[23] For critics with socialist leanings, it is tempting to read *Bartholomew Fair* as a proto-Brechtian work, as if Jonson were criticizing the early signs of capitalism from the left.[24] But insofar as the play satirizes the commercial world, it does so from the right. One must remember that even (and especially) in Marxist terms, capitalism was the progressive force in Jonson's day, since it was working to dissolve centuries of antiquated feudal privilege and unleash unprecedentedly productive forces. At first glance, Jonson's view of capitalism in *Bartholomew Fair* thus seems reactionary. Turning his back on his own class origins and scorning the original source of his theatrical success, he identifies with an aristocracy we now know to have been dying. *Bartholomew Fair* shows how chaotic and morally dubious the new world of trade and money looked to the old order it was displacing. In Jonson's portrait, the marketplace is basically a den of thieves and flouts all conventional notions of morality, decency, and fair play. One character, Ezekiel Edgworth, is a professional cutpurse, but Jonson does not present him as the only criminal among a group of honest tradespeople. On the contrary, almost all the fair merchants are directly implicated in the activities of Edgworth, identifying victims for him, setting them up for the actual robberies, and helping him to dispose of the stolen goods.

Even when the merchants of Bartholomew Fair are not participating in outright thievery, Jonson presents them as looking to cheat their customers. He makes the familiar charge that the merchants adulterate their products to increase their profits.[25] Many of the tradespeople deal in suspicious merchandise (see, for example, 2.2.3–9), but the prize for adulteration at the fair goes to Ursula the pigwoman, who also does a thriving business in alcohol and tobacco on the side and instructs her assistant Mooncalf on how to stretch their supplies and increase their sales:

> But look to't, sirrah, you were best; threepence a pipeful I will ha' made of all my whole pound of tobacco, and a quarter of a pound of coltsfoot mixed with it too, to eke it out.... Then six and twenty shillings a barrel I will advance o'

> my beer, and fifty shillings a hundred o' my bottle-ale; I ha' told you the ways how to raise it. Froth your cans well i' the filling, at length, rogue, and jog your bottles o' the buttock, sirrah, then skink out the first glass, ever, and drink with all companies, though you be sure to be drunk; you'll misreckon the better, and be less ashamed on't. But your true trick, rascal, must be to be ever busy, and mis-take away the bottles and cans in haste before they be half drunk off, and never hear anybody call (if they should chance to mark you) till you ha' brought fresh, and be able to forswear 'em. (2.2.86–99)

The density of detail in this passage suggests that Jonson was uncannily familiar with the dark side of Renaissance commerce.

But Jonson is not interested only in aberrations of the market principle, moments when unscrupulous individuals depart from the decent norms of business. His satire goes right to the heart of the market principle itself. He is extremely skeptical about the way products are merchandised and displays a surprisingly sophisticated understanding of how tradespeople are able to prey upon the desires of potential customers. Jonson's portrait of the fair suggests a world that has gone mad with consumerism, and the young fool, Bartholomew Cokes, is the maddest of them all—Jonson's image of everything that can go wrong when a market liberates the desires of its customers.[26] He is particularly struck by the power of what we would call advertising. Jonson shows the customers at the fair continuously bombarded by the din of the merchants hawking their wares: "What do you lack? What is't you buy? What do you lack? Rattles, drums, halberts, horses, babies o' the best? Fiddles of the finest?" (2.2.28–32).

Cokes's tutor, Humphrey Wasp, describes him as mesmerized by the power of advertising—the many signs displayed at the fair (1.4.102–6). As a result, Cokes has his desires awakened, and he cannot control his appetites (1.5.100–106). In Cokes, Jonson creates an unforgettable portrait of the helpless consumer, caught in the webs of advertising and overwhelmed by the wealth of goods now available in the Renaissance marketplace: "And the three Jew's trumps; and half a dozen o' birds, and that drum (I have one drum already) and your smiths (I like that device o' your smiths very pretty well) and four halberts—and (le'me see) that fine painted great lady, and her three women for state, I'll have" (3.4.67–71).

Wasp sees the logical conclusion of Cokes's infinite desire: "No, the shop; buy the whole shop, it will be best, the shop, the shop!" (3.4.72–73). Cokes recognizes the truth of Wasp's charge—"I do want such a number o' things" (3.4.82)—and finally asks one merchant: "What's the price, at a word, o' thy whole shop, case and all, as it stands" (3.4.129–30). Without skipping a beat, Leatherhead calculates the sum: "Sir, it stands me in six and twenty shillings sevenpence halfpenny, besides three shillings for my ground" (3.4.131–32). Here is the new world of capitalism in a nutshell—everything has its price in money and everything is up for sale. To emphasize the point and suggest that even human flesh can be bought in the marketplace, Jonson makes prostitution an integral part of the fair. He presents the marketplace as a deeply confused and confusing realm, a topsy-turvy world in which moral values are inverted and characters lose their bearings. As the consumer par excellence, Cokes ends up completely bewildered and disoriented by his experience at the fair: "By this light, I cannot find my gingerbread-wife nor my hobby-horse man in all the Fair, now, to ha' my money again. And I do not know the way out on't, to go home for more. . . . Dost thou know where I dwell?" (4.2.20–22, 25). Assaulted from all sides by thieves, charlatans, and advertisers, Cokes utterly loses his sense of identity: "Friend, do you know who I am?" (4.2.71).

III

Jonson develops a strong case against the market in *Bartholomew Fair*. He shows the amorality, venality, lawlessness, and even criminality of the unregulated marketplace. And he includes in the play characters who vehemently condemn the fair and call for its regulation. But for once Jonson asks the follow-up question: Who are these would-be regulators, and are they fit to impose law and order on the sprawling marketplace they profess to despise? This is not a trivial question, and just by posing it Jonson takes a significant step toward arguments that eventually were to be developed by economists such as Adam Smith in favor of free markets. The fact that an unregulated market may have its faults and disadvantages does not in itself prove that a regulated market will be any better: it may have its own faults and disadvantages and perhaps end up producing an even worse situation. In *Bartholomew Fair* Jonson finally gets around to scrutinizing the proponents of law and order to see if they really are capable of living up to their promise of improving the world.

The simplest case Jonson examines is Humphrey Wasp, who is devoted to restraining the appetites of his charge Cokes. Given how freely young Bartholomew spends his money, one can sympathize with Humphrey's attempts to be strict with him. But Wasp responds to Cokes's excesses with moral indignation, and indeed indignation is the hallmark of his character. As his name indicates, Humphrey is waspish, always ready to fly off into fits of anger and quarrel with anyone in sight. It is thus by no means clear that his disposition is preferable to Cokes's or any less passionate and excessive. Bartholomew is a fool, but he is a relatively harmless fool and unlikely to cause much trouble for others. By contrast, Wasp is always provoking conflict and getting himself and others into difficulties. Other characters, such as John Littlewit, feel compelled to caution him: "Be civil, Master Numps" (1.4.53). His reply is not promising: "Why, say I have a humour not to be civil; how then? Who shall compel me?" (1.4.54–55). Incivility seems to be fundamental to Wasp's character. Mistress Overdo views him as an enemy of the "conservation of the peace" (1.5.12) and eventually pleads with him: "govern your passions" (1.5.21). Here is the irony of Wasp's role in the play: he sets himself up as the governor of his charge's passions, yet he cannot govern his own. He presents himself as the champion of law and order, yet he is in fact one of the chief forces for disorder in the play.

The game of "vapours" that breaks out in act 4 is very funny and borders on absurdity, but it may reflect a serious threat Jonson sensed in his world. In his image of people contradicting each other merely for the sake of contradicting each other, Jonson offers a comic reflection of Elizabethan and Jacobean society—a community riven by all sorts of competing claims and authorities, political and religious. With the benefit of historical hindsight, we can read *Bartholomew Fair* today and see the forces at work in the London of the play that were in a few decades to plunge Britain into civil war. But Jonson himself evidently saw the Puritan Revolution coming or at least had an inkling of what might spark it. As the game of vapours gets out of hand and starts to become dangerous, Mistress Overdo sees the direction in which Humphrey's waspishness is leading him: "Are you rebels? Gentlemen? Shall I send out a sergeant-at-arms or a writ o' rebellion against you?" (4.4.128–29). The threat of revolution seems to be hovering in the background of *Bartholomew Fair*, and Jonson traces it not to the childish appetites of a Bartholomew Cokes but to the fiery indignation of a Humphrey Wasp.

In fact, the only way to contain Wasp's rebellious anger turns out to be to place him in the stocks. In another ironic twist, the would-be restrainer ends up in restraint. The irony is not lost even on the dim-witted Bartholomew; learning of his tutor's disgrace, Cokes is no longer disposed to honor his authority: "Hold your peace, Numps; you ha' been I' the stocks, I hear" (5.4.88). Wasp immediately recognizes the implications for his continued rule over his charge: "Does he know that? Nay, then the date of my authority is out; I must think no longer to reign, my government is at an end. He that will correct another must want fault in himself" (5.4.90–91). Wasp's last statement may represent Jonson's great discovery in the course of thinking through and writing *Bartholomew Fair*.[27] The principle that only a superior, indeed a perfect, person has the right to regulate others does not apply just to Wasp in the play. In fact it is the governing principle of Jonson's critique of all the would-be forces of law and order in the play, and especially of Zeal-of-the-Land Busy.[28]

IV

The fact that a fanatical Puritan is one of the chief critics of the marketplace in *Bartholomew Fair* is a good indication that Jonson may be reconsidering his earlier attacks on the new economic freedom of his era.[29] Jonson's portrayal of Busy makes it clear that arguments against free markets are often ultimately based in religion, not economics. Busy's objections to advertising and to the products displayed at the fair are rooted in his Puritanism and specifically his hatred of idolatry (3.6.27–35). Busy is convinced that the economic activity at the fair is not merely disordered and unregulated but sinful and evil. For him the fair is "wicked and foul" and "fitter may it be called a foul than a Fair" (3.6.79–80). He claims to know what is good for his fellow human beings and what is bad for them. Thus he arrogates to himself the right to tell people what they can and cannot do in the marketplace. Jonson himself had a strong streak of moralism, and in many of his plays he sets himself up as the arbiter of good and evil. But his creation of the character of Busy seems to reflect a growing doubt about the social consequences of moralistic attitudes.

Busy is a busybody, constantly meddling in other people's affairs and trying to reorder their lives. He criticizes pride but he is exceedingly proud himself and enjoys lording it over others. It surely was not lost on Jonson that it was people like Busy who were attacking the London theaters and constantly trying to shut them down. Anyone who condemns attempts to please consumers is eventually going to get around to condemning the theater. In short, if the Puritans were enemies of the marketplace, Jonson may have begun to wonder if the marketplace was his friend.

Jonson portrays Busy as an overreacher, a man who sets himself up as a god over his fellow human beings and fails to live up to his inflated self-image. But he also shows that Busy is a hypocrite. He condemns the moneymaking activities of the marketplace, yet he is obsessed with moneymaking himself.[30] In general, as if he were anticipating Max Weber's *Protestant Ethic and the Spirit of Capitalism*,

Jonson shows the Puritans devoting themselves quasi-religiously to the acquisition of wealth. In the fifth act, Dame Purecraft finally reveals that she is "worth six thousand pound" (5.2.46)—a huge sum in those days—and goes on to explain the devious means by which she accumulated the money:[31]

> These seven years I have been a willful holy widow, only to draw feasts and gifts from my entangled suitors. I am also by office an assisting sister of the deacons, and a devourer, instead of a distributor, of the alms. I am a special maker of marriages for our decayed brethren with rich widows, for a third part of their wealth, when they are married, for the relief of the poor elect; as also our poor handsome young virgins with our wealthy bachelors or widowers to make them steal from their husbands when I have confirmed them in the faith, and got all put into their custodies. (5.2.48–57)

Here the Puritan Dame Purecraft begins to sound a good deal like one of Jonson's con men in earlier plays.

But Purecraft defers to Busy as the chief moneymaker of them all. In his scheming to exploit legacies, he sounds even more like Volpone: "Our elder, Zeal-of-the-Land, would have had me, but I know him to be the capital knave of the land, making himself rich by being made feoffee in trust to deceased brethren, and cozening their heirs by swearing the absolute gift of their inheritance" (5.2.59–63). Jonson gives Busy mercantile origins; the fact that he began as a baker (1.3.107–12) stresses his kinship to the tradespeople he later condemns. Toward the end of the play, in Busy's debate at the puppet show, the Puppet Dionysius points out that the Puritans are heavily involved in the clothing trade and are thus implicated in the very luxuries they rail against (5.5.75–84).[32]

By revealing the Puritans to be hypocrites, Jonson undermines their authority as advocates of law and order. He further shows that Busy is willing to bend the law to suit his own purposes.[33] Despite their claim to adhere strictly to religious law, the Puritans turn out to be extremely flexible when it comes to interpreting the law in accord with their own desires. When Win Littlewit expresses her deep longing for roast pig at the fair, her mother at first urges her to resist the temptation, but she soon is willing to endorse the desire "if it can be any way made or found lawful" (1.6.27–28). Dame Purecraft enlists her spiritual advisor Busy to find a way of pronouncing Win's appetite lawful. Busy sets to work interpreting the law, but it is a difficult case: "Verily, for the disease of longing, it is a disease, a carnal disease, or appetite, incident to women; and as it is carnal, and incident, it is natural, very natural. Now pig, it is a meat, and a meat that is nourishing, and may be longed for, and so consequently eaten; it may be eaten; very exceeding well eaten. But in the Fair, and as a Bartholomew pig, it cannot be eaten, for the very calling it a Bartholomew pig, and to eat it so, is a spice of idolatry" (1.6.43–49). Purecraft urges a liberal understanding of the law on her fellow Puritan: "Good Brother Zeal-of-the-Land, think to make it as lawful as you can" (1.6.54–55). Busy proves equal to the task: "It may be eaten, and in the Fair, I take it, in a booth, the tents of the wicked. The place is not much, not very much, we may be religious in midst of the profane, so it be eaten with a reformed mouth, with sobriety, and humbleness; not gorged in with gluttony or greediness" (1.6.63–67).

The ease with which Busy is able to interpret the law to permit him to do whatever he desires raises doubts about the status of law in the play. The advocates of the law present it as the moral alternative to the marketplace. The law is supposed to be immutable and incorruptible, as opposed to the mutable and corrupt marketplace, where everyone is on the make and values and prices change from minute to minute. But Jonson shows the Puritan characters making and remaking the law before our eyes. The law loses much of its prestige when it is revealed to be changeable and even pervertible according to the dictates of desire. In the puppet show debate, lawfulness turns out to be a matter of semantics, the product of mere wordplay and not of any fundamental principle. The puppet has an easy answer to Busy's charge that the theater lacks lawfulness:

> BUSY. I mean no vocation, idol, no present lawful calling.
> PUPPET DIONYSIUS. *Is yours a lawful calling?* . . .
> BUSY. Yes, mine is of the spirit.
> PUPPET DIONYSIUS. *Then idol is a lawful calling.*
> LEATHERHEAD. He says, then idol is a lawful calling! For you called him idol, and your calling is of the spirit.
> (5.5.49–50, 52–55)

By the time Jonson is through ringing changes on the word *law* in *Bartholomew Fair*, the term has become virtually meaningless.[34] The law no longer appears to stand majestically above the marketplace and hence to be entitled to regulate it. Rather, the law is negotiated and renegotiated just like any other item at the fair.

Jonson's antipathy to the Puritans led him to probe deeper into their hostility to the marketplace. The gamester Quarlous notes that Busy, as a Puritan, rejects all tradition and claims to remain true to a purified notion of an original faith: "By his profession, he will ever be i' the state of innocence, though, and childhood; derides all antiquity; defies any other learning than inspiration; and what discretion soever years should afford him, it is all prevented in original ignorance" (1.3.129–33). Busy's hatred for the marketplace grows out of his Puritan hostility to tradition.[35] For Busy the marketplace is the locus of business as usual, where men and women go about satisfying the desires they have always had. By catering to what people want, the market stands in the way of the moral reformation Busy is striving for. Unlike the merchants of Bartholomew Fair, he will not accept human beings as he finds them but rather wants to remake them in one grand revolutionary effort. That is why Busy images the moral reformation of the world in terms of an apocalyptic abolition of the marketplace. He defines himself as "one that rejoiceth in his affliction, and sitteth here to prophesy the destruction of fairs and May-games, wakes and Whitsun ales, and doth sigh and groan for the reformation of these abuses" (4.6.78–80). This passage embodies a profound insight into Puritan psychology and into the political and economic reformer's mentality in general. Jonson understands that Busy rejects the world as such and wants to see it fundamentally remade. His hostility to life as usual dictates his hostility to business as usual and hence demands the overthrow of the marketplace as the center of existing abuses. Jonson saw how deeply revolutionary the Puritan mentality was, and events in a few decades were to prove him right.

The Puritan revolutionary impulse manifests itself even on the level of language. Refusing to accept the common names of things, the Puritans become involved in a laughable process of trying to rename everything, including themselves: "O, they have all such names, sir; he was witness for Win here—they will not be called godfathers—and named her Win-the-fight. You thought her name had been Winifred, did you not?" (1.3.116–19). In a play in which signs are often more important than substance, the impulse to rename things is tantamount to the impulse to remake them. Thus, although Busy appears to be an advocate of law and order, like Wasp he turns out to be a force for disorder. He too is guilty of incivility, as Quarlous makes clear in his final summary of the Puritan character: "Away, you are a herd of hypocritical proud ignorants, rather wild than mad, fitter for woods and the society of beasts than houses and the congregation of men. You are . . . outlaws to order and discipline" (5.2.38–41).

V

Like Wasp and Busy, Adam Overdo claims to devote himself to repressing passions and correcting excesses in others, yet he is in the grip of passion himself and goes from one excess to another.[36] Overdo is another busybody and would be a petty tyrant if he had his way. Though he presents himself as a disinterested servant of "the public good" (2.1.9; see also 5.2.84), Jonson suggests that he may be just a social climber who uses his office to advance his own cause. Wasp reproaches Mistress Overdo: "Why mistress, I knew Adam, the clerk, your husband, when he was Adam scrivener, and writ for twopence a sheet, as high as he bears his head now, or you your hood, dame" (4.4.141–43). Overdo is a little man who puffs himself up with the thought that he is better than his fellow human beings and seeks to prove it by imposing order on their lives.

Unfortunately for Overdo, he is not equal to the task he sets himself as the overseer of law and order. He prides himself on his judgment of human nature and his ability to spy into the souls of men. But Jonson shows him making one mistake after another.[37] He thinks that the robber Edgworth is in fact a "civil" young man and tries to become his patron (2.4.30). Overdo is particularly susceptible to anyone who will flatter his ego. This tendency becomes evident in his encounter with Trouble-All, a man who went mad when Overdo dismissed him from his position in the Court of Piepowders at the fair. Trouble-All is unwilling to do anything without a written warrant from Overdo, a form of madness that initially strikes the justice as evidence of Trouble-All's wisdom: "What should he be, that doth so esteem and advance my warrant? He seems a sober and discreet person!" (4.1.23–24). Overdo's continuing misjudgment of the other characters in the play makes him a laughingstock and ultimately undermines his authority. The complete collapse of his regime occurs when he goes to punish a group of prostitutes and discovers that one of them is his own wife in disguise.

When Overdo speaks out against the fair's merchandise, chiefly alcohol and tobacco, one might be tempted to sympathize with his criticism, but Jonson goes out of his way to caricature Overdo's complaints and make them sound foolish. Busy inveighs against the products of the fair because he is trying to save the souls of its customers; Overdo is trying to save their bodies. He cautions against alcoholic beverages: "Thirst not after that frothy liquor, ale; for who knows when he openeth the stopple what may be in the bottle? Hath not a snail, a spider, yea, a newt been found there?" (2.6.11–14). Overdo is also on an antismoking crusade: "Neither do thou lust after that tawny weed, tobacco... Whose complexion is like the Indian's that vents it! ... And who can tell, if, before the gathering and making up thereof, the alligator hath not pissed thereon?" (2.6.21–26). Overdo may be raising slightly different doubts about the safety of alcohol and tobacco products than we hear today, but the basic principle is the same. He distrusts anything exotic and loves to dwell on the worst-case scenario. He goes on to lament the amount of money he thinks is wasted on these luxury products: "Thirty pound a week in bottle-ale! Forty in tobacco! And ten more in ale again" (2.6.77–78). At times Overdo sounds much like a contemporary campaign against smoking: "Hence it is that the lungs of the tobacconist are rotted, the liver spotted, the brain smoked like the backside of the pig-woman's booth here" (2.6.39–41).

Overdo thus offers a puritanism of the body to correspond to Busy's puritanism of the soul. In either case, the result is the same: strict government control over the everyday activities of ordinary people, with prohibition as the ultimate goal. If it is not clear from the way Jonson has the justice characteristically overdo his tirade against alcohol and tobacco that the playwright is making fun of this health-conscious puritanism, one might recall that Overdo's attack on drinking and smoking is identical to Puritan strictures against theatergoing ("it's bad for you," "it wastes your money," and so on). Evidently by the time of writing *Bartholomew Fair*, Jonson had begun to wonder whether concern for saving souls and bodies would result in the end of the entertainment business as he knew it.

Perhaps the most remarkable aspect of Jonson's critique of authority in *Bartholomew Fair* is his anticipation of Hayek's theory about the benefits of dispersing knowledge in society. Overdo's scheme to disguise himself and spy out enormities at the fair is an attempt to gain the knowledge he would actually need to regulate the marketplace. Modeling himself on "a worthy worshipful man" (2.1.11–12), probably "Thomas Middleton, the reforming Lord Mayor of London in 1613–14,"[38] Overdo uses his masquerade to seek out a synoptic, even a panoptical view of the economic world of London: "Marry, go you into every alehouse, and down into every cellar; measure the length of puddings, take the gauge of black pots and cans, aye, and custards with a stick; and their circumference with a thread; weigh the loaves of bread on his middle finger; then would he send for 'em, home; give the puddings to the poor, the bread to the hungry, the custards to his children; break the pots and burn the cans himself; he would not trust his corrupt officers; he would do't himself" (2.1.16–24). As Overdo describes the mayor's procedures, they seem a model of regulating the economy. He oversees all economic activity in the city, down to the last detail, and he uses his comprehensive knowledge to correct all injustices, with a particular care to redistributing goods to the poor and needy. The actions of Overdo's model are in fact what most people have in mind when they talk about correcting the failures of the market.

But *Bartholomew Fair* is a comedy, and Overdo is one of the chief targets of its satire, not a model of enlightened rule in Jonson's eyes. There is more than something faintly absurd about the justice's view of a centrally planned economy. Indeed he inadvertently reveals the impossibility of the task. For a government to regulate the economy successfully, it would need knowledge of every detail of its working, all the way down to weighing every single loaf of bread to the ounce. But in fact this knowledge in all its complexity of detail is never available to any one person or centralized authority, as Jonson's example suggests. The mayor's idea of regulating the economy is to do every job himself, a telling image for the ultimate consequences of government intervention in the economy. The mayor violates the principle of the division of labor, which is the foundation of any advanced economy. In fact, the market works precisely by dispersing knowledge of economic phenomena among a myriad of people and using the pricing mechanism to coordinate their efforts. The central thrust of entrepreneurial activity is the creation, or at least the ferreting out, of economic knowledge, and this process works best precisely when it is not centralized but pits many individuals against each other in active competition (with success rewarded and failure punished in financial terms).[39]

Jonson specifically presents the problem of government regulation of the economy as a problem of knowledge. Overdo's model mayor has ambitious plans for restructuring the economy, yet he himself does not "trust his corrupt officers"; hence he gets involved in the hopeless task of doing everything in the economy by himself. Overdo realizes the limitations of his knowledge as a government official: "For (alas) as we are public persons, what do we know? Nay, what can we know? We hear with other men's ears; we see with other men's eyes; a foolish constable or a sleepy watchman is all our information; he slanders a gentleman by virtue of his place, as he calls it, and we by the vice of ours, must believe him. . . . This we are subject to, that live in high place; all our intelligence is idle, and most of our intelligencers, knaves; and by your leave, ourselves thought little better, if not arrant fools, for believing 'em" (2.1.24–34). By impeaching his sources of knowledge, Overdo undermines his authority to regulate the marketplace. Realizing the incompetence and unreliability of the officials he depends on, he ought to realize the futility of his plans. He points out all the reasons why government officials are not in a position to know the relevant economic facts, and his scheme to gain access to that knowledge proves to be a complete and humiliating failure for him. Overdo's noble-sounding vision of an all-seeing and all-knowing government turns out to be a fantasy and a farce. Government officials are limited and fallible human beings themselves and just as likely to make mistakes as merchants in the marketplace. The difference between civil servants and private businessmen is that when a central planner makes a mistake he is likely to disrupt the whole economy and not just a single business.

VI

The madman Trouble-All provides the inverted mirror image of an all-seeing, all-knowing government. He is the perfect subject of a panoptical regime,[40] the man who will not make a move without express warrant from a government official: "he will do nothing but by Justice Overdo's warrant: he will not eat a crust, nor drink a little, nor make him in his apparel ready. His wife, sir-reverence, cannot get him make his water or shift his shirt without his warrant" (4.1.51–54).[41] Trouble-All provides the reductio ad absurdum of the regulatory ideal. In a total command economy, people would insanely and slavishly refuse to do anything without explicit government approval. Even Overdo is appalled at what he has done to transform Trouble-All into a figure wholly dependent on authority for guidance: "If this be true, this is my greatest disaster!" (4.1.55).

Overdo's encounter with Trouble-All teaches him a Hayekian lesson, what one might call the law of unintended consequences: "To see what bad events may peep out o' the tail of good purposes!" (3.3.12–13). Jonson seems to measure his characters by the results of their actions, not their motives. The do-gooders in *Bartholomew Fair* are the cause of most of the difficulties in the play and all the near-disasters. And the reason is that in Jonson's view, life in general and the marketplace in particular are just too complicated for these simplistic and moralistic regulatory schemes to work successfully. Actions have unanticipated consequences and efforts to control events succeed only in producing disorder and eventually chaos. Overdo must learn to accept life for what it is, admit his own limitations, and abandon his plans for perfecting and reforming the world.[42] As Quarlous tells him in the end: "remember you are but Adam, flesh and blood! You have your frailty; forget your other name of Overdo, and invite us all to supper. There you and I will . . . drown the memory of all enormity in your biggest bowl at home" (5.6.93–97). Jonson presents the festive spirit of comedy as the triumph of humanity and freedom over petty moralism and officious government.[43]

The advocates of authority in *Bartholomew Fair* want to contrast the ordered and stable world of law with the chaotic and unstable world of the marketplace. But Jonson's satiric view of the would-be regulators suggests a different perspective. He seems to contrast the rigid and stultifying world of law with the fluid and vibrant world of the marketplace. As happens in many comedies, in *Bartholomew Fair* Jonson portrays the dead weight of the law as the obstacle standing in the way of the characters satisfying their normal human desires. The law appears in the first speech in the play proper, appropriately in stilted legal language: "Here's Master Bartholomew Cokes, of Harrow o'the hill, i'the county of Middlesex, Esquire, takes forth his license to marry Mistress Grace Wellborn of the said place and county" (1.1.3–5). The first manifestation of the power of law in *Bartholomew Fair* significantly takes the form of a marriage license.[44] Jonson emphasizes the way the law gives power to some human beings to dispose of the lives of others, with men usually ruling over women, and parents over children. Jonson makes one of the marriage plots turn on the fact that Grace Wellborn is the legal ward of Adam Overdo and thus his to dispose of in marriage.[45] In Grace's statement of her position, Jonson stresses the arbitrariness of her status and her dissatisfaction with it. When asked how she became Overdo's ward, Grace bitterly replies: "Faith, through a common calamity: he bought me, sir; and now he will marry me to his wife's brother, . . . or else I must pay value o' my land" (3.5.260–62). Evidently, human beings are bought and sold in the legal world just as commodities are bought and sold in the marketplace.[46] Far from providing an alternative to the venality of the market, the law seems to operate according to the same principles. Indeed in Jonson's presentation, the law seems worse than the market: it gives people the right to buy and sell other human beings, and not just commodities.

Women especially do not fare well in the legal world of *Bartholomew Fair*. In their homes, they seem to be the chattel property of their husbands, fathers, and guardians. That perhaps explains why the women in the play are particularly eager to go to the fair. For them, entering the marketplace represents a kind of liberation. Jonson suggests this point comically when several of the women quite literally enter the marketplace—that is, are enlisted into prostitution. He certainly is not advocating prostitution as a way of life, but he approaches the subject with greater freedom and less moralism than Justice Overdo does. Half jokingly, Jonson has the bawd Captain Whit try to teach Win Littlewit that she ought to prefer the life of a prostitute to that of a married woman: "de honest woman's life is a scurvy dull life" (4.5.26–27). The chief reason Whit offers for his claim is that a wife leads "de leef of a bondwoman," whereas he tells Win: "I vill make tee a free-woman" (4.5.29–30). The cutpurse Edgworth reinforces the point to Win later in the play: "Is not this a finer life, lady, than to be clogged with a husband?" (5.4.53–54). In *Bartholomew Fair*, the legal institution of marriage is presented as a form of slavery, while entering the marketplace as a prostitute appears to be a form of freedom.

Viewed from one perspective, prostitution is one of the chief vices of the fair, but in the full context of the play it is difficult for the advocates of law and order to use prostitution as an argument against the marketplace. Jonson does everything he can to efface the distinction between prostitutes and married women, as he shows men buying women in marriage.[47] Quarlous thinks of the legal institution as in fact a way to marry money itself: "Why should not I marry this six thousand pound . . . ? And a good trade too, that she has beside, ha? . . . It is money that I want; why should I not marry the money, when 'tis offered me? I have a license and all; it is but razing out one name and putting in another" (5.2.69–75). Quarlous also reveals the arbitrariness of legal documents: they are supposed to embody the sanctity of the law, but it is an easy matter to doctor them.[48] A legal document can mean almost anything, depending on how the writing is altered. There are a number of "blank checks" in the form of legal documents circulating in *Bartholomew Fair*,[49] including the open warrant Overdo thinks he is giving to the madman Trouble-All but that actually falls into the hands of Quarlous. He immediately grasps the possibilities of having the justice's signature on a blank document: "Why should not I ha' the conscience to make this a bond of a thousand pound, now?" (5.2.112–13). But Quarlous finds a better use for this blank document: to certify transferring Grace as a ward from Overdo to himself. Thus he, not Overdo, becomes the beneficiary when Grace must pay money to her guardian for the right to marry Winwife.

Jonson's criticism of the law is double-edged. On the one hand, the law appears to be too rigid; with its iron hand, it tries to define all human relationships and keep people confined to the straight and narrow path. But on the other hand, the law appears to be too flexible and arbitrary; with a stroke of a pen, a man can alter a legal document and redefine a human relationship. Ultimately in Jonson's portrayal the problem with the law is its mindless legalism. The law tries to codify the fluidity of life into binding rules, but as Jonson shows in *Bartholomew Fair*, once a legal document is written down it can all too easily be rewritten. As Jonson presents it, the law seems to alternate between defining the terms of human life too tightly and defining them too loosely. In either case, the law gives some human beings a despotic power over others.

Jonson's sympathy for the free market in *Bartholomew Fair* makes the play unusual if not unique in his dramatic output.[50] As we have seen, in other plays he can be highly critical of the marketplace and its effect on society. But it seems that for once in this play he decided to give the market its due and explore what kind of case could be made for economic freedom, or at least against economic regulation. If this seems like an implausible concern for Jonson, one must remember that by participating in the English Renaissance theater he was experiencing one of the most sophisticated and advanced segments of the economy of his time, and also one that was heavily regulated by the government. Jonson's experience in the theater in fact put him in an excellent position to examine the question of government regulation of the economy, of the law versus the marketplace. Jonson's newfound sympathy for the marketplace seems to have grown out of his recognition that his theater world was inextricably intertwined with the emerging market economy of his day.

NOTES

A different version of this essay was published under the title "In Defense of the Marketplace: Spontaneous Order in *Bartholomew Fair*" in *Ben Jonson Journal* 8 (2001): 23–64. The author wishes to thank the journal for permission to reprint substantial portions of that essay.

1. T. S. Eliot claimed that *Bartholomew Fair* has "hardly a plot at all." See his "Ben Jonson," in *Selected Essays* (New York: Harcourt, Brace, 1950), 134. See also Richard Levin, *The Multiple Plot in English Renaissance Drama* (Chicago: University of Chicago Press, 1971), 202: "We cannot find any central line of action which holds everything together." In his *Introduction to English Renaissance Comedy* (Manchester: Manchester University Press, 1999), Alexander Leggatt quotes Terry Hands, who, in connection with his 1969 production of the play for the Royal Shakespeare Company, described it as "an enormous canvas with no particular focus" (138). I quote *Bartholomew Fair* from the edition of Gordon Campbell in Ben Jonson, *The Alchemist and Other Plays* (Oxford: Oxford University Press, 1995), with citations incorporated in the body of the essay.

2. See Levin, *Multiple Plot*, 208, and Eugene M. Waith, ed., *Ben Jonson: Bartholomew Fair* (New Haven: Yale University Press, 1963), 2.

3. Martin Butler says that Jonson manages "to give an illusion of randomness which is carefully and rigorously premeditated." See his *Selected Plays of Ben Jonson* (Cambridge: Cambridge University Press, 1989), 2:147.

4. See Waith, *Bartholomew Fair*, 20.

5. See Leggatt, *English Renaissance Comedy*, 136–37; E. A. Horsman, ed., *Bartholomew Fair* (Manchester: Manchester University Press, 1960), xi; and Anne Barton, "Shakespeare and Jonson," in *Essays, Mainly Shakespearean* (Cambridge: Cambridge University Press, 1994), 294: "[*Bartholomew Fair*] maintains the most delicate balance between order and chaos, between structure and a seemingly undisciplined flow which is like the random, haphazard nature of life itself."

6. For information on the actual Bartholomew Fair and Renaissance fairs in general, see Peter Stallybrass and Allon White, *The Politics and Poetics of Transgression* (Ithaca:

Cornell University Press, 1986), especially chap. 1. Stallybrass and White correctly emphasize the modernity of the fair and its role as a harbinger of developing market principles, and they criticize a nostalgic view of the fair as a backward-looking medieval institution. For the role of fairs in the developing market economy of the Renaissance, see Jean-Christophe Agnew, *Worlds Apart: The Market and the Theater in Anglo-American Thought, 1550–1750* (Cambridge: Cambridge University Press, 1986), 17–56, and especially for Bartholomew Fair, 47.

7. See Waith, *Bartholomew Fair*, 3, and William W. E. Slights, *Ben Jonson and the Art of Secrecy* (Toronto: University of Toronto Press, 1994), 149, 152, and 211 n. 34.

8. Nearly a year and a half after writing the first draft of this essay, I discovered that its central claim had already been advanced by Jean-Christophe Agnew, who writes of *Bartholomew Fair* in his *Worlds Apart*, 120–21: "There are plenty of plots in the play but no plot to it; no one, villainous or virtuous, appears to be in charge.... [T]he fair itself is the engine that precipitates the action of the play.... Jonson's market operates, in effect, as an 'invisible hand,' diverting private vices to the public benefit.... [T]he forms and conventions that Jonson introduced to achieve his dramatic purposes in the play do adumbrate the solutions that Adam Smith would later propose to those who feared the divisive social consequences of unrestricted competition. Like *The Wealth of Nations*, *Bartholomew Fair* imagined the market as a power capable of generating its own legitimacy through a negotiated process of mutual authorization. By making the fair itself the occasion of countless private calculations and, at the same time, the vehicle of their ultimate public reconciliation, Jonson was taking a step, however tentative, toward a functionalist legitimation of a free and placeless market." (I thank my colleague Katharine Eisaman Maus for calling my attention to this passage and for other help with this essay.) My analysis may be regarded as a working out in detail of Agnew's original insight, though, for what it is worth, I did arrive at the point independently, and my use of Austrian economics, rather than Marxist, to analyze Jonson's view of the market leads me to emphasize different aspects of the play.

9. See Stallybrass and White, *Transgression*, 66; Jonas Barish, *Ben Jonson and the Language of Prose Comedy* (Cambridge, MA: Harvard University Press, 1967), 212–13; and Katharine Eisaman Maus, *Ben Jonson and the Roman Frame of Mind* (Princeton: Princeton University Press, 1984), 132.

10. For a concise statement of the theory of spontaneous order, see Hayek's essay "The Results of Human Action but Not of Human Design," in his *Studies in Philosophy, Politics and Economics* (New York: Clarion, 1969), 96–105.

11. For examples of government regulation during the Elizabethan period that proved disastrous to the theater companies and to Jonson in particular, see David Riggs, *Ben Jonson: A Life* (Cambridge, MA: Harvard University Press, 1989), 33–34.

12. For an excellent attempt to sketch out the structural pattern of *Bartholomew Fair*, see the section on the play in Levin's *Multiple Plot*, esp. 211–12.

13. Friedrich Hayek, *The Fatal Conceit: The Errors of Socialism* (Chicago: University of Chicago Press, 1988), 90, 91, and 93. For similar thoughts on how the new market economy was imaged in terms of sorcery, see Agnew, *Worlds Apart*, 57–59, 70–72.

14. I do not have the space to deal adequately with the vexed question of exactly when capitalism "began." Arguments have been made that certain principles of the market economy can already be observed in the medieval period. See, for example, Henri Pirenne, *Medieval Cities: Their Origins and the Revival of Trade*, trans. Frank D. Halsey (Princeton: Princeton University Press, 1952), and Robert S. Lopez, *The Commercial Revolution of the Middle Ages, 950–1350* (Cambridge: Cambridge University Press, 1976). See also Agnew, *Worlds Apart*, 27–28, 44. But however "protocapitalist" the Middle Ages may have been, England was clearly entering a new phase of economic life in Jonson's day, and he and his contemporaries had trouble coming to terms with the radical changes in market organization that occurred during their lifetime.

15. This is one of the main themes of David Riggs's biography of Jonson; see especially *Ben Jonson*, 4–5.

16. On Jonson's ambition, see Riggs, *Ben Jonson*, 2–3.

17. See ibid., 24–25.

18. On Jonson's motives for bringing out the 1616 Folio, see Jonas Barish, *The Antitheatrical Prejudice* (Berkeley: University of California Press, 1981), 138; Leggatt, *English Renaissance Comedy*, 135; and Stallybrass and White, *Transgression*, 75.

19. For the tension running throughout Jonson's theatrical career, see Riggs, *Ben Jonson*, 63–64, 69, 234; Stallybrass and White, *Transgression*, 66–79; Barish, *Antitheatrical Prejudice*, 132–54; and Kate McLuskie, "Making and Buying: Ben Jonson and the Commercial Theater Audience," in *Refashioning Ben Jonson: Gender, Politics and the Jonsonian Canon*, ed. Julie Sanders, Kate Chedgzoy, and Susan Wiseman (London: Macmillan, 1998), 134–54.

20. See Waith, *Bartholomew Fair*, 205; Butler, *Selected Plays*, 148; Leggatt, *English Renaissance Comedy*, 136; and Campbell, *Alchemist*, 503.

21. See Horsman, *Bartholomew Fair*, xii–xiv; Butler, *Selected Plays*, 149; and Julie Sanders, *Ben Jonson's Theatrical Republics* (London: Macmillan, 1998), 92–93.

22. See McLuskie, "Making and Buying," 144–45.

23. This was L. C. Knights's view of Jonson and his "fellows" in his famous book, *Drama and Society in the Age of Jonson* (London: Chatto and Windus, 1937). See esp. 7: "The standards of judgement that they brought to bear were not formed in that new world of industrial enterprise. They belonged to an older world which was still 'normal,' a world of small communities." Knights's view of Jonson is effectively countered by Don E. Wayne in his essay "Drama and Society in the Age of Jonson: An Alternative View," *Renaissance Drama* 13 (1982): 103–29. Wayne points out that Knights's view of Jonson as reactionary depends crucially on the fact that he omits *Bartholomew Fair* from his discussion (104). Wayne goes on to show how Knights's interpretation itself rests on a kind of academic nostalgia (127–29).

24. See Jonathan Haynes, *The Social Relations of Jonson's Theater* (Cambridge: Cambridge University Press, 1992), 135; he calls *Bartholomew Fair* "this most Brechtian of Renaissance plays."

25. See ibid., 123.

26. On the stimulation of desire in Renaissance fairs, see Stallybrass and White, *Transgression*, 38–40.

27. This point is reinforced by the fact that the Wasp-Cokes story in *Bartholomew Fair* may reflect events that actually happened when Jonson accompanied Sir Walter Raleigh's son Wat as his tutor on a trip to Paris. See Riggs, *Ben Jonson*, 206–7; Barish, *Prose Comedy*, 213; and Butler, *Selected Plays*, 137: "during this trip the pupil triumphantly exposed his mentor to public view in a cart while he was prostrated in a bout of drunkenness." See also Luke Wilson, *Theaters of Intention: Drama and the Law in Early Modern England* (Stanford: Stanford University Press, 2000), 226, 314 n. 25.

28. On the parallels between Wasp and Busy, see Levin, *Multiple Plot*, 204–5.

29. Riggs (*Ben Jonson*, 195) suggests that in creating the character of Zeal-of-the-Land Busy, Jonson may have had a personal score to settle with a particular Puritan preacher named Robert Milles. In her *Politics of Mirth* (Chicago: University of Chicago Press, 1986), Leah Marcus points out that *Bartholomew Fair* appeared during a period of "a fierce concentration of anti-Puritan rhetoric in performances at court, including the revival of works like Ben Jonson's *Alchemist*" (28).

30. See Slights, *Art of Secrecy*, 158.

31. See ibid., 159.

32. See Leggatt, *English Renaissance Comedy*, 139.

33. See Slights, *Art of Secrecy*, 157–58.

34. See Marcus, *Politics of Mirth*, 40, 50–51.

35. See ibid., 51–52; Marcus argues that Busy "has, in effect, undertaken the disestablishment of history."

36. See Levin, *Multiple Plot*, 206–7.

37. See Leggatt, *English Renaissance Comedy*, 149; Marcus, *Politics of Mirth*, 56; and Slights, *Art of Secrecy*, 154, 169.

38. Gordon Campbell's note in his edition (*Alchemist*, 507, line 12). See also Butler, *Selected Plays*, 137 and 530. The claim that the mayor referred to was Thomas Hayes can be found in Horsman, *Bartholomew Fair*, xviii–xix, and Michael Jamieson, ed., *Ben Jonson: Three Comedies* (Harmondsworth: Penguin Books, 1966), 481, 483. Slights (*Art of Secrecy*, 153, 209 n. 14) settles the identification in favor of Middleton. For more on the relevance of the Lord Mayor's activities to *Bartholomew Fair*, see Marcus, *Politics of Mirth*, 39, 272 n. 27.

39. For Hayek's key contribution on the problem of knowledge, see his "The Use of Knowledge in Society," in his *Individualism and Economic Order* (Chicago: University of Chicago Press, 1948).

40. Leggatt, *English Renaissance Comedy*, describes Trouble-All as a "citizen of an authoritarian state" and "a figure Kafka might have invented" (150–51). See also Marcus, *Politics of Mirth*, 56. For a contrary view of Trouble-All and his obsession with warrants, see Wilson, *Theaters of Intention*, 119.

41. See also 4.2.4–5, 86–87, 98–99, and 4.6.4, 114–15.

42. See Horsman, *Bartholomew Fair*, xii.

43. See Barish, *Prose Comedy*, 236; and Maus, *Roman Frame of Mind*, 134.

44. On the importance of the marriage license in the play, see Sanders, *Ben Jonson's Theatrical Republics*, 90–91; and Slights, *Art of Secrecy*, 161–62.

45. On the issue of legal wards in the play, see Wilson, *Theaters of Intention*, 131–34.

46. See Leggatt, *English Renaissance Comedy*, 145.

47. See ibid., 147; Slights, *Art of Secrecy*, 160, 163, 166; and Agnew, *Worlds Apart*, 129.

48. For good discussions of the dubious status of legal documents in the play, see Slights, *Art of Secrecy*, 154, 170; and Marcus, *Politics of Mirth*, 40.

49. See Leggatt, *English Renaissance Comedy*, 140.

50. It is quite possible that this sympathy begins to surface in Jonson's earlier works, such as *The Alchemist*, but for the moment I wish to confine myself to what I can demonstrate in the space available, namely its strong presence in *Bartholomew Fair*. In a longer study of the play, which overlaps considerably with this essay, I take up the ways in which *Volpone* and *The Alchemist* anticipate the treatment of the marketplace in *Bartholomew Fair*. See Paul Cantor, "In Defense of the Marketplace: Spontaneous Order in *Bartholomew Fair*," *Ben Jonson Journal* 8 (2001): 23–64, esp. 55. But even if *Bartholomew Fair* is not Jonson's only defense of the marketplace, it is fair to say that it is his most cogent and thoroughgoing. I should also state clearly that I am not claiming that writing *Bartholomew Fair* permanently altered Jonson's attitude toward the marketplace. His doubts resurface in later works. I am basically arguing that, in its economic views, *Bartholomew Fair* is anomalous among Jonson's works, although exactly how anomalous can legitimately be debated and requires further study.

THREE

Ben Jonson and London Courtrooms

Frances Teague

Critics have provided compelling answers to the question, "Why is *Volpone* set in Venice?"[1] The setting draws on the conventional associations that early modern English culture made generally between Italians and vice and specifically between Venice and exotic luxury.[2] Venice suggested wealth, wonders, and wickedness, a combination thoroughly appropriate for Jonson's satire. Yet to the best of my knowledge, no one has explored the parallel question, "Why is *Volpone not* set in London?" That question is one I will examine in this essay. Specifically, I want to argue that the courtroom scene, were the play set in London, might be too topical, given the recent investigation and prosecution of the Gunpowder Plotters. Setting the courtroom scenes in Venice, then, becomes a way to *avoid* setting such scenes anywhere in London, where legal action against those suspected in the Gunpowder Plot might well have troubled even someone who was sympathetic to the government's position.

The city setting of *Volpone* is integral to the play's dramatic effect. Richard Dutton remarks that "*Volpone*, set in Venice, is the first of the comedies with a clearly articulated urban landscape."[3] The urban landscape that the dramatist chose, however, was not the one he knew best, although he would favor London settings in his later works. After writing *Volpone*, Jonson clearly signaled his preference for setting his comedies in London. During the central phase of his career, from James I's accession in 1603 until the publication of the folio *Works* in 1616, all of the comedies that he wrote are set in London. His early play *Every Man in His Humor* (ca. 1598) was set in Italy at first; Jonson radically revised the play to change that setting to London.[4] Aside from *Volpone*, Jonson's other major comedies, *Epicoene* (1609), *The Alchemist* (1610), and *Bartholomew Fair* (1614), all employ London settings. A central joke in *Epicoene* is the noisiness of the city. The resolution of *Bartholomew Fair* requires that Adam Overdo preside over the Piepowders court peculiar to the Smithfield Fair in London. "The Prologue" to *The Alchemist* boasts about the excellence of the London setting for a satirical comedy:

> Our *Scene* is *London,* 'cause we would make known,
>   No country's mirth is better than our own.
> No clime breeds better matter, for your whore,
>   Bawd, squire, imposter, many persons more,
> Whose manners, now called humours, feed the stage;
>   And which have still been subject for the rage
> Or spleen of comic writers.
>   (5–11)[5]

This mock braggadocio claims London's superiority as a site for displaying the laughable humors of rascals. While this passage finds London a particularly useful setting to expose "your whore, / Bawd, squire, imposter," Jonson could also have said that he found London particularly useful as a setting for judges and lawyers to pass judgment on those rascals as they reveal themselves in legal proceedings, for legal personnel appear in all these plays save *The Alchemist* (and in that play, Lovewit "hears" the complaints of the neighbors and gulls in 5.1–3, then hands down judgment).

Indeed, this device of the public hearing, which brings together the play's characters, reveals the various conflicts, and resolves the play, is central to Jonson's dramaturgy (rather like the pervasive metatheatrical device of the play-within-a-play in Shakespeare's plays). A hearing offers a dramatist like Jonson the chance to bring together a group of characters, each of whom tells a version of the events to an authority that tries to sort out some version of what the audience has seen happen. The pleasure for the audience lies in the various accounts of what they have witnessed and in the errors that the authority can make in this hunt for what happened. William Slights has remarked, "Jonson had used trial scenes in his comical satires as a way to present in orderly fashion key issues such as courtly pretension (*Cynthia's Revels*) and false art (*Poetaster*)," and he goes on to argue that in *Volpone* the device of the hearing is even more integral to dramatizing the play's concerns than in Jonson's earlier work.[6] Before I consider why *Volpone*, a play that depends for two acts upon this device of the hearing, is not set in London, as one might expect given Jonson's other comedies, I want to analyze what happens in that play's courtroom scenes because my understanding of those dramatic events is rather different from that of other critics.

In Jonson's canon, *Volpone* makes the most extensive use of a courtroom setting, since acts 4 and 5 are set principally in the Scrutineo where the Avocatori hear the case that sets Celia and Bonario against Volpone and his allies. Critics have commented on the judges' venality. Stephen Greenblatt declares that in the Scrutineo, "judgment fails"; we witness "corruption" in the judges, for example, and Slights would trace that failure to the Avocatori's "obtuseness."[7] Anne Barton is vehement: she thinks not only that the Avocatori are "obtuse magistrates" but also that if they "were left to their own devices, [they] would have expended their energies in competing for Mosca as son-in-law."[8] Certainly it is true that the Avocatori lack the dispassionate freedom from bias that one seeks in a judge. The trial has begun before their entrance in 4.5. The play's courtroom scenes begin in medias res, as it were, for the judges have already heard the charges made by Celia and Bonario. Thus when the trial *scenes* begin (as opposed to the trial itself), the judges seem to display great prejudice against Volpone and Mosca and in favor of Celia and Bonario when they enter discussing the testimony they have already heard. Despite their predisposition to judge Volpone and Mosca guilty, however, they hear the rest of the case, and Voltore's arguments persuade them that they have been mistaken in their initial assessment. At that point, despite their initial prejudice, they issue a judgment against Celia and Bonario. Not until act 5, when the court reconvenes for the sentencing, does Avocatore 4 (and only that character) consider Mosca, putative heir to Volpone, as a prospective son-in-law. In their general conduct of the case, then, the Avocatori are neither venal nor obtuse judges. The critics who complain about these characters think that they do not respond to the evidence of the case; I think that they do and that Jonson's audience would have recognized that they do.

Moreover, any seventeenth-century observer would begin with the expectation that the Avocatori were sound judges. "Venice," as David McPherson reminds us, "had a special reputation for justice."[9] Richard Perkinson demonstrates that Jonson's principal source of information for the trial scenes is Lewis Lewkenor's translation of Cardinal Gasparo Contarini's *De magistratibus et Republica Venetorum*.[10] Contarini's work was originally published in 1589, and Lewkenor's translation appeared in 1599; it is this work to which Sir Politic refers (4.1.40) when he boasts of reading Contarini. Sir Pol also mentions Bodin (4.1.26), referring to a second likely source: Jean Bodin's *Les six livres de la Republique* (published 1576, English translation by Richard Knolles, 1606). Both Contarini and Bodin stress the excellence of Venetian courts. The former, for example, says that Avocatori "behaue themselues with great sharpnesse, vehemence, and seuerity" for "the duty and function thereof being to defend the lawes pure and inuiolable without suffering them in any one point to be blemished, . . . their authority and power is much like vnto that of the Tribunes of the Romaine people, but that they were to defend the liberty of the people, and ours onely the force of the lawes."[11] The standard work on Venice, then, and a work that Jonson knew and alluded to in his play, praises the high ethical standards of the court. The play itself presents a trial in which we can see the Avocatori decide in favor of those who make their case more effectively and who attempt to support what they say with testimony and evidence.

Yet the Avocatori reach an incorrect judgment, as the audience fully realizes. Despite the audience's knowledge that Celia and Bonario are innocent, the Avocatori find them guilty because of the immense superiority of the case that Voltore presents on Volpone and Mosca's behalf. Having first listened to Bonario and Celia's account of events, the court turns to the other side. As Avocatore 3 remarks to Bonario, "You had your hearing free, so must they theirs" (4.5.140). The judges allow Voltore to present his version of events (4.5.29–92), then hear his "proofs" (4.5.93, 102), namely the various witnesses who testify as to what occurred. Not only is Voltore's initial speech gripping (with its internal consistency and its dreadfully sensational details of adultery and patricide), but so also are the long line of witnesses. The father testifying to his son's criminality is the first, and so compelling is Corbaccio that Bonario sits down in silence without rebutting his testimony. Next the husband takes the stand to detail his being cuckolded. As Bonario refuses to contradict his perjured father, so Celia is unable to contradict her husband because she swoons. Mosca is the third witness for Voltore and provides not only testimony but the physical evidence of his wound. If the Avocatori think that Corbaccio, Corvino, and Mosca all have a vested interest in disguising what they have been up to, the fourth witness, Lady Politic Would-be, seems to have no such involvement. She appears disinterested as she testifies that Celia has seduced her husband. Finally, the appearance of Volpone and his seeming inability to testify completes Voltore's case.

Of course, the Avocatori decide against Celia and Bonario. Who wouldn't? Within the world of the play, the decision is perfectly plausible: Celia and Bonario provide no evidence save their avowals, while Voltore, who argues Volpone's case, provides physical evidence (Mosca's wound, Volpone's appearance as an invalid), damning testimony from Corvino and Corbaccio that goes unrefuted (Celia faints, Bonario refuses to speak against his father), and independent confirmation of Celia's lasciviousness from the relative stranger Lady Politic Would-be. Given the evidence presented, the Avocatori could reach no other decision in the case.

That does not mean that the Avocatori have no flaws. They enter the courtroom prejudiced in favor of Celia and Bonario and against Volpone, they show themselves to be greedy and overconcerned with social rank, and they render final judgments that strike many as unduly harsh. One cannot, however, gainsay their initial finding against Celia and Bonario, a decision that they reach despite their initial bias in favor of the two. Moreover, when Voltore begins his distracted confession of his deceit (5.10.3), they move immediately to investigate by summoning Mosca (5.10.20). When Voltore tries to retract his confession and when others enter conflicting accounts, they recognize that "These things can ne'er be reconciled" (5.12.1) and refuse to proceed with the sentencing until the various confessions are straightened out. After they learn that they have been deceived with perjured testimony, they act swiftly to punish the perjurers despite wealth and social rank, although they do reserve the harshest punishment for the servant who was "the chiefest minister" rather than the master who is "By blood and rank a gentleman" (5.12.8, 17). Ultimately the Avocatori reach the correct conclusion because "The knot is now undone by miracle!" (5.12.95). The Avocatori do their best to render a correct judgment in this case, but finally their human best is not adequate. Justice triumphs in this play only because "Heaven could not long let such gross crimes be hid" (5.12.98).

Volpone treats the personnel of the law courts with more respect than do *Every Man in His Humor*, *Bartholomew Fair*, and *Epicoene*. The lawyers in *Epicoene* are outright frauds, Justice Clement in *Every Man in His Humor* spends a fair amount of act 5 merrily quarreling as he hears the various cases, and Adam Overdo is, as he himself acknowledges at the end of *Bartholomew Fair*, unable to function as justice of the peace. Yet one cannot say that the Avocatori are more sympathetic than the officials in the other plays. The different effect has an obvious cause. While the lawyers and judges in the other plays may be eccentric individuals, the Avocatori in *Volpone* are not: they generally act as a group, lacking even personal names. (Only Avocatore 4 shows much individuality in his bid to make Mosca his son-in-law.) But they do take part in a legal process that proceeds with great correctness to render a totally unjust verdict.[12] Critics who object to the Avocatori in *Volpone* miss the point: in this play justice is done *despite* the legal process. By suggesting that even competent judges may be subject to prejudice or may be led astray by perjury or false confessions, Jonson suggests that the legal process is flawed. To make that argument, he carefully distances the play from London and from himself.

— Ben Jonson wrote *Volpone* in five weeks during the winter of 1605–6.[13] The period when he wrote the play followed several hectic and frightening months. In September 1605, after offending the king with his depiction of Scots in *Eastward Ho*, he had written to a number of important men asking to be released from prison. Following his release from prison, his mother announced to the assembled company at a supper party that she had planned to poison her son and commit suicide if he was not freed, suggesting the gravity of the charges against him. Though Jonson regained his freedom, his livelihood was in abeyance, for on October 5, 1605, the theaters closed because of the plague.

Around October 9, Jonson attended another supper party, this one at the Irish Boy in the Strand with a group of Catholics.[14] The supper was given by Robert Catesby, who was completing his plans to blow up the king, Prince Henry, and others at the opening of Parliament; most of the guests at the supper party—Francis Tresham, Thomas Winter, Lord Mordaunt—took part in this plot. On November 5, their plot failed when Guy Fawkes was discovered guarding the gunpowder they had stored under Parliament. Fawkes refused to provide any useful information about the men with whom he had plotted. On November 6, therefore, King James had ordered that "the gentler Tortures are to be first used unto him *et sic per gradus ad ima tenditur*," yet Fawkes continued uncooperative. Because of Fawkes's silence, the Privy Council seems to have recruited Jonson as a special agent, probably at the instigation of Robert Cecil, Earl of Salisbury, one of the men to whom Jonson had appealed for release from prison. On November 7, Jonson agreed to work for Privy Council by searching out a "certaine priest" and offering that priest a warrant from the Privy Council guaranteeing his safety. Jonson wrote to Salisbury on November 8 about his lack of success but promised to continue his search.

After torture, Fawkes began to confess late on November 7 and made two more confessions on November 8 and 9. Afterwards Father Thomas Wright, the priest who is generally believed to have converted Ben Jonson to Catholicism, was brought to Fawkes:

> [T]he Lords of the Councel, requested that a Priest should be appoynted to perswade and assure *Fauxe* (a chiefe agent in it) that he was bound in conscience to vtter what he could of that conspiracie, and M. Tho. Write a learned

>Priest did hereupon come to the councell, and offer his best seruice herein, and had a warrant to that purpose subsigned with 12.priuie Councellors hands, which he shewed vnto me, and I am witness of his hauing such a warrant. But as he said, *Faux* had confessed all they could wish before he could come vnto him.[15]

Father Wright's warrant sounds remarkably like that issued to Jonson on November 7: it bears a guarantee of safe conduct to which the Privy Councillors have sworn upon their honors. Since "Faux had confessed all they could wish," Father Wright must have seen the prisoner after he had made his third confession on November 9, 1605. Since Jonson's letter to Salisbury, saying he had not yet located the priest, was written on November 8, 1605, Jonson may well have succeeded after all. As the investigation proceeded, the various conspirators either died or were arrested; also arrested were innocent people who nonetheless fell under suspicion.

The official trial began in January, although, as Fraser points out,

> The decision was never in doubt. The mere fact that these men were on trial for high treason meant that they would inevitably be found guilty, and equally inevitably be sentenced to death. Refinements such as defending counsel were unknown. In the nineteenth century, Lord Macauley would describe the process as "merely a murder preceded by the uttering of certain gibberish and the performance of certain mummeries." Yet one should be wary of too much anachronistic indignation. There were the rules of a treason trial at the time, proceedings which were quite literally intended as a show trial.... The real trial had already taken place in the form of interrogations before the Privy Council. (218–19)

Sir Edward Coke prosecuted the case, and all of the defendants were indeed found guilty, on the basis of the evidence gathered by the Privy Council's interrogations. It seems likely that Jonson, as a recusant Catholic who was acquainted with Catesby and his circle, was one of those interrogated between November and January when the trial began. Nevertheless, he was in good odor with the government, for the Earl of Suffolk, the Lord Chamberlain, commissioned (for his daughter's wedding) *Hymenaei* from Jonson; the masque was performed January 6, 1606, about three weeks before the trial began.

Riggs argues that Jonson and his wife had reconciled, probably in late October, and had begun attending Anglican services soon after the Gunpowder Plot revelations. Despite his attendance, Jonson continued as a Roman Catholic when the inevitable backlash against Catholics occurred in the early months of 1606; however, his punishment for remaining in that faith was relatively light. This rush of events—Jonson's imprisonment for *Eastward Ho*, his supper meeting with the Gunpowder Plotters, his service to the Privy Council against the conspiracy, and his investigation as a Roman Catholic—not only occurred before and during Jonson's composition of *Volpone* but also marked several months when he was simultaneously within the law and outside it, a hunter and a fox.

Jonson's imprisonment in the autumn of 1605 did not mark his first brush with the law. He had been imprisoned for coauthoring *The Isle of Dogs* (1597); convicted of and branded for the murder of Gabriel Spencer (1598); prosecuted and imprisoned for debt (1600); examined by Sir John Popham, the Lord Chief Justice, for *Poetaster*; and investigated for "popery and treason" in *Sejanus* (either 1603 or 1605) before he was imprisoned for satire in *Eastward Ho* (1605).[16] As a playwright he was subject to constant scrutiny from the Lord Chamberlain's office lest his work prove offensive, while as a convert to Catholicism he was also at odds with the law, for under the 1559 Act of Uniformity he was forbidden to practice his faith. The pressure of his position as a Catholic intensified after the revelations of the Gunpowder Plot, but the affair may have also suggested the rewards available to one who served powerful men.[17]

The London public generally responded with horror and anger to the news that certain Catholics had sought to blow up the king, the royal family, and many members of Parliament. Thus, when King James spoke to Parliament about the plot, he explicitly warned his people against the persecution of Catholics in retribution for the Gunpowder Plot, since the vast majority of recusants were innocent. Providence had intervened, James said, and a divine miracle had preserved the state. In passing he referred to the Monteagle letter, the now infamous anonymous missive that warned Lord Monteagle to stay away from the opening of Parliament on November 5 lest he be blown up. Lord Monteagle took this letter to the government, and it may have contributed to the discovery of Guy Fawkes. The problem, however, is that to this day no one knows the source of the letter. Was it from one of the conspirators? Or was Monteagle himself a conspirator who had developed cold feet? Or was the letter a plant from the government, specifically from Salisbury, who may have had men serving as agents provocateurs to entrap the conspirators?

Nor is the Monteagle letter the only disturbing part of the Gunpowder Plot investigation. When the plot was discovered, men were tortured to extract confessions; the various confessions conflicted and could not be reconciled. Moreover, confession took on a particularly unsavory connotation when it was learned that a few priests had known in advance about the plan to blow up Parliament but had remained silent because they had been told of it under the seal of the confessional. The argument that one of them, Father Henry Garnet, made—that it was acceptable to equivocate rather than to break the seal of the confessional—was treated by the London public with especial scorn.[18] Finally there was the execution of the men who were convicted of treason. Their deaths were horrible: first they were dragged through the streets tied to hurdles; then each was hanged, cut down alive, drawn, and quartered. After they were dead and the executioners had burned the organs of their bodies removed during the drawing, pitch was poured over what was left of their quartered corpses to preserve the remains for public display

— Jonson's role in the plot and its investigation is obscure, but his concern with the Gunpowder Plot is manifest from the poems he wrote about the events. His poem praising William, Lord Monteagle, suggests that whether or not he accepted the story of the letter as genuine, Jonson felt Monteagle's warning had helped to save the country (Epigram 60). He was greatly relieved by the survival of the king (Epigram 51). His poem to Sir Edward Coke, who prosecuted the case against the Gunpowder Plotters, provides a useful index to Jonson's attitude toward the law at this point in his life and suggests that the case of the Gunpowder Plot had helped to alter his outlook. Coke, he declares, has the sort of eloquence that "Stood up thy nation's fame, her crown's defence." As Lord Chief Justice, Coke was "like Solon's self," in the way that he "explait'st the knotty laws / With endless labors" (*Underwood*, 46.14, 17). Now in conjunction with Epigrams 51 and 60, the poem on Coke is obviously a poem praising him, yet the phrase "knotty laws" is just as obviously a play on words that suggests Jonson thinks some of the laws being enforced are "naughty." As a Catholic forced to worship outside the law, Jonson disapproves of some laws; as a man witnessing a horrible act of attempted treason, Jonson is deeply grateful for the law that protects the state.

It would be a mistake, I think, to argue that Jonson's changing attitudes toward the legal system stemmed solely from his experiences concerning the Gunpowder Plot. As I have suggested, he had used legal scenes in his plays before 1605–6, and he would do so repeatedly throughout his career. His own legal troubles began in the 1590s. In several poems about members of the legal system, he addresses others than the government lawyers and judges involved in the Gunpowder Plot. Thus in the Chevril epigrams or in the epigram "On Spies" (Epigrams 37, 54, 59), he shows open contempt for corrupt lawyers or for the practice of setting spies to gather evidence. In "An Epigram to the Counsellor that Pleaded and Carried the

Case," Jonson describes lawyers as "hirelings, wranglers, stitchers-to of strife," / Hook-handed harpies, gownèd vultures" (*Underwood*, 33.8–9). He admits in this poem, however, that one exceptional attorney (almost certainly Sir Anthony Benn) has made him "conceive a lawyer new" so that "Thy sincere practice breeds not thee a fame / Alone, but all thy rank a reverend name" (38.14, 39–40). Similarly in the second epigram to Thomas, Lord Ellesmere, Jonson speaks of how the judge's good example repairs the bad impression left by "great foes, / Both armed with wealth and slander to oppose" (*Underwood*, 32.7–8). Neither Benn nor Ellesmere is a figure concerned in the Gunpowder Plot trial. The point of these examples is that Jonson's concern with or shifting view of the legal system, while it was quite certainly affected by the events of the Gunpowder Plot, was not affected solely by these events. The law was a topic of continuing concern for Jonson. Generally, he preserved a discreet silence on religion, however, and reserved his open criticism for corrupt lawyers and judges or for judicial practices he considered unethical (like spying on the accused). He was also deeply interested in the practice of rhetoric by attorneys and judges. Finally, he was taken with the potential absurdities of a hearing in which various accounts of an event were given and then reconciled, to judge from his repeated use of that device in his comedies.

Were *Volpone* set in London, one could perhaps link it to the government's proceedings against the Gunpowder Plotters. To begin with, the play seems to pun on the name of the most notorious of the conspirators, Guy Fawkes: like Jonson's Fox, Fawkes was a villain who was surprised in his crimes, supposedly by providence.[19] The play features an investigation by the state in which perjury is a central issue and in which false confessions complicate matters greatly, and both of these issues (perjury and conflicting confessions) complicated the Gunpowder Plot investigations. Finally, it is a play in which the sentences issued are very harsh. Difficult investigations, false confessions, and harsh sentences were all part of the legal proceedings that followed the Gunpowder Plot.

For a patriotic recusant Catholic, the case inevitably created conflicts in loyalty. Yet what is more important is that if *Volpone* were supposed to recall the Gunpowder Plot, it would have to be considered a critique of the government's actions. Nothing in the rest of Jonson's writing suggests that he saw the government's actions as anything other than justified. Furthermore, he had gone to considerable care in his presentation of the scenes of the Scrutineo, for Venetian justice had a particularly good reputation for integrity. I argued earlier that the play makes it plain that the Avocatori, as the government's agents, were acting in good faith. To read *Volpone* as covert criticism of or complaints about the government's case in the Gunpowder Plot is counter to everything else that we know about what Jonson said and did during the winter of 1605–6.

With the Gunpowder Plot, Ben Jonson, who had been in and out of prison and trouble most of his adult life, was asked to serve the authorities as their agent. From September 1605 until April 1606, Jonson had to think intensely about the rule of law as it affected himself, his friends, and his nation. Though he began outside the law as a practicing Roman Catholic, he moved back into sympathy with the law as he realized what had been planned: regicide, murder of many innocent people, and civil war. His sympathy for the legal system was not, however, without question or reservations. The rule of law, although clearly superior to the rebellion offered by Catesby and the other plotters, had weaknesses, especially in the way it dealt with those Catholics who tried to follow their consciences but who were not involved in the plot; in the way that interrogators used torture; and in the brutal treatment that the guilty parties received for a crime that had not taken place.

Moreover, Jonson would have recognized that any legal system, English or Venetian, was fallible. It could not overcome badly made laws, perjured testimony, or false confessions. Yet the Gunpowder Plot raised precisely these points. From Jonson's point of view, the Act of Uniformity was a bad or "naughty" law. Indeed, the laws against the practice of Roman Catholicism in England had not prevented the Gunpowder Plot but rather had led to it. Virtually every historian agrees that some of the testimony in the case was perjured (especially that about Monteagle's letter) and that those involved in the case knew that. Finally, the validity of confessions obtained after torture is always questionable.

Perhaps the most troubling—or comforting—aspect of the case for a seventeenth-century citizen was the way that the plot had come to light. The Monteagle letter was presented to the public as an act of providence. (In fact, Salisbury may have known about the plan in advance, as many contemporary historians suspect, and arranged for the letter. Even if he did not, Monteagle or one of his kinsmen might not have been able to stomach the prospect of unsuspecting members of Parliament, Catholic as well as Protestant, dying in an explosion.) But the letter was not the only remarkable circumstance in the case. The capture of Fawkes on the day before the explosion was to occur did seem to be a miracle, the result of providential intervention in England's affairs. Only a miracle had saved England; God's favoring of the nation had preserved the king. In King James's speech, this point of view is clearly in evidence. As he thought about these points, Jonson had to recognize that ultimately the law—and the nation—relied on providence. Given the threat to order posed by men who sought to do harm, sometimes "the knot [must be] undone by miracle," as the Avocatori exclaim in *Volpone*, using the same pun as *Underwood* (46). While that faith in providence may seem naive, especially since the miraculously undone knot in *Volpone* comes from a falling out among thieves, while the marvelous intervention in the Gunpowder Plot may well have originated in Salisbury or Monteagle, the prospect certainly has its attractions. For a man who took his faith seriously—so seriously that he remained a Roman Catholic for five more years and who accepted the penalties he had to pay when he operated outside the law—trust in providence was far easier to contemplate than a nation without law.

NOTES

1. See, for example, David McPherson, *Shakespeare, Jonson, and the Myth of Venice* (Newark: University of Delaware Press, 1990); Richard Perkinson, "*Volpone* and the Representation of Venetian Justice," *MLR* 35 (1940): 11–18; Ralph Cohen, "The Setting of *Volpone*," *Renaissance Papers* (1978): 65–75. For the English views of Venice during the Renaissance, see John Lievsay, *The Elizabethan View of Italy* (Ithaca: Cornell University Press, 1964).

2. Herford and Simpson discuss the Venetian setting in terms of the cultural associations that the city had for Jonson; Venice is "in the front rank for [Italy's] sinister repute." C. H. Herford and Percy Simpson, *Ben Jonson* (Oxford: Clarendon Press, 1925–52), 2:53–54.

3. Richard Dutton, *Ben Jonson, Authority, Criticism* (London: Macmillan, 1996), 121.

4. The date when he revised *Every Man in His Humor* is uncertain, according to Gabriele Bernhard Jackson, but the revision definitely occurred after the composition of *Volpone*. Herford and Simpson think the revision occurred around 1612, but Jackson is inclined to say 1607–8. See Gabriele Bernhard Jackson, ed., *Every Man in His Humor* (New Haven: Yale University Press, 1969), Appendix 2.

5. I shall cite Jonson's works from the following editions: *The Alchemist*, ed. F. H. Mares (Cambridge, MA: Harvard University Press, 1967); *Volpone*, ed. Alvin Kernan (New Haven: Yale University Press, 1962); and the poems from *Ben Jonson*, ed. Ian Donaldson (Oxford: Oxford University Press, 1985).

6. William Slights, "The Play of Conspiracies in *Volpone*," in *Ben Jonson's "Volpone, or the Fox,"* ed. Harold Bloom (New York: Chelsea House, 1988), 125.

7. Stephen Greenblatt, "The False Ending in *Volpone*," in Bloom, *Ben Jonson's "Volpone,"* 31, 41; Slights, "Play of Conspiracies," 125.

8. Anne Barton, *Ben Jonson, Dramatist* (Cambridge: Cambridge University Press, 1984), 117.

9. McPherson, *Myth of Venice*, 36.

10. Perkinson, "Venetian Justice," 14.

11. Lewis Lewkenor, *The commonvvealth and gouernment of Venice* (London: Iohn Windet, 1599), 85.

12. Whether such a concatenation of special conditions and coincidences could occur offstage is another matter. Dutton argues that in the play's Preface Jonson is "very provocatively running together the 'rules' of poetry and the 'laws' of state" so that "his entire vocabulary . . . is, if not positively ironic, at least double-edged" (*Ben Jonson*, 93–94). That position is tempting. I shall argue below in this essay, however, that Jonson is trying to avoid anything in *Volpone* that might be regarded as a link to London events because he wishes to create a secure poetic position from which to contemplate the process of hearing and weighing evidence.

13. See the appendix entitled "Text and Sources" in Kernan, *Volpone*, 229. My account of the events in Jonson's life draws on material from Herford and Simpson's life and their supplementary material, *Ben Jonson* (Oxford: Clarendon Press, 1925–52), vols. 1 and 11; I have also benefited from David Riggs's *Ben Jonson: A Life* (Cambridge, MA: Harvard University Press, 1989) and from Dutton, *Ben Jonson*.

14. For accounts of the Gunpowder Plot, there is an embarrassment of riches. The official government account is *The King's Book*, which is officially titled *His Maiesties speach in this last session of Parliament [. . .] of this late intended treason* (London: Robert Barker, 1605), and the standard history is S. R. Gardiner's account, both in *The History of England* (London: Longmans, Green, 1883) and in *What the Gunpowder Plot Was* (London: Longmans, Green, 1897); all of these are firmly anti-Catholic. A corrective to Gardiner is John Gerard's *What Was the Gunpowder Plot?* (London: Osgood, McIlvaine, 1897), which is deeply sympathetic to the conspirators. The best lay histories that I have found are Paul Durst, *Intended Treason* (pro-Gardiner but suspicious of Robert Cecil's role; London: W. H. Allen, 1970), and Antonia Fraser, *Faith and Treason* (very detailed, sympathetic to the conspirators; New York: Doubleday, 1996). Finally, anyone concerned with Jonson's attitude toward the Gunpowder Plot owes a debt to Barbara De Luna's *Jonson's Romish Plot* (Oxford: Clarendon Press, 1967), although I interpret the evidence very differently. Of some use, also, is Eric Linklater's *Ben Jonson and King James* (New York: Jonathan Cape, 1931), especially chap. 8, 144–58.

15. Richard Broughton's *English Protestants Plea and Petition for English Preists [sic] and Papists* (1621, STC 3895.5 and 3895.7), 59. To the best of my knowledge, no one has previously argued that Jonson was ultimately successful in his efforts to locate the unnamed priest.

16. David Riggs *(Ben Jonson)* gives a good account of these events, but see also Dutton's remarks, in *Ben Jonson*, on the Epistle to *Volpone*, 85. Although Dutton is concerned with the Preface, as an example of literary criticism, rather than the play itself, I have found his analysis of how *Volpone* fits into Jonson's career and canon very useful.

17. I simply see no compelling evidence that Jonson was a government spy or one of Salisbury's secret agents. Thus I would disagree with both Paul Durst *(Intended Treason)* and Barbara de Luna *(Jonson's Romish Plot)* in their analyses of Jonson's role in the Gunpowder Plot.

18. It is allusions to equivocation that allow scholars to date *Macbeth* after 1606. See Kenneth Muir's Arden edition of *Macbeth* (Cambridge, MA: Harvard University Press, 1966), xv–xviii, for an account of Shakespeare and the Gunpowder Plot.

19. Slights, "Play of Conspiracies," points out the pun, 115. He thinks that the Gunpowder Plot and *Volpone* are linked and that Jonson was satirizing the atmosphere of suspicion and anxiety that followed the revelations of the plot. I would not deny such a reading, which he makes with elegance, but I am less convinced that Jonson wanted his audience to make the connection to topical events. It seems far more likely to me that he preferred that they not do that, hence the play's Venetian, rather than London, setting.

LEGAL RHETORIC AND
THEATRICAL PRESSURE

FOUR

"They took from me the use of mine own house"
Land Law in Shakespeare's *Lear* and Shakespeare's Culture

Heather Dubrow

I

The status of legal analysis among students of early modern literature in the United States is as fraught and contradictory as the status of women in early modern culture. On the one hand, the law has hardly been neglected by these critics; witness, for example, the career of that indubitably distinguished and no less indubitably controversial scholar Stanley Fish. Other developments, however, have on occasion delimited the degree of interest bestowed on the law and deflected, even distorted, that interest when it does arise. In particular, our current version of cultural history, influenced as it still is by Foucault, has encouraged those critics who do study the law to focus on its outré manifestations rather than its quotidian workings. Thus, for example, witchcraft has received far more attention than burglary; yet this and other forms of thievery were not only the most commonly prosecuted crimes but also the nexus of cultural attitudes on subjects ranging from gender to geography.[1]

Studying land law, and particularly the regulations associated with property disputes, crystallizes the significance of quotidian legal practices. These perspectives are intended, however, not as a substitute for the issues in cultural history that engage so many critics today, but rather as a supplement (in all the fraught senses of that term). Indeed, in this as in so many other instances, the foul rag and bone shop of social history and the circus animals of cultural history are closely, even symbiotically, allied. For questions about such current topics as gender and fear of foreign Others, I will demonstrate, can fruitfully be reinterpreted in terms of daily legal events.

II

Though land law is slower and less appealing reading than, say, regulations governing sexual behavior, studying it raises no fewer methodological problems. To begin with, this legislation tells only part of the story about how property was passed on: long-standing local practices, particularly manorial customs, remained more powerful than legislation in many cases, and the laws that did exist were, as I will suggest shortly, frequently circumvented. Regional differences again complicate analyses. Although literary critics sometimes assume the hegemony of primogeniture, an alternative system for sharing land among children known as gavelkind survived in Kent. A practice called tenant right, which differed significantly from leasehold and copyhold (a system under which members of the lower social strata acquired certain property rights), was the principal form of land tenure for the relevant social groups in Cumberland and Westmorland; it also had some sway in Northumberland and county Durham.[2] And again both geographical and temporal distinctions demand attention; for example, Cynthia B. Herrup demonstrates that land disputes increased in the 1620s and 1630s, apparently in part at least in response to local economic tensions.[3]

Bearing these caveats in mind, one can generalize that many uncertainties attending on land ownership in early modern England, with the concomitant danger of loss of home, stemmed from the movement away from feudal conceptions of property. That system of land tenure in effect denied ownership in the senses it is conceived today in that property granted by a feudal lord technically could not be alienated (sold) or willed to an heir since it did not really belong to the person granted it. (Indeed, the cognate assumption that all English land is the king's shaped land law well into the modern period.) But these generalizations also immediately call for their own caveats: medieval practices about the passing on of real property were themselves far from monolithic and were in fact under attack throughout the very period that bald historical surveys would confidently label feudal. The Middle Ages saw the development of many ways of circumventing feudal conceptions of ownership and the feudal rights and payments such as wardship that went with them. Moreover, disputes about title, often involving the type of trespass known as "forcible entry" and resulting in violence, were very common in the later Middle Ages in particular.[4] The recognition that medieval landowners strenuously resisted feudal privileges can challenge simplistic assumptions about the monolithic dominance of that economic system and about the radical break between medieval and early modern England. The countervailing myth of a feudal culture in which land holdings were secure and the social relationships they symbolized and enabled equally stable is one of the many symptoms of the pastoral nostalgia suffered by academics.

Hence what the sixteenth century witnessed was not the initiation but rather the intensification of the conflict between two assumptions about land ownership and the financial interests attached to each. The king wanted to preserve the financial benefits of his feudal land privileges; many of his subjects were no less eager to avoid those payments and to have the right freely to pass land to heirs of their choosing. In addition, the concept of selling land for gain, not merely passing it on, was growing, though not without resistance.[5] And the fact that an early modern king attempted, with partial though by no means complete success, to retain those privileges, an instance of what has been termed "fiscal feudalism," similarly warns us to nuance generalizations about protocapitalism with a recognition of the survival of both the discourses and the practices of a feudal economy, a point to which we will return shortly when exploring *King Lear*.[6]

The conflict between the king and landowners came to a head in a series of statutes of the 1530s. Described by one legal historian as "perhaps the most important addition that the legislature has ever made to our private law,"[7] the Statutes of Uses and Enrolments (1535–36) attempted to control what the Crown perceived as the abuses that had burgeoned in medieval law. The use was a way of transferring land by creating a trust and in so doing avoiding feudal obligations such as wardship; it also allowed a landowner to avoid losing property if convicted of treason and to pass it to people who would not traditionally inherit it, such as younger sons and widows, or to religious orders that would otherwise be unable to receive it because of limitations on their ability to own property.[8] Having failed in earlier attempts to negotiate with peers for the restoration of feudal payments, Henry VIII attempted through the Statute of Uses to control what he perceived as the loss of income rightfully owed him: it restored the king's feudal payments and redefined uses in a way that abolished the power to devise, in other words to pass on property through wills. So unpopular was this legislation that it contributed to the 1536 rebellion known as the Pilgrimage of Grace. If Henry was not a man to give in on the subject of matrimony, he apparently recognized the stubbornness of those who wanted to will their property, and the Statute of Wills (1540) effected a compromise, restoring to landowners the power to devise but retaining for the king some feudal rights.

The legislation in question complicated English land law considerably, adding further uncertainties and ambiguities, and thus challenged lawyers to continue to craft further loopholes. Observing that "every legal transaction [concerning land laws] was subject to dispute," Alice T. Friedman traces how these quarrels strained the already tense marriage of two members of the family she studies, Sir Francis Willoughby and his wife Lady Elizabeth, a woman who from some perspectives appears long-suffering and from others merely insufferable.[9] Francis Bacon, generally known more for trenchant observation than florid overstatement, laments situations like those the Willoughby family confronted when lecturing at Gray's Inn on the Statute of Uses, which he calumniates as "a law whereupon the inheritances of this realm are tossed at this day, as upon a sea, in such sort that it is hard to say which bark will sink, and which will get to the haven: that is to say, what assurances will stand good, and what will not."[10] In short, the laws in question opened the door, as it were, to new threats to one's dwelling, but they provided in addition new ways of protecting it.

If these statutes encouraged continuing manipulation and litigation throughout the sixteenth century, so too did the shifting practices for settling title disputes. Central to English common law is the concept of a "real action"—that is, an action concerning land, which is defined as "real" in the sense of perpetual and hence always able to be recovered, as goods might not be. Such cases were notoriously cumbersome to litigate; for example, small technical mistakes in wording could determine the outcome. The Tudor period saw the growth of an alternative method of disputing title, the use of the action of ejectment.[11] This was a version of the laws concerning trespass, a large and amorphous category that comprised the situation of someone stepping onto the property of someone else but also a range of other imputed actions, including certain crimes against the person. This legal strategy was originally developed for the benefit of lessees, who could not pursue real actions because they were merely leasing the property in question. In the sixteenth century, however, freeholders began to use this device in lieu of real actions, attracted by its less rigid and less technical rules and its provision of a jury trial.

Doing so initially involved a maneuver that would entitle the would-be owner of the property to deploy procedures designed for lessees: he would lease the land to someone, who would then assume the role of plaintiff when the adversary trespassed on the land. Thus if A and B disputed each other's rights to land, A would lease it to C, who would then take out an action of ejectment against B, the current occupant of the land, who would be incited to eject C. As the early modern period progressed, however, the law recognized that such leases were pro forma and worked out a fictional formula involving an imaginary lessee.

One of the signal differences between real actions and actions of ejectment intensified the insecurities of property ownership: the former provided a definitive decision on who owned the property in question and the possibility for continuing enforcement of that decision, but because an action of ejectment merely involved a single instance of trespass, it could be tried again with a different instance—and not infrequently was, a situation Chancery attempted with only limited success to rectify at the beginning of the seventeenth century. In any event, such cases could linger in the courts and in the lives of their participants. Witness one of several cases involving the Townshend family of Norfolk, an episode that started in the late fifteenth century but is typical of situations that recurred in the succeeding century too. When Sir Thomas overturned an earlier entail granting property to his second wife, Elizabeth, in favor of his son and that child's wife, Elizabeth's retaliation included suing her stepson for trespass and taking possession of the disputed property. Though she instituted that suit in 1484, it grew more complex and was not eventually resolved until 1502, twelve years after her death.[12] Her case reminds us that women as well as men might be deeply and even continuously involved in attempting to protect their property in early modern England. And this instance reminds us too that the repeated threats of loss that structure so many Shakespearean plots not coincidentally mime the anticlosural indeterminacies of contemporary land law.

The action of ejectment concerned the laws of trespass, a loose and flexible term. Trespass in the more precise and more germane sense of invasion was involved in many of these cases as well as many other land disputes. A common strategy for pursuing land disputes in the sixteenth century—and in so doing in some instances at least depriving one party of what was considered home— included forcible entry onto property someone else was claiming. Another case involving the Townshends is telling. The Paston family, no strangers to litigation, became embroiled with the Townshends in such a controversy about the manor of East Beckham. The dispute, which lasted from 1498 to 1503, involved, according to Paston, an episode of forcible entry.[13]

Though the Townshends and Pastons were prosperous gentry, the less privileged were not immune from disruptions and threats to their home because of disagreements surrounding property. To be sure, the Middle Ages and early modern period saw the expansion of the rights of leaseholders and of those living under that arrangement for occupying property, common among the lower social strata, called copyhold. Yet they were in a less happy situation if, as was so often the case, two parties disputed about the ownership of the land on which they were dwelling. At times their only alternatives were the costly one of giving rent to both disputants or the risky option of paying only one party in the knowledge that the other might threaten their right to continue to reside there.

In short, then, in the sixteenth and seventeenth centuries property rights were unstable for many reasons; land and the home it both contained and represented could readily be lost, and often realized or anticipated loss was associated with prolonged uncertainty. Lear's counterpart in the sixteenth century would have needed teams of lawyers to divide his property in the ways he did—and in heeding their advice might have gotten into even more trouble than Lear, that example of the complications of early retirement, endured. Recognizing these legal complexities and perils offers a further perspective on a subject of interest to many students of the period, fears of invasive Others, an issue typically studied primarily in terms of national politics. Arguably such anxieties about deceptive Spaniards, dark-skinned women, and disloyal priests intensified, figured, and were figured by fears of invasion by one's own neighbors in the course of a land dispute.

Similarly, acknowledging the instability of land ownership complicates the commonplace associations between real estate and women. In early modern England such property had the instability associated with the female body, thus helping to explicate why and how both land and the edifices on it were often though not invariably gendered female. Even more pertinent to misogynist anxieties is how readily a seemingly amiable neighbor could gain access to the property in question by trespassing on it. These local legal conditions, I maintain, gloss a speech by Leontes in *The Winter's Tale* that is customarily read simply in terms of more generalized fears of adultery:

> There have been
> (Or I am much deceiv'd) cuckolds ere now,
> And many a man there is (even at this present,
> Now, while I speak this) holds his wife by th'arm,
> That little thinks she has been sluic'd in 's absence,
> And his pond fish'd by his next neighbor—by

Sir Smile, his neighbor. Nay, there's comfort in't,
Whiles other men have gates, and those gates, open'd,
As mine, against their will.
(1.2.190–98)

Sluice, defined by the *Oxford English Dictionary* as "to let *out;* to cause to flow *out*,"[14] invokes the associations between the female body and fluid that have been noted by so many feminist scholars. That definition also establishes a connection with Leontes' telling question in the next act: "How came the posterns / So easily open?" (2.1.52–53). Indeed, like the references to the sexualized gates and the pond within this speech, "sluic'd" (194) yet again establishes connections between displacement, especially a reversal of inside and outside, a threat to property, home, and sexuality. Those connections have implications as well for recent studies of protocolonialist tracts: if, as many critics have suggested, the gendering of newly discovered land female asserts the sexual and political power of the would-be conqueror, this habit also carries the reminder that golden lands were as liable to successive waves of invasion and conquest as golden ladies.

Studying land law also encourages a reinterpretation of the references to displacement in a number of plays, notably *As You Like It* and *The Tempest*. In the current critical climate, such references are often glossed in terms of colonialist imperialism. Although Shakespeare's countrymen were aware of Spain's colonialist enterprises, and although their own early voyages of discovery indubitably both reflect and generate imperialist paradigms, English colonialism was, as Meredith Anne Skura has reminded us, still very rudimentary at the end of the sixteenth and beginning of the seventeenth centuries.[15] When Caliban complains that the original sovereign of his island was displaced by that displaced duke Prospero, and when Jaques similarly challenges the process of turning landowners into venison, their lines gesture toward the results of actions of ejectment and other land disputes at least as much as toward colonialist ventures. Shakespeare's recurrent preoccupation with exile and displacement includes sources that are in more senses than one close to home.

Cognate issues about property arise in many other Shakespearean texts as well. Gaunt's references to Richard as a landlord of course are rooted primarily in his economic practices, but they implicitly remind us that he and Bolingbroke are engaged in a type of land dispute, with Gaunt's heir deprived of home and homeland. It is telling that his exile denies him the right to guard his dwelling place and land when the king seizes them; on his illicit return, he asserts that he is returning to protect what is his by right. Power is again associated with the ability to protect—and, as in the instance of dominating husbands, power is again augmented by the excuse that its agenda is merely the benign guardianship of one's precious possessions. From another perspective, Bolingbroke in effect trespasses into England because the king has trespassed on his own inherited property. In no Shakespearean play, however, are the issues raised by actions of ejectment and related shifts in land law more significant than in *King Lear*, the text that opens on the division of property and pivots on its alienation in many senses of that word.

III

The outcasts in *King Lear* are literally cast out of their dwellings. Man—and woman—are "unaccommodated" (3.4.106–7), not only in the respect critics usually assume, that is, deprived of all trappings, but also in the more specific sense of deprived of all lodgings, a usage of *accommodation* that is arguably present in *Othello* (1.3.238) as well.[16] Indeed, not the least of the many connections among the ethical characters in the play is that virtually all of them lose their homes.[17] Thus the key episodes on which the play pivots involve dwellings. The deprivation or contamination of them regularly accompanies and signals other reversals of fortune; and, in a textbook instance of anagnorisis, when Lear awakens to recognize Cordelia in several senses of both verbs, Kent glosses the moment with the assurance that Lear is indeed home ("In your own kingdom, sir" [4.7.75]).

More specifically, throughout the play the loss of that material version of protection the abode creates and represents the denial of the ability to protect and be protected in other respects, though at the same time the loss in question may engender new forms of guardianship. Hence here, as in *Cymbeline*, literal shelters trope broader questions of safety, responsibility, and subjectivity. In particular, several different versions of protection and guardianship, notably that involved in hospitality, are played against recurrent threats of trespass. Yet this tragedy's propensity for first offering, then snatching away forms of comfort and reassurance is evident in how the episodes in question ironize and complicate the desire to be sheltered and lend shelter to others.

In representing imperiled dwellings, then, *King Lear* repeatedly engages with seventeenth-century cultural and social pressures, notably the concerns about trespass and dispossession intensified by actions of ejectment. As many Shakespeareans have observed, the most influential readings of the play produced during the first seven decades of the century, notably interpretations by John F. Danby and Maynard Mack, emphasized larger metaphysical and philosophical issues—

the nature of mankind, the nature of nature—at the expense of more immediate historical and political questions.[18] We should not, however, endorse without qualification the temptingly easy historiography of the profession that firmly locates in the final two decades of the twentieth century the birth—bloody, painful, but triumphant—of an awareness of cultural history. Important exceptions present themselves; in an essay published as early as 1958, for example, Jonas A. Barish and Marshall Waingrow analyze service from perspectives that would interest new historicists.[19] During the 1970s, Rosalie L. Colie, though readily pigeonholed as a formalist in overviews of Shakespeare studies, connected the play to changes in the economic and political position of the aristocracy, while Paul Delany positioned it in relation to social and economic changes resulting from the weakening of feudalism.[20] Nor should we ignore the many connections between political readings of the plays and the transhistorical questions favored by many earlier scholars; lost abodes and cognate issues about lost guardianship bridge both perspectives. In any event, more recent Shakespearean criticism, notably studies by Jonathan Dollimore and Stephen Greenblatt, has rooted the play in socioeconomic developments, notably anxieties about inheritance and the support of elderly artisans and farmers.[21] Yet by and large the housing crisis in the play, neglected in earlier analyses, has received relatively little attention even in the materialist studies of recent years.[22]

A short passage, the Fool's jingle about the cuckoo who invades the nest of another bird, aptly introduces the play's perspectives on that crisis and on its relationship to protection:

"The hedge-sparrow fed the cuckoo so long,
   That [it] had it head bit off by it young."
So out went the candle, and we were left darkling.
                        (1.4.215–17)

These lines activate the social and legal history that lies just below the surface of *King Lear*, the reliance on actions of ejectment and other forms of trespass in early modern England: the cuckoo enters a nest where it does not belong, displacing its rightful inhabitants and in effect gaining title. The episode culminates in violence, as land disputes in the culture often did, and involves as well a travesty of familial ties.

Appearing early in *King Lear*, the jingle about the cuckoo provides a kind of dumbshow of subsequent actions and perspectives. The child who does not have, as it were, a legitimate place in the nest trespasses, displacing the legitimate occupant and destroying its putative parent. Hence the mother who should be caring for the child instead needs to be preserved from its threats, a paradox that draws attention to the significance of protection throughout the play and to the limitations of the maternal body as its putative source.[23] In biting the head that feeds it, our avian interloper performs the outlaw desires that Edmund attributes to his brother, a plot that consciously manipulates what may be a projection of his own unconscious fantasies, and the cuckoo anticipates as well the behavior of Lear's "pelican daughters" (3.4.75). Moreover, the ungrateful cuckoo is, like Tarquin, a guest who takes over; the bird's literal transgression anticipates the violations of hospitality that the play, with varying degrees of probability, will shortly attribute to the retainers and Cornwall, in so doing commenting as well on anxieties about hosts and guests germane to its own culture. The nest is at once the literal dwelling place of our unfortunate hedge-sparrow and a symbol of the family, much as the text itself will merge disorder in and destruction of a literal dwelling place, a particular family, and a family line ("Ask her forgiveness? / Do you but mark how this becomes the house!" [2.4.152–53]).

At the same time, the abode of the birds figures a nation liable to invasion: nowhere in the canon is there a better example of the imbrication of national and domestic anxieties. In a culture that expressed fears of foreign troops invading from abroad, foreign citizens living in its cities, and arguably though not indubitably foreign races as well, the trespass that threatened domestic abodes is performed by a bird of a different species. These concerns are troped generically, as cultural concerns so often are: activating potential connections between home and the pastoral genre, the jingle also anticipates the transformation of place to space, garden to heath.

The nest of that unfortunate bird is, as I have suggested, far from the only dwelling subject to threats in the play: the fortunes of many characters may be mapped in terms of their changing relationships to actual and potential buildings. Often they lose their homes in the course of a lengthy process that arguably gestures toward the interminable property disputes of Renaissance England. This process of loss generally entails a cancellation of agency, whose lack is both created and signaled by the loss of the dwelling. The victims in question then generally regain some measure of agency, either by deploying homelessness to their own ends, as Edgar does throughout, or by attempting to redefine the inhospitable dwellings into which they are cast, as Lear famously does in the speech beginning "No, no, no, no! Come let's away to prison" (5.3.8). That recovery is frequently signaled by the restoration of the ability to guard others, most notably in the instance of Kent.

Our first instance of these patterns, Lear's parody of a royal progress through his kingdom, demonstrates the many connections between abandoning his political and social place as king and variously surrendering and being denied literal dwelling places. To an audience assuming that its nobility, let alone its royalty, may well possess more than one dwelling place, Lear's decision to surrender not only "cares of state" (1.1.50) but quite literally all his castles must have seemed more striking than it has to modern Shakespeareans. Surely it would not have been difficult for him to divest himself of most property but with the "reservation" (1.1.133) of both one hundred knights and a castle or two in which to house them. One explanation is that establishing a situation in which someone else takes care of him, a role he anticipates assigning to Cordelia, is a way of asking yet again that love be publicly shown.[24] Moreover, in not retaining a castle here and there, he manifests both his characteristic attraction to the extravagant and absolute gesture (a predilection echoed linguistically in the superlative adjectives tellingly prominent in 1.1) and his no less characteristic inconsistency: just as it is problematical to demand "the name, and all th' addition to a king" (1.1.136) without any other trappings of power, so it is problematical to maintain a household but not a house. Whatever his motives, however, he anticipates that he will "set [his] rest" (1.1.122), a phrase that could refer to choosing a permanent abode, through a decision that destroys rest in the sense of both dwelling place and peace of mind.

Lear's surrender of all his lodgings is more immediately relevant to his retainers as well. Their dismissal indicates that in giving up his castles he also culpably surrenders his ability to protect those who protect him. If, as I have argued elsewhere, the role of guardian, so central to early modern male subjectivity, translates and transforms feudal relationships, *King Lear* demonstrates the workings of such relationships and their intimate relationship to housing.[25] Male subjectivity, this strand of the plot demonstrates, is in no small measure formed by the ability to shelter and deformed by its absence, and once again that literal shelter the house represents these processes.

The Fool's observations repeatedly gloss Lear's surrender of a dwelling place. His several references to land remind us that such a locale is associated with revenue: the power to protect others is connected with and enabled by more material power. Even more telling, however, is his explanation of why a snail, unlike Lear, has a house: "Why, to put 's head in, not to give it away to his daughters, and leave his horns without a case" (1.5.30–31). Here, as later in the play, the reference to a head connects the physical shelter offered by dwellings, their role in guarding reason and good sense, and the social position of leader. Behind the curious reference to horns may lie a suggestion that a house also serves to keep the shameful private. This is a play of public humiliation (which may go some ways toward explaining why it is so often staged by theater companies directed by English public school boys), a play of stocks, of verbal insults delivered before a crowd.

Pastoral is the genre of lost and recovered abodes and, as the very concept of a shepherd insists, the genre of failed and successful protectors; Lear's scenes on the heath activate all of these resonances. The heath, that externalization of Lear's tumultuous mind and of the horrors of not having a home, is in the most precise senses *unheimlich*. Peter Brook's 1971 film of *King Lear* demonstrates this through its shots of fetuslike creatures apparently drowned in the tempest. Thus, as is so often the case with the *unheimlich*, this locale brings Lear home to his worst fears, to the dark and dank cellars that, as Bachelard reminds us, are also part and parcel of a house even after the most determined spring cleaning.[26]

Critics have debated to what extent these scenes on the heath should be labeled antipastoral.[27] Some of these disagreements are rooted in a false dichotomy, the assumption that the antipastoral will reject all pastoral norms. *King Lear* is antipastoral in its denial of the succour often associated with nature, a point that it reinforces through exploring pastoral themes and adducing pastoral topoi. More specifically, this play, like *Cymbeline*, twists pastoral topoi: an inhospitable court is succeeded not by its antithesis, a welcoming pastoral home, but rather by the inhospitality of nature.[28] Both texts thus resist and problematize the pastoral agenda of replacing a defective civilized world (whose defects are signaled in part by the contamination of a home by evil stepmother and daughters respectively) with an ideal natural one. In so doing they also participate in so-called hard pastoral, the version of the genre that evokes a harsh landscape.

As the scenes on the heath demonstrate, *King Lear* connects housing and its absence with the loss and restoration of Lear's mind, his dignity, and his power. Tellingly, when he awakens he signals his confusion by confessing, "nor I know not / Where I did lodge last night" (4.7.66–67) and proceeds to ask if he is in France. When he sees Cordelia, he briefly assumes that she is a spirit (4.7.48), a line that at once gestures toward her spiritual significance in the play, anticipates her death, and, more to our purposes here, demonstrates that Lear, denied a pastoral haven on the heath, fantasizes his presence in that other and more reliable pastoral dwelling place, heaven. The line quoted earlier, Kent's "In your own kingdom, sir" (75), gestures toward a return to home in other senses: a land where he has place in its many senses and power.

Other characters are deprived of housing in ways that mime the nexus of questions about guardianship and displacement raised by Lear's fall—Kent, Cordelia, and Edgar all lose both places and place. But it is in the narrative of Gloucester's misfortunes that we most clearly witness the subterranean but significant links between this play and the issues raised by English land law. To understand the horror of what he endures, it is important to remember the nobility of his title: if seeing a king wandering on the heath would persuade an audience that all germanes had indeed broken, seeing an earl subjected to what Gloucester endures would have been very troubling as well. To begin with, then, Edmund's insistence that he will have his father's lands prefigures the many kinds of loss associated with property in Gloucester's life and that of the other characters. Shortly afterwards Gloucester in effect surrenders his house to Cornwall and Goneril in a gesture that links this type of loss of a dwelling with the loss of dignity and self-respect.[29]

Gloucester's deprivation of his abode and the ability to receive and lend shelter commences when his guests each tell their host, "Shut up your doors" (2.4.304, 308). I chose the verb *tell* with care, because the ambiguity of the English imperative, a verb form that can encompass speech acts ranging from a suggestion to a command, embodies the ambiguity of this situation. To what extent are these guests protecting their host, assisting him with a sensible suggestion that involves not only Lear but also Gloucester's own comfort (Cornwall, after all, observes, "'tis a wild night" [308] immediately after uttering the phrase in question)—and to what extent are they beginning to assert their power tyrannically, to move from the role of guests to that of trespassers?

Though the scene in question does not provide a firm answer, Gloucester's complaint to Edmund that "they took from me the use of mine own house" (3.3.3–4) persuasively links him to the characters who have lost their houses in other senses. And, of course, in the horrifying blinding scene, Gloucester repeatedly reminds his tormentors that they are violating the relationship that should link a host and his guests; far from protecting or being protected by those guests, he desperately needs protection from them. Shortly afterwards Gloucester, deprived of his rights within his own dwelling, is finally literally deprived of it as well:

> Reg. *Out,* treacherous villain!
> . . . .
> Go thrust him *out* at gates.
> (3.7.87, 93; italics added)

The guest taking over the house, effecting a Bakhtinian reversal of roles, is of course a familiar and transcultural comedic turn. But to Shakespeare's audience the situation would also have signaled the insecurity of dwelling places in their own historical moment. Like the rogues who are depicted as invaders in the extensive literature of roguery and like antagonists in property disputes, Cornwall and his distinctively unladylike lady trespass in Gloucester's house. And in this instance it is the female, so often associated with the insecurity of land tenure and the invasions of fire, who repeats the cruel command to thrust the owner of the house outdoors.

These resonances are, however, complicated by an undertow. When those ministers of evil and fear Cornwall and Goneril are Gloucester's guests, two status systems coexist. Within his own home he should certainly retain a certain sovereignty. Yet his guests are his superiors politically and socially, and, to the extent that the king's daughter and son-in-law are themselves sovereigns in the region, all property in one sense belongs to them. From that perspective arguably Gloucester is the unruly guest: the reversal of roles that Cornwall and Goneril effect has already been established by feudal models of land tenure, some of which survived into the Renaissance. These paradoxes remind the audience that the ownership of land and home in early modern England was not simply liable to sporadic depredations from trespassers but rather continuously and inherently unstable.

The subplot involving Gloucester also crystallizes the questions about hospitality that run through the play, counterpointing the threat of trespass; Gloucester and Lear, like our maternal hedge-sparrow, are victims of the tragic travesty of hospitality, and a version of its repair emerges in the resonances of "host" when Edgar urges, "Here, father, take the shadow of this tree / For your good *host*" (5.2.1–2; italics added). Hospitality is so central to the play in part because it offers a test case for broad problems and issues at the core of this drama—social responsibilities, bonds of many types, guarding and being guarded. At the same time the play both celebrates and interrogates hospitality as a putative alternative to a more local and immediate problem, its culture's anxieties about property ownership.

On one level, then, hospitality offers an alternative to trespass and other versions of the forceful seizure of property, reminding one of the theories that its codes exist in no small part to neutralize the potential threats posed by Others. Hospitality also provides a deeply conservative version of redistribution that maintains traditional social norms and values. The nostalgic reappropriation of feudal values in the play, discussed by many critics, finds its analogue in the treatment of guest-host relationships.[30] In such bonds, there is no question to whom property belongs, no threat to preexisting principles of ownership, and no risk of an unwelcome visitor entering without invitation, as do the participants in an action of ejectment. Rather, one person graciously gives and the other gratefully receives. Although the more extreme defenses of redistribution advocated by the Levellers and other groups some thirty years later were not current at the beginning of the seventeenth century, other types of political theory, notably the English and continental utopian writing that enjoyed a considerable vogue during the sixteenth century, variously involved versions of what has been termed Christian communism and of other models of egalitarian redistribution of property.[31] The interpretation of the speeches in which Lear and Gloucester famously demand better treatment of the poor (3.4.28–36 and 4.1.67–71) is fraught, with some critics finding in these passages a radical abhorrence of poverty and even an ideal of the redistribution of wealth and others a demand for charity that involved no threats to conventional assumptions about the ownership of property.[32] However one resolves that issue, hospitality appealed so much to Shakespeare, I suggest, because it provided a model for protecting others while at the same time avoiding both the dangers of hostile trespass and the more extreme and permanent forms of distribution. At the same time, this ideal, like so many others in the play, does not escape unchallenged: as the behavior of Cornwall and Goneril demonstrates, the bonds and rules linking host and guest prove as unstable in the play as those linking parent and child.

The relationship of land law to the lawless world of *King Lear* is, then, as subterranean as it is significant. Contemporary tensions about property ownership lie behind the anxieties about housing and displacement that run throughout the play, often surfacing only as a hint of internal slant-rhyme in a stanza with a different prosodic pattern. But in certain episodes, notably the events culminating in Gloucester's ejectment from his home, early modern fears of trespass become more intense, acquiring the haunting and haunted insistence of the rhymes of a sestina.

NOTES

I am indebted to Sarah Armstrong, Kimberly Huth, Jason Siegel, and A. W. B. Simpson for valuable assistance with this essay.

1. For a fuller discussion of the privileging of the more extreme and unusual legal actions over quotidian ones, see Heather Dubrow, *Shakespeare and Domestic Loss: Forms of Deprivation, Mourning and Recuperation* (Cambridge: Cambridge University Press, 1999), 6 and chap. 2.

2. On alternatives to primogeniture, see J. H. Baker, *An Introduction to English Legal History* (London: Butterworths, 1971), 145; Theodore F. T. Plucknett, *A Concise History of the Common Law*, 5th ed. (Boston: Little, Brown, 1956), 530. On tenant right, see R. W. Hoyle, "Lords, Tenants and Tenant Right in the Sixteenth Century: Four Studies," *Northern History* 20 (1984): 38–63.

3. Cynthia B. Herrup, *The Common Peace: Participation and the Criminal Law in Seventeenth-Century England* (Cambridge: Cambridge University Press, 1987), 39–40.

4. See Maurice Keen, *English Society in the Later Middle Ages, 1348–1500* (London: Allen Lane, 1990), 203–6.

5. See Garrett A. Sullivan Jr., "'Arden lay murdered in that plot of ground': Surveying, Land, and *Arden of Faversham*," *ELH* 61 (1994): 231–52.

6. On fiscal feudalism and its relationship to literary and cultural studies, see esp. Michael McKeon, *Origins of the English Novel, 1600–1740* (Baltimore: Johns Hopkins Press, 1987), 176–77.

7. W. S. Holdsworth, *A History of English Law*, 17 vols. (Boston: Little, Brown, 1903–72), 4:409.

8. The use is described in ibid., 4:407–80; Plucknett, *Concise History*, bk. 2, pt. 3, chap. 7. For a briefer and less technical explanation, see Joyce Youings, *Sixteenth-Century England* (Harmondsworth: Penguin Books, 1984), 53.

9. Alice T. Friedman, *House and Household in Elizabethan England: Wollaton Hall and the Willoughby Family* (Chicago: University of Chicago Press, 1989), esp. 57–59. The sentence quoted appears on 57.

10. Francis Bacon, *The Works of Francis Bacon*, ed. James Spedding, Robert Leslie Ellis, and Douglas Denon Heath, 15 vols. (1857–74; reprint, New York: Garrett Press, 1968), 7:395.

11. For a useful overview of this procedure, see Holdsworth, *History of English Law*, 7:4–23; A. W. B. Simpson, *A History of the Land Law*, 2nd ed. (Oxford: Clarendon Press, 1986), 144–47. Simpson also tellingly describes the social consequences of one dispute about land in his book *Leading Cases in the Common Law* (Oxford: Clarendon Press, 1995), 13–44.

12. C. E. Moreton, *The Townshends and Their World: Gentry, Law, and Land in Norfolk c. 1450–1551* (Oxford: Clarendon Press, 1992), 95–100.

13. Ibid., 91–95.

14. *OED*, 1st ed., s.v. "sluice." The italics, though germane to my argument, do appear in the dictionary itself.

15. Meredith Anne Skura, "Discourse and the Individual: The Case of Colonialism in *The Tempest*," *Shakespeare Quarterly* 40 (1989): 42–69.

16. For other examples of this usage in Shakespeare's period, see *OED*, 1st ed., s.v. "accommodation." That source includes the relevant passage in *Othello* as an instance of the definition "Room and suitable provision for the reception of people ... lodgings"; the context, however, is Othello's request that his wife be provided for, so the word might also be glossed with some of the other definitions the *OED* provides, such as "entertainment." Linda Woodbridge arrives independently at this connection between "unaccommodated" and housing in *Vagrancy, Homelessness, and English Renaissance Literature* (Urbana: University of Illinois Press, 2001), 234.

17. Albany might appear to be an exception, but one could argue that his dominating wife threatens his sovereignty within his home, if not his literal possession of that

"They took from me the use of mine own house"

97

dwelling. I am grateful to Donald Rowe for this insight, as well as many other useful suggestions about this essay.

18. John F. Danby, *Shakespeare's Doctrine of Nature: A Study of "King Lear"* (London: Faber and Faber, 1949); Maynard Mack, *King Lear in Our Time* (Berkeley: University of California Press, 1965). Similarly, writing on Shakespearean tragedy, Larry S. Champion divides his own intellectual kingdom into chapters on "cosmic dimensions," "private dimensions," and "social dimensions" and inserts *King Lear* in the first of these sections (*Shakespeare's Tragic Perspective* [Athens: University of Georgia Press, 1976]).

19. Jonas A. Barish and Marshall Waingrow, "'Service' in *King Lear*," *Shakespeare Quarterly* 9 (1958): 347–55.

20. Rosalie L. Colie, "Reason and Need: *King Lear* and the 'Crisis' of the Aristocracy," in *Some Facets of King Lear: Essays in Prismatic Criticism*, ed. Rosalie L. Colie and F. T. Flahiff (Toronto: University of Toronto Press, 1974); Paul Delany, "*King Lear* and the Decline of Feudalism," *PMLA* 92 (1977): 429–40.

21. Jonathan Dollimore, *Radical Tragedy: Religion, Ideology and Power in the Drama of Shakespeare and His Contemporaries*, 2nd ed. (Durham: Duke University Press, 1993), 195–202; Stephen Greenblatt, "The Cultivation of Anxiety: King Lear and His Heirs," *Raritan* 2, no. 1 (1982): 92–114.

22. After completing a draft of this argument, I read chap. 6 of Woodbridge, *Vagrancy*, virtually the only exception to my point that most critics have ignored or downplayed the question of abodes in the play, and found that we arrived independently not only at the significance of housing in the play but also at many specific interpretations. Her study, however, differs from my essay in several respects, notably its fuller exposition of the relationship between homelessness in the play and poverty in its culture; my reading, on the other hand, focuses more on the relationship of homelessness to hospitality and rivalry.

23. Robert Bechtold Heilman, one of the relatively few critics who comment on their lines at all, briefly suggests that they evoke an upside-down world (*This Great Stage: Image and Structure in "King Lear"* [1948; reprint, Seattle: University of Washington Press, 1963]).

24. Northrop Frye suggests that Lear wants to separate himself from his social context at the beginning of the play, and one might adduce his surrender of all his dwellings to support that observation; as I am arguing, however, the resulting necessity of dwelling with others involves reinserting himself in new social contexts and on new and troubling terms (*Fools of Time: Studies in Shakespearean Tragedy* [University of Toronto Press, 1967], 103).

25. On guardianship and masculinity, see Dubrow, *Shakespeare and Domestic Loss*, esp. 55–56. Woodbridge, *Vagrancy*, 210, points out that the knights are themselves rendered homeless in the process; I am grateful to her for this and other insights.

26. Gaston Bachelard, *Poetics of Space*, trans. Maria Jolas (Boston: Beacon Press, 1969), 17–26.

27. Thus, e.g., Mack, *King Lear*, 65–66, emphasizes the antipastoral elements, and Rosalie L. Colie responds that a focus on antipastoral may distract readers from the presence of pastoral patterns throughout the text (*Shakespeare's Living Art* [Princeton: Princeton

University Press, 1974], 302–16). Other discussions of the role of pastoral in the play include Nancy R. Lindheim, "*King Lear* as Pastoral Tragedy," in Colie and Flahiff, *Some Facets of King Lear*; David Young, *The Heart's Forest: A Study of Shakespeare's Pastoral Plays* (New Haven: Yale University Press, 1972).

  28. Colie also notes that both plays present a strikingly inhospitable nature (*Shakespeare's Living Art*, 304, 315).

  29. The violation of hospitality here is briefly noted in Colie, "Reason and Need," 193; William R. Elton, *"King Lear" and the Gods* (San Marino, CA: Huntington Library, 1966), 288. Mark Koch cites hospitality as an instance of the feudal values that the play contrasts with an alternative system of exchange, an argument that ignores the centrality of hospitality to many cultures other than feudal ones ("The Shaking of the Superflux: *King Lear*, Charity, Value, and the Tyranny of Equivalence," *Upstart Crow* 10 [1990]: esp. 87). These studies do not, however, explore the issue at any length.

  30. The most important of these discussions is found in Richard Halpern, *The Poetics of Primitive Accumulation: English Renaissance Culture and the Genealogy of Capital* (Ithaca: Cornell University Press, 1991), chap. 6, though I part company with some of the author's interpretations, such as his finding feudal values in Edmund's behavior (see esp. 246).

  31. On these utopian traditions, see J. C. Davis, *Utopia and the Ideal Society: A Study of English Utopian Writing, 1516–1700* (Cambridge: Cambridge University Press, 1981), esp. chaps. 2 and 3.

  32. For example, Woodbridge, *Vagrancy*, 213–18, argues for radical implications. On the other hand, in *"King Lear* and the Decline of Feudalism" Delany argues that the play does not really move toward a radical political analysis, and Judy Kronenfeld maintains that the language seems more radical to twentieth-century readers than it would have to Shakespeare's contemporaries ("'So distribution should undo excess, and each man have enough': Shakespeare's *King Lear*—Anabaptist Egalitarianism, Anglican Charity, Both, Neither?" *ELH* 59 [1992]: 755–84).

FIVE

Sycorax's "Thing"

Ernest B. Gilman

> So when they did design
> The *Capitol's* first Line,
> A bleeding Head where they begun
> Did fright the Architects to run.[1]

These lines from Marvell's "Horatian Ode" remind us of a commonplace going back as far as Pliny, and applicable not only to the foundations of Rome but to the founding of any civic order. The "first line" marks, not the beginning of the enterprise, but the dividing line between what the architects construct and its prior foundation. In the long view Marvell here invokes—a view that also informs Shakespeare's history plays, Roman and English—political institutions rest on bleeding heads. Acts of violence, buried and forgotten, underlie acts of statecraft. Insofar as the "design" of states is an *ars* like that of architecture or poetry, its very regularity of "line" serves to conceal the bloody lineage beneath. Marvell's insight is that such concealment is part of the "design" of the state. No sooner is the head discovered than it is incorporated into a prophetic vision in which "the State / Foresaw its happy Fate." States have designs on us. Their interest in repressing the origin on which, and from which, civic institutions are later constructed is unearthed in the attempt: the buried *caput* retains its bloody outline even in the finished judicial forms of the "Capitol," the head of state: still in Pliny's time, those condemned for capital crimes against the state were hurled to their death from the Tarpeian Rock on the south face of the Capitoline Hill. Virgil's Rome could not be founded until Turnus had been killed by Aeneas, or Cromwell's Protectorate until it had taken the head of Charles. To invoke a Shakespearean quibble appropriated by Marvell in the same poem, "plots" of land betray the "plots" of their designers. Shakespeare's most telling instance of this same point occurs in *The Tempest*, in Antonio's gibe at the attempt of Gonzalo to sketch out the lines of the perfect commonwealth he would establish on the island, if he "were the king on't" (2.1.146).[2] When, at the conclusion of his account, Gonzalo declares that there is to be "No sovereignty" (2.1.157), Antonio acidly remarks that "The latter end of his commonwealth forgets the beginning" (2.1.159). What else has *The Tempest* forgotten about its own beginning?

For the discussion of the law and *The Tempest* that follows, I would like to take this moment as an epitome of the play as a whole, and the play itself as the epitome of a more deeply buried narrative, unseen but insistently implied, concerned with the fate of Sycorax. The overt plot of this, the briefest of Shakespeare's plays, occupies three or four hours of a single afternoon but marks the latter end of a long history of events—some more recent, like Prospero's banishment from Milan, and others, like the voyages of the primordial political refugee, Aeneas, barely glimpsed in the "dark backward and abyss of time" (1.1.50). The present state of Prospero's commonwealth on the island has as its undramatized prologue an unscripted "beginning" that must be recalled for the play to reach its conclusion. In the process of its completion, *The Tempest* reconnects Miranda's "brave new world" (5.1.183), including the prospect of a return to Milan after act 5, to old worlds faintly but profoundly invoked. Prospero's world-weary reply to his daughter, "Tis new to thee" (5.1.184), opens a dual perspective in which the future is to be regarded as an aspect of its past. The past must be not only remembered, as Miranda is prompted to remember the fleeting impressions of her childhood, but represented, as Prospero re-presents the treacherous plot of his brother in the dramatic plot that unfolds as the afternoon's brief spectacle on the island. Antonio's unlawful design on his brother's sovereignty is now reenacted under Prospero's legitimate control and as part of his sovereign artistic, as well as political, design. In turn, if part of that dramatic design involves the need closely, even neurotically, to observe the laws of dramatic place and time—it is as if Prospero were somehow aware of the rigid Aristotelian requirements imposed on him by his creator—then it follows that what came before the play emerges from the realm of the unlawful, from the recollection of that which had to be excluded in the first place for the drama to proceed legitimately from its "first line." An unacknowledged but powerful need to exclude is bound up with, and fuels, the play's powerful desire to remember.

— *The Tempest* has always compelled attention to what it excludes. We have come to the theater too late, it would appear, to see a tragedy that might have been entitled "The Fall of Prospero, or the Duke Unduk'd." Another prefatory drama—the dark mirror of Shakespeare's early comedies—might have been called "The Marriage of Claribel." It turns on a daughter caught between loyalty to her father, the King of Naples, and her own loathing for the Tunisian bridegroom to whose distant shore, "Ten leagues beyond man's life" (2.1.245), it is her fate to be "banished" (2.1.124), as if to her death. One such virtual play has subsequently been produced, as it were between the lines of Shakespeare's text. *Une tempête*, by the Caribbean liberationist writer Aimé Césaire, records long, subversive conversations between Prospero's two colonial subjects, Caliban and Ariel.[3] These are imaginary conversations, to be sure, but they are imagined as the voices of the politically excluded who might have been heard in *The Tempest* if the play had not been so completely under the sway of their master, Prospero.

My own interest, however, lies with a less celebrated omission, the Algerian courtroom drama that, as Prospero pointedly reminds Ariel, determined the fate of the unspeakable Sycorax years before:

> This damned witch Sycorax,
> For mischiefs manifold and sorceries terrible
> To enter human hearing, from Algiers
> Thou know'st was banished—for one thing she did
> They would not take her life. Is this not true?
> (1.2.263–67)

Sycorax's manifold crimes, presumably rehearsed at her trial but too terrible for our present hearing, were mitigated by the unspecified "thing" that she did, which in turn led to the commutation of her death sentence and her subsequent exile to Prospero's (or perhaps, strictly speaking, *her*) island. All this provides the material for a virtual fore-play or antimasque that might be entitled "The Trial of Sycorax, or the Witch Banish'd," a courtroom drama once performed on the same African margin of *The Tempest*'s geography as that on which, more recently, the unfortunate Claribel was abandoned by the Neapolitan wedding party.

Among this shadow company of the (dramatically and politically) dislocated, my emphasis on Sycorax is intended, first of all, to give her role its due among those characters, as Orgel notes of Prospero's wife, "conspicuous by [their] absence from the play."[4] This is, in part, an attempt to shift the balance of attention from the postcolonial Caliban—Césaire's heroic "esclave nègre révolté"—who has loomed so large in recent criticism and productions of *The Tempest*.[5] My contention is that most critical renditions of these colonial "encounters" are incomplete insofar as they simplify the kind of cultural double vision by which the European imagination constructs a "new" world as a *re*-encounter with the old. Working through a history of Sycorax as the symbol of that re-encounter, I will want to argue that the matrix of the past produces, and is re-produced in, the protocolonial future. In what follows I will want to read against the critical grain by emphasizing the play's imagined *pre*history, starting with the matter of Sycorax—the *res*, or judicial "thing," that determines her fate. The plight of Caliban, for all his compelling presence in the play, must be understood in relation to that of the other marginal or absent characters, and chiefly in relation to his mother. In a play that "tempts us to fill in its blanks, to create a history that will account for its actions,"[6] creating a history of Sycorax reminds us first of all that, although the stage is peopled—save for the crucial exception of Miranda—entirely by men, the "blank" spaces around the edges of the drama are almost exclusively the province of dead women. Their influence, like the gravitational pull of a black hole upon a nearby star, is powerful but unseen.

My second goal will be to dig deeper into what Shakespeare's audience might have understood or surmised about the two key legal issues underlying Sycorax's judicial banishment from Algiers, and their import for the drama unfolding on the island where she now lies buried. Condemned for terrible sorceries, the one "thing" Sycorax did to save her life, according to most if not all critical conjecture, was to "plead the belly," and part of my concern will lie with the legal and social context of this plea in the early modern period. (Her "thing," then, would be both the means by which she got herself pregnant, to which in the recounting Prospero is much too fastidious to do more than allude, and the legal "thing," the *res* or claim for leniency on which Sycorax was therefore able to establish her defense.) The other legal issue is that of her being "banished"—not simply cast out into the wilderness like a biblical exile, but, it would appear, purposefully *transported* to the island as part of her sentence: "This blue-eyed hag was hither brought with child, / And here was left by th' sailors" (1.2.269–70). Her death sentence thus commuted to transportation, Sycorax both benefits by and suffers from two judicial practices first linked in Shakespeare's day and later more commonly applied in the cases of errant women before the law. In this respect, Sycorax is the distant forebear among English literary malefactresses of Moll Flanders's mother, of whom Defoe tells us that she "pleaded her Belly, and being found quick with Child, she was respited for about seven months," after which she was "call'd Down" again "to her former Judgment, but obtain'd the Favour of being Transported to the Plantations."[7] In this perspective, any allegorical history of Caliban as colonial subject must be incomplete without an awareness of his coming to the island in the first place as the beneficiary of an actual colonial practice that determined his mother's fate.

— What happens, in the "dark backward and abyss of time," when the family histories of Prospero and Sycorax intersect? We have already noted Orgel's emphasis on the "conspicuous absence" of Prospero's wife, the mother Miranda cannot recall. Prospero's only reference to her—"Thy mother was a piece of virtue, and / She said thou wast my daughter" (1.2.56–57)—commemorates her virtue only to call it into question, however facetiously, in a gesture that seems to dismiss her memory as soon as it is evoked. Orgel sees this "absent presence" as "a space that is filled, for Prospero, with surrogates and a ghostly family: the witch Sycorax and her monster child Caliban, who is so often and so disturbingly like the other wicked child, the usurping younger brother Antonio; the good child-wife Miranda, and adolescent and libidinous Ferdinand."[8] This *coincidentia oppositorum* of the play's two absent mothers, paragon and hag, implicates those characters as more tangibly present. Miranda stands between them as the daughter in this "ghostly" genealogy, as her island stands between Milan and Algiers. Both dead before the play begins, these two mothers will be succeeded by Miranda, whose anticipated role as the mother of Milan's future dukes will not begin until the play ends. In this way, motherhood is strongly marked as part of the play's past and future but excluded from the play itself: Miranda can be Prospero's "child wife," in Orgel's phrase, because she is only a child and cannot be a wife, and all due precautions are taken to protect her innocence. Insofar as Sycorax casts a maternal shadow over Miranda, furthermore, Caliban's threat to Miranda's virtue—his plot to people the isle with Calibans—seems all the worse for being incestuous, a "brother's" design on his own "sister." Likewise Prospero's ultimate acknowledgment of Caliban as "mine" seems all the more resonant as an acceptance of paternal responsibility for this "thing of darkness" (5.1.275–76). These substitutions themselves follow a witchly logic of the changeling child, as if Sycorax in her absence still held sway over the disposition of the characters on the island.

These relationships are often seen from a psychoanalytic point of view as case histories concerning mothers, fathers, and children. I believe they need to be seen as well in the light of those legal cases by which Sycorax's undocumented but evidently notorious career as a witch can be reconstructed. The history of European witchcraft suggests two connections in particular—with treason and with sexual desire, the twin motives of Caliban's revolutionary politics—that bridge the gaps in the prehistory of *The Tempest* between its scattered peripheral characters. As Deborah Wallis has shown, charges of witchcraft were "frequently combined with accusations of treason or conspiracy against the state": "Shakespeare's first tetralogy focuses on a number of such politically embedded witchcraft cases: Joan of Arc, Eleanor, Duchess of Gloucester, Margery Jourdain, Margaret, Queen Elizabeth, and Jane Shore are all accused—and some convicted of witchcraft."[9] From Elizabethan times the offense of witchcraft had been exempted from the benefit of the Queen's General Pardon along with such other offenses as high treason, slander against the government, and (after the Essex affair) "all Rebellions and Insurrections whatsoever." In this context, witchcraft seems to be proscribed as much for fear of its offense against the Crown as for any inherent evil.[10]

The link between witchcraft and treason strengthens the connection between the unspecified "mischiefs manifold" of which Sycorax stands convicted in Algiers ("terrible to enter human hearing") and the very explicit treachery of Antonio in Milan—a tale that would "cure deafness" (1.2.106). His own betrayal, as Prospero recognizes, was not merely that of an evil brother seizing a Machiavellian *occasio* to advance himself when Prospero left the dukedom unattended. Prospero's responsibility for Antonio seems more direct, for his own neglect of worldly ends and the closeness of his private studies "Awaked an evil nature" in his "false brother":

> and my trust,
> Like a good parent, did beget of him
> A falsehood in its contrary as great
> As my trust was.
>
> (1.2.92–96)

In the Milanese tragedy that precedes the action of *The Tempest*, Prospero's fatherly trust begat its "contrary," an evil born of Prospero himself. By the logic of the changeling, Antonio's treachery would figure as an attack on the father by the parricidal monster-child of his own brain and would thus prefigure Caliban's insurrection against Prospero later in the play. Even as Prospero engenders his "contrary" in Antonio, he also evokes his other contrary, the Algerian witch who pleads the belly and begets Caliban. Alike practitioners of secret arts, both Prospero and Sycorax conceive an "evil nature," and they do so in a like attempt—however different their circumstances and intentions—to free themselves from the strictures of legal responsibility.

The sexual implication of this thing that Prospero did to engender his banishment from Milan, the begetting of his own undoing, also reflects upon the deeply ambiguous eroticism attributed to the witch. The name Sycorax is linked etymologically to that of the seductress Circe, who was also exiled to a Mediterranean island.[11] As a witch she is marked by her rampant sexual desire, both through her general European reputation and, in this play, specifically through Sycorax's African connection. The authors of the *Malleus maleficarum* are convinced that "[a]ll witchcraft comes from carnal lust, which is in women insatiable." Witches have been observed "lying on their back in the fields or the woods, naked up to the very navel," writhing in furious copulation with devils invisible to all but themselves—a pertinent fact in the case of Sycorax if, as Prospero charges, Caliban was "got by the devil himself / Upon thy wicked dam" (1.2.319–20).[12] To these discoveries James I adds his own speculation, in the *Demonologie*, as to whether the devil comes to his witchly paramours "onelie as a spirite, and stealing out the sperm of a dead bodie, abuses them that way" or whether "he borrowes a dead bodie" and so appears to them "visiblie."[13]

In the case of Sycorax, the presumed lustfulness of the witch must be imagined as all the more torrid because of her African origins, in that dark and abysmal space on the margin of the European imagination whose very heat fuels the cauldron of witchcraft. As John Gillies argues, Shakespeare's Africa figures as the scene of an undifferentiated and threatening exoticism in which (as in the character of Othello), Moorish, Turkish, Egyptian, and Indian are commingled.[14] According to Leo Africanus, the inhabitants of Barbarie (Sycorax's Algiers) "leade a beastly kinde of life," having "great swarms of harlots among them," while neighboring Fez is rife with "women-witches" who "have a damnable custome to commit unlawfull Venerie among themselves."[15] Algiers may have its own more deeply buried amorous history as the putative site of Dido's Carthage. That history in turn foreshadows Cleopatra's later role as the wily temptress of Roman virtue, her "gypsy's lust" (*Antony and Cleopatra* 1.1.10) reflecting the popular association of Egyptians with Gypsies, whose lewd and vagabond ways were the subject of Elizabethan legal suppression. The history of Egypt, as Jonathan Haynes notes in his reading of

George Sandys's *Relation of a Journey* (1610), is a history of "endless and inglorious degeneration which does not lend itself to a comprehensive narrative," a history "unknown except in fragments," concealed in hieroglyphs and revealed only enigmatically in the riddles of the Sphinx.[16] Africa keeps its secrets, which can be alluded to mysteriously, as in Prospero's dark allusion to Sycorax's "thing," but which can never brought fully to light or comprehended in a rational history. Sycorax appears in the play only as a representative of the silent dead—speechless and unspoken, the mute counterpart to Prospero's loquacity. With his mother's blood in his veins, Caliban's twin ambitions of killing Prospero and raping Miranda combine treason with unlawful venery, a powerful lust with a lust for power. These desires fuse the political and sexual threats of witchcraft and so represent the African dangers from which the European magus and his daughter must be protected.

On the other hand, as the *Demonologie* also insists in its exposé of the witch's amours, in whatever shape her demon lover comes to her, the witch cannot conceive. For all his ingenuity, the devil is sterile: "Indeede, it is possible to the craft of the Deuill to make a womans bellie to swel after he hath that way abused her, which he may do, either by steiring vp her own humor, or by herbes, as we see beggars daily doe."[17] Her pregnancy might well have been, in the words of the play, a "falsehood in its contrary as great" as the true pregnancy of a woman great with child in the ordinary fashion. For the tradition that James reflects, as for Milton later, demonic sex is fruitless. (Knowing this, those charged with determining whether a convicted witch was truly pregnant when she pled the belly would need to approach their task with the most acute discrimination.) Even worse, her sexual vigor not withstanding, the witch threatens to blight the principle of fertility itself. The infamous papal bull of 1484 warned that witches "have slain infants yet in the mother's womb, as also the offspring of cattle, have blasted the produce of the earth, the grapes of the vine, the fruits of trees . . . vineyard, orchards, meadows, pastureland, corn, wheat and all other cereals. [They] hinder men from performing the sexual act and women from conceiving, whence husbands cannot know their wives nor wives receive their husbands."[18] While Pope Innocent VIII had included "many persons of both sexes" in this indictment, the subsequent experts in the field, beginning with the authors of the *Malleus* five years later, emphasize the doleful influence of women's sexuality, if for no other reason than, as James I estimated, for every man there are "twentie women giuen to that craft."[19] Women were, of course, also held responsible for infanticides, exposures, and the mutilation of infants. (Sycorax's imprisoning the disobedient Ariel in a cloven pine is, in this light, only a more magically innovative version of a maternal abandonment.) From the mid-sixteenth century onward such crimes are represented with increasing frequency in the English legal record, often in association with the charge or suspicion of witchcraft. A full quarter of all the indictments brought against witches in England from the fourteenth through the eighteenth century involved the bewitching of infants.[20]

With this legacy, Sycorax even in her absence haunts the "marriage blessing" of Prospero's masque, in which Juno's hope of fertility for the betrothed couple is echoed in Ceres' call for "Earth's increase, foison plenty" (4.1.110). The dead witch seems to have transferred her powers of enchantment to Venus, the goddess excluded from the celebration for her attempt to cast "Some wanton charm upon this man and maid" (4.1.95). If Venus had succeeded in disrupting the festivities, all vows of chastity would be broken and all of Prospero's designs ruined, including the dynastic future envisaged in the betrothal of Ferdinand and Miranda. The sexual politics of witchcraft offers a ground on which we can understand Prospero's obsession with dampening the lust that he projects onto Ferdinand while meeting the threat posed by Caliban, the spawn of the witch who carries the coupled tendency of her race toward sexual depravity and political sedition.

The danger of a blighted union is further intensified, in Shakespeare's play, by the same association of Sycorax with Africa that we considered before an aspect of her licentiousness. It is from this region, we are reminded by *The Tempest*'s deepest historical echoes, that Aeneas fled the coils of Dido to pursue his destiny to Rome; and to this region, in the play's immediate prehistory, that the unfortunate Claribel was consigned in a loathsome union with the King of Tunis. The nuptials of Claribel and Miranda bracket the play: the unseen marriage at Tunis before the first line of the drama foreshadows the marriage of Ferdinand and Miranda in Milan after its close and, like that later marriage, may have seemed to hold the promise of a fertile political union (in this case, a mutually advantageous maritime alliance between Naples and a notoriously piratical African kingdom). Yet Claribel's marriage, more dire for her than a foreign captivity, amounts to a virtual death sentence, in effect a ghastly exile "contrary" both to her own wishes and to any sense of marriage as a fulfillment and a beginning. Claribel now "dwells / Ten leagues beyond man's life" (4.1.245) in a land, as Antonio argues, from which she can never return: "Say this were death / That now hath seized them"—that is, both Claribel and her brother Ferdinand, who is presumed to be drowned—"why, they were no worse / Than now they are" (2.1.258–59). In fact Sebastian holds her father, Alonso, responsible for Ferdinand's death, seeing it as a just rebuke for the fate to which Claribel has been consigned:

> Sir, you may thank yourself for this great loss,
> That would not bless our Europe with your daughter,
> But rather lose her to an African,
> Where she, at least, is banished from your eye,
> Who hath cause to wet the grief on't.
>
> (2.1.121.25)

This speech follows immediately upon the banter between Sebastian and Antonio about the "widow Dido" and the speculation as to the proximity of Tunis to the site of ancient Carthage, as if to suggest that this is a marriage already shadowed by a history of "great loss" and death. Antonio's ironic allusion to the "miraculous harp" of Amphion that raised the walls of Thebes (2.1.85) juxtaposes a resonant image of civilization building with a reminder of its destruction, in this case the obliteration of Carthage that makes its very location a matter of dispute. The architects of Tunis may well have built their city on the buried ruins of Carthage, and now Alonso's design for a political alliance between Naples and Tunis sealed by the marriage of Claribel seems to totter on the same perilous foundation. In the long view, this blighted union threatens to undo the Virgilian project by exiling a European daughter to the very shore from which Aeneas had to free himself in order to "bless our Europe" with a new marriage and a new political order at Rome. In Prospero's wedding masque, Claribel's African exile is given its mythic counterpart in the abduction of Proserpine to the underworld kingdom of "dusky Dis" (4.1.89), with the consequent loss of the world's fecundity until her return. Antonio's "Say this were death / That now hath *seized* them [emphasis mine]" takes on, in this context, the suggestion of the sexual violence suffered by the bride at the hands of her dark lover. In the changeling logic governing the movement of women in this play, it is as if Africa demanded its Claribel as a captive in exile under sentence of death in return for commuting the death sentence of Sycorax, who, in her exile to the very island on which Claribel's father is shipwrecked, returns if only in death as the "daughter" in a ghostly family reunion.

Of the various nations peopling the "Africa" of the Renaissance imagination, we will return to the Egyptians/Gypsies below in the context of penal transportation. Here I would suggest that Sycorax also has an unspecified but compelling association with the elusive nation of the Amazons. Everyone knew about Penthesilea, the heroic Amazonian queen celebrated in Jonson's *Masque of Queens*: "She lived and was present at the war of Troy, on their part against the Greeks, where (as Justin gives her testimony), 'among the bravest men great proofs of her valor were conspicuous.'"[21] Louis Montrose reminds us of Ralegh's speculation in the *Discoverie . . . of Guiana* (1596) "on the existence of Amazons near the river named after that mythical but seemingly international tribe of 'warlike women': 'The memories of the like women are very ancient as well in Africa as in Asia. . . . In many histories they are verified to have bene, and in divers ages and provinces'; [Ralegh] then speaks of 'the Amazones' as if 'they' were at once the very ancient contemporaries of the Trojans and the actual women before his eyes: 'if they conceive, and be delivered of a sonne, they returne him to the father.'"[22] Associated with both the New and the Old World (where even the "memories" of them are "very ancient"), the Amazons are, like Sycorax, conspicuous by their absence. They are, and always have been, everywhere, their existence is "verified" in "in many histories," their hold on the memory is strong, and the "proofs of [their] power" are great; but, with the exception of Penthesilea's campaign at Troy, they remain unseen. As Ralegh notes, however, we are aware of their customs when it comes to the disposal of superfluous male children. According to Kathryn Schwarz, "[I]n various accounts they kill them, mutilate and enslave them, or send them to fathers who, having been seduced in the dark, have to guess which child belongs to whom based on accidents of resemblance."[23] Infanticide and the mutilation of infants are practiced in common by Amazons and their witchly African co-regionalists. The return of the male child to an unwitting father would seem to be a well-known, and uniquely Amazonian, habit. This inversion of European child-rearing practices is part of what Montrose aptly terms the "Amazonian anticulture," a structure of "analogy and antithesis" between European patriarchy and Amazon matriarchy that also aligns the relationship of Prospero and Sycorax, his antagonist and alter ego. Insofar as some such memory as Ralegh invokes may lurk in Sycorax's African origins, the action of the play is underwritten by an Amazonian subplot hinged on the "return" of Caliban to Prospero. Having conceived in Algiers and pled the belly to secure her own deliverance, Sycorax is "delivered of a sonne." Lawless by Algerian standards, in her exile Sycorax fulfills her Amazonian responsibility, if only posthumously and symbolically, by returning that son to the "father" who in the end acknowledges him—this "thing of darkness" (5.1.275), this "thing" conceived in darkness, this dark "thing" of Sycorax's—as his "own."

— So far I have been arguing for the unseen but pervasive influence of Sycorax upon the action she does not survive to witness. I have wanted to point to some of the ways in which, paradoxically, she makes her absence felt—rather like the invisible demon lover of witchcraft lore whose commerce with the woman writhing in the field can be registered through her but not directly perceived. I want now to suggest, further, that these unseen lines of force connecting Sycorax to the main characters of the play converge in the "one thing" she did so that they "would not take her life." This, in turn, will lead to some conclusions about what I will call the "law" of *The Tempest*'s dramatic design, in which Sycorax's prehistory in the Algerian legal system plays a crucial role

Of this "one thing," Orgel observes in his note on Prospero's speech that the "problematic element in the passage is not its meaning, but the obliqueness of Prospero's reference to it."[24] In fact, its meaning would be obvious enough to a contemporary audience if not to later commentators,[25] and Prospero could merely gesture in its direction—we may suppose, if we like, out of a sense of delicacy about Miranda's feelings—without fear of being misunderstood. Shakespeare's age would have had no doubt that Sycorax secured her own deliverance by "pleading the belly." In *1 Henry VI* Joan declares herself to be suffering from this same "infirmity" (5.4.60) at the eleventh hour, just as she is about to be carried off to the stake. In his own (very likely apocryphal) account of Joan's machinations, Holinshed summarizes the legal procedure that followed upon her claim of pregnancy: "For triall, the lord regents lenitie gave hir nine moneths staie, at the end of which," no child having appeared, the original sentence was carried out. She was "thereupon delivered over to the secular power, and so executed by consumption of fire in the old market place at Rone."[26]

Some few in Shakespeare's audience would also have been familiar with what is surely the most spectacular illustration of this provision of early modern European law, the engraved title page of Vesalius's treatise on anatomy, the *De humani corporis fabrica* of 1543. In this famous depiction of the anatomy "theater," the drama focuses upon a female cadaver opened to reveal the abdominal cavity and "drawn," says Vesalius, to indicate "the position of the uterus and bladder exactly as they occurred in this woman." This woman, Vesalius continues, "in fear of being hanged had falsely declared herself pregnant. However, by order of the judge she was interrogated by midwives who declared her not at all pregnant."[27] Hanged after all, she suffered the final indignity of being displayed on the anatomist's table, as if to confirm by the ghastly but incontrovertible testimony of the woman's own vacant womb that the midwives had been correct in their diagnosis.

Holinshed's Joan and the anonymous subject of Vesalius's anatomy, as well as Sycorax and, later, Moll Flanders's mother, may be taken to stand for thousands of women from the Middle Ages until modern times who, falsely or truthfully, but all surely in equal despair of their lives, sought the reprieve of a death sentence before European (and American) courts by entering this plea. In England, the calendars of assize records for the reign of Elizabeth and that of James I reveal that during this period nearly half the women convicted of felony "pleaded that they were pregnant, and thirty-eight percent successfully maintained that claim."[28] Since some women convicted of felony would be beyond the age at which such a claim could plausibly be made, the percentage of those pleading the belly among those biologically eligible would be even higher. If the pregnancy was proven (in England, upon examination of the woman by a "jury of matrons"), a reprieve was granted until the woman was delivered, on the grounds that the unborn child should not pay for the sins of the mother. By the letter of the law, the original death sentence was then to be carried out, as it is in the chronicler's account of the execution of Joan of Arc. However, in practice justices tended to be lenient with pregnant women, or at least to avail themselves of the extra time provided by the reprieve to evaluate the prisoner's case more fully. In some jurisdictions, a successful plea of pregnancy was tantamount to a pardon in the end. Overall, the evidence suggests that many if not most of the English women who escaped hanging initially through "benefit of the womb" were later pardoned, either outright or conditionally upon transportation.[29]

If we may suppose that the legal system of Shakespeare's "Algiers" is similar to that of England, then we may assume that Sycorax's pregnancy was certified by a jury of matrons after her conviction. In her case, the same or a similar committee of women would already have been called upon before her trial to certify for the purpose of evidence that her body bore the marks of the witch. The *Malleus maleficarum* had recommended just such a procedure: "While the officers are preparing for the questioning," the woman accused of witchcraft "should be led to the penal cells and there stripped by honest women of good reputation," who then conduct a "search for any instrument of witchcraft sewn into her clothes."[30] In England and America, as James C. Oldham goes on to point out in the seminal study of the matron's juries, the "inspection was for a different purpose—to search the accused's body for any 'witch's teat' or 'witchmark' used to suckle her familiars."[31] In *The Tempest* Miranda has no recollection of her mother, but she does recall, "far off, / And rather like a dream than an assurance," that she had "Four or five women once that tended me" (1.2.45–47). It is intriguing to imagine that, emerging from the "dark backward and abyss of time" (1.2.50) in which Sycorax also dwells, these memories not only recall the handmaidens attending upon her but, in the absence of her own mother, betray the ghostly presence of the matrons tending upon the witch-mother who has taken her place.

In England, the record of documented cases of condemned women successfully pleading the belly, and so gaining a postponement of their sentence, goes back at least to the fourteenth century. The origins of the plea go back even farther: under the Roman republic, the execution of a pregnant woman was similarly postponed until she had given birth. However, the link between the pardon of pregnant felons and the condition of transportation, common by the end of the seventeenth century in England, was just being forged in Shakespeare's time as part of a broader interest in peopling the colonies with exported criminals, vagabonds, and indigents. In 1583, Sir George Peckham's *True Reporte* included a prefatory poem by John Hawkins that saw the resettlement of England's surplus population to the Virginia colony as a means of ridding the country of a pestiferous and suffocating horde:

> But *Rome* nor *Athens* nor the rest, were neuer pestered so,
> As *England* where no roome remaines, her dwellers to bestow,
> But shuffled in such pinching bondes, that very breath dooth lack:
> And for the want of place they craul one ore another's backe.[32]

If the want of a place at court might impel some few gentlemen to try their fortunes in the new world, Virginia might also relieve the more threatening social problem of the lower orders choking the kingdom by their very numbers. These verses read as if an aristocratic anxiety about limited room at the top were being projected downward—as if, indeed, releasing the pressure from below would create more breathing space for those above. For high and low alike, the new world offers a "place" where men will not need to "crawl one o'er another's back."

In 1597, Parliament authorized, in the case of dangerous or incorrigible individuals, the transportation of rogues and vagabonds, including traveling con men, beggars, "and all such persons not being Fellons wandering and pretending themselves to be Egipcyans, or wandering in the Habite Forme or Attyre of counterfayte Egypcians."[33] Six years later, in the first year of his reign, James I followed up on this initiative by designating "The New found Land" as a destination for "incorrigible and dangerous rogues." It appears that few were actually transported as a result of these early edicts. They were, nevertheless, unopposed as an advantage of colonial policy, for they were based in an urgent, if unrealized, hope that (as the Records of the Virginia Company put it) transportation would relieve the kingdom of this "Surcharge of necessitous people, the matter or fewell of daungerous insurrections."[34] The State Papers contain a 1609 letter from Lisbon reporting that the Portuguese were shipping fifteen hundred indigent children as young as ten to the East Indies, and recommending a similar policy for Virginia.[35] In the same year preparations were made for the Virginia Company to follow suit; Smith estimates that several hundred poor children were shipped to Virginia and, later, to New England, by the time of the English Civil War.

Beneath the openly expressed fear of insurrection by the poor and the criminal classes lay a deeper anxiety about their very rootlessness, their lack of a fixed place. The 1597 statute specified as candidates for transportation scholars or seafaring men "going about the Country begging," minstrels, tinkers, and peddlers "wandring abroade," and those who "travayle begging."[36] It is thus not merely the begging or even the itinerant flimflam artistry of those who conduct "unlawful Games or Playes" on the road that provokes concern but the very fact of their wandering, going about, and traveling. Toward the end of the seventeenth century, the "mob" will get its name from its mobility: vagrant in its allegiances as well as in its physical movement. Transporting the reprobate among these vagabonds not only relieves the kingdom of their presence but transplants them to a fixed abode from which they may not re-move themselves under penalty of death. In *Richard II* Shakespeare's Bolingbroke banishes Exton with a sentence of biblical exile: "With Cain go wander thorough shades of night" (5.6.43). But under a policy of colonial transportation, the fate of exile for the wanderer is no longer imagined as prolonging the errant life—a Dantesque punishment of having to do forever the thing for which you were condemned—but as restricting it. In *The Tempest*, the exhilaration of Ariel's freedom of movement after having been confined by Sycorax in a tree replays, and reverses, the underlying thematics of the judicial policy of transportation by which Sycorax was originally banished to the confinement of the island.

The transportation of Sycorax anticipates Crown policy by several years and surely reflects the drift of opinion about the uses of the New World. Traditionally, the only mitigation of the automatic death sentence attached to more than three hundred crimes classified as felonies was either a royal pardon or one of two pleas on the part of the condemned: the "pleading of clergy"—in effect, mercy granted for passing a literacy test—and "pleading the belly," the latter, as we have seen, leading in its strictest application only to a postponement of the original sentence. On January 24, 1615, the king addressed a commission to the Privy Council expressing "our desire that Justice be tempered with mercie": "Soe likewise it is our care soe to have our Clemency applied at that greate and notorious malefactors may not be encouraged, and yet the lesser offenders adjudged by lawe to dye may in that manner be corrected, as that in theire punishment some of them may live and yield a profitable service to the Common wealth in parts abroade where it shall be found for to imploie them." The council was authorized "to reprive and stay from execucon such and soe many persons as nowe stand attaynted or convicted of or for any robberie or felonie, (wilful murder rape witchcraft or Burglarie onlie excepted) whoe for strength of bodie or other abilities shall be thought fitt to be ymploied in forraine discoveries or other services beyond the Sea."[37] That same year saw the implementation of the king's mercy, and the beginning of a two-hundred-year history of English colonial transportation for felons, when some twenty convicts were handed over to Sir Thomas Smith, governor of the East India Company, destined for either the Indies or Virginia. It is a minor irony but an inevitable one, given James's lifelong antipathy to witchcraft, that "Algerian" law seems to be more lenient on this point than English law, under which the king's edict specifically exempts the likes of Sycorax from the merciful benefit of transportation. Indeed, one reason as good as any other to account for the "obliqueness of Prospero's reference" to the "one thing" (1.2.266) Sycorax did to save her life may well have been Shakespeare's prudent reluctance in a play performed at court to emphasize the disposition of a case so obviously offensive to James's published views.

— Such, I believe, is a plausible brief account of Sycorax's unwritten legal history. What is gained by the attempt to fill this gap—when, it might be observed, the number of things Shakespeare did *not* write about is surely very large? As we have already seen, key pieces of that history substantiate and clarify the hidden alliance between Sycorax and Prospero that lurks beneath the play's investment in asserting their opposition. Working against the difference between the beneficent theurge and the horrid witch, this alliance projects and displaces the darker shadows of Prospero's magic onto Sycorax. The "unmitigable rage" (1.2.276) that, in Prospero's account, drove Sycorax to confine Ariel in a tree for refusing her commands is an emotion to which he himself is all too prone when he feels his authority challenged. Renouncing his magic in the end, Prospero sides with his "nobler reason 'gainst [his] fury" (5.1.26)—the same fury embodied as one of the pack of hounds he had earlier unleashed against Caliban, Stephano, and Trinculo: "Fury, Fury! There Tyrant, there! Hark hark!" (4.1.258). Orgel draws attention to the "similarities between the two sorcerers," pointing to Prospero's rage as well as to "the demand for unwilling servitude, the continual threats of constriction and painful imprisonment" that he shares with Sycorax.[38] In the light of these similarities, Prospero's account of the neglect of his dukedom in Milan—

that he was "transported / And rapt in secret studies" (1.2.76–77)—takes on an apt connotation. The *furor platonicus* that lifted him in transport to the heights of philosophy and ultimately to the island of his exile also recalls the judicial "transportation" to the same island that was Sycorax's parallel fate in Algiers, and with it the double valence of that nascent legal policy in England. Prospero was "transported" and then transported. The force of the word alone, in its new sense, momentarily places Prospero, however incongruously, in the company of those "incorrigible and dangerous rogues" who were to be sent to "parts abroade." At the same time it holds the promise of salvation in a new world where "he may live and yield a profitable service." Transportation effects a generic sea change, turning what might have been the tragedy of Prospero's death at the hands of his brother into the comic prospect of a fresh beginning.

Sycorax's African association with Egyptians/Gypsies doubly implicates Prospero as well. Gypsies first appeared in England in the early sixteenth century, having willingly or not already been transported, as the Elizabethans supposed, from their native Egypt. By the end of the century they were again regarded as candidates for transportation, not merely because they were tainted by lust, cunning, and deceit, as their reputation had it, but because they were entangled with dramatic pretense. Transportation for these "Egyptians," first from their putative homeland into a European diaspora and now again from Europe to the colonies, could be rewritten as a continuing typological drama in which an apparently punitive measure turns out to be a great mercy, an act of royal clemency in which the king extends his free pardon in the name of a merciful God. Like the pardon extended to the woman pleading the belly, the case of the Gypsies reveals how the law transcends itself by freeing those captive to sin from their "Egyptian" bondage to the law, tempering justice with mercy, and transporting them (albeit over oceans, not deserts) to the promised land of their salvation. In this view, peopling the colonies with Gypsies (or a Mediterranean island with an ingathering of exiles from north and south) carries forward the redemptive work of history.

At the same time, the parliamentary edict of 1597 cited above betrays a disquieting ambiguity when it speaks of persons "pretending themselves to be Egipcyans," or wandering "in the Habite Forme or Attyre of counterfayte Egypcians." How is the law to tell the difference between authentic Gypsies, who make their living by cozenage and deceit (*lewdness, divining, murder, roguery,* and *juggling* are all terms commonly associated with Gypsies in contemporary usages listed in the *OED*) and those pretending to be Gypsies? The law cannot easily discriminate counterfeiting Gypsies from counterfeit Gypsies, non-Gypsies of a certain entrepreneurial spirit and theatrical flair whose dress and habits and talent for playing the role of Gypsies makes them indistinguishable from the "real" thing. The authentic and the theatrical meet in the notion of the Gypsy counterfeit, an unstable and dangerous compound. In the 1597 edict, "counterfayte Egypcians" as candidates for transportation are lumped into the same category as beggars "pretending losses by Fyre or otherwise," persons "fayning themselves to have knowledge" of physiognomy or palmistry; and "comon Players of Enterludes."[39] Thus it is not begging, fortune-telling, or *being* an "Egypcian" that primarily worries the law but begging under false pretenses, pretending to be a physiognomist, or counterfeiting the role of an "Egipcyan." This dramatic flair, and not merely the shared fact of their vagrancy, joins the beggar, the fortune-teller, and the "comon Player" with the counterfeit Egyptian—all practitioners of the actor's craft, roaming the countryside and threatening to turn the world into a stage. A Gypsy-Sycorax similarly threatens any firm distinction between Prospero's role as the master illusionist and cozener of those who come under his sway on the island and hers as the purveyor of "mischiefs manifold" in Algiers. Magus and witch, the real and the counterfeit, are joined in a mutual theatricalism, his "secret studies" (involving, for their display, the use of a magic garment, a staff, and a promptbook) and her "sorceries terrible" mirroring one another as the two aspects of one dramatis persona.

The sense that Prospero and Sycorax share a single role is heightened by the eerie effect of Prospero's great renunciation speech at 5.1.33–57, in which the account of his powers, including the claim that he can raise the dead, closely follows the language of Ovid's Medea in book 7 of the *Metamorphoses* and so recalls the witch who stands behind the figure of Sycorax as well. Jonathan Haynes, writing of George Sandys's travels through Egypt and the Holy Land in 1610, says that the future translator of Ovid saw the Ovidian image of Medea in native women wherever he went, the same image Shakespeare's audience would have seen in Sycorax: the "Medean witch who for thousands of years has been exercising her dark powers in the same place—at the edge of the European psyche—whether that place is called Colchis or Carthage."[40] A witch like Sycorax and an abandoned lover like Dido, Medea also speaks for all the absent women still working their magic "at the edge" of *The Tempest*'s world. Just after the passage Shakespeare uses, Ovid's Medea goes on to appeal to "*Pluto* and his ravisht wife the sovereigne states of Hell" (7.325)[41] to spare old Aeson's life, further connecting her narrative with both that of the abduction of Proserpine recalled in Prospero's masque and that of Proserpine's latter-day counterpart, the unfortunate Claribel, now the ravished wife of a "dusky" Tunisian husband—both, like Aeson, not quite dead but in the place of the dead, ten leagues beyond man's life. Orgel's comment is apt: "In giving up his magic, Prospero speaks as Medea. He has incorporated Ovid's witch, prototype of the wicked mother Sycorax, in the most literal way—verbatim, so to speak—and his 'most potent art' is now revealed as translation and impersonation. In this context, the distinction between black and white magic, Prospero and Sycorax, has disappeared."[42]

But it is important to realize that, even as "Prospero speaks as Medea," in Ovid Medea speaks at cross-purposes to Prospero's appropriation of her language. The thrust of Prospero's speech is to abjure his magical powers. Medea's purpose is to invoke hers once again for the purpose of raising the dead: she seeks an herbal juice that will restore the youth of Jason's aged father, Aeson, to snatch him back from death's door. In the practice of her magic she has "compelled streames to run cleane backward to their spring" (7.268). She now calls upon those same powers to rejuvenate Aeson, restoring "To flowring prime of lustie youth old withred age" (7.285). Prospero's purpose is just the opposite, to give up his art—with the attendant irony, however, that this revocation is a powerful evocation at the same time, recalling not only Sycorax's magic but also, as it were, raising Medea from the dead, along the intervening poets who preserved her resounding voice, Ovid and Golding. In the "dark backward" of Shakespeare's Ovidian source, then, Prospero's speech finds its echo in Medea's power to run "backward" in order to restore, for the future, the "flowering prime" of Aeson's youth. Prospero does not merely "impersonate" or "incorporate" Ovid's Medea. Rather, in Ovid's own terms, the passage that lies behind Prospero's speech is the "spring" to which Prospero returns to make Ovid flower again. The magus will "bury" his staff "certain fathoms in the earth," perhaps just as deep as Sycorax is buried, and drown his book "deeper than did ever plummet sound" (5.1.55–56), returning the implements of his art to the "abyss of time" from which they emerged. In its intertextual richness, however, Prospero's speech resurrects its buried literary history even as he repudiates it.

That this is also, crucially for the connection to Sycorax, a *legal* history is suggested by the word that is Prospero's alone, not Ovid's—that he will "here *abjure* [emphasis mine]" this "rough magic" (5.1.50–51). The moment of Prospero's renunciation takes on the solemnity of a judicial proceeding. To abjure is to make a formal recantation or retraction on oath. To "abjure the realm" is to swear before the court, as felons granted transportation must do, to leave the kingdom and never return. Thus the legal language of Prospero's renunciation enacts the same double gesture in relation to Sycorax's case as the renunciation itself in relation to the literary history it evokes: Prospero's abjural, even as it legally disclaims Sycorax's arts, implicitly repeats and completes Sycorax's "thing," assuming her position before the law when, in accepting the penalty of transportation, she would have had to abjure the realm of Algiers. (Such oaths must be witnessed to have binding force, and although Prospero is alone on stage at that moment, the judicial import of the scene casts the audience as the court, a role the audience will play once more in the Epilogue when Prospero begs its "pardon.") The pattern of the replay casts Prospero's upcoming return to Milan, with all its promise of a new beginning, as a voyage of exile nonetheless—"Every third thought shall be my grave" (5.1.311)—and one in which the very gesture of detachment and renewal reconfronts the thing left behind.

— What would James have made of all this, if indeed he was paying attention during the performance of the play at Whitehall "before the kinges maiestie" noted in the Revels accounts for Hallowmas night, 1611? Would he have been flattered to find his own reflection in Prospero as a monarch able to control the forces of nature and raise the dead? Readers of the *Demonologie* would be left in no doubt that, for the royal author, there could be no difference between Prospero and Sycorax, or at least no difference in what they deserved. There are inequalities in power—"Witches ar servantes onelie, and slaues to the Devil; but the Necromancers are his maisters and commanders"—and they practice their craft from different motives. Magicians are learned. Enticed by a desire "to satisfie their restles mindes," they mount "from degree to degree, vpon the slipperie and vncertaine scale of curiosity"; "their knowledge, for all that they presume thereof, is nothing increased, except in knowing evill, and the horrors of Hell for punishment thereof as *Adams* was by the eating of the forbidden tree."[43] Witches tend to be unlearned women acting out of revenge and greed. For both alike, however, the penalty is death, "according to the Law of God, the ciuill and imperial law, and the municipall law of all Christian nations," nor may their children be spared. It is wrong for the prince or magistrate to "to spare the life, and not to strike when God bids strike."[44]

Against such an unbending application of the law, *The Tempest* may be read as abjuring the practice of magic, and with it everything for which magic had stood in earlier years. Prospero's breaking his staff would figure as a forceful if tacit acknowledgment of James's point, an acknowledgment of Sycorax's guilt as "mine," indeed the collapse of Sycorax back into Prospero despite the magician's strenuous efforts to maintain their opposition. The disavowal of magical power would thus signal a loss of faith in the dream of extending the dominion of the mind over a world responsive to the sheer force of the desire to command it and compel it to give up its secrets. Like the demented Glendower, the magician can "call spirits from the vasty deep," but, as Hotspur observed acidly at the time, there is a serious possibility that they will not "come when you do call for them" (*I Henry IV* 3.1.52–54). In such a narrative, the iconoclastic breaking of the staff would register a larger cultural break between the age of Dee, Bruno, and the other enthusiasts who likely provided the matter of Prospero's secret studies and a more skeptical age ripe for Protestant fideism, Baconian science, and Cartesian rationalism. As Dryden will observe in 1670, apologizing in the Prologue to his revision of *The Tempest* for the Bard's use of supernatural magic, "Those Legends from old Priesthood were receiv'd / and he then writ, as people then believ'd." Yet Dryden goes on in the same Prologue to praise Shakespeare's theatrical magic: "Within that Circle none durst walk but he."[45] The connection between Prospero's discredited art and Shakespeare's dramatic power "sacred as a King's" suggests that magic has not died but has rather been transported from the realm of belief to the kingdom of the theater, where its Medean powers remain undiminished. As Prospero's "secret studies" nourish his magical practice, Dryden sees his own version of *The Tempest* as a "new reviving Play" sprung from the "secret root" of his predecessor that "Lives under ground." Prospero does not renounce his powers until the moment of their exhaustion, not until they have been fully exercised in, and by, the play itself. The power to raise the dead, to call up the spirits of Sycorax, the Widow Dido, Prospero's wife, and the unfortunate Claribel, is the power of drama that *The Tempest* itself commands, and that it cannot so easily abjure except in a last-minute appeal for pardon when the spell is broken.

    A subtler narrative is thus possible, one more closely attuned to what Elizabeth Mazzola has recently described, in the case of the Reformation's discarded religious beliefs, as the age's "sophisticated methodologies for the burial and retrieval of cultural knowledge." The discards and fragments of broken symbols and practices "do not simply disappear from the mental landscape" but can "find their powers increased by occupying the margins of accepted ideas, shadowing the background of the imagination." These "remains," like the ghost of Hamlet's father still hovering near (an officially discredited) purgatory, reappear as "boundary" figures that "linger at imaginative limits or haunt cognitive thresholds." They are filed away, in Mary Douglas's phrase, in "pigeonholes of oblivion," (memory) places occupied by things that can no longer be thought but that continue to shape what can be thought.[46] Such anthropological and psychological accounts of a secret alliance between the unspeakable and what is spoken, and the consequent view of a cultural history that unearths murky but powerful continuities beneath what appear on the surface to be clean breaks, can also be redescribed in the legal terms of this essay. As the means, and the emblem, of Sycorax's survival, the "thing" she did—pleading the belly—mitigates a death sentence with a reprieve. She is transported to an island at the limit of the (Algerian) world, to such a place on the colonial margin as the designers of English transportation policy would already foresee as littered with the monstrous, the felonious, the rebellious, and the merely rootless excess of their own island. Prospero's own exile transports him "backward" to a dead past mirrored in his journey to the place where Sycorax lies buried. The journey makes possible a new beginning through the repudiation of an old world that is never left completely behind.

Evoking a comparably liminal state in the alchemical language Prospero would understand from his secret studies, Donne declares in the "Nocturnall upon S. Lucies Day" that from "nothingnesse," he is "re-begot / Of absence, darknesse, death; things which are not."[47] Within the magic circle of the island, what is begot appears as re-begot of the absence of Prospero's wife, the darkness of Claribel's exile, and the death of Sycorax—all "things which are not." Prospero's reduction of Sycorax's "thing" to nothing—to a thing unspoken, banished to the realm of the obscene and the unlawful—follows what we might call the play's own exclusionary legal code, circumscribing the order of things by attempting to mark it off from the realm of things which are not. The gesture recurs again and again in other works of the same period: Donne's own circumscriptions of private amatory worlds from which the larger world is forcibly excluded, Jonson's moral demarcation of Robert Sidney's estate by what it rejects ("Thou art not, PENSHVRST, built to enuious show"); Marvell's ironic appraisal, in "Upon Appleton House," of his own patron Fairfax's attempt to exclude a world of chaos and civil war "without," only to have it recur "within" the walls of Appleton House; ultimately Milton's attempt to imagine a paradise ordered by the absence within it of everything in the fallen world to which we ourselves have been exiled. Adam and Eve were spared from death, their exclusion from Eden re-begot as the beginning of history. Thus were our first parents saved from the rigors of the law and then transported, in history's first recorded instance of the happy fate that would await Sycorax in Algiers. The idea of a (trans)portable paradise, of an exile pregnant with the seed of renewal, is adumbrated in the excluded judicial proceeding in *The Tempest*. It turns out that Prospero and his discarded magic are less potent as the begetters of a nascent colonialism than his alter ego, Sycorax, in whose matrix this specific idea of the colonial becomes thinkable.

NOTES

1. Andrew Marvell, *The Poems and Letters of Andrew Marvell*, ed. H. M. Margoliouth, 3rd ed., vol. 1 (Oxford: Clarendon Press, 1971).
2. All quotations from *The Tempest* are taken from the Oxford Shakespeare edition, ed. Stephen Orgel (Oxford: Clarendon Press, 1987).
3. Aimé Césaire, *Une tempête* (Paris: Éditions du Seuil, 1969).
4. Stephen Orgel, "Prospero's Wife," in *Rewriting the Renaissance: The Discourses of Difference in Early Modern England*, ed. Margaret W. Ferguson et al. (Chicago: University of Chicago Press, 1986), 1.
5. J. S. Phillpotts, writing in 1876, was perhaps the first to see *The Tempest* as the augury of that future: "If Prospero might dispossess Caliban, England might dispossess the aborigines of the colonies" (quoted in William Shakespeare, *The Tempest*, ed. H. H. Furness, New Variorum, vol. 9, 7th ed. [Philadelphia: J. B. Lippincott, 1892], 383). Building on the work of Leo Marx, Frank Kermode, Stephen Greenblatt, Stephen Orgel, Paul Brown, and Peter Hulme among many others, Kim F. Hall notes in her 1995 study *Things of Darkness: Economies of Race and Gender in Early Modern England* (Ithaca: Cornell University Press, 1995) that "[c]olonialist readings of *The Tempest* have shown the text to be a fertile ground for exploring issues of race, cultural contest, and authority in English encounters with the 'new world'" (141). See also Leo Marx, *The Machine in the Garden* (New York: Oxford University Press, 1964); William Shakespeare, *The Tempest*, ed. Frank Kermode (Cambridge, MA: Harvard University Press, 1958); Stephen Greenblatt, *Marvellous Possessions: The Wonder of the New World* (Chicago: University of Chicago Press, 1991) and *Shakespearean Negotiations: The Circulation of Social Energy in Renaissance England* (Berkeley: University of California Press, 1988); Paul Brown, "'This thing of darkness I acknowledge mine,'" in *Political Shakespeare: New Essays in Cultural Materialism*, ed. Jonathan Dollimore and Alan Sinfield (Manchester: Manchester University Press, 1985), 48–71; and Peter Hulme, *Colonial Encounters: Europe and the Native Caribbean, 1492–1797* (New York: Methuen, 1986).
6. Orgel, *Tempest*, 11.
7. Daniel Defoe, *Moll Flanders*, ed. Edward Kelly (New York: Norton, 1973), 8.
8. Orgel, *Tempest*, 18.
9. Deborah Willis, "Shakespeare and the English Witch-Hunts: Enclosing the Maternal Body," in *Enclosure Acts: Sexuality, Property, and Culture in Early Modern England*, ed. Richard Burt and John Michael Archer (Ithaca: Cornell University Press, 1994), 99.
10. David Dean, *Law-Making and Society in Late Elizabethan England: The Parliament of England, 1584–1601* (Cambridge: Cambridge University Press, 1996), 58–60.
11. See Frank Kermode, ed., *The Tempest*, Arden Edition, 6th ed. (Cambridge, MA: Harvard University Press, 1958), 26.
12. The *Malleus* is quoted in Camille Naish, *Death Comes to the Maiden: Sex and Execution, 1431–1933* (New York: Routledge, 1991), 26–27.
13. James I, *Demonologie*, ed. G. B. Harrison (1597; reprint, New York: Barnes and Noble, 1966), 67.

14. John Gillies, *Shakespeare and the Geography of Difference* (Cambridge: Cambridge University Press, 1994), 32.

15. Johannes Leo Africanus, *A Geographical Historie of Africa*, trans. and ed. John Pory (London, 1600), quoted in Hall, *Things of Darkness*, 34, 36.

16. Jonathan Haynes, *Humanist as Traveler: George Sandys's Relation of a Journey Begun An. Dom. 1610* (London: Associated University Press, 1986), 90, 85.

17. James I, *Demonologie*, 68.

18. Quoted in Naish, *Death Comes to the Maiden*, 25.

19. James I, *Demonologie*, 43.

20. P. C. Hoffer and N. E. H. Hull, *Murdering Mothers: Infanticide in England and New England, 1558–1803* (New York: New York University Press, 1981), 29.

21. Ben Jonson, *Selected Masques*, ed. Stephen Orgel (New Haven: Yale University Press, 1970), 365.

22. Louis A Montrose, "The Work of Gender in the Discourse of Discovery," *Representations* 33 (1991): 26.

23. Kathryn Schwarz, "Missing the Breast: Desire, Disease, and the Singular Effect of Amazons," in *The Body in Parts*, ed. Carla Mazzio and David Hillman (New York: Routledge, 1997), 15.

24. Orgel, *Tempest*, 116.

25. Among others in the nineteenth century, Charles Lamb regarded this unspecified "thing" as deeply mysterious: "How have I pondered over this, when a boy! How have I longed for some authentic memoir of the witch to clear up this obscurity!—was the story extant in the Chronicles of Algiers? . . . The blue-eyed hag,æcould *she* have done anything good or meritorious?" Writing in 1823 in *The London Magazine*, Lamb offers a long account of a witch who delivered Algiers from a siege by predicting, or producing, a tempest that sank the enemy fleet: "Can it be doubted for a moment that the dramatist had come fresh from reading some *older narrative* of this deliverance of Algiers by a witch, and transferred the merit of this deed to his Sycorax, exchanging only the 'rich remuneration,' which did not suit his purpose, to the simple pardon of her life?" (quoted in Furness, *Tempest*, 60–61).

26. Geoffrey Bullough, *Narrative and Dramatic Sources of Shakespeare* (New York: Routledge and Paul, 1957–75), 3:77.

27. Quoted in C. D. O'Malley, *Andreas Vesalius of Brussels, 1514–1564* (Berkeley: University of California Press, 1964), 143.

28. J. S. Cockburn, quoted in James C. Oldham, "On Pleading the Belly: A History of the Jury of Matrons," *Criminal Justice History* 6 (1985): 10.

29. See J. A. Sharpe, *Crime in Early Modern England, 1550–1750* (New York: Longman, 1984), 68; and Oldham, "On Pleading the Belly," 19.

30. Quoted in Oldham, "On Pleading the Belly," 8.

31. "Polymasty" or "polythely," extra breasts or nipples, is, in the words of one modern expert, "not quite so uncommon as the layman might think." Their discovery by the

matrons would be considered proof positive of witchcraft, but even in the absence of such startling evidence, "any wart or sore could be interpreted as a witch's mark" (E. Peel, quoted in Oldham, "On Pleading the Belly," 8).

32. George Peckham, *True Reporte, of the Late Discoueries* (London, 1583).

33. Statute 39 Eliz., c.4, quoted in Abbot Emerson Smith, *Colonists in Bondage: White Servitude and Convict Labor in America, 1607–1776* (Chapel Hill: University of North Carolina Press, 1947), 137.

34. Quoted in Smith, *Colonists in Bondage*, 138.

35. C. S. P. *East Indies*, 1571–1616, no. 432; quoted in Smith, *Colonists in Bondage*, 147.

36. Quoted in Smith, *Colonists in Bondage*, 136–37.

37. Quoted in ibid., 92–93.

38. Orgel, *Tempest*, 19.

39. Smith, *Colonists in Bondage*, 136–37.

40. Haynes, *Humanist as Traveler*, 119.

41. Ovid, *The Metamorphoses*, trans. Arthur Golding (1567), in *Shakespeare's Ovid, Being Arthur Golding's Translation of the Metamorphoses*, ed. W. H. D. Rouse (New York: Norton, 1961).

42. Orgel, "Prospero's Wife," 11.

43. James I, *Demonologie*, 9–11.

44. Ibid., 77–78.

45. John Dryden and William Davenant, *The Tempest, or the Enchanted Island* (London, 1670).

46. Elizabeth Mazzola, *The Pathology of the English Renaissance: Sacred Remains and Holy Ghosts* (Boston: Brill, 1998), 1–9.

47. John Donne, The *Poems of John Donne*, ed. Herbert J. C. Grierson (Oxford: University Press, 1912), 1:44.

SIX

The Witch of Edmonton and the Guilt of Possession

Dennis Kezar

> These are no jestes, for they be written by them that were
> and are judges upon the lives and deaths of those persons.
> —Reginald Scot, *The Discoverie of Witchcraft*

>   I have heard
> That guilty creatures sitting at a play
> Have by the very cunning of the scene
> Been strook so to the soul, that presently
> They have proclaim'd their malefactions:
> For murther, though it have no tongue, will speak
> With most miraculous organ.
>   —*Hamlet*

No Renaissance art form calls more loudly for our ethical response than that representing the persecution and execution of witches; and none raises more clearly the analytical problem of "guilt" or "responsibility" in historical discussions of early modern texts. If, more than any other literary genre, drama interacts with a culture's ways of seeing, the theater of witchcraft involves an epistemology in which looks really can kill. Yet though works of dramatic journalism such as *The Late Lancashire Witches* (1634)[1] may have influenced the legal process in offstage witch trials, we search in vain for an actual corpse with which to accuse Renaissance drama's fascination with the subject.² Though there is much to suggest that early modern skeptics such as Reginald Scot and Samuel Harsnett recognized the function of theatricality in the cultural production of the bewitched and bedeviled, moreover, these skeptics never charge the institution of the stage with responsibility for persecution and execution. In fact, as Stephen Greenblatt has demonstrated, the opposite is the case: the "freely acknowledged fictionality" of the theater provides Renaissance skeptics with a zone of inconsequentiality where otherwise dangerous witch beliefs can be safely contained. In the Renaissance, only a thoroughgoing antitheatricalist like Stephen Gosson, suspicious not of the theatricalization of evil but of the evil of theater, seems willing to blame plays for performing the devil's work: "The Devil is the efficient cause of plays."³

But Gosson's voice, though muffled, is audible in criticism implicitly concerned with the instrumentality of the stage in perpetuating and enabling social persecution. Etta Soiref Onat's response to *The Late Lancashire Witches* illustrates what has for some time been the fashion of displacing ethical with formal criticism when confronted with the damningly orthodox representation of witches. Observing that the play was produced between the examination of the accused and their pardon by King Charles, and that the playwrights "undoubtedly knew the rumors which were circulating about the pardon and the suspicions of the good faith of the . . . chief witnesses for the prosecution," Onat struggles with the dramatists' decision to represent the accused as unquestionably bewitched:

> Such a choice is, of course, entirely within the province of the playwright; even when he is working with sources of such topical nature, he does not work like a reporter. . . . We do have the right, however, to ask that, once having made a choice, he should not be superficial in his portrayal. Thus, without agreeing that the authors "had *pendente lite*, done their utmost to intensify public feeling against witches," we may regret perhaps that *The Late Lancashire Witches* is so completely orthodox and positive in its presentation of the popular superstitions. But we cannot really censure the authors for making that choice. What we can censure them for is that their portrayal is superficial and trivial; throughout the entire play the emphasis is upon the sensational for its own sake.⁴

In earlier debates over Shakespeare's troubling dramatization of witches, the underlying assumption that such representation can have harmful social consequences seems to inform the desire to exculpate Shakespeare for authorial responsibility, even if this defense requires aesthetic condemnation. Joan la Pucelle in *1 Henry VI*, for instance, has been indignantly labeled "un-Shakespearean"—a product of a disintegrated text that does not reflect Shakespeare's intentions and does not, therefore, require his accountability;[5] the "interpolated" witches' song in *Macbeth*, a crowd-pleasing round taken from Thomas Middleton's *The Witch*, has similarly appeared "spurious"—a dismissal that has until quite recently foreclosed analysis of Shakespeare's employment of it.[6]

The bold questions beneath such partial indictments and defensive strategies have recently been brought into open air by Greenblatt, who responds to feminist and psychoanalytic recognition of *Macbeth*'s "radical excision of the female"[7] by asking why the play should not be equated with such socially consequential texts as the witch-mongering *Malleus maleficarum*:

> Why should we not say that the play, with immeasurably greater literary force, undertakes to reenchant the world, to shape misogyny to political ends, to counteract the corrosive skepticism that had called into question both the existence of witches and the sacredness of royal authority? . . . Why should we not say that this play about evil is evil? . . . What is the point of speaking at all about the historical situation of works of art if ideological entailments and practical consequences are somehow off-limits, and if they are not off-limits, how can we avoid moral judgments?[8]

Inevitable objections present themselves to such questions, which Greenblatt himself finally disregards as "smug moral critique":[9] post-Enlightenment rationalism and tests of "progressive politics" are notorious impediments to historical empathy with early modern texts; assessing the artistic intentions and social consequences of a play such as *Macbeth* requires missing biographical and historical evidence; and, perhaps most importantly, subjecting *Macbeth* to a modern-day inquisition ignores the ways in which the play "questions from within itself its own theatrical representation of witchcraft."[10]

Metadramatic reflexivity would indeed seem to offer the theater a powerful defense against such probing questions: How can we indict the stage for substantiating the theatricalism for which and by which witches were killed, after all, if the theater clearly designates such imaginary enchantment as manipulative illusion? Does the explicit and self-conscious dramatization of witchcraft not always provide its own skeptical critique? Interestingly, such questions are posed forcefully by the very play Greenblatt chooses to contrast with *Macbeth* in an effort partially to exonerate Shakespeare's play; unlike *Macbeth*, he claims, *The Witch of Edmonton* apparently "sanction[s]" the legal prosecution and execution of witches.[11] The following essay argues largely to the contrary—suggesting that Thomas Dekker, John Ford, and William Rowley collaboratively produce in *The Witch of Edmonton* (1621) one of the most radical dramatic challenges to the legal and cultural production of witches in the Renaissance. Complicating this argument, however, is the coextensive claim that such a reading—which locates invitations to skepticism within a text—should not necessarily disentangle or exculpate a text from its acknowledged legal and cultural complicities. Calls for light within a theater can have enchantments of their own; they can also cast long shadows of guilt across the text that gives them being. Greenblatt's analytical attempt to contrast an ethically free and even virtuous "skepticism" with fear-mongering is, therefore, in the context of this essay, dubious and itself subject to suspicion.

Nevertheless there is an undeniably important contribution lying within Greenblatt's reading of *Macbeth* in "Shakespeare Bewitched." That reading lies in its articulation of the possibility that witchcraft drama might be socially consequential and ethically accountable—an anxiety harbored not only by critics of this drama but also by Renaissance playwrights. By identifying the terms by which theater can both collude with and skeptically destabilize a culture's witch beliefs, Greenblatt subjects to historical analysis the question of literary responsibility. If his essay has a disabling omission, however, it appears in an inattention to the textual experience of this responsibility. When asked to choose whether a play like *Macbeth* "*is*" evil" or "is *about* evil," the latter proves more demonstrable, and more historically responsible, than the retrospective ascription of guilt. And that is presumably why Greenblatt's analysis of the play's "political and ethical consequences" becomes increasingly attenuated by qualification until Shakespeare is finally placed "on the side of a liberating, tolerant doubt."[12] But if, in an historicist reading of *Macbeth*, "objective" guilt ultimately proves inapplicable, the formal defense of reflexivity would at least seem limited; reflexivity, after all, does not automatically exculpate a text from the consequences of what it self-consciously performs, any more than a flickering expression of social conscience justifies attendant, strategic evil:

> If th'assassination
> Could trammel up the consequence, and catch
> With his surcease, success; that but this blow
> Might be the be-all and the end-all here,

> But here, upon this bank and [shoal] of time,
> We'ld jump the life to come. But in these cases
> We still have judgment here, that we but teach
> Bloody instructions, which, being taught, return
> To plague th'inventor.
> (*Macbeth*, 1.7.2–10)

Even to imply that the author of a witchcraft play could consider his part in and responsibility for "teach[ing] / Bloody instructions," though, is to supply the missing category in Greenblatt's analysis—the category of subjective guilt.

This category is accessible to historical analysis precisely because it is produced by, and respondent to, historical and cultural pressures. In the following reading of *The Witch of Edmonton*, I will suggest that listening for expressions of subjective guilt can expand the possibilities of metadramatic reflexivity to include not only skeptical challenges to the theatricalization of witchcraft but also complex confessions of the theater's capitalization on this phenomenon. Such a reading will concern the playwrights' acknowledged complicity with the fairly diffuse economy that supported witch-mongering in Renaissance England; and we will see the ways in which this complicity is "redistributed"[13] in the play's deceptively collaborative plots and in the terrible collusion they reveal between the tragicomedy of religious punishment and forgiveness and the entertainment industry of the stage. First, though, I want to consider the chief complicity Dekker, Ford, and Rowley undertook the moment they chose the subject of their play—a complicity with the law that had already provided for Elizabeth Sawyer's representation and execution.

The Law's Eye and the Theater's Capital

Though in obvious ways the playwright does not, in Onat's words, "work like a reporter," authors of Renaissance witchcraft dramas had special reason to meditate upon the mediation performed by their texts. Their subjects could be unusually topical, recognizable as offstage persons unprotected by the laws against libel and slander that customarily governed the stage. As a legal category, the Renaissance "subject" of witchcraft was for several more specific reasons exposed to acute theatrical vulnerability. In early modern England, where uniquely in Europe the jury (rather than the bench) was charged with "finding fact" in the adjudication of guilt or innocence, the theater could influence not only the court of public opinion but also the generic perspective of potential jurors.[14] When we consider a related legal distinction between Renaissance England and the rest of Europe—that in England criminal trials were typically public and well-reported affairs, while on the Continent they were conducted in relative secrecy[15]—the epistemological analogies between courtroom and drama further suggest consequential social connections.

Indeed, if the English theater occupied a position of what we might call "culpable mediacy" in a culture that created and killed witches, it was because these analogies placed the stage on the verge of the legally produced "real": the epistemological conviction deliberated by jurors and required of spectators sought to alter the ontology of the accused and the staged.[16] The plea we hear in *Henry V*'s Prologue to see more than meets the eye, for instance, echoes in John Gaule's mid-seventeenth-century call for evidentiary latitude in judging a witch: "Neither is it requisite that so palpable evidence for conviction should here come in, as in more sensible matters. It is enough if there be but so much circumstantial proof or evidence, as the substance, matter, and nature of such an abstruse mystery will well admit."[17] In 1616, John Cotta similarly recommends a fantastically "curious view" of witchcraft cases, since (as Duke Theseus observes of the theatergoer's need for epistemological charity in *A Midsummer Night's Dream*) such cases are "neither manifest to sense, nor evident to reason"; without the active engagement of the juror's "presumptions," Cotta suggests, the theatrical mysteries of witchcraft will fail to convince.[18] Five years later another interpretive community is enjoined "from suspicion to proceed to great presumptions," a reliance upon the evidence of things not seen that produces both a witch "on whose body law was justly inflicted" and a made-for-theater account.[19] In *The Wonderful Discoverie of Elizabeth Sawyer a Witch, Late of Edmonton, Her Conviction and Condemnation and Death*, the minister Henry Goodcole provides a catalog of witnesses and transcripts of testimony in defense of the prosecution—"thereof to stop all contradictions of so palpable a verity" as that which he represents in narrative and dialogue (388). As hard as he strives to leave nothing to the imagination in his proof of Sawyer's guilt, however, Goodcole must finally resort to the imagination as he confronts the airy nothing of her possession. To ascribe to Sawyer the agency that will define a host of unfortunate events as her evil acts, Goodcole must demonstrate that she really trafficked with a spirit unwitnessed by anyone else in the courtroom; to do so he requires that Sawyer produce against herself a convincing bit of theater that renders tangible the privately spectacular: "Did you ever handle the Devil when he came unto you? (I asked of her this question because some might think this was a visible delusion of her sight only)" (*Wonderful Discoverie*, 396).[20] Goodcole never comes closer to fantasizing of the special effects—the talking dog, the touching "familiar"—with which the authors of *The Witch of Edmonton* give the devil a local habitation and a name in the play.

But the circumstantial proof and spectacularly produced "real" of the theater always, at the final curtain, discredit themselves as insubstantial pageantry. In fact we might take *any* theatrical representation (however orthodox or unreflective) of an embattled legal belief structure as a subversive call to skepticism; Thespis, after all, has always made Solon nervous—perhaps by drawing attention to the uncomfortable homologies between courtroom and drama, legal fiction and theatrical illusion.[21] The Renaissance stage, moreover, was especially well situated to expose the machinery and motivations of illusion-mongering, the contingency and capitalism of credibility. When, for example, two characters in *The Witch of Edmonton*'s comic subplot propose adding a make-believe witch to the cast of their morris dance, we are reminded with a metadramatic wink that the play's "real" witch is really a counterfeit too:

> YOUNG BANKS. I'll have a Witch; I love a Witch.
> 1. MORICE-DANCER. Faith, Witches themselves are so common now a days, that the counterfeit will not be regarded. They say we have three or four in *Edmonton*, besides Mother Sawyer.

Such winks, however (and the play is replete with them), can also produce a blind eye: by establishing a distant focal point on the obvious fiction of a play-within-the-play (here, the carnivalesque morris), the dramatist also blurs those categories by which his spectators maintain distinction between the framing action and the real world that frames it. The self-conscious deployment of an act of make-believe, as the mannered mimesis of *The Murder of Gonzago* famously illustrates, can paradoxically contribute to the making of consequential belief—especially when accompanied by appeals to the process of legal conviction. By reifying "the play" as the conscience-catching "thing," Hamlet joins his spectators in a theater transformed by the judicial discovery of fact and production of evidence; *Hamlet* performatively authenticates itself by producing, in a case of conscience, an *authentes* or "murderer" who interrupts the theatrical counterfeit of his crime with a disillusioning call for light.[22] *The Witch of Edmonton*, first published with the subtitle "A known true Story,"[23] achieves an even firmer referential authenticity by borrowing from the specific legal precedent represented by Goodcole: "For my part I meddle here with nothing but matter of fact, and to that end produce the testimony of the living and the dead, which I hope shall be authentical for the confirmation of this Narration" (*Wonderful Discoverie*, 381).

I say "borrowing" because the Prologue attached to a revival of the play, acknowledging the fact that Edmonton has already provided the theater with diabolical source material,[24] describes the transaction in these terms:

> The Town of Edmonton hath lent the Stage
> A Devil and a Witch, both in an Age.
> (Prologue, 1–2)

In the scene of the Young Banks's morris preparations, this conception of the witch as theatrical capital appears in the diabolical "Spirit's" distinction between comic subplot and the play's more serious economy:

> We'll sport with [Young Banks]; but when reckoning call,
> We know where to receive: th'Witch pays for all.
> (3.1.75–76)

Certainly these lines reveal the terrible calculus of scapegoating—a symbolic math that the play frequently graphs metadramatically: "The Witch must be beaten out of her Cock-pit" (5.1.49).[25] More specifically, they unravel the twisted logic of a culture whose king (the play was performed not only "often at the Cock-pit" but "once at Court, with singular Applause")[26] authored both the *Book of Sports* and *Daemonologie*—the first an advocation of the kind of spirited civic revelry represented by the morris, the latter a complex legitimization of the prosecution of witches that accommodates skepticism.[27] When sanctioned play threatens to undo such cultural work, a scapegoat typically gets stuck with the bill. Thus when Young Banks unwittingly contaminates the morris with the evil familiar, thereby confirming the Puritan argument that such festivities transform their participants into "deuils incarnate," a genuine crime intercedes to excuse his "deuil's dance" as innocent.[28] "This news of Murder," he exclaims when informed of the main plot's homicide, "has slain the Morrice" (3.4.63–64); and the investigation of this crime, after false accusations, leads to Sawyer's conviction as the efficient cause. But if "th'Witch pays for all" as the price of playing, the expense of spirit that satisfies social accounts, she also provides credit as a convincing spectacle—a commercial resource of theatrical prejudice. As capital, Elizabeth Sawyer offers the stage a prepaid product of its genuinely forensic counterpart, already examined and convicted for capital crimes by the jury that theatergoers can only approximate.

That the transactions between legal and fictional representation can challenge the former's legitimacy appears in Goodcole's explanation of his desire

> to defend the truth of the cause, which in some measure hath received a wound already, by most base and false ballads, which were sung at the time of our returning from the Witch's execution. In them I was ashamed to see and hear such ridiculous fictions of her bewitching corn on the ground, of a ferret and an owl daily sporting before her, of the bewitched woman braining herself, of the spirits attending in the Prison: all which I knew to be fitter for an Ale-bench than for a relation of proceeding in Court of Justice. And thereupon I wonder that such lewd Balladmongers should be suffered to creep into the Printers' presses and people's ears. (*Wonderful Discoverie*, 381–82)

Here as throughout the narrative Goodcole acknowledges the vulnerability of "the cause" to parodic devolution and textual circulation;[29] indeed in a few instances he is surprisingly willing to concede the dubiety of specific aspects of Sawyer's trial in order to contain the more radical skepticism that would expose his *Wonderful Discoverie* as tragic or farcical misapprehension.[30] When relating the town's superstitious method of determining who was responsible for "the death of nurse-children and cattle," for instance, Goodcole interjects an editorial note that anticipates the commonsense objection to such a test: "And to find out who should be the author of this mischief, an old ridiculous custom was used, which was to pluck the thatch of her house and to burn it, and it being so burned, the author of such mischief should presently come out: and it was observed, and affirmed to the Court, that Elizabeth Sawyer would presently frequent the house of them that burnt the thatch which they plucked of her house, and come without sending for" (*Wonderful Discoverie*, 382–83). Goodcole similarly acknowledges the uncomfortable fact that in prison Sawyer has confessed to him the murder of the two nurse-children "for the which I was now indicted and acquitted, by the Jury"; on the other hand, she has remained resolute to the gallows that she is innocent of the death of one "Agnes Ratcliefe," "for which [she was] found guilty by the Jury" (*Wonderful Discoverie*, 391).

For Goodcole the "old ridiculous custom" of thatch burning, like the "ridiculous fictions" of the "lewd Balladmongers," must be dutifully marked as suspect and counterfeit if his audience's limited credulity is to be reserved for, and focused upon, the central drama of his narrative. If in the faithful representation of this drama Goodcole must also admit the potential fallibility of the jury that pronounced Sawyer guilty, moreover, he defends all the more firmly the fundamental justice of her conviction and execution. By converting the body and speech of the accused into self-incriminating evidence, the courtroom becomes an authentic and providentially directed theater:

> The Bench commanded officers appointed for those purposes, to fetch in three women to search the body of Elizabeth Sawyer, to see if they could find any such unwonted mark as they were informed of. . . .
> That tongue which by cursing, swearing, blaspheming, and imprecating, as afterward she confessed, was the occasioning cause of the Devil's access unto her . . . and to claim her thereby as his own, by it discovered her lying, swearing, and blaspheming as also evident proofs produced against her, to stop her mouth with Truth's authority. . . . Thus God did wonderfully overtake her in her own wickedness, to make her tongue to be the means of her own destruction, which had destroyed many before. (*Wonderful Discoverie*, 387, 383–84)

Like the authors of *The Witch of Edmonton*, Goodcole advertises the marvelous fact of his discovery—a fact established by Sawyer's essential role as a legible body and a possessed tongue—by distinguishing it parenthetically from untenable fiction and corrupting superstition. In their similar and often complementary attempts to render Sawyer's case "A known true Story" with a future stage history, *The Wonderful Discoverie* and *The Witch of Edmonton* in fact suggest a cooperation between legal apology and self-authenticating theater. If in the defense of the law the condemned must be convincingly made-for-theater, the theater's appropriation of this product can involve a "loan" that respects the principle as the immutable stipulation of the borrower. Indeed, Greenblatt's argument that *The Witch of Edmonton* actually sanctions the legal execution of witches suggests how such a loan may be repaid with interest: theatrical representation, with its potential for limitless reproduction, can contribute to the process whereby an individual legal case lives in history as a constantly relevant and applicable precedent.[31]

Goodcole's strategies of incorporating skepticism for the purpose of authentic conviction at least provide the playwrights with a representational model. In a scene that may recall the morris dancers' rejection of a "counterfeit" witch for their festivities, the Justice examining Sawyer dismisses the bogus proofs of witchcraft offered by Young Banks's father and a group of rustics:

> 1. COUNTRY-MAN. This Thatch is as good as a Jury to prove she is a Witch...
> OLD BANKS. . . . a Witch: to prove her one, we no sooner set fire on the Thatch of her House, but in she came running...
> JUSTICE. Come, come; firing her Thatch? ridiculous: take heed Sirs what you do: unless your proofs come better arm'd, instead of turning her into a Witch, you'll prove yourselves starke Fools.
>
> (4.1.25, 34–36, 39–41)

Like Hamlet, the playwrights' Justice (whose localized skepticism, sensitivity toward the judicially "ridiculous," and empirical focus upon the body of the accused transcribe Goodcole) will have "grounds / More relative than this" (*Hamlet*, 22.603–4). And the play obliges by arming its proofs against such popular superstitions and dubious juries; the play, in fact, enlists its spectators as jury, resolving into spectacle some of the evidentiary ambiguities raised by Goodcole's narrative.

The instant Sawyer is left alone in the scene above, for example, the "Familiar" enters to "have the Teat" ("dri'd up / With cursing and with madness") and to inform Sawyer that he has lamed a horse "and nip'd the sucking-childe" (4.1.151, 153, 159–60). In this very brief exchange, the playwrights compress the damning anatomical examination reported in *The Wonderful Discoverie* (387–88); they also establish Sawyer's role in the death of at least one of "those two nurse-children"—a crime of which she has been acquitted (apparently erroneously) in Goodcole's account. Such *maleficia* typically, as in *The Wonderful Discoverie*, can be reconstructed only in the confession of the accused or in the charges of the prosecution. Onstage, though, the Witch's commands to her familiar reveal what even a skeptic must acknowledge as a crime of intention. In a passage to which we shall return, moreover, *The Witch of Edmonton* redresses a further ambiguity in Goodcole's account by representing the consequences of Sawyer's cursing of Agnes Ratcleife: her commands that the Dog "pinch that Quean to th'heart" and "Touch her" are followed (post hoc if not propter hoc) by "Anne Ratcliff's" madness and suicide (4.1.71–207). Though the playwrights' witch, like Goodcole's, will deny in the end any responsibility for this crime (5.3.33–35), our witnessing of this scene amplifies and confirms the "insight" of those who have examined Sawyer's body for witch's marks in *The Wonderful Discoverie*: "This view of theirs . . . gave some insight to the Jury, of her: who upon their consciences returned the said *Elizabeth Sawyer*, to be guilty, by diabolical help, of the death of *Agnes Ratcleife.* . . . And thus much of the means that brought her to her deserved death and destruction" (388). One cannot read substantial portions of the play without sensing the commercial value of this "insight" to the theater. As a satisfying supplement to interpretive appetizers offered in the courtroom, such a gaze endows the observed with enough agency to register the significance of its appropriation by the observer: "she has done killing now, but must be kill'd for what she has done: she's shortly to be hang'd" (*Witch of Edmonton*, 5.1.101). As a solution to any perceived antagonism between the licit and the entertaining, legal and theatrical imperatives merge in a play that invites its spectators to continue the law's work.

Of course, reliance upon theatrical prejudice to establish and perpetuate the essential justice of legal precedent entails obvious liabilities. In *Measure for Measure*, Angelo's desire to execute a sex offender as a future warning to the rest of Vienna requires an admission of juristic hypocrisy that will return to haunt him:

> I do not deny
> The jury, passing on the prisoner's life,
> May in the sworn twelve have a thief or two
> Guiltier than him they try. What's open made to justice,
> That justice seizes.
>
> (2.1.18–22)

The Witch of Edmonton involves theatrical exposures of legal abuse similar to the Duke's ultimate discovery of Angelo; the play's Justice may peremptorily claim, in response to Sawyer's indictment of socially tolerated forms of ruinous "Inchantment," "Yes, yes, but the Law / Casts not an eye on these" (*Witch of Edmonton*, 4.1.117–18), but it is the panoptic privilege of theater to examine just such inequities. My foregoing analysis of *The Witch of Edmonton*'s substantial connivance with the law, however, has aimed at revealing the central complicity that defines much of the play's remarkable social criticism as self-criticism. If the play finally allows no uncomplicated scapegoating, the text forbids even itself the purifying displacement of its social implications. Before recognizing *The Witch of Edmonton*'s representation of the social guilt that underlies local blame, then, I wish to exemplify the play's reflection on the culpability of its own representations.

My example focuses on what we have seen as the playwrights' intertextual self-consciousness, their awareness of Goodcole's prior account as authenticating source and theatrical capital. Any latent tension between these two conceptions of their legal source has thus far, in my analysis, been resolved in the playwrights' "supplemental" representation of Sawyer's case. In the scene of Anne Ratcliff's bewitching, however, the dramatists depart from Goodcole's narrative in an especially significant way; they create, in fact, a glaring intertextual contradiction that exposes the exploitative nature of Goodcole's account and their dramatization of it. In his trenchant discussion of cultural conflict in the play, Anthony Dawson has described this contradiction as "in essence an addition to the source":

> In Goodcole's pamphlet, Agnes Ratcliffe dies bewitched, a victim of Mother Sawyer's revenge for a petty neighborly trespass. In the play she runs mad and subsequently commits suicide. The difference may seem slight, motivated perhaps by the opportunity the change offered the dramatists for a theatrically effective mad scene. But I think there is more to it than that.... As a social critic, she is allied with her enemy in the same scene, Mother Sawyer.... So, Anne Ratcliffe, victim of witchcraft, is linked in her madness to the transgressive marginality of witchcraft itself. She thus joins hands with Mother Sawyer.[32]

Dawson's sensitivity to the passage's theatrical opportunism and legal satire is illuminating;[33] but his premise that the exchange is "an addition to the source" leads him to conclude with what I consider a distorted sense of the dramatists' ventriloquized social criticism and sympathy in this passage. In this part of the scene the dramatists have not, strictly speaking, added to their sources; they have instead incorporated those "most base and false ballads" whose "ridiculous fictions ... of the bewitched woman braining herself" Goodcole mentions in his pamphlet only to discount:

> and nothing in her mouth being heard, but the Devil,
> the Witch the Witch, the Devil; she beat out her own brains,
> and so she died.
> (*Witch of Edmonton*, 4.1.205–7)

What can seem (and what on one level is) a dramatic liberty taken to enhance social protest and marginal sympathy is actually (or perhaps, is also) an intrusive reminder of the commercial interests of theater.[34]

"Performance," writes Harry Berger, "asks us to submit to its spell, and the text asks us to examine the implications of that submission."[35] Like the authors of *The Witch of Edmonton*, Goodcole avails himself of illusionistic strategies—such as present-tense dialogue—whereby a text can become a script. In so doing he strives mightily to distinguish his production and distribution of numerous "written copies of this . . . Declaration" from the "lewd Balladmongers . . . suffered to creep into the Printers' presses and people's ears" (*Wonderful Discoverie*, 381–82). To the extent that Goodcole makes us forget that "as Ordinary at Newgate [he] heard the dying confessions of the prisoners [and] eked out his livelihood by publishing the details of their trials and confessions,"[36] this performance is successful. But as the profitable packaging of a prior performance, his text exposes itself and its consumers as implicated in a potentially insidious yellow journalism. If this self-interrogation appears only as an unwelcome by-product of Goodcole's text, moreover, it seems volunteered by a play that registers its own textual (and intertextual) self-consciousness. We can attribute this self-consciousness to the fact that the dramatists' capitalization on their sources is less easily effaced or ignored than the clerical reporter's and to the ways in which their script authenticates itself on Goodcole's precedent even as it challenges the legitimizing disclaimers of his text. By considering those plots in *The Witch of Edmonton* less obviously implicated in *The Wonderful Discoverie*, however, we can understand the play's self-consciousness as a more general product of tensions between social criticism and the conventions of dramatic representation.

Things of Darkness, Acknowledgments, and the Communion of Guilt

In 1658, Jacobean performance becomes Protectorate text when *The Witch of Edmonton* first appears in print. The date speaks both to the play's ideological adaptability and to its ability to satisfy theatrical appetites even without the stage.[37] On the title page of this publication, in type larger than the play's title, appears a generic identification every bit as arresting as this date: "Composed into A TRAGI-COMEDY." We cannot know for certain whether the playwrights ever intended this specific label, though in its homiletic closure and gestures toward social reintegration the text seems to anticipate such an advertisement.[38] The final scene's orgy of forgiveness, which pointedly excludes Mother Sawyer, defines the murdering bigamist Frank Thorney as the central spectacle of a communal drama of redemption. In the eyes of his father, Frank approaches his execution lost only to the law, not to this drama:

> Here's the sad Object which yet I must meet
> With hope of comfort, if a repentant end
> Make him more happy then mis-fortune would
> Suffer him to be.
>
> (5.3.53–56)

In contrast to Sawyer, whose "resol[ution] / To die in my repentance" waivers as her zealous accusers tempt her with anger and despair (5.3.21–51), Frank is guided along an ideal *preparatio mortis*. Upon hearing evidence of his penitence, Winnifride (the surviving victim of the bigamy plot) informs him that "this Repentance makes thee / As white as innocence" (5.3.94–95). When asked for forgiveness, Winnifride acknowledges her required role ("'Tis my part / To use that Language" [5.3.106–7]), just as Sir Arthur Clarington, Frank's evil counselor in the bigamy plot, renounces his prior "part in thy wrongs" (5.3.127).

The metadramatic hypostatization of these roles opens up a skeptical space in which the scene's scapegoating can appear mechanically imposed; but the self-conscious assignment of "parts" in this scene also reveals the playwrights' participation in *The Witch of Edmonton*'s ambiguous tragicomic machinery. Such machinery was exactly what Harsnett had marked off as fraudulent theater when he described John Darrel's exorcism of William Sommers (which included accusations of witchcraft): "of all the partes of the tragicall Comedie acting between him and *Somers*, there was no Scene in it, wherein *M. Darrell* did with more courage and boldnes acte his part, then in this of the discouerie of witches."[39] Elsewhere Harsnett refers more generally to the "tragi-comedy" of exorcism,[40] but his linking of witchcraft and exorcism in the exposure of Darrel seems especially apposite to *The Witch of Edmonton*'s final scene—where the community (and specifically the murderer Frank) is effectively exorcised through the identification of a witch as the all-responsible "instrument of mischief" (5.3.21).

Recognizing the resonance of Harsnett's "tragi-comedy" in this play certainly helps us recalibrate any generic expectations derived from John Fletcher's bloodless definition: "A tragi-comedy is not so called in respect of mirth and killing, but in respect it wants deaths, which is enough to make it no tragedy, yet brings some near it, which is enough to make it no comedy: which must be a representation of familiar people, with such kind of trouble as no life be questioned."[41] Reading *The Witch of Edmonton*'s witchcraft scenes within the context of an exorcistic tragicomedy also provides an interesting explanatory model for the play's tenuously connected structure and puzzling emphases: the witch plot's subordination to the bigamy-murder-repentance-forgiveness plot may suggest that the play should be understood primarily as an exploration of the social act of exorcism;[42] as the scapegoat (she is unconvincingly accused of everything from Frank's murder of Susan to Old Banks's unnatural interest in his cow and an epidemic of male impotence and female promiscuity) Sawyer is also the symbolically exorcised, the thing of darkness whose violent removal makes the community "white as innocence." While "witchcraft" and "possession" should not be conceptually conflated—since the first ascribes agency while the second records its absence—there is in fact reason to allow some analogical intercourse between the terms in our analysis of this play. The possession/exorcism model best describes the *social* and *theatrical* transactions that mark the identification and persecution of witches. When these transactions are viewed from the social level, the community behaves like a possessed body and the witch like the threatening demon; for the community to regain possession of itself, it must effectively exorcise the witch. When these transactions are viewed through the playwrights' eyes, the witch is always the possessed—always speaking words and performing acts not her own. Conceiving witchcraft as possession, in other words, results from the same kind of social criticism and dramatic reflexivity I claim for the authors of *The Witch of Edmonton*.

But Harsnett's skeptical dismissal of the "tragicall Comedie" of exorcism, while relevant to *The Witch of Edmonton* and certainly to the play's 1658 appearance in print, does not provide us with clear criteria for assessing the social function of the tragicomedy that appears on stage and page. If by labeling exorcism a "tragi-comedy" Harsnett assumes that the mere acknowledgment of theater kills belief, the title of one of Goodcole's surviving pamphlets reveals a comfortable faith in tragicomic theater's service to belief in killing: "A True Declaration of the happy Conuersion, contrition, and Christian preparation of Francis Robinson, Gentleman. Who for covnterfetting the Greate Seale of England, was drawen, Hang'd, and quartered at Charing Crosse."[43]

For Harsnett, exposing the theatricality of exorcism in *A Discovery of the Fraudulent Practices of J. Darrel* (1599) is to employ the skeptical strategy of Reginald Scot's *Discoverie of Witchcraft* (1584)—a strategy of tearing illusion into actors and roles. For Goodcole, however, the same rhetoric of "Discoverie" can stage Sawyer's witchcraft as an essential role; what the skeptic discovers as rough magic, the smooth magician discovers as wonderful fact:

Here Prospero discovers Ferdinand *and* Miranda *playing at chess.*

Paulina draws a curtain, and discovers Hermione *standing like a statue.*[44]

The shared rhetoric, the reliance upon theater both to challenge and to create credibility, present little difficulty in distinguishing between a Harsnett and a Goodcole: one writes a text against performance, the other a text in defense of performance. In a text intended *for* performance, however, skepticism itself has a tendency to become labile as the theater asserts its will to belief. If by marking off the conventional "parts" of their characters the authors of *The Witch of Edmonton* shine daylight on the social theater of scapegoating, they also write these parts for social consumption—a digestion that begins with the actor's internalization of his or her role and leads finally to Paulina's imperative to all witnesses of spectacle: "It is required / You do awake your faith."[45]

Thus Sawyer's introduction to the stage, a soliloquy remarkable for its anatomy of scapegoating, also presents Renaissance drama with its only example of an actor being possessed by the witch's part:[46]

> And why on me? why should the envious world
> Throw all their scandalous malice upon me?
> 'Cause I am poor, deform'd and ignorant?
> And like a Bow buckl'd and bent together,
> By some more strong in mischiefs then my self?
> Must I for that be made a common sink,
> For all the filth and rubbish of Men's tongues
> To fall and run into? Some call me Witch;
> And being ignorant of my self, they go
> About to teach me how to be one: urging,
> That my bad tongue (by their bad usage made so)
> Forespeaks their Cattle, doth bewitch their Corn,
> Themselves, their Servants, and their Babes at nurse.
> This they enforce upon me: and in part
> Make me credit to it.
>
> (2.1.1–15)

With Dawson we can read Sawyer's partial "credit" as the cooperation of a conscious victim with the terms of her misrepresentation: "She complies with the process of social representation—indeed, what else can she do?—even as she insists on its injustice. Hers is a strong case of labeling."[47] We can go even further: hers is a strong case of theatricalized power, which requires a Faustian pact with representation—a submission that in Sawyer's case promises the power of transgression, the ability to curse her enemies "to death or shame." Sawyer's "possession" involves the deceptive ownership of method acting: in owning her role, she is owned by it. But it would be a mistake to treat this passage's dramatization of such possession simply as another facet of its penetrating but unimplicated social criticism—for the simple fact that Sawyer's role here is "in part" a product of the dramatists' own "bad usage." Indeed, this soliloquy, which both analyzes the scripted fictions of the witch's part and prepares us for Sawyer's convincing performance of it, establishes the ethical problem that *The Witch of Edmonton* puts not only to its audience but to itself: when a thing of darkness is acknowledged upfront as "mine," at once a product and a possession of theater, all subsequent representation and interpretation is charged with the responsibility of ownership. When the play itself both admits the injustice of social representation and complies with it ("'Tis all one, / To be a Witch, as to be counted one" [2.1.114–15]), the guilty self-consciousness that troubles Goodcole not in the least becomes an inevitable consequence of dramatic participation.

In the last section of this essay I shall return to the partial "credit" Sawyer gives to her own representation, coordinating this unstable belief with the playwrights' problematic "loans" from their legal sources, and with a final discussion of self-reflexive tensions in *The Witch of Edmonton*'s tragicomic machinery. But here I pause to suggest that allowing Sawyer's soliloquy to criticize not only social representation but also the specific dramatic representation of which it is a part reveals the self-consciousness beneath what Dawson describes as "the play's dividedness" and the text's "ambivalence." That grounds can be found in *The Witch of Edmonton* for both the skeptical discovery and the theatrical perpetuation of witch belief seems clear; nearly as persuasive is Dawson's claim that the play's conclusion reveals how "the text and its authors, in speaking to the predominantly upper-class audience for whom the play was first performed . . . , were seeking to assuage anxieties that they were at the same time raising about social division and conflict."[48] But even such a pliant containment model does not accommodate disturbances introduced by the play's self-criticism—disturbances produced by the text's complicity with the same "bad usage" it dissects. The metadramatic self-consciousness we have already seen surrounding the morris provides the most glaring example of such disturbance, and I would like briefly to consider the reflexive function of this interlude in the play's complication of tragicomedy.[49]

Dawson insightfully demonstrates that *The Witch of Edmonton* dramatizes a breakdown of communal charity that in fact motivated many accusations of witchcraft in the period.[50] From this perspective, witchcraft accusations are compensatory: "[T]he accused is first a victim [of an emergent 'individualistic set of values'], and the accuser is assuaging his social guilt by proclaiming her evil, and hence undeserving of charity."[51] When Dawson applies this insight to *The Witch of Edmonton*'s deployment of the morris, however, he has a difficult time reconciling the play's subversive exposure of such scapegoating with the apparently conservative intentions of the text and its authors. On the one hand, he claims social criticism as a possible accident of the text:

> The morris *can be seen* as a comic alternative to witchcraft.... But the text's yoking of morris and witchcraft reveals, *perhaps unwittingly*, contradictory ideological positions in regard to value and change; that is, the playwrights, exactly like King James, treat the morris as a positive, if naïve, force for communal solidarity and witchcraft as antisocial, but at the same time, by focusing on the similar social dynamics that give rise to these diverse practices, they undermine the stability of the opposition they seek to assert. (my emphases)

On the other hand, he suggests that "the text's support for the morris" serves to enable the displacement enacted by witchcraft accusations with a simple and purposed "gesture aimed at assuaging social guilt."[52] More recently Leah S. Marcus has powerfully argued that *The Witch of Edmonton*'s probing of "a hypothetical connection between old holiday customs and demonism" "cannot be read as either advocacy or condemnation of the Stuart position" but that the play "repeatedly employs Stuart themes to undo the Stuart idealisation of the countryside and to expose the oversimplicity of the standard Stuart dichotomy between urban vice and pastoral virtue."[53] While I agree with Dawson that the communal and comically clownish morris dance provides a seductive alternative to the failures of charity that result in Sawyer's persecution, Marcus's argument offers an important corrective: what is intentionally revealed in the morris is not a clear ideological program but the fallacies and collapses that prevent the plausible displacement and limitation of a pervasive social guilt.

I place Dawson and Marcus in dialogue, however, because the terms introduced by each can extend the reading of the other in an important new direction. If we agree that *The Witch of Edmonton*, in its representation of the morris, subverts the strategies of containment, we must also acknowledge the play's repeated emphasis upon the theatricality of social guilt—an emphasis that does not limit the play's criticism to "contradictory ideological positions" but intentionally includes the textual instabilities produced by its own negotiation with these positions. Adapting Dawson's terms, we can read the morris as a self-conscious gesture aimed at assuaging theatrical guilt, a gesture that metadramatically exposes itself as culpably complicit with the social maneuvers criticized by the play. Thus *The Witch of Edmonton*'s generic and economic discrimination between plots ("We'll sport with [Young Banks]; but when reckoning call, / We know where to receive: th'Witch pays for all"), like its acknowledgment of generic imperatives ("The Witch must be beaten out of her Cock-pit"), advertises a performance at once conventional and untenable. As we have already seen, the morris—which the play presents as a carefully marked zone of innocence—is infiltrated by Dog (the Familiar) and interrupted by the "news of Murder" from the main plot. This prophylactic failure certainly reveals "the oversimplicity of the standard Stuart dichotomy between urban vice and pastoral virtue"; but we should add here that the morris's failure to defend itself from the play's ambient evil also admits evidence of the play's indefensibility.

The "news of Murder" that kills the morris comes from the author's most substantial addition to their legal source.[54] In the bigamy plot, Frank kills his second wife after being touched by Dog (3.3.15); though Dog's part in Frank's crime has not been authorized or even recognized by Sawyer, the Familiar's role in this murder incriminates her in the eyes of the town. That Dog serves as the only real suture between bigamy and witch plot (and indeed, comic subplot) elicited a revelatory complaint from Algernon Swinburne:

> The want of connection between the two subjects of the play, Mother Sawyer's witchcraft and Frank Thorney's bigamy, is a defect common to many plays of the time . . . but in this case the tenuity of the connecting link is such that despite the momentary intervention of her familiar the witch is able with perfect truth to disclaim all complicity with the murderer. Such a communion of guilt might easily have been managed, and the tragic structure of the poem would have been complete in harmony of interest.[55]

In calling for firmer causal links and a "tragic structure" "complete in harmony of interest," Swinburne seems actually to wish for a play that would justify the social scapegoating that *The Witch of Edmonton* performs critically;[56] his formal criticism establishes criteria for ignoring or containing the play's unsettling social criticism. But Swinburne's dissatisfaction with the play's structure is also a symptom of the play's self-criticism. By disrupting the morris with Dog, and with news of the crime he seems to have caused, the playwrights reveal the tenuity of the plot connections they also serve; their dramaturgic desire to portray a communicable guilt, passed from Sawyer to Thorney through Dog, is undercut by the genuine and less exclusive "communion of guilt" in which they knowingly participate. The morris disappears from the play, then, as its enabling distinctions between social guilt and theatrical innocence collapse; though rendered unsustainable, however, it remains in the text as evidence of a desire for such distinctions that the playwrights share with their audience. Swinburne's reading of the play as a collaborative failure can therefore be redirected from artistic dismissal or bibliographic conjecture to a complex level of signification: *The Witch of Edmonton*'s "want of [simplifying] connection" between plots, like its generic antagonisms and its vacillations between skepticism and belief, self-consciously reflects upon the theater's collaboration with its audience. By producing a connective "want" (desire and lack), the play confronts expectations that it creates but refuses entirely to meet.

In a discussion of the counterfeit witch's exploitation of credibility, Scot suggests how a desire for plot and unambiguous causality provides ideal customers for theater: "Men in all ages have been so desirous to know the effect of their purposes, the sequele of things to come, and to see the end of their fear and hope; that a seelie witch, which had learned anie thing in the art of cousenage, may make a great manie jollie fooles." And as Greenblatt has shown, an important strategy in Scot's response to this desire is to disenchant witchcraft by revealing it as a metaphor that only the "carnallie minded" would murderously literalize. The tenor is a culturally pervasive tendency to misprision: "the world is now so bewitched ... with this fond error"; the baud's "eie infecteth, entiseth, and (if I maie so saie) bewitcheth"; "illusions are right inchantments."[57] In *A Mirrour of Monsters* (1587), the antitheatricalist writer William Rankins turns such rhetoric against plays, accusing them of "inchaunting Charmes, and bewitched wyles," and urging his readers to "arme ourselves against the damnable enticings of these hellish feendes [the players] with the wise regard of prudent Ulises."[58] In both the bigamy and the witch plot, the authors of *The Witch of Edmonton* deploy strikingly similar metaphors in an apparent effort to divest witchcraft and demonism of literal power and to distribute guilt across the community. Thus Frank Thorney, who conceives the bigamy stratagem as an evil necessitated by his financial need for a paternal blessing, figures "beggery and want" as "Two Devils that are occasions to enforce / A shameful end" (1.1.18–20); thus Sir Arthur Clarington describes Frank's sexual desire for his first wife as "the nimble devil / That wanton'd in [his] blood" (1.1.78–79), a prelude to Frank's father calling his dishonest son "A Devil like a Man" (1.2.154). Thus Sawyer in her defense powerfully presents courtiers as "more Witch-like" than herself, just as she indicts the female "painted things" at court for "Inchantments" that "burn Mens Souls in sensual hot desires" and reduce "Lordships" "To Trunks of rich Attire" (4.1.88, 103, 105, 109–10). Sawyer's parting shot at "Men-witches" who "without the Fangs of Law" enchant women out of their honor elicits an anxious response from Clarington, who has seduced Frank's first wife in just such a manner; the threatening incontinence of her metaphor and its obvious application to him leads Sir Arthur to insist upon the literal fact of Sawyer's witchcraft (4.1.138–46).[59]

Clarington's emphatic literalism certainly appears suspect in a play that follows Scot in warning the superstitious that their gullibility may "prove" them "starke Fools"; but it also reminds us of the morris dancers' distinction between "real" witches and the "counterfeits" who "will not be regarded" by a community both suspicious of representation and desirous of authentication. The morris dancers' savvy sense of theatrical "regard" in fact reflects the playwrights' commercial interest in satisfying the "carnallie minded" with an utterly convincing body—a body resistant to the disenchantment and dilution of Scot's skeptical wordplay. This commercial interest, we should note, is hardly conducive to what Swinburne calls dramatic "harmony of interest": the desire to convince, enchant, and concentrate the figure of witchcraft actually contradicts the play's skeptical distribution of evil and illusion through metaphor; and in this contradiction, I argue, the playwrights confront the culpability of their own dramatic needs.

In the character of Dog—an avatar of the demonic that provides the play with an apparent criterion for the real—the playwrights incarnate evil as an instrument of plot. To the extent that the Familiar establishes the guilt of Sawyer and Frank Thorney, the innocence of the morris, it presents the audience with the same literalistic escape desired by Sir Arthur. Ontologically distinct from the play's figurative distribution of evil, Dog offers a seemingly unshakable justification for scapegoating and for the play's carefully calibrated degrees of guilt. But while *The Witch of Edmonton* acknowledges the theatrical and social desirability of such a justification, the playwrights admit antitheatrical evidence against its validity. They self-consciously present the Familiar, in fact, as a hallucinatory product of theater—a product that reveals once again the theater's capitalization on legal sources, its exploitation of tragicomic expectations, its collaboration with cultural fantasies of persecution.

The Hair of the Dog

Renaissance spectators clearly brought a wide range of reflexes to a theater that represented demonism with similar variety. If a play such as *Doctor Faustus* could incite a few of the hypercredulous to see more devils than the actors onstage might account for, it no doubt reassured a great many more with the palpable theatricality—if not the completely safe fictionality—of its diabolic representations. When compared with the awesome otherness of Marlowe's devils, *The Witch of Edmonton*'s furry Familiar would hardly seem a character designed to trade upon the credibility and anxiety of such an audience. Renaissance England's broad cultural recognition of "the familiar" notwithstanding, the obvious contortions necessary for an actor to play a devil-dog in fact suggest an element of farce;[60] and indeed in some of his comic interactions, such as his enticement of Young Banks into a muddy pond, Dog conjures up the disenchanting "low" burlesque that appears especially in the B text of *Faustus*. I therefore need to qualify my claim that Dog offers the playwrights a criterion for the real and a body resistant to metaphorical disenchantment, since both the canine and the diabolical status of this character constantly reveal themselves as ludicrously contrary to fact, bark the actor as he may. That Dog presents so many obstacles to complete plausibility need not prevent us from observing his dramatic service to the interpretive desire—"Resolve me of all ambiguities"—that cues the devil's entrance in *Faustus*.[61] As a domestication of the supernatural, this Familiar introduces to the play a means for distinguishing Sawyer's guilt from that circulating in much of the play's community;[62] her pact, which enlists Dog as an instrument of revenge, defines even the hypocritical Banks as supernaturally innocent and invulnerable (2.1.152–61). We can certainly interject that the very implausibility of Dog's supernatural agency exposes such a distinction to skeptical critique; but to do so is both to ignore the play's substantial support for this distinction and to foreclose analysis of the dramatists' more subtle interrogation of its construction.

The legal and dramatic allure of the diabolic pact lies in the possession of the soul of the accused. Proof of such a pact provides the courtroom with evidence that its execution of justice upon the body of the accused reflects, and is confirmed by, divine punishment; proof of such a pact provides the theatergoer with the experience of soteriological access, an experience that offers body and spirit as properties of the stage. If the pact promises a kind of spiritual ownership not simply to its demonic signatory but to its judicial and theatrical witnesses, an interesting contrast appears in the release of ownership that is forgiveness. In *The*

Witch of Edmonton, Frank Thorney prepares us for the forgiveness that will render his soul "As white as innocence" by confessing his murder to Winnifride (his surviving wife) as a microcosm of the courtroom:

> for thou my evidence art,
> Jurie and Judge: sit quiet, and I'll tell all.
> (4.2.108–9)

Winnifride is not alone in her quick forgiveness: the father of Frank's victim pronounces Frank "well prepared to follow" her to heaven (5.3.116), and one of the men Frank has blamed for his own crime laments the fact that such a redeemed character must still "Make satisfaction to the Law" (5.3.122). By forgiving Frank and collaboratively preparing his spirit for its divine reception, the community assembled onstage in the final scene makes a proprietary distinction between his body (which still belongs to the law and the theater) and his soul (which belongs now to heaven alone). That this distinction does not apply to Sawyer, who is forced by the same community to spend her last words "in bawling" rather than in the resolution and prayer she desires (5.3.48–49), suggests a tenacious grasp on the absolute possession she has become.

In important ways the play allows Sawyer to speak against this presumed legal and theatrical ownership of the spirit of the possessed. In a debate with the Justice over the charges of Old Banks, her chief persecutor, Sawyer invokes the socioeconomic oppression critically represented by the play to reveal the materialist component of Banks's accusations:

> By what commission can he send my Soul on the Divel's Errand,
> more then I can his? is he a Landlord of my Soul, to thrust it when
> he list out of door?
> (4.1.82–84)

And in a complaint against the baying community that surrounds her in the final scene, Sawyer employs a rare metaphorical adaptation of her Familiar to describe Edmonton's effort to possess her spirit:

> These dogs will mad me: I was well resolv'd
> To die in my repentance.
> (5.3.41–42)

Sawyer's language here may also recall the bear-baiting image through which Malvolio figures his exorcistic victimization in *Twelfth Night*,[63] but in *The Witch of Edmonton* the "propertied" victim of tragicomedy is the much more secure possession of a community that has underwritten the diabolic pact. This community becomes a figurative pack of "Dogs" not as evidence against Sawyer's literal forfeiture of her soul but as testimony to the social appropriation of this demonic deal.

That the play does not enjoy a position of complete critical detachment from the community it represents, however, appears most clearly in the only other clear instance I find of a metaphorical adaptation of the Familiar. In her first scene—shortly after Old Banks has attacked her for gathering "a few rotten sticks" on the land of which he is lord, and after the morris dancers have fled from her while threatening, "Away with the Witch of Edmonton"—Sawyer describes Banks as

> this black Cur,
> That barks, and bites, and sucks the very blood
> Of me, and of my credit.
>
> (2.1.112–14)

Here Sawyer may recall Shylock, another tragicomic victim of a play that largely excludes him from its ethic of Christian forgiveness while preying upon his "credit"; but in Sawyer's case the justification for persecution is presented not only in the dubious social terms of the play's community but also in the equally suspect dramatic terms of the play itself. Banks's social power to scandalize Sawyer and suck "the very blood" of her credit in the community merges, just a few lines later, with the playwrights' exploitation of the theatrical credit offered by the witch to the stage: the moment Sawyer's metaphorical complaint ends, the literalized Dog enters to suck her blood, an act accompanied by thunder and lightning and witnessed only by the play's spectators. We have seen that such parasitism characterizes *The Witch of Edmonton*'s self-conscious borrowing of legal credit, and I want to suggest now that the portrayal of Dog reveals the dramatists' indictment of themselves (and not simply the community they represent) as guilty landlords of Sawyer's soul.

In Goodcole's dialogue with Sawyer, several particulars emerge in her confession that she withheld at her trial ("thereby hoping to avoid shame" [*Wonderful Discoverie*, 397]). Among the details dramatically useful to the playwrights, such as those having to do with her method of nursing the familiar, Sawyer's disclosure that the devil-dog appeared to her in "two colours, sometimes of black and sometimes of white," receives special interest. When she was praying to the dog in the perversion of the Lord's Prayer he taught her,[64] Sawyer relates, "he then would come to me in the white colour" (*Wonderful Discoverie*, 391, 397). In the play, this detail is imported but also italicized as the kind of textual disturbance I have ascribed to the playwrights' intertextual self-consciousness. No mention or indication is made of Dog's whiteness, for instance, when Sawyer prays to him in acts 2, 3, and 4; and when she conjures him with prayer at the beginning of act 5, she seems baffled by his chromatic transformation:

> SAWYER. Why dost thou appear to me in white, as if thou wert the Ghost of my dear love?
> DOG. I am dogged, list not to tell thee, yet to torment thee.
> (5.1.34–36)

Dog goes on to explain that his whiteness is meant to put Sawyer "in minde of thy winding Sheet," that the devil's paradoxical appearance "as a Lamb" signals her imminent death (5.1.37, 40). When Dog briefly attempts to account for his peculiar metamorphosis by referring Sawyer to the explanation provided in Goodcole's pamphlet, she still insists upon the novelty of this episode:

> DOG. Why am I in white? didst thou not pray to me?
> SAWYER. Yes, thou dissembling Hell-hound: why now in white more then at other times?
> (5.1.44–46)

Only after Sawyer's reiteration of the question raises Dog's color to a pressing interpretive issue does he provide an answer that allows us to make sense of the exchange:

> Be blasted with the News; whiteness is days Foot-boy, a
> forerunner to light; which shews thy old rivel'd face: Villaines
> are strip't naked, the Witch must be beaten out of her Cock-pit.
> (5.1.47–49)

In these lines, Dog reveals his lamblike appearance "in white" as a costume change that serves the play's grinding tragicomic machinery. Here, in other words, Dog discovers himself as a theatrical invention, a special effect created by the playwrights' alteration of their source for their own dramatic needs—needs that generically reflect the desires of the community they represent.

As a spokesperson for genre, the white Dog, like the black Dog that substitutes himself for Old Banks in 2.1, admits the role of theater in shaping fantasies of persecution; as the protean connection between plots, he identifies Sawyer as an expendable property of the stage while adumbrating a conclusion that will render Frank's guilt "As white as innocence." The devil's desertion of the possessed as death approaches may be a common occurrence in Renaissance witch lore, but we should note that Dog's forsaking of Sawyer speaks powerfully (and, if my argument has persuaded, self-consciously) to the playwrights' "bad usage" of the subject they have borrowed from Edmonton:

> Out Witch! Thy tryal is at hand:
> Our prey being had, the Devil does laughing stand.
> (5.1.76–77)

Such laughter is of course an impossible emotional response to the scenes that follow, despite some last-ditch foolery from Young Banks and Old Cartwright's concluding effort to leave us "as merry as we can" (5.3.169). But the dramatists' occupational proximity to Dog, whose whiteness Sawyer describes as a "puritan-paleness" (5.1.54), has created an alliance that causes shivers in their text. That alliance is not simply with Minister Goodcole and his commodified confession; nor is it simply an accedence to the dictates of genre. It also lies in a tense cooperation with the enemy: not Satan, but the Puritan appetites that in 1658 would provide *The Witch of Edmonton* its readership. This is not to imply that the play, first performed for altogether different audiences, ever had such a reception as its specific intention; nor is it to claim that Puritans ever cornered the market on the persecution performed by the play. Instead, it is to suggest how the play survived the closing of the theaters and the scrutiny of England's most antitheatrical period: suspicious of its own theatricalism and the economies it serves, *The Witch of Edmonton* also exploits its customers' desire for material possession—a desire satisfied not by plays but by texts.

NOTES

1. I suggest that Thomas Heywood's and Richard Brome's *The Late Lancashire Witches* may have influenced the trial on which it was based because the play was actually performed before the verdict of this trial. Any argument directed toward this drama's

influence on the judicial process is complicated, however, both by a lack of critical consensus on the play's attitude toward witchcraft and by the ultimate pardon that the "Lancashire witches" received from Charles I. For accounts of the Lancashire trials of 1634, see George Lymman Kittredge, *Witchcraft in Old and New England* (Cambridge: Cambridge University Press, 1929), 270–71; Wallace Notestein, *A History of Witchcraft in England from 1558 to 1718* (Washington, DC: American Historical Association, 1911), 146–60; and A. M. Clark, *Thomas Heywood, Playwright and Miscellanist* (Oxford: B. Blackwell, 1931), 122–26. In Etta Soiref Onat's summary (*The Witch of Edmonton: A Critical Edition* [New York: Garland, 1980], 47–48): "Although the jury was convinced of the guilt of seventeen of the accused, the judges had doubts about the matter and reported the case to the King and the Privy Council. The London authorities then brought in seven of the convicted—among them Margaret Johnson, Frances Dicconson, and Mary Spenser, who appear in our play—to be questioned by Dr. Bridgeman, Bishop of Chester. . . . After an examination for witchmarks by a committee headed by the King's physician, Harvey, which produced negative results, Charles I granted pardons to all those surviving; there had been no executions, but three or four had died in prison. Finally the young instigator of the scare confessed that his story had been a fabrication, so that he would not be punished by his father for some disobedience."

    2. Such causality is of course difficult to prove in any analysis of "media ethics" (witness even the much debated cause of Princess Diana's recent death). If *The Late Lancashire Witches* influenced the jury that moved to keep the "real" Lancashire witches in prison, however, then we have an actual case in which Renaissance drama was directly involved in killing its object of representation—since "three or four" of the supposed witches died in prison.

    3. Stephen Gosson, *Plays Confuted in Five Actions*, quoted in Stephen Greenblatt, *Shakespearean Negotiations: The Circulation of Social Energy in Renaissance England* (Oxford: Clarendon Press, 1988), 116. In *Shakespearean Negotiations*, 94–128, Greenblatt considers Harsnett's skepticism, his banishment of exorcism to theater, and Shakespeare's exploitation of the resources of exorcism. In a separate essay, Greenblatt traces the development of skepticism toward witchcraft through Scot ("Shakespeare Bewitched," in *New Historical Literary Study: Essays on Reproducing Texts, Representing History*, ed. Jeffrey N. Cox and Larry J. Reynolds [Princeton: Princeton University Press, 1993], 17–42).

    4. Onat, *Witch of Edmonton*, 51–52; the quote within the quote is from A. W. Ward and A. R. Waller, eds., *Cambridge History of English Literature* (New York: G. P. Putnam's Sons, 1907–17), 7:118–19.

    5. In *Saint Joan* (1924; reprint, New York: Random House, 1956), 24, George Bernard Shaw offers one of the more famous defenses of Shakespeare's representation of Joan by claiming that Shakespeare, after attempting to fashion her as "a beautiful and romantic figure," "was told by his scandalized company that English patriotism would never stand a sympathetic representation of a French conqueror." E. M. W. Tillyard, acknowledging the "queer reluctance to allow Shakespeare to have written ill," and designating "the way he treats Joan of Arc" as "the chief reason why people have been hostile to Shakespeare's

authorship [of *1 Henry VI*]," finds such hostility analogous to "arguing that Shakespeare could not have written *King John* because he does not mention Magna Carta" (*Shakespeare's History Plays* [London: Chatto and Windus, 1948], 162). Recently Kathryn Schwarz has taken this critique further in a brilliant reading of the ideological disintegration that has Joan at its epicenter: "The gesture that defines Joan la Pucelle as 'not Shakespeare's' is not merely a defense of chivalry or good historicism but a symptomatic reproduction of the play's own logic, logic that identifies the familiar through the power of the contrary example: if idealized Englishness is constructed against France's Joan, then the idealized Shakespeare, in controversies over the authorship of this play, has been constructed against a Joan who belongs to someone else entirely. By this logic, to allow Joan into the canon is to endanger the most important bond of all—that which links Shakespeare to his readers and thus to the 'Shakespearean.' In metatextual negotiations, as with those that take place onstage, the terms in which Joan is defined suggest the fragility of privileged systems of connection" ("Fearful Simile: Stealing the Breech in Shakespeare's Chronicle Plays," *Shakespeare Quarterly* 49 [Summer 1998]: 152). For discussions of *1 Henry VI* and some of the problems and motivations of assigning authorship, see Leah Marcus, *Puzzling Shakespeare: Local Reading and Its Discontents* (Berkeley: University of California Press, 1988), 51–105; and Gary Taylor, "Shakespeare and Others: The Authorship of *Henry the Sixth, Part I*," *Medieval and Renaissance Drama in England* 7 (1995): 145–205.

6. In the Arden *Macbeth* (New York: Random House, 1962), 4.1.43 n., Kenneth Muir complains of this passage: "It is to be hoped that this song was altered for *Macbeth*, as some lines are relevant only to the plot of Middleton's play. But the 1673 edition of *Macbeth* prints them without alteration. No exit is marked for Hecate and the spurious witches; but the sooner they depart the better." In "Shakespeare Bewitched" (41 n. 42), however, Greenblatt persuasively argues that this moment seems "a deliberate quotation, a marking of the demonic as theatrical"—and, I would add, a marking of the theatrical as appropriative.

7. Janet Adelman, "'Born of a Woman': Fantasies of Maternal Power in *Macbeth*," in *Cannibals, Witches, and Divorce: Estranging the Renaissance*, ed. Marjorie Garber, English Institute Essays (Baltimore: Johns Hopkins University Press, 1987), 103.

8. Greenblatt, "Shakespeare Bewitched," 20–21.

9. Ibid., 31.

10. Ibid., 21, 31.

11. Ibid., 20. In a note to this essay, Greenblatt suggests more subtly that "the most powerful theatrical acknowledgment of the weakness and vulnerability of witches is in Dekker's *Witch of Edmonton*, a play that nonetheless stages without protest the witch's execution" (38 n. 15). It is informative to note that the ethical distinctions made between Shakespeare's and Dekker's play in this essay (what would a "protest" really look like?) seem to have collapsed in Greenblatt's subsequent General Introduction to the *Norton Shakespeare*, where he writes, "It is sobering to reflect that plays like Shakespeare's *Macbeth* (1606), Thomas Middleton's *Witch* (before 1616), and Thomas Dekker, John Ford,

and William Rowley's *Witch of Edmonton* (1621) seem to be less the allies of skepticism than the exploiters of fear" (*Norton Shakespeare*, gen. ed. Stephen Greenblatt [New York: W. W. Norton, 1997], 29). What does Greenblatt mean by skepticism, and what does he really mean by the exploitation of fear, in 2004?

12. Greenblatt, "Shakespeare Bewitched," 22, 36. By the end of this essay, Shakespeare occupies "the position neither of the witchmonger nor the skeptic" but instead "the position of the witch" (36). In what may be an unintentionally mystifying transformation, the potential "evil" of Greenblatt's opportunistic and persecutorial playwright has been displaced by the persecuted and harmless enchanter whose illusions have no identifiable consequences. The preceding logic of this essay, though, has identified in *Macbeth* currents of both skepticism and witch-mongering, two positions taken in the legal and theological discourse of the Renaissance; to identify Shakespeare with the subject of this discourse is to move from an analysis of the social function of his art to a figurative description of the technique of that art. Greenblatt's earlier questions about *Macbeth* being "evil," however, are not entirely siphoned off in this essay—though it is interesting to note that the contrast with *The Witch of Edmonton* serves to identify a more culpable black magic against which Shakespeare's play looks more benign. But I think that for Greenblatt such questions linger as the honest response of a reader for whom the ethical problems of Shakespeare's dramatic opportunism remain suspect and unresolved. Such a response, in the context of my own chapter, must be labeled generational.

13. I borrow here from Harry Berger Jr., *Making Trifles of Terrors: Redistributing Complicities in Shakespeare*, ed. Peter Erickson (Stanford: Stanford University Press, 1997). My difference with Berger lies in my assumption that dramatic "acknowledgment" and "complicity" include not only the audience but also the playwright and the social community outside the playtext.

14. In *Verdict According to Conscience: Perspectives on the English Criminal Trial Jury, 1200–1800* (Chicago: University of Chicago Press, 1985), Thomas Andrew Green distinguishes between the Renaissance legal systems of France, Italy, and Germany, where judges decided the question of guilt or innocence, and that of England, where the judges were restricted to "finding law" (determining the relevant precedents and statutes), while the jury "found fact" (delivered a verdict on the individual case). See also Katharine Eisaman Maus, *Inwardness and Theater in the English Renaissance* (Chicago: University of Chicago Press, 1995), 106–7.

15. In *Inwardness and Theater*, 106, Maus notes that in the rest of Europe the execution was typically presented as public spectacle, while the judicial deliberations leading up to it were kept secret; by contrast England publicized the trials of capital cases but typically kept executions "relatively unspectacular affairs."

16. Even today the label *convicted* designates a real change in the legal status of the formerly "accused"—a change wrought by the consensus of juries and judges. As Mother Sawyer's first soliloquy in *The Witch of Edmonton* reveals, legal "conviction" can also involve convincing the accused that she is what her accusers say she is; in this speech, the

causal relation between epistemology and ontology is represented in a scene of method acting by a person who is a spectator of herself.

17. John Gaule, *Select cases of conscience touching witches and witchcraft* (London, 1646), 194 (this and the following passage from John Cotta are quoted in Maus, *Inwardness and Theater*, 112, 114).

18. John Cotta, *The triall of witch-craft, shewing the true methode of their discovery* (London, 1616), 18. Cotta's call for a "curious view" recalls for me the alternative skeptical warning of Horatio, who warns Hamlet against considering "too curiously" the avenue by which a king might be digested by a beggar.

19. Henry Goodcole, *The Wonderful Discoverie of Elizabeth Sawyer a Witch, Late of Edmonton, Her Conviction and Condemnation and Death* (in Onat, *Witch of Edmonton*, 381–400 [381, 399]). This and future references to Goodcole's *Wonderful Discoverie* appear in Onat's edition and are henceforth cited parenthetically by page number.

20. In Goodcole's account, the words I place in parentheses are actually a marginal gloss. Here as throughout his account, Goodcole attempts to preempt frequently voiced skepticism toward witchcraft and possession. For the skeptical position specifically addressed here—that possession is simply psychological delusion—see Greenblatt, *Shakespearean Negotiations*, 100–106; and Sydney Anglo, "Melancholia and Witchcraft: The Debate between Wier, Bodin, and Scot," in *Folie et deraison à la Renaissance: Colloque international*, ed. Fédération internationale des instituts et sociétés pour l'étude de la Renaissance (Brussels: University of Brussels, 1976), 209–28. The possibility that witchcraft might be produced by self-delusion, or by the "phantasms and illusions of demons," appears as early as Reginone of Prum's tenth-century *De ecclesiasticis disciplinis*.

21. In *Renaissance Minds and Their Fictions: Cusanus, Sidney, Shakespeare* (Berkeley: University of California Press, 1985), Ronald Levao recreates the Plutarchan story of "the archetypal confrontation between the Athenian lawmaker Solon and the first man of the theater, Thespis," recording "the former's distress at the latter's lying and his fear, despite assurances that all is play, that its subversion would spill over into life." See also A. M. Nagler, *A Source Book in Theatrical History* (1952; reprint, New York: Dover, 1959), 3.

22. The word *authentic* derives from the Greek word *authentes*, which can mean "murderer" or "one who does something himself." In "*Hamlet*: Equity, Intention, Performance," Luke Wilson has brilliantly discussed the complex ways in which Shakespeare's play achieves performative authenticity by appealing to early modern conceptions of intention as understood in classical and Renaissance theories of legal interpretation; his analysis includes a discussion of "The Mousetrap" to which I am indebted (*Studies in the Literary Imagination* 24 [Fall 1991]: 91–113 [98]).

23. The play's 1658 title page is reproduced by Onat, *Witch of Edmonton*, 171. According to this title page, the play was "never printed until now," a claim that if true speaks for a cultural need for the theatrical representation of witches that survived the official closing of the theaters; indeed, this play may have been printed to satisfy that need.

24. The date of this revival is debated. Gerald Eades Bentley (*The Jacobean and Caroline Stage* [Oxford: Clarendon Press, 1941–68], 1:251–52) assigns it to 1635 or 1636, but

Onat (*Witch of Edmonton*, 162, 281) argues for a date as early as 1634. The Prologue refers to the anonymous play *The Merry Devil of Edmonton* (1603?), ascribed to Dekker, Drayton, and Heywood (and sometimes Shakespeare).

25. It is surprising that this reflexive reference to the Cock-Pit Theater in Drury Lane goes unremarked by Onat and other commentators. After the March 4, 1617, sacking of the Cock-Pit by London apprentices celebrating Shrove Tuesday, the theater reopened as the Phoenix. But the 1658 title page describes this 1621 play as acted "often at the Cock-pit," and the name *Cock-Pit* clearly continued, after 1617, to refer to the theater renamed the Phoenix. In an indirect but powerful way, however, *The Witch of Edmonton*'s reference to "the Cock-pit" may refer us to the potentially destructive social energies—those of cockfighting, if not those that destroyed the Cock-Pit—that must "beat out" the witch if the theater (and the community represented by the morris) is to survive.

26. This detail also appears on the 1658 title page: "Acted by the Princes Servants, often at the Cock-Pit in *Drury-Lane*, once at Court, with Singular Applause."

27. As James VI of Scotland, the king had become involved in the great prosecution of 1590–97. For a long time scholars believed him responsible for fanning the flames of witch belief in England (in 1604 Parliament passed a statute against witchcraft even more severe than that of 1563), but Kittredge "has . . . effectively shown that James was not responsible for the passage of the Act, and that the witch-mania did not mount in intensity when the author of the *Daemonologie* came to the throne of England" (Onat, *Witch of Edmonton*, 7). In fact there were more executions for witchcraft in the last twenty-two years of Elizabeth's reign than during the twenty-two years of James's reign. The *Daemonologie*, moreover, is far from a simple defense of persecution; it devotes much of its space to skeptical attacks on "impostures" and to exposures of farcical legal proceedings. As with Goodcole's account of Elizabeth Sawyer's trial, however (and as with *The Witch of Edmonton*, for that matter), the incorporation of skepticism can strengthen the legitimacy of "valid" witchcraft trials. For analyses of potentially subversive energies given "license" in the *Book of Sports*, see David Underdown, *Revel, Riot, and Rebellion: Popular Politics and Culture in England, 1603–1660* (Oxford: Clarendon Press, 1985), 63–68; and Leah Marcus, *The Politics of Mirth: Jonson, Herrick, Milton, Marvell, and the Defense of Old Holiday Pastimes* (Chicago: University of Chicago Press, 1986), 7–8, 22; Marcus's study also addresses James's attempt to moderate the prosecution of witches (90–92, 280).

28. Philip Stubbes, *Anatomie of Abuses*, ed. Frederick J. Furnivall (London: New Shakspere [sic] Society, 1879), 1:147.

29. In the margin of *The Wonderful Discoverie*, 396, Goodcole returns to this complaint when he asks Sawyer if the devil has visited her in prison: "I asked this question because it was rumoured that the Devil came to her since her conviction, and shamelessly printed and openly sung in a ballad, to which many gave too much credit." Goodcole's concern to disprove the rumor that Sawyer was possessed "since her conviction" seems designed further to authenticate her testimony against herself.

30. Goodcole's dismissal of the ballads circulating after Sawyer's execution actually aligns him with skeptics such as Harsnett—who in response to a fraudulent exorcism

complains that ballads serve to popularize and further mystify the fiction by spreading it to the credulous masses (see Greenblatt, *Shakespearean Negotiations*, 102). The skepticism allowed and even encouraged in Goodcole's homiletic account is genuinely surprising, but each concession serves to mask and strengthen his underlying polemical position; consider, for example, his first admission: "The publication of this subject whereof now I write, hath been importunity [sic] extorted from me, who would have been content to have concealed it, knowing the diversity of opinions concerning things of this nature, and that not amongst the ignorant, but among some of the learned. For my part I meddle here with nothing but matter of fact" (*Wonderful Discoverie*, 381).

31. Again I am indebted in a rather oblique way to Wilson's observation of the concordance between law and dramatic script (as initial intentions), equity and performance (as anticipated "supplemental" intentions), in "*Hamlet*" (especially 91–99).

32. Anthony B. Dawson, "Witchcraft/Bigamy: Cultural Conflict in *The Witch of Edmonton*," *Renaissance Drama* 20 (1989): 84–85. Dawson is right to point out that madness and witchcraft were rarely directly associated in the Renaissance (see Alan Macfarlane, *Witchcraft in Tudor and Stuart England: A Regional and Comparative Study* [London: Routledge, 1970], 183). However, Mother Sawyer's "madness" (4.1.153) is a source of interest in *The Witch of Edmonton*. The play similarly conflates demonic possession and witchcraft, topics with a complex relation in the period (see Keith Thomas, *Religion and the Decline of Magic* [London: Weidenfeld and Nicolson, 1971], 470–85).

33. When Sawyer informs Ratcliff she is a lawyer, Ratcliff begs "let me scratch thy Face" (4.1.181). This antilegal satire also reflects a witch belief held well into the nineteenth century: a victim of witchcraft was thought to be able to free herself from a curse by drawing blood from the witch "above the breath."

34. Anne's madness and its apparent causal indeterminacy have aroused critical interest. David Atkinson observes that "the play does not make it entirely clear whether or not the witch really is responsible for the death of Anne Ratcliff," suggesting that "the episode was probably imperfectly assimilated from the source" ("Moral Knowledge and the Double Action in *The Witch of Edmonton*," *Studies in English Literature* 25 [Spring 1985]: 431). Michael Hattaway writes: "[T]he text makes it legitimate to conjecture that [Anne's] madness arose independently of the devil's action," the "motives for action aris[ing] out of social transactions" that leave the "chains of causation ... incomplete" ("Women and Witchcraft: The Case of *The Witch of Edmonton*," *Trivium* 20 [May 1985]: 53). I think that this debate can be accommodated by my argument that the question of causality and responsibility is a product of the playwrights' revision of their legal source—a revision that makes the play itself a responsible party to Anne Ratcliffe's manner of dying.

35. Berger, *Making Trifles of Terrors*, 103.

36. Onat, *Witch of Edmonton*, 158. Onat notes that the titles of Goodcole's two surviving pamphlets "suggest that they were calculated to appeal to the readers' sensations" and that "it is not unlikely that he, like the Prince's men, desired to capitalize on the events [of Sawyer's execution] by publishing a pamphlet for which there was an ample reading public."

37. Reginald Trevor Davies has claimed that the play's late publication date reflects its advocacy of witch-mongering policies held in check (through print censorship) by the Stuarts but supported more firmly by the Protectorate (*Four Centuries of Witch-Beliefs* [London: Methuen, 1947], 112–17). Onat (*Witch of Edmonton*, 157–58) points out the obvious flaws in this argument, but it is worth noting that the play-text did have relevance and commercial value in the Protectorate period—despite any skepticism and anti-Puritan satire we detect in it. The play's appearance *as* a text may respond simply to the unavailability of public theater in this period, but the ways in which that text is interpreted (for publication advertisement) are nonetheless significant.

38. On the play as homiletic drama, see Henry Adams, *English Domestic or Homiletic Tragedy, 1575–1642* (New York: Columbia University Press, 1943), 141; Andrew Clark, *Domestic Drama: A Survey of the Origins, Antecedents and Nature of the Domestic Play in England, 1500–1640*, 2 vols. (Salzburg: Universitat Salzburg, 1975), 1:209–10; and Viviana Comensoli, "Witchcraft and Domestic Tragedy in *The Witch of Edmonton*," in *The Politics of Gender in Early Modern Europe*, ed. Jean R. Brink, Allison P. Coudert, and Maryanne C. Horowitz (Kirksville, MO: Sixteenth-Century Journal Publishers, 1989), 43–60. The tragicomic note is struck at the play's conclusion by Old Cartwright's attempt to balance Frank's execution with the promise of marriage—"So let's every man home to *Edmonton* with heavy hearts, yet as merry as we can, though not as we would" (5.3.167–69)—and by Winnifred's Epilogue, which acknowledges her widowed status but looks forward with "modest hopes" to a figurative second marriage that will be affirmed by the "noble tongues" of a "gentle" audience (Epilogue, 5–6).

39. Samuel Harsnett, *A Discovery of the Fraudulent Practices of J. Darrel . . . concerning the pretended possession and dispossession of W. Somers, etc.* (1599), 142, quoted in Greenblatt, *Shakespearean Negotiations*, 186 n. 9. For Harsnett's comments on witchcraft and its relation to exorcism, see *A Declaration of egregious Popish Impostures* (London: Iames Roberts, 1603), 135–36. In any discussion of Harsnett's skepticism and its relation to a play such as *The Witch of Edmonton*, it is important to realize that Harsnett rarely if ever expresses sympathy with the "victims" of theatrical fraud. In "Shakespeare and Harsnett: 'Pregnant to Good Pity'?" (*Studies in English Literature* 38:2 [1998]: 251–64), Amy Wolf argues that sympathy with the "victims" of exorcism is a Shakespearean contribution to Harsnett's skepticism (which tends to treat the exorcised as conspirators). This distribution applies equally well to any sympathy with Sawyer we find in *The Witch of Edmonton*: though it may come from Scot, it does not come from Harsnett.

40. See Harsnett, *Declaration*, 150; and *Discovery*, 142.

41. John Fletcher, "To the Reader," *The Faithful Shepherdess*, in *The Beaumont and Fletcher Canon*, ed. Fredson Bowers (Cambridge: Cambridge University Press, 1976), 3:497. Cyrus Hoy argues of Fletcherian tragicomedy that its weakness "lies in the formal arbitrariness of the definition" (*The Hyacinth Room: An Investigation of the Nature of Comedy, Tragedy, and Tragicomedy* [New York: Knopf, 1964], 210). But Alastair Fowler notes that Fletcher "certainly knew that Shakespeare's plays and his own explored more subtly and

pervasively mixed actions containing apparent or virtual deaths, of a sort hardly covered by the popular definition he offers" (*Kinds of Literature: An Introduction to the Theory of Genres and Modes* [Cambridge, MA: Harvard University Press, 1982], 188; see also 26, 31, 185–87, 244). For an example of a quasi-Fletcherian witchcraft tragicomedy, see Thomas Middleton's *The Witch*. For a discussion of Harsnett's idea of tragicomedy and its relevance for the Renaissance stage, see Herbert Berry, "Italian Definitions of Tragedy and Comedy Arrive in England," *Studies in English Literature* 14 (1974): 179–87.

42. Before the Prologue of *The Witch of Edmonton*, "The whole Argument" of the play is presented in "this Dystich": "Forc'd Marriage, Murder; Murder, Blood requires: / Reproach, Revenge; Revenge, Hells help desires." Much of the play's criticism responds to the tenuous connections between bigamy and witch plots. Dawson's "Witchcraft/Bigamy" goes the furthest toward exploring the "semantic asymmetries" in this distich, the connective gaps and leaps in the play's structure—and the complex social negotiations they perform.

43. This pamphlet survives in the British Museum. I quote its title from Onat, *Witch of Edmonton*, 158.

44. Stage directions from *The Tempest* (after 5.1.171) and *The Winter's Tale* (after 5.3.20). Paulina's advice to Leontes—that he "awake" his "faith" and "resolve" "For more amazement"—requires that she deny occult powers (5.3.86–91, 94–95).

45. *The Winter's Tale*, 5.3.94–95.

46. Dawson notes "that none of the other witch plays of the period display the witch in the process of turning to witchcraft" ("Witchcraft/Bigamy," 80).

47. Ibid., 81.

48. Ibid., 94.

49. The picture illustrating the title page of the 1658 edition of the play suggests that Young Banks's comic subplot balanced any tragedy produced by the witch plot: in the lower left-hand corner of the illustration, Banks stands waist-deep in a pond (a victim of the Familiar's fairly benign fooling), exclaiming, "Help help I am Drownd"—a quotation of 3.1.90. In the upper left-hand corner appears the black Dog, speaking his first line to Sawyer in the play ("Ho haue I found thee Cursing"). In the upper right-hand corner, Mother Sawyer repeats the oath the Familiar teaches her. This illustration suggests a reading that the text largely supports: that the Banks subplot is much less consequential than the main plot. The seriousness of this main plot would have rested, for a Renaissance audience, in the power with which oaths and curses were invested in the period.

50. Dawson reaches his insight by applying Macfarlane's observation that most witchcraft accusers in the early modern period had acted against the unwritten rules of charity by refusing the accused a gift or donation (*Witchcraft*, 150–55, 195–97). Citing other historical sources, Viviana Comensoli makes a similar point in an article published the same year as Dawson's ("Witchcraft and Domestic Tragedy").

51. Dawson, "Witchcraft/Bigamy," 83.

52. Ibid., 91. Even in the second quotation, Dawson seems uncertain about intentionality; the sentence reads, "The text's support for the morris (like that of the society it represents) *can in fact be read* as a gesture aimed at assuaging social guilt."

53. Leah S. Marcus, "Politics and Pastoral: Writing the Court on the Countryside," in *Culture and Politics in Early Stuart England*, ed. Kevin Sharpe and Peter Lake (London: Macmillan, 1994), 159. Marcus supports her argument, which does not explicitly address Dawson, by observing that the play represents moral turpitude in James's bucolic countryside and by showing that the ambiguous morris does not apparently reintegrate the community according to the Jacobean program announced in the *Book of Sports*.

54. Katharine Mary Briggs has suggested a possible source for Frank Thorney's murder of Susan in a ballad published between 1640 and 1655 (see *Pale Hecate's Team: An Examination of the Beliefs on Witchcraft and Magic among Shakespeare's Contemporaries and His Immediate Successors* [New York: Humanities Press, 1962]), 96. This attribution, if correct, further reflects the playwrights' contamination of their "legal" source with the "lewd Balladmongers" Goodcole condemns.

55. Algernon Charles Swinburne, *The Complete Works*, ed. Sir Edmund Gosse and Thomas J. Wise (London: W. Heinemann, 1925–27), 12:395.

56. As Dawson has shown, the very tenuity of the play's connection between witchcraft and bigamy provides the necessary space for a social criticism to which Swinburne here seems deaf.

57. Scot, *Discoverie of Witchcraft*, 197, 507, 3, 172, 9, quoted in Greenblatt, "Shakespeare Bewitched," 24–25. While I am indebted to Greenblatt in this part of my paragraph, I disagree with his assertion that Scot's wordplay "ironically re-enchant[s] what he most wishes to disenchant." I would agree, however, to such a reading of a dramatic work like *The Witch of Edmonton*, which marks witchcraft off as metaphor only to literalize it.

58. William Rankins, *A Mirrour of Monsters*, ed. Arthur Freeman (New York: Garland, 1973), E.i. Like Stubbes, Rankins may be investing the theater with a literally demonic power here; writing just a few years after the publication of Scot's *Discoverie*, however, Rankins seems to be appropriating the figurative disenchantment of skepticism for his own antitheatricalist argument.

59. Diabolical powers of divination were conventionally ascribed to witches capable of such perspicuous charges, but I think it is more interesting to read Clarington's response as an anxious and gendered reaction to Sawyer's threatening category of "Men-witches."

60. On the cultural conception of the familiar in Renaissance England, see Barbara Rosen, ed., in her introduction to *Witchcraft* (London: Edward Arnold, 1969), 17–18; and Thomas, *Decline of Magic*, 530–31. Onat devotes some time to the question of whether Dog was represented on two or four legs and reminds us that *The Witch of Edmonton*'s audience "did not think of the devil-dog onstage as either a real dog or as a real devil" (*Witch of Edmonton*, 308). The play clearly has some fun with the implausibility of an actor playing a dog; in 4.1, for instance, Young Banks questions his father's identification of Dog's barking as "the voice of a dog": "The voice of a Dog? if that voice were a Dog's, what voice had my Mother?" (247–48). Young Banks then proceeds to imitate Dog's barking, claiming to have produced the barking his father heard. For accounts of twentieth-century productions of the play that describe the portrayal of Dog, see *Three Jacobean Witchcraft Plays*, ed. Peter Corbin and Douglas Sedge (Manchester: Manchester University Press, 1986), 27–28.

61. Christopher Marlowe, *The Tragical History of the Life and Death of Doctor Faustus*, 1.1.81, ed. Irving Ribner (New York: Odyssey Press, 1966).

62. Dawson describes Sawyer as innocent on the "natural" level but guilty on the "supernatural" level ("Witchcraft/Bigamy," 83). For a discussion of natural and supernatural categories of action, see Peter Stallybrass, "*Macbeth* and Witchcraft," in *Focus on Macbeth*, ed. John Russell Brown (London: Routledge, 1982), 206.

63. See *Twelfth Night*, 5.1.378.

64. In Goodcole's narrative, the prayer is *"Sanctibicetur nomen tuum,"* and Sawyer goes on to declare herself ignorant of any more Latin (*Wonderful Discoverie*, 395). In the play, the quarto's various spellings of the prayer also suggest an imperfect grasp of Latin, though in one instance the playwrights intriguingly show Sawyer parrying with Dog in passable Latin and declaring "I'm an expert Scholar; / Speak Latine, or I know not well what Language, / As well as the best of 'em" (2.1.177–79).

LAW STAGED AND
THEORY TROUBLED

SEVEN

"Paper Bullets"
Texts, Lies, and Censorship in Early Modern England

Debora Shuger

Hony soit qui mal y pense.

I

Most studies of censorship in early modern England, while diverging over how stringently controls on the press were enforced, assume that their primary object was "to prevent the circulation of dangerous ideas," "controversial opinions," and other "attempts to deliver the truth."[1] Tudor-Stuart censorship is thus viewed as a mechanism for stifling uncomfortable truths and principled dissent—an assessment strongly corroborated by Milton's *Areopagitica*, which condemns censorship on precisely these grounds.

Yet *Areopagitica* deals primarily with *religious* heterodoxy. While early modern English governments may have endeavored to suppress heretical ideas, the ban evidently did *not* extend to secular theorizing, since by 1641 virtually every major text of classical republicanism had been printed in a licensed English translation—a state of affairs Hobbes thought responsible for the Civil War but no one else seems to have minded. The claim that early modern censorship attempted to suppress dangerous *political* truths runs into two problems. First, one can easily find works in which patently subversive passages survive the censor untouched, while apparently innocuous lines succumb to the red pencil. Such puzzling and quite common "incidents of *noncensorship*" suggest that ideological controls governing the press and stage were lax or at least inconsistent.[2] The second problem cuts deeper. I began thinking about censorship in the course of reading various seventeenth-century biographies and autobiographies; I had expected that those written after the collapse of the licensing system in the 1640s would, like *Areopagitica*, have celebrated the new freedom of political self-expression. What I instead found was the reverse: acute misgivings voiced across the political spectrum and invariably for the same reasons. In 1642 Thomas Fuller thus denounced the "scurrilous scandalous papers" issuing from the unregulated press: "They cast dirt on the faces of many innocent persons, which dryed on by continuance of time can never after be washed off. . . . [T]he Pamphlets of this age may passe for Records with the next (because publickly uncontrolled) and what we laugh at, our children may believe."[3] Fuller was, of course, a royalist author, but John Rushworth, Cromwell's secretary to the Council of War from 1645 on, makes the same assessment in his *Collections of Private Passages of State* (1659); he compiled his massive documentary history of the period, Rushworth explains, because some

> mens Fancies were more busie then their Hands, forging Relations . . . relating Battels which were never fought, and Victories which were never obtained; dispersing Letters which were never writ by the Authors. . . . [Thus] the impossibility for any man in After-ages to ground a true History, by relying on the Printed Pamphlets in ourdays [sic] which passed the Press whilst it was without controul, obliged me . . . to make a great *Collection*; and whilst things were fresh in memory, to separate Truth from Falshood.[4]

The unregulated circulation of printed falsehood also disturbed the Levellers, who protest that the Long Parliament allowed the press "to print, divulge and disperse whatsoever books, pamphlets and libels they please, though they be full of lies."[5]

I have not doctored the evidence here, quoting only authors troubled by the results of press deregulation and omitting those who praised such freedom of expression; I simply did not come across *any* instances of the latter stance. "Freedom of expression" is, of course, a misleading phrase: the texts cited above do not deplore freedom but falsehood. But their strikingly un-Miltonic outlook raises the possibility that virtually all modern accounts of censorship have built on anachronistic premises. The concerns articulated following the collapse of the licensing system suggest that earlier Tudor-Stuart efforts to police both spoken and written words might themselves have aimed to check the circulation of falsehood rather than either information the Crown wished to conceal or ideas it deemed objectionable. As I shall try to argue in what follows, this hypothesis not only makes sense of numerous specific instances of government censorship but also illuminates broader issues pertaining to the early modern politics of discourse.

II

Examining the sixteenth-century laws regulating spoken and written materials, one begins to grasp the serious threat that false reports might pose in eras before more or less objective journalism and the sorts of "hard" evidence supplied by photographs and fingerprinting. Royal proclamations, in particular, shed light on the cultural contexts framing government attempts to regulate discourse. Time and again, they endeavor to allay the fears stirred up by oral or printed rumors. A 1560 proclamation, for example, condemns those spreading "seditious and slanderous tales, importing to simple people a fear that cattle unmarked should be forfeited."[6] In such instances, "censorship" manifestly does not concern transgressive ideas, but even the proclamations attacking seditious books insist upon their factual inaccuracy rather than their ideological threat. Thus the 1579 proclamation attacking Stubbs's *Gaping Gulf*—a Puritan denunciation of the French match—vehemently objects to its "heap of slanders ... bolstered up with manifest lies," its "fardel of false reports," and its rehearsal "of hearsays uncertain or of vain guessings and suposals ... maliciously forged against manifest truth."[7] A 1573 proclamation condemned *A Treatise of Treasons*, a libel against Cecil and Bacon, as "false calumnies" and "manifest untruths"; Cardinal Allen's incendiary *Admonition* was likewise denounced as "most false and abominable lies" that "slander and dishonor her majesty."[8]

It remains to be seen, of course, whether these accusations were themselves false—whether, that is, the government's claim that these works were at bottom a "fardel of false reports" was not doublespeak for the Crown's real objection: that such texts publicized dangerous truths and revolutionary ideologies. Before we turn to this critical issue, however, a second feature of the proclamations deserves mention. The proclamations repeatedly characterize the "lies" disseminated by rumor and print as "slander" or "defamation"; that is, they identify political dissent with attacks on specific individuals, whether the queen, her counselors, or her prospective husbands.

The same identification informs sixteenth-century common law, which did not recognize either holding or publishing dissident opinions (other than heresy) as a punishable offense. While seditious doctrine per se could be prosecuted under special felony statutes, these proved paper tigers and, lapsing at Elizabeth's death, were never reenacted.[9] In general, language became actionable only if it involved treason, *scandalum magnatum* (spreading "false and horrible" lies concerning the great men of the realm), or either ecclesiastical, civil, or criminal defamation.[10] Tudor laws, that is, chiefly criminalized slanderous attacks on individuals. The laws, like the proclamations, responded to the peculiar nature of early modern political discourse: the reliance on slander to discredit one's opponents. As Sir George Buc, the Jacobean master of revels, observed, "to make an innocent man culpable . . . is an old and stale strategm and court juggling."[11]

It is important not to confuse such defamation with the impolitic revelation of the faults and follies of the powerful. A small but telling instance suggests the extent to which this mix-up distorts our picture of early modern censorship. The 1601 quarto of Jonson's *Cynthia's Revels* omits lines in which a courtier boasts that his graceful dancing is "the very high way of preferment." Subsequent critics have, quite plausibly, read the passage as a satire on Sir Christopher Hatton, whom his enemies referred to as "the dancing chancellor," this allegedly being his sole qualification for office. A recent study of Tudor-Stuart censorship thus concludes that the passage was cut because "its strain of truth" proved offensive.[12] But did the censor (if the passage was, in fact, censored) delete these lines for revealing the truth about Hatton? In his magisterial *The Elizabethan Puritan Movement*, Patrick Collinson remarked, somewhat optimistically, "[W]e have discarded the legend of the dancing chancellor and a proper estimate of . . . [Hatton's] abilities now includes an appreciation of one of the great parliamentary orators of the age."[13] If Jonson's lines satirized Hatton, they were defamatory, and the censor may have excised them precisely because they rehearsed "malicious reports of hearsays uncertain."

Other scholars have surmised that Jonson himself tactfully dropped the passage. This seems plausible, especially since Tudor-Stuart dramatists generally shared the government's view of defamation. The protheatrical *apologiae* embedded in various early-seventeenth-century plays insist that the stage does *not* slander individuals. In Massinger's *Roman Actor* the performers thus assert that they are not guilty of "traducing such / That are above us."[14] So too in *Poetaster*, both Horace (Jonson's alter ego) and the concluding "Apologeticall Dialogue" decry slanderous attacks on individuals: the poet should "spare men's persons and but tax their crimes." When the jurist Trebatius warns Horace of the legal penalties assigned those who "wrong men's fames with verses lewd," the poet responds by praising the "just decree" that punishes libels "aimed at persons of good quality." This justification of censorship does not, moreover, advocate a poetics of spineless conformity. In the fifth act, Virgil distinguishes between the "wholesome sharpe morality, / Or modest anger of a satiric spirit" and its "sinister application" to particular individuals, a distinction that affirms the dramatist's right to engage in sociopolitical commentary; a "sharp morality" that castigates social injustice is not, Virgil insists, that which "hurts or wounds the body of a state."[15] The play implies that poets attain the authority and privilege to speak dangerous truths by refraining from scandalous lies.

Both the attacks on the stage for slandering individuals and the playwrights' pleas of innocence are well-known but rarely given much weight, since the whole issue of defamation has seemed only marginally relevant to the *politics* of early modern drama and hence to the political operations of censorship. Gossip about Chancellor Hatton's dancing has never been seen to have much bearing on the great ideological struggles culminating in the Civil War. But this distinction between defamation and politics seems singularly unhelpful in any attempt to understand either early modern political discourse or the attempts made to regulate it. As recent historians have pointed out, well into the Jacobean age, opposition to authority was far less a matter of "generalized political principles" than specific "rights, grievances, and personalities."[16] "Personalities" is crucial here. In Tudor-Stuart England personal honor and reputation remained *central* cultural values. A man's "good name," Coke avers, "ought to be more precious to him than his life."[17] For the ruling classes, personal reputation constituted "the very essence of their ability to govern."[18] As Coke rhetorically queried, "What greater scandal of government can there be than to have corrupt or wicked magistrates to be appointed and constituted by the king?"[19] Defamation became an effective political weapon precisely because in early modern England the political was personal. Robert Darnton's observation on eighteenth-century French politics applies equally to the Tudor-Stuart period; it is, he notes, "easy to underestimate the importance of personal slander . . . because it is difficult to appreciate that politics took place at court, where personalities counted more than policies. Defamation was a standard weapon of court cabals."[20]

III

It is equally easy to underestimate the effectiveness of slander and related brands of falsehood, if only because most Americans cannot imagine life before newspapers and National Public Radio. By contrast, most early-seventeenth-century persons seem to have been quite ill informed about national and international events; as Henry Radeclyffe complained to his brother, the Earl of Sussex, "We haue euery daye seuerall newes, and sometyme contraryes, and yet all put out as true."[21] People outside the tiny elite circle that made policy learned about events either from the occasional royal proclamation or by the unofficial channels of gossip, ballads, private correspondence, and contraband pamphlets.

If the former category provided rather meager fare, the latter, insofar as we can reconstruct it, shows a marked propensity toward conspiratorial paranoia and partisan virulence, qualities often ignored in modern discussions of this material. In his groundbreaking *Freedom of the Press in England*, Frederick Siebert thus explains that John Stubbs's *Gaping Gulf* (1579) made Elizabeth "furious" because the author had dared "to discuss in public print . . . [a] matter of state policy."[22] What Stubbs had done, in fact, was considerably less innocuous. He begins his criticism of the French match by explaining that the Duc d'Alençon is "the old serpent in shape of a man." We later learn that Alençon's morals pass the "worst of Heliogabalus." Equally bad, the gentleman comes from France, and "the French," as it turns out, "do account as fair virtues all foul lies, treasons, poisonings, massacres, and turning of realms upside down." And to cap matters, Stubbs has somehow discovered that Alençon really has no intention of marrying Elizabeth at all but intends to wed Mary Stuart, after which the pair will together lead a rebellion to usurp the English throne.[23] This is not "discussing public policy"—at least not in the current sense of the phrase—but *scandalum magnatum*, the crime for which Stubbs was convicted and that cost him his right hand.

The majority of texts condemned by the Elizabethan proclamations are, like Stubbs's, packed with defamatory lies. Most were products of the Roman Catholic slander machine on the Continent, which seems to have been operating at capacity throughout the late sixteenth and early seventeenth centuries. Mark Pattison provides a vivid sketch of one of these tracts, Carolus Scribanius's 1605 *Ampitheatrum honoris*: "It must suffice to say that it is one of the most shamelessly beastly books which have ever disgraced the printing press. The leading characters among the Reformed are brought up one after another, and the most filthy imputations alleged against them, without the smallest evidence, or the pretence of it.... It is a cesspool of filth, in which sectarian hate and an impure imagination do not seek to disguise themselves by any arts of composition."[24] Such texts still haunt Richard Baxter three-quarters of a century later, stirring up painful images of the posthumous attacks that he feared would destroy his own "stock of reputation" in the same way as men like Scribanius "have made the world believe that Luther consulted with the devil, that Calvin was a stigmatised Sodomite, that Beza turned Papist etc., to blast their labours."[25]

Pattison's characterization of this material fits most of the Roman Catholic pamphlets singled out in the Elizabethan proclamations. Cardinal Allen's *Admonition*, multiple copies of which were packed into the Armada to be distributed upon landing, is the most "shamelessly beastly." Concerning the queen's relation with the Earl of Leicester, Allen relates that "she took [him] up ... only to serve her filthy luste," to which end, "he (as may be presumed, by her consent) caused his owne wife cruelly to be murthered." Moreover, with "divers others she hathe abused her bodie ... by unspeakable and incredible variety of luste." The cardinal then supplies the moral to be drawn from these fables: the English queen "deservethe not onelie deposition, but all vengeaunce bothe of God and man."[26]

The first of Allen's accusations repeats calumnies previously detailed in *Leicester's Commonwealth* (1584). Neither modern scholars nor sixteenth-century polemicists can, of course, *know* whether Leicester had his first wife, Amy Robsart, murdered; she was found dead at the bottom of some stairs, and the coroner's jury ruled "death by mischance." D. C. Peck's meticulous study of *Leicester's Commonwealth*, however, found the charge distinctly implausible: at the time of her demise Robsart was dying of breast cancer; if Leicester had wished her dead, he need only have waited a few months.[27] *Leicester's Commonwealth* is the work of exiled English recusants. Its contents were based on rumors spread by the Howard clan, whose members blamed the earl for their own political eclipse; recognizing that Leicester's "power depended upon attractive personal qualities, [they] sought to make him unattractive."[28] Like so many of the texts that the Elizabethan authorities sought to suppress, the work is a "heap of slanders ... bolstered up with manifest lies." The accession of James did not interrupt the Roman Catholic libel campaign against the English monarchy. To take just one example: in 1615 there appeared the anonymous *Is. Casauboni corona regia*,[29] which purports to be a panegyric on King James by the great Protestant scholar Isaac Casaubon, who had died the previous year. The work is, in fact, a vicious and clever satire on the king. In a characteristic passage "Casaubon" informs James that, since "the origin of kings should be traced to piety, not blood," Scotland's Puritan divines decided that their papist queen, Mary Stuart, was "unworthy to bear a king." Hence they covertly exchanged her own child for "one conceived by a minister of the Divine Word," a substitution that ensured their future ruler would be "pious, learned, and a guardian of the Church's interests." From this "Casaubon" triumphantly concludes that, since James is not Mary's son, "no law of nature, no sacred obligation, prevented you from neglecting, hating, and even (if necessary) killing her."[30] This mock-encomium both ridicules the king's taste for theological controversy and, in the final lines, mocks his failure to avenge his mother's execution, its double-pronged attack setting up a cruel and witty dilemma: either the allegations concerning James's parentage are true, in which case the king is a usurper, or they are false, rendering him accessory to matricide.

The piece, which was printed in Brussels, caused a major diplomatic uproar: the English government mounted an investigation that may have been "the most detailed and expensive ever conducted to determine the author of a book"; between 1618 and 1624 alone, the English agent in Brussels doled out over 765 pounds trying to ferret out the desired information.[31] Modern studies of Jacobean censorship have, however, largely ignored the *Corona regia*, focusing instead on the threats posed by Puritan oppositional writings. Since these contributed to the demise of Stuart absolutism, and since this has generally been viewed as a positive outcome, most of these studies have viewed such critiques favorably. Yet their tactics differ little from those employed by the papal propagandists. The hotter sort of Jacobean Protestants attacked the Spanish match with the full arsenal of defamation, forgery, and partisan distortion.[32] By the 1620s the anti-Spanish party was circulating "bitter and slanderous critiques" of the Jacobean court, raising dark suspicions among the king's Protestant subjects.[33] As Alastair Bellany notes in his important study of early modern libelous politics, such material fostered expectations "that popery might be accompanied by witchcraft, that the sexually lax might favour Arminians, that the enemy of Parliaments might poison his rivals," all these being "recognisable symptoms of the corruption associated with the alien, and especially with popery."[34]

The most scurrilous fantasies occur in the verse libels of the period, which exhibit considerably more interest in the sex life of the Buckinghams than "threats to habeas corpus or to the subject's liberties": one, for example, recounting how the elderly Countess of Buckingham played "the fucking game" with Bishop Williams, along with similar information about the female relatives of other pro-Spanish courtiers.[35] Early-seventeenth-century news diaries preserve similar verse libels, as well as reports of court intrigue and imaginary papist plots. William Davenport's diary thus transcribes a newsletter implicating the Earl of Somerset and various Catholic noblemen in treason, which Davenport considered to be "accordinge to the truest reporte," together with two related documents—both Puritan forgeries—exposing the perfidious machinations of Spanish diplomats.[36] Newsletters, both printed and manuscript, likewise warned of impending Catholic massacres, of the king's imminent submission to Rome, of powerful courtiers betraying their country to the Antichrist for Spanish gold.[37]

Forgery seems to have been a particularly effective political weapon. Thomas Scott, a Puritan minister, was the undisputed master of this genre; two of the items Davenport copied into his news diary—the council speech of Archbishop Abbot and the Spanish king's letter—were probably Scott's work. His other accomplishments include a "Dutch" pamphlet describing Spanish aggression in the Netherlands; a list of secret articles agreed upon by the College of Cardinals; and the brilliantly effective *Vox populi* (1620) and *The Second Part of Vox populi* (1624), both purporting to be translations of top-secret Spanish documents that revealed how the English had been tricked into furthering Spain's pursuit of global empire. Scott, of course, fabricated the reports—out of what cannot always be ascertained. One of the few modern historians to investigate the matter concludes that Scott was "in no position to have any accurate notion of what was going on"; the two parts of *Vox populi* mix "exaggerations, errors of fact, and ludicrous excesses . . . to stir up anti-Spanish and anti-Catholic hatreds."[38]

Yet the *Vox populi* tracts were widely accepted as genuine. Simonds D'Ewes, a university-educated Puritan M. P., noted in his journal that the works had been "generally approved of, not only by the meaner sort that were zealous for the cause of religion, but also by all men of judgement that were loyally affected to the truth of the Gospel."[39] As has long been known, the *Vox populi* tracts also provide the "historical" underpinnings for Middleton's *A Game at Chess,* among the most overtly topical of all English Renaissance dramas, which played to packed houses for nine consecutive days before being shut down by royal command. The play has frequently been commended for its political boldness: Margot Heinemann's *Puritanism and Theatre* describes it as a "sophisticated critical satire" voicing the "radical, sceptical, plebeian opposition of ordinary Londoners" to Jacobean policy; Albert Tricomi's *Anticourt Drama* similarly argues that *A Game* introduced "unapproved categories of political thought," pressuring the Crown "to bring *its* manner of seeing the world into line with reality."[40]

"Reality," however, seems an ill-chosen label. Insofar as the play makes specific allegations about historical events and persons, its version of events does not square very well with those given by modern historians. The character representing Gondomar in the play, for instance, boasts of having inveigled the English into a naval campaign against the Algerian pirates—pirates who preyed upon *Spanish* shipping.[41] A recent historian describes the episode somewhat differently: when James ordered Sir Robert Mansell to attack the Barbary pirates, "the Spanish were aghast. In the state of Spain's naval preparedness such a fleet could bombard her coasts at will"; Gondomar thus made "frantic efforts to stop it."[42] The White King's Pawn presents similar difficulties. Most scholars read the character as figuring Lionel Cranfield, the Lord Treasurer, who had been impeached in May of 1624 for opposing England's entry into the Thirty Years' War.[43] Middleton's hostile portrait, which represents Cranfield as a Spanish agent and "most dangerous hypocrite," reflected the political temper of the time.[44] As before, however, its "reality" is dubious. Akrigg summarizes the received view of modern historians: "[I]f ever there was a man who had served King James well, it was Cranfield." That Tricomi praises Middleton's libelous portrait of the ex-Lord Treasurer for taking "us beyond events to a public labeling of the psychic essence of court figures" suggests some justification for Jacobean strictures against representing public persons on the stage.[45]

The same queasy relation to reality can be discerned in other plays dealing with contemporary events. As Sir George Buc, Master of the Revels from 1610 to 1622, noted in the margin of the dangerously topical *Sir John van Olden Barnavelt*, "I like not this: neithr do I think that the prince was thus disgracefully used."[46] Subsequent research has justified Buc's reservations. According to its modern editor, Wilhemina Frijlinck, the play "gives a representation of the facts which is not at all in keeping with the historical truth." Its authors (perhaps Fletcher and Massinger) may not have meant to defame Barneveld; the problem lay in their sources. "After Barneveld's arrest," Frijlinck reports, "there was a deluge of the most villainous pamphlets. . . . [People] were aghast as they heard how the Advocate had for years been the hireling of Spain . . . . [yet they] believed it, and hated him accordingly."[47] It is clear from Frijlinck's research that *Barnavelt* took its "historical" material from these pamphlets. The work, like *A Game at Chess*, exemplifies the politicized textual circuitry that connects the theater to early modern libelous politics.

Buc's laconic skepticism about the play's accuracy points to his own alertness to the politics of representation. Perhaps as a result of his experiences in the Revels office, Buc had become seriously interested in the problematic relation between truth, politics, and historical narrative. These meditations dominate Buc's own revisionist *History of King Richard the Third*, completed around 1619—the same year that *Barnavelt* came under his scrutiny. This text would therefore seem to shed light on the issues that troubled at least one Jacobean censor. *The History* attempts to disprove the received version of Richard's character. What Buc argues is that the stories of Richard's depravity were slanders, fabricated by his old enemy Bishop Morton and popularized by Morton's ally Sir Thomas More, who availed himself of a poet's "privilege to tell false tales." Buc construes these stories in the standard terms of early modern censorship: they are "libels and railing pamphlets," "slanderously" bismirching Richard with "false accusations" to make "his memory infamous forever."[48] The bishop's motives, as Buc makes clear, were political, Morton having led the revolt against the Yorkist king. But political opposition, here as elsewhere, takes the form of personal attacks on another's character. Moreover, these attacks had little basis in truth, being mostly "but fables and fictions and poetical inventions"—a view of fiction that may reflect Buc's encounters with contemporary topical/historical drama. Like all defamatory fabrications, the charges against Richard proved no less dangerous for being untrue, since "to the world it is all one to seem and to be."[49]

Buc's own project, conversely, implies a *positive* notion of censorship, one curiously reminiscent of Milton's *Areopagitica* insofar as both require the reader to take upon himself the responsibility of censuring suspect texts. Buc thus instructs his audience "to consider and examine what they read, and make trial of such doubtful things are as [sic] written before they give credit unto them." In particular, "suspicion supposeth many times men to be guilty and culpable of crimes whereof they are not. So that an innocent may as easily be condemned as a malefactor." For this reason, "just judges . . . require strong evidence of the accuser, or else they pronounce the accuser guilty of condemnation." As this final clause implies, for Buc the duty of a censor—condemning false accusers—was inseparable from the historian's obligation "to make truth (hereby concealed and oppressed and almost utterly suppressed) present herself to the light."[50]

I want to skip now to the crisis of 1641–42 and the virulent resurgence of libelous politics—a phenomenon to which revisionist historiography has called attention. There exists surprisingly little evidence of radical, republican, or even constitutionalist opposition to Caroline rule; rather, it would seem that a considerable portion of the English people took up arms against their king because they believed widely disseminated rumors implicating Charles, Henrietta Maria, the bishops, and a good number of leading courtiers in various sinister popish plots.[51] Antipopery was, in Peter Lake's eloquent metaphor, the "cloud of unknowing through which contemporaries blundered into civil war."⁵² In his first speech to the Long Parliament, Pym thus warned of schemes "woven by Jesuits, bishops, popish courtiers and prelates acting in concert," informing the Commons that the French were preparing to invade Portsmouth, assisted by "divers persons of eminency about the Queen." Similar rumors spread panic in the localities: the mayor of Norwich told the Privy Council that twelve thousand papists were poised to attack the city, while a gentleman from Derbyshire reported that Catholics had been stockpiling hatchets with which to slaughter their Protestant neighbors. Lurid reports of atrocities committed against Ulster Protestants intensified the mood of distrust and fear; as Baxter would later recall, the horrific stories of Irish cruelty "filled all England with a fear both of the Irish and of the Papists at home.... And when they saw the English Papists join with the king against the parliament, it was the greatest thing that ever alienated them from the king."⁵³ Parliamentary newsletters told of "enormous and largely mythical reinforcements of savage Irish Catholics... hurrying to join the King," of cavalier banners bearing "the Popes Motto." Sinister rumors spread across the country that Henrietta Maria, and perhaps even Charles, had ordered the Irish massacres.⁵⁴

The collapse of the licensing system in 1641 has, rather obviously, some bearing on this outpouring of lies that helped precipitate a civil war—a result that raises questions not addressed in *Areopagitica*, although it helps explain the puzzling phenomenon Blair Worden once noted, namely that virtually no one in seventeenth-century England, radical or royalist, defended freedom of the press per se.⁵⁵ Moreover, this *habitual* use of falsehood, slander, hearsay, and forgery in political controversy calls into question recent claims to the effect that the oppositional texts of the period gave birth to a Habermasian "public sphere" in which "power came to be constructed not out of adherence to the authority of special persons, but by the conditions of rational public discussion."⁵⁶ Rather, precisely because power remained inseparable from adherence—that is, from trust and loyalty—to persons, resistance expressed itself in the language of defamation rather than political theory. As Darnton remarks, again with regard to eighteenth-century France, slander proved "more dangerous propaganda than [Rousseau's] *Contract social*. It severed the sense of decency that bound the public to its rulers."⁵⁷

— One final instance of early modern "libelous politics" may serve to illustrate Darnton's point. As is well known, Sir Thomas Overbury died in the Tower of London on September 13, 1613, killed by a poisoned clyster. Frances Howard, Countess of Somerset, subsequently confessed to having orchestrated the murder to prevent Overbury from thwarting her marriage to the royal favorite, Robert Carr.[58] Evidence that Overbury had been murdered first surfaced in the summer of 1615. During the next six months, Coke presided over the trial and conviction of the various shady characters responsible for executing Howard's scheme. Their confessions implicated Howard and, indirectly, Carr, both of whom were placed under house arrest in October. Howard confessed and pleaded guilty; Carr maintained his innocence. They were tried in May of 1616, Bacon, then attorney-general, directing the prosecution before the House of Lords. Convicted and sentenced to death by their peers, the couple subsequently received a widely unpopular royal pardon.

Thirty-five years later, two versions of the Overbury murder appeared in print: the rather elliptical account sketched in Sir Anthony Weldon's *The Court and Character of King James* (1650) and Sir Arthur Wilson's more coherent narrative included in his *The Life and Reign of King James I* (1653). In these, Overbury's death, scandalous enough in itself, assumes more sinister dimensions. Wilson and Weldon both link Overbury's murder to the death of Prince Henry in 1612; moreover, both implicate the king in his son's alleged poisoning as well as in Overbury's demise.

Wilson's narrative is particularly illuminating. Tracing the chain of events that led to Overbury's murder back to their origin, Wilson begins his account by describing how Prince Henry, now approaching adolescence, "put forth himself in a more Heroick manner than was usual with Princes of his Time . . . which caught the Peoples Eyes." He then strikes the first ominous note: although James still trusted his son, Wilson continues, "how far the King's Fears (like thick Clouds) might afterwards blind the Eye of his Reason, when he saw him (as he thought) too high mounted in the Peoples Love . . . to decline his Paternal Affection to him . . . may be the Subject of my Fears, not of my Pen." The predicted estrangement of father and son began when Carr became the royal favorite, "for the Prince being a high-born Spirit, and meeting a young Competitor in his Father's Affections . . . gave no Countenance, but Opposition to it." The prince's hostility intensified when both young men find themselves attracted to Frances Howard, in which rivalry, Wilson observes, "the Viscount got the Mastery, but to his Ruine."

Prince Henry then died, "poisoned," it was rumored, "with a Bunch of Grapes" or "the venemous Scent of a pair of Gloves." The murder occurred, Wilson adds, because the prince's light "cast so radiant a Lustre, as (by darkning others) it came to lose the Benefit of its own Glory"—a veiled allusion to the king's complicity, reinforced in the next clause, which reminds the reader that "jealousy is like Fire that burns all before it, and that Fire is hot enough to dissolve all Bonds that tends to the diminution of a Crown." The oblique phrasing here hints at dark recesses of the royal psyche, where tangled oedipal and political motives ignited the king's jealous rage against his "manly" son. Alongside this account, however, Wilson gives another, incompatible, scenario in which Overbury, at Carr's instigation, murdered Prince Henry—which murder James then avenged by having Overbury poisoned. The account Henry's death concludes with Wilson's elliptical remark that "some that knew the Bickerings betwixt the Prince and the Viscount muttered out dark Sentences." The next few pages describe Overbury's murder and the subsequent trials, making no overt reference to the prince's death until Wilson turns to the story of Coke's behavior during the abortive trial of Sir Thomas Monson in December 1615. According to Wilson, Coke discovered that Northampton had at one point said that "the making away of Sir *Tho Overbury* would be acceptable to the King." On the basis of this or "some other secret Hint receiv'd," Coke intimated in open court "that *Overbury's* untimely Remove had something in it of Retaliation, as if he had been guilty of the same Crime against Prince Henry." Following this injudicious outburst, Monson's trial was suddenly dropped, putting, Wilson notes, "strange Imaginations into Mens Heads." At the close of Wilson's history, an obscure poetic justice asserts itself in the king's own death—once again by poison, this time administered by the new favorite, Buckingham, who, having displaced Carr in James's affections, now suspected that he too was on the way out.[59]

These poisoning narratives, although not printed until the Interregnum, rehearse gossip that had been circulating for over three decades. Coke's trial notes from 1615 show that he suspected a conspiracy linking Prince Henry's death to Overbury's. In his journal, Simonds D'Ewes conjectured that Carr, on Overbury's advice, had murdered the prince and that Buckingham had poisoned his royal master, the latter charge echoed by Lucy Hutchinson, who also thought it likely that Charles "had favour'd the practise."[60] That such slander could persuade highly educated persons like Coke, D'Ewes, and Hutchinson that their country was governed by poisoners and parricides suggests why, while waiting out the dark years of the Interregnum, Peter Heylyn might have desired to consign Wilson's "most infamous Pasquill" to an "*Ignis expurgatorius.*"[61]

Wilson's allegations are unproven, implausible—and Tacitean. His narrative is, in fact, a pastiche of the *Annals'* life of Tiberius: the same section, interestingly enough, that Jonson dramatized in *Sejanus*. A glance at the play's "Argument" indicates the similarities: "Aelius Seianus ... grew into fauour with [Tiberius].... Which greatnesse of his, Drusus, the Emperors sonne, not brooking, after many smother'd dislikes (it one day breaking out) the Prince strooke him publikely on the face. To reuenge which disgrace . . . Seianus practiseth . . . to poyson Drusus." The poison has the desired effect. Emboldened by this success, Sejanus then plots to murder Germanicus, Tiberius's valiant and popular younger son, to which end "he deuiseth to make Tiberius selfe, his meanes: & instill's into his eares many doubts, and suspicious . . . . which Caesar iealously hearkning to, as couetously consenteth to . . . [his son's] ruine."[62] Sejanus then poisons Germanicus. Shortly thereafter, however, Tiberius turns against the favorite and "hath him suspected, accused, [and] condemned." According to Suetonius, Tiberius himself died from poison administered by his successor; in Tacitus's *Annals,* alternatively, the emperor was instead murdered by a new favorite—smothered under a pile of laundry.

The two incompatible explanations for Prince Henry's death given by Wilson—James's jealous fear of his popular and "manly" son *versus* Carr's preemptive strike against a hostile rival—correspond to those that Jonson, drawing on the Roman historians, offers for the deaths of Germanicus and Drusus. The parallel between Tiberius and James's death at the hands of the new favorite is equally obvious. Wilson's *Life and Reign,* in fact, averts to its own Tacitean subtext in its final paragraph, which begins, "some Parallel'd . . . [King James] to *Tiberius.*" The remainder of the passage, however, veers in an unexpected direction, Wilson concluding his venomous narrative with perhaps the most astonishing (and self-incriminating) early modern reflection on the origin and effects of libelous politics:

> [Y]et Peace was maintained by . . . [James] as in the time of *Augustus:* And Peace begot Plenty, and Plenty begot Ease and Wantonness, and Ease and Wantonness begot Poetry, and Poetry swelled to that Bulk in his time, that it begot strange Monstrous Satyrs against the King's own Person, that haunted both Court and Country. . . . And the Tongues of those Times more fluent than my Pen, made every little Miscarriage (being not able to discover their true Operations, like small Seeds hid in earthy Darkness) grow up, and spread into such exuberant Branches, that evil Report did often pearch upon them. So dangerous it is for Princes, by a remiss Comportment, to give Growth to the least Error: for it often proves as fruitful, as Malice can make it.[63]

Wilson's genealogy summarizes basic early modern assumptions about the form and content of oppositional discourse: that it concerned persons rather than ideas; that it was composed of "hearsays uncertain," "vain guessings" and "supposals . . . maliciously forged against manifest truth"; and that such slanders, although false, had "dangerous" consequences "for Princes."

IV

Up to this point, I have argued that Tudor-Stuart press controls attempted to suppress falsehoods. Yet this is clearly not the whole story. Throughout the period, there seems to have been a fairly widespread consensus that some facts (or at least educated guesses) should not be disseminated. This attitude no longer finds much support; we tend rather to assume that one of the free press's primary functions is to expose precisely the information that someone (or everyone) wishes to hide: *The Pentagon Papers*, for example. Early modern persons seem to have viewed the ethics of disclosure somewhat differently, subordinating the public right to know to the moral prohibition against exposing one's neighbors' failings. Thomas Fuller, a moderate royalist and Anglican priest, thus deplored "scurrilous scandalous" pamphlets, for, even granting "the things true they jeer at," Christians ought not "to play upon the sinnes and miseries of others."[64] A Puritan biographer similarly explained that he had not attempted to record his subjects' "weaknesses, [or] to discover their shame, for this is a poysonous disposition."[65]

The term most often used for such reticence is *charity*. The 1559 *Injunctions for Religion*, which enact the Elizabethan licensing system, thus open by condemning "slanderous words and railings whereby charity, the knot of all Christian society, is loosed."[66] As a popular sixteenth-century catechism explains, "[E]verie man is bound to have a charitable opinion and good conceit of his neighbour, with a desire of his good name and credit."[67] The church courts thus prosecuted defamation as a violation of "charity within the Christian community"—whether or not the allegation was in fact true.[68] Baxter's *Autobiography* movingly intimates the relation between these precepts of charity and the practice of censorship; reviewing his own literary output, he concludes, "I have a strong natural inclination to speak of every subject just as it is, and to call a spade a spade.... But I unfeignedly confess that it is faulty ... [and shows] some want of honour and love or tenderness to others; or else I should not be apt to use such words as open their weakness and offend them. And therefore I repent of it, *and wish all over-sharp passages were expunged from my writings,* and desire forgiveness of God and man."[69] Such moral reservations about telling the whole truth, while shaped by Christian values, did not express a narrowly clerical viewpoint. Samuel Daniel, a deeply intelligent and much underrated poet, thus avers that "*gratitude,* and *charity* / ... keepe no note, nor memory will haue, / Of any fault committed." Even a sophisticated and disillusioned courtier like Fulke Greville similarly insists that "bashfull Truth vayles neighbours errors too"—a particularly interesting line, since "Truth" here must mean troth, not veracity.⁷⁰ One omits certain facts not to avoid legal reprisal but to maintain the communal bonds of troth and charity.

The hermeneutic counterpart to the demand that authors conceal what it would be uncharitable to disclose is the legal rule that words should be interpreted *in mitiori sensu*. This rule held that if a statement could be construed in both a defamatory and an innocent sense, the latter should be considered its true meaning: "*verba semper accipienda sunt in mitiori sensu.*"⁷¹ *Mitior sensus* was a theological hermeneutic adopted by the common law in the late sixteenth century to adjudicate the rapidly increasing numbers of defamation cases, many of which the judges considered spiteful fabrications and hence attempted to discourage by refusing to label defamatory any statement that could possibly be given a more charitable interpretation.⁷² Poets and playwrights subsequently transposed this axiom to defend their own words against what Jonson calls

> ... the sinister application
> Of the malicious, ignorant, and base
> Interpreter: who will distort, and straine
> The generall scope and purpose of an authour,
> To his particular, and priuate spleene.⁷³

The dramatists' reiterated attacks on readers who quarry dangerously topical meaning from their works invoke this hermeneutic of the *mitior sensus*. Like the legal and ecclesiastical authorities, that is, the playwrights treat charity as a *categorical* imperative.

Overt topicality could, of course, expose a writer to legal sanctions, but it does not follow that fear of punishment alone motivated self-censorship. Rather, authors explain that they have "tread ... tenderly on the graves" of departed noblemen,⁷⁴ even though "no power remaines ... to hold / The tongues of men, that will be talking now."⁷⁵ The terrible vulnerability of these once-powerful figures to slanderous attack haunts Daniel's elegy on the Earl of Devonshire, for "the Lyon being dead euen Hares insult." Yet, Daniel continues,

> The worthier sort, who know we do not liue
> With perfect men, will neuer be so vnkinde;
> They will the right to the diseased giue,
> Knowing themselues must likewise leaue behind,
> Those that will censure them. . . .

> And will not vrge a passed error now,
> Whenas he hath no party to consult,
> Nor tongue, nor aduocate, to shew his minde.[76]

Sir Robert Naunton's *Fragmenta regalia*—a series of thumbnail biographies of Elizabethan statesmen and courtiers—likewise announces its unwillingness to publicize the "passed error" of these dead lions, since "modesty . . . forbids the defacement of men departed." In Naunton, however, the aristocratic honor code outweighs specifically Christian motives for self-censorship. As he quite elegantly puts it: "I had rather incur the censure of abruption than to be conscious . . . of sinning by eruption and in trampling on the graves of persons at rest which living we durst not look in the face or make our addresses to them otherwise than with due regard to their honors and reverence to their virtues."[77] Such self-confessed abruption is less a response to government censorship than an affirmation of the moral and social values that authorized such restrictions. We may or may not consider this reverence for dead noblemen legitimate, but numerous early modern writers apparently did—and were, moreover, perfectly explicit about the silences this respect imposed. The "cultural bargain between writers and political leaders," to which Patterson has called attention, that allowed the former to offer political and social criticism *if* decently veiled, was perhaps, as Patterson herself notes, less a bargain than a "joint project," one that proved, on the whole, mutually satisfactory because both parties thought the communal bonds of honor, troth, and charity worth protecting.[78] That the legal restrictions on speech and print embodied widely shared cultural sentiments may help explain why several of the most notorious victims of early modern censorship—for example, Stubbs and Hayward—were not radicalized by this experience: Stubbs entered the service of Lord Burghley, writing (presumably with his left hand) anti-Catholic pamphlets in his patron's defense; Hayward was appointed royal historiographer and knighted. Even the incendiary Thomas Scott remained chaplain to the English garrison at Utrecht until his death.

The protocols of charitable interpretation aimed at fostering civil harmony, which sufficiently explains their appeal to Tudor-Stuart authorities. But their cultural plausibility also rested, at least in part, on specifically Christian assumptions about human nature and human knowledge: in particular, the possibility of moral/spiritual transformation and the impossibility of intersubjective scrutiny. The relation between these postulates is implicit in Hooker's restatement of what he terms "the safest axioms for charity to rest itself upon": namely, "It becometh not us during this life altogether to condemn any man, seeing that (for any thing we know) there is hope of every man's forgiveness, the possibility of whose repentance is not yet cut off by death." No person, Hooker continues, has "sufficient means to comprehend" nor "leave to search in particular" the state of other men's souls, this knowledge having been reserved "only unto God, who seeth their hearts and understandeth all their secret cogitations."[79]

This sense of the unfixity and opacity of moral/spiritual selfhood, in turn, underlies some of the narrative conventions characteristic of Tudor histories and history plays. Neither chroniclers nor playwrights extenuate the sins of kings and magistrates, but they deal generously with their souls. In Fabyan, Edward II, although formerly dominated by "the appetite and pleasure of his body," after his deposition "tooke great repentaunce of his former lyfe."[80] Even the tyrannical Richard III is extended the possibility, albeit remote, of repentance; Holinshed thus grudgingly refrains from passing final judgment: "but to God, which knew his inward thoughts at the houre of his death, I remit the punishment of his offenses commited in his life."[81] The discontinuities in Marlowe's portrayal of Edward II and Shakespeare's depiction of Richard II and Wolsey—all of whom become markedly more sympathetic in their plays' last scenes—presuppose the discontinuous selfhood of pastoral theology, as well as the axiom of charity it underwrites.

Like the theologians, the chroniclers tend to shrink from analyzing the motives impelling their characters, a reticence Buc commends, invoking the "divine epigram" "Leave secret things to God, who knows all hearts."[82] *Holinshed's Chronicles* registers the same conviction that the heart is not available for human inspection; rather, the historian's gaze reaches only to matters "publicklie doone" and "the truth of that outward act."[83] As Worcester's ghost complains in *Mirror for Magistrates*, "Thus story [i.e., history] writers leave the causes out, / Or so rehears them, as they wer in dout"—a complaint echoed in Gabriel Harvey's disparaging remark that Tudor chroniclers know nothing of "the art of depicting character."[84]

The chroniclers do not altogether refrain from alleging possible motives for things "publicklie doone," but they evince considerable discomfort with such explanations, often citing several incompatible motives (compiled from various sources) for the same act to emphasize their conjectural status. This incorporation of divergent voices does not, I think, obliquely advocate "the idea of an open society in which dissent must be spoken," as Patterson has suggested.[85] It seems rather to register the chroniclers' sensitivity to the problem of defamation, their awareness that motives cannot be known but only imputed and that such imputations may be slanderous. Such concerns suffuse Holinshed's account of the death of King John's nephew Arthur: "But now touching the maner in verie deed of the end of this Arthur, writers make sundrie reports. . . . Some have written . . .

[that] he fell into the riuer of Saine, and so was drowned. Other write . . . [that] he pined awaie. . . . But some affirme, that king Iohn secretlie caused him to be murthered. . . . [B]ut verelie king Iohn was had in great suspicion, whether worthilie or not, the lord knoweth."[86] The historian must perforce rely on contemporary witnesses, "but such was the malice of writers in times past" toward King John that every unfortunate occurrence "was still interpreted to chance through his default, so as the blame still was imputed to him." Yet, whatever John's failings, "to thinke that he deserued the tenth part of the blame wherewith writers charge him, it might seeme a great lacke of aduised consideration in them that so should take it."[87] The chronicler sets down the incriminating allegations found in his sources because some may have been true, but, like the narrator of *Paradise Lost*, he attempts to educate his readers to consider advisedly charges purveyed by talking snakes.

The chronicles' peculiar formulas for depicting character—the sudden repentance of wicked rulers, the unselective rehearsal of contradictory interpretations, the unwillingness to probe the occulted causes impelling the "outward act"—assume the possibility *(gratia adiuvante)* of radical moral change and the impenetrability of "the soul's most subtle rooms."[88] These assumptions underwrite the chroniclers' efforts to deal gently and generously with the souls of famous men, as well as the legal hermeneutic of the *mitior sensus* and Hooker's axioms of charity. Such protocols seem to have been emphasized during the Tudor-Stuart era in response to political concerns, but concerns apparently shared by both authors and authorities over the depredations of the Blatant Beast.

V

Yet if these protocols had wide currency, they were also contested. In particular, the Roman historians of the Silver Age, widely imitated from the late sixteenth century onwards, sanctioned representational procedures fundamentally at odds with habits of charitable and honorable reticence.[89] Tacitus and Suetonius take for granted that a person's moral nature is essentially fixed from childhood: the young Domitian, for example, "would spend hours alone every day doing nothing but catch flies and stabbing them with a needle-sharp pen."[90] If Tiberius and Nero temporarily manage to hide their true natures, the repressed always returns in the end. Hence, for these Roman historians, the "art of depicting character" is to capture (or conjecture) this core selfhood, disclosing its presence beneath the stately masks that power uses to conceal its guilt.

But, in Tacitus especially, the attempt to expose the dark secrets of empire has problematic entailments. Tacitean Rome is a nightmare world of spies, informants, and conspirators: *delatores* hide in corners, listening for whispers of discontent; rumors circulate about ghastly misdoings within the imperial palace; senators betray their colleagues to the wrath of paranoid emperors. But the historian, in publishing these rumors and probing the vicious secrets of the court, becomes himself a *delator*, a defamer.

Taciteanism, that is, blurs the distinction between history and libel, which may have been one reason why, particularly after the publication of Hayward's *Henry IIII*—the first experiment in English Taciteanism—Tudor-Stuart authorities kept particularly close watch over this genre. Tacitus provided a dangerous model—not, I think, because of his republican sympathies, which he shared with Aristotle, Cicero, and Livy, but rather because Taciteanism configured "court politics . . . as a factious pursuit of personal advantage, shaped by jealousy, malice and fear," its obsession with "unsavoury gossip" reinforcing "diffuse cynicism" and "a highly conspiratorial interpretation" of political events.[91] The "unsavoury gossip" that fills the pages of both Tacitus and Suetonius tells of princes poisoned by their royal father, of unnatural lusts, domestic intrigues, and vicious favorites—materials not lost on seventeenth-century libelers who adapt these stories to delegitimize the Stuart monarchy.

But there is also a more radical sense in which Taciteanism violated the obligation to believe honorably of one's betters and charitably of all men. The Tudor chronicles record similarly vicious rumors about English kings, but by keeping within the bounds of charitable representation they implicitly ratify the bonds of trust and respect that weave the fabric of Christian community. Tacitus depicts a world in which such bonds have been replaced by the politics of the gaze. In the *Annals*, rulers and subjects eye each other with grim hostility; those in power spy upon the secret crimes of their subjects, who in turn observe their superiors with an attentive hatred, watching for evidence of political murders and sexual perversities—the historian viewing all parties with cold contempt. A sentence from Ralegh's *On the Seat of Government* brilliantly conveys the seditious optics that structure Tacitean political relations: "Certainly the unjust magistrate that fancieth to himself a solid and untransparable body of gold, every ordinary wit can vitrify and make transparent pieces, and discern their corruptions; howsoever, because not daring, they cover their knowledge: but in the meanwhile it is also true, that constrained dissimulation, either in the proud heart or in the oppressed . . . where the fear of God is not prevalent, doth in all the leisure of her lurking but sharpen her teeth."[92] Resentment, hypocrisy, and barely contained violence here *typify* the relations between rulers and their subjects. Like Tacitus, Ralegh configures this relation in terms of the politics of the gaze, whereby the capacity to detect—or avoid detection—constitutes power.

This reciprocal construction of power and knowledge radically alters the nature of censorship. In Tacitean histories, the state's obligation to "cover" certain items no longer derives from any moral ground, with the result that censorship aims merely at silencing dissent, and self-censorship serves only to deflect punishment. Moreover, for Ralegh censorship suppresses, not rumors or conjecture, but *knowledge*, an entailment of his claim that people can be "vitrified," their secret motives and acts laid open to inspection. The object of state surveillance, consequently, becomes truth rather than slander. In Tacitus (and, implicitly, Ralegh as well) censorship thus becomes a confrontation between the transgressive author and the coercive state—and hence synecdoche for the larger struggle between freedom and tyranny.

VI

In this final section, I want to return to Wilson's identification of poetry with the sort of unsavory gossip that delegitimized the Stuart monarchy. Louis Montrose has recently broached the interesting possibility that in the late Tudor period "the art of characterization seems to have undergone a dramatic change ... [that coincided] with the keen interest of the late Elizabethan sociopolitical and intellectual elites in the employment of Tacitean/Machiavellian paradigms in order to speculate upon the acquisition of power and the legitimation of authority.... And the increasing concern of players and dramatists with individual characterization in the motivation of dramatic action suggests that this mode of drama was especially congenial to Tacitean/Machiavellian views of historical process."[93] Montrose's conclusion—that this drama "*formally* contested the dominant ideological assertions of the Elizabethan state"—oddly resembles Wilson's claim that Jacobean poetry begot "monstrous Satyrs against the King's own Person, that haunted both Court and Country."[94] The two observations differ, however, in that Montrose construes the political modality of literature in terms of ideology rather than defamation. Yet since Montrose identifies the Taciteanism of early modern drama with its "art of depicting *character*," what he terms ideological contestation may share considerable common ground with the defamatory representations of libelous politics. But if this is the case, could not one argue that Tudor-Stuart literature, particularly the drama, contributed to the breakdown of trust and "good opinion" that rent the fabric of English society?[95] More than one recent scholar has traced a straight line from the theaters of London to those of war. As Gary Taylor puts it: "In 1624 Middleton put King James on a stage; in 1649 Parliament put King Charles on a scaffold. One might well say of *A Game at Chess* . . . '*C'ést déjà la Revolution.*'"[96] Already in 1613 Sir Henry Wotton experienced such premonitions; writing to Sir Edmund Bacon concerning a performance of Shakespeare's *Henry VIII*, Wotton worriedly concludes that such stagings of "pomp and majesty" might be "sufficient in truth within a while to make greatness very familiar, if not ridiculous."[97]

Yet to claim that, in general, this drama functioned primarily to demystify or subvert royal power seems untenable. While I have not done the arithmetic, I suspect that the majority of Tudor-Stuart plays keep within the limits of charity and honor, including *Henry VIII*. Shakespeare allows the corrupt and self-seeking Wolsey to die in the odor of sanctity; he likewise interprets the king's own actions *in mitiori sensu*, passing in decent silence over his role in the deaths of Anne and Cranmer; instead Henry becomes both symbol and source of communal charity, reconciling his factious nobles and defending the innocent Cranmer from slanderous attack. *Henry VIII* is not a Tacitean work; especially the final two acts, which dramatize the triumph of royal "love, truth, [and] terror"—a very un-Tacitean conjunction—over a dissident nobility, seem almost deliberate inversions of the "Tacitean/Machiavellian paradigm."[98]

I cannot figure out why this play in particular disturbed Wotton, nor does it seem possible to determine to what extent Tacitean plays and "monstrous Satyrs" sapped the moral bases of royal power. But clearly much of the best literary scholarship over the past three decades has been devoted to uncovering the politically subversive implications of Tudor-Stuart literature. With very few exceptions, this scholarship assumes that "good" literature challenges political elites and orthodoxies by telling dangerous truths, the state, in turn, deploying the formidable powers at its disposal to ban such poetic license. The title of Janet Clare's recent book on early modern censorship provides an elegantly Shakespearean version of this paradigm: *Art Made Tongue-Tied by Authority*.

Yet Tudor-Stuart poets do not seem to have sanctioned transgression as "an imperative peculiar to literature,"[99] mostly because they, like the authorities, took defamation seriously. One gets a sense that they found art's complicity in libelous politics both real and disturbing. In Jonson's *Poetaster*, for example, a paranoid tribune slanderously attacks the leading Augustan court-poets, Horace and Virgil; but this informant receives assistance from various playwrights and actors, who conspire to defame the pair out of malicious envy. Augustus dismisses the charges, assigning Horace and Virgil to choose the appropriate punishment. While they refrain from tongue-tying the offenders, they do make the playwrights vomit up their words.

Only a few years earlier, Spenser had portrayed a similar episode of state literary censorship. As Artegall and Prince Arthur approach Mercilla's resplendent throne in book 5 of *The Faerie Queene*,

> they saw
> Some one, whose tongue was for his trespasse vyle
> Nayled to a post, adjudged so by law:
> For that therewith he falsely did revyle
> And foule blaspheme that queene for forged guyle
> Both with bold speaches which he blazed had,
> And with lewd poems which he did compyle;
> For the bold title of a poet bad
> He on himselfe had ta'en, and rayling rymes had sprad.[100]

Here art is quite literally tongue-tied by authority: not, however, for dangerous ideas but for "wicked sclaunders" (5.9.26) and false railings against the queen. The scene is not ironic. Throughout *The Faerie Queene*, but especially in the second half, the most terrible Spenserian monsters personify the workings of defamation: Error, Sclaunder, Ate, and above all the Blatant Beast, whose battle with Calidore, the knight of courtesy, occupies the final canto of the 1596 edition of the poem. The beast has a thousand tongues, "Which spake reprochfully, not caring where nor when." These spew forth

> licentious words and hatefull things
> Of good and bad alike, of low and hie;
> Ne kesars spared he a whit, nor kings,
> But either blotted them with infamie
> Or bit them with his banefull teeth of injury.

But as the monster reviles his opponent "with bitter termes of shamefull infamy," Calidore, in what might almost be read as an allegory of censorship, "did him suppresse, and forcibly subdew" (6.12.27–33). The Blatant Beast, of course, signifies not unlicensed printing but simply defamation, yet it was precisely the conviction that the latter profoundly threatened the foundations, political and moral, of Christian society that made it possible to perceive early modern censorship as a discipline of Spenserian courtesy. And if poets were sometimes the Blatant Beast's victims, they also supplied him with effective shock troops.

Quite obviously, neither Jonson nor Spenser allows Sidney's claim that "though he would . . . a poet can scarcely be a liar." For Sidney, the poet *cannot* lie because he does not represent "what men have done" but ranges freely "only within the zodiac of his own wit. . . . He nothing affirms, and therefore never lieth." Poetry names characters only to make the "picture the more lively, and not to build any history." That is, Sidney posits—perhaps even invents—the notion of "imaginative literature" to deflect the charge that "the poets give names to men they write of, which argueth a conceit of an actual truth, and so, not being true, proves a falsehood." The link here between falsehood and naming connects the issue of poetic lies to that of defamation; for Sidney, literature (what he calls "poetry") is precisely that class of writings that affirms nothing concerning actual persons, that has no dealings with the Blatant Beast. Unlike mocking rhymes or monstrous satires, poetry cannot, by definition, engage in libelous politics; it does not pose the sort of threat Tudor-Stuart authorities struggled to contain. By conceptualizing poetry as "imaginative literature" or "art," Sidney implicitly exempts it from most forms of early modern censorship. Poets have license to range *freely* precisely because each remains "only within the zodiac of his own wit."[101]

Sidney's defense of poetry against moral and, by implication, political censure requires that "the poet (as I said before) never affirmeth." This defense will not serve Spenser's rayling rhymer and Jonson's poetasters, whose offense consists of making slanderous affirmations. Nor is Sidney's defense an option for recent historicist criticism, which holds that literature has "considerable historical specificity," that it "participates in . . . the political management of reality."[102] Insofar as this criticism "refuses easy distinctions" between the "workings of power" and "symbolic acts," it also refuses the easy opposition between authority and art.[103] Early modern Englishmen understood, perhaps better than we, the full implications of Stephen Greenblatt's memorable claim that power is the ability "to impose one's fictions upon the world."[104]

Sidney's view of poesy as imaginative literature, which cannot lie because it nothing affirmeth, won the day—a victory implicit in our unhesitating condemnation of attempts to tongue-tie it. Poesy thus understood is patently fictional and hence does not impose upon the world, which is to say that it is relatively powerless. To the extent, however, that fiction approaches imposture—to the extent that its rhetoric seeks rather than suspends belief—it has very real power,[105] including the very real power to harm others, and would therefore seem prima facie no less subject to regulation than cars, whiskey, advertisements, guns, and other instruments of potential harm. *Mein Kampf* and *Protocols of the Elders of Zion* are still banned in Germany.

Early modern persons seem to have credited such fictions with a power no less than and not very different from that of sticks and stones. The Restoration historian John Nalson spells out their potential cost with a passionate unambiguity:

> I know not any one thing that more hurt the late King then the paper bullets of the press; it was the scandalous and calumniating ink of the Faction that from thence blackened him, and represented all his words and actions to the misguided People, who would difficultly have been persuaded to such a horrid Rebellion, if they had not been first prepossessed by the tongues and the pens of the Faction, of strange and monstrous designs, which they said the King and his evil Councilors the Bishops and Malignants, who were all by these pamphlets styled papists and atheists, had against their lives, liberties, and religion.[106]

As a statement of the causes of the English Civil War, Nalson's analysis might be thought somewhat partial, and to modern ears it does run roughshod over the distinction between words and actions on which First Amendment jurisprudence depends. Yet Darnton's point regarding the political *libelles* in prerevolutionary France holds equally for Nalson's paper bullets: these materials shaped the way people viewed events, and "the contemporary view of events was as important as the events themselves; in fact, it cannot be separated from them. It gave them meaning, and in so doing it determined the way people took sides."[107] Moreover, as Nalson observes, "[T]he number of the malicious and seditious pamphlets did far exceed those that had any thing honest in them." Early modern English writers return again and again to this dishonesty: to the prevalence of forgery, false news, and libel. The royal proclamations, which lay out the government's reasons for suppressing works viewed as *politically* offensive, make precisely the same objections. These proclamations identified pervasive characteristics of Tudor-Stuart oppositional writing—ones widely recognized at the time by men of such different political conviction as Nalson and Rushworth.

No one denies that Tudor-Stuart political censorship failed. What has been far more difficult to keep in focus is the actual offensiveness of the offending texts;

our instincts are on the side of contestation and dissent, and even in the state of innocence, the devil could persuade Eve regarding an apple that

> [the] forbidding
> Commends thee more, while it infers the good
> By thee communicated.[108]

Whatever Satan's role in the matter, there is for us a cultural resistance to noting the extent to which Tudor-Stuart oppositional writing purveyed fear and falsehood. This misrecognition, by making the state's efforts to outlaw such paper bullets transparently illegitimate, closes off the possibility of understanding the early modern regulation of language. The point of calling attention to the problematic character of Tudor-Stuart oppositional writing is not to defend censorship but to legitimate posing the questions with which this essay is primarily concerned: questions about what values the system that collapsed in 1641 might have attempted to safeguard and what sort of real dangers it sought to contain.

NOTES

This essay subsequently evolved into a book-length project, now in print as *Censorship and Cultural Sensibility: The Regulation of Language in Tudor-Stuart England* (Philadelphia: University of Pennsylvania Press, 2006). I have made some last-minute revisions to the essay to correct factual errors, but on the whole it reflects a somewhat earlier stage in my thinking on this topic.

1. Christopher Hill, "Censorship and English Literature," in *The Collected Essays of Christopher Hill*, vol. 1, *Writing and Revolution in Seventeenth-Century England* (Amherst: University of Massachusetts Press, 1985), 32–33; Anne Castanien, "Censorship and Historiography in Elizabethan England: The Expurgation of Holinshed's *Chronicles*" (PhD diss., University of California, Davis, 1970), 34; Annabel Patterson, *Reading Holinshed's Chronicles* (Chicago: University of Chicago Press, 1994), 263.

2. Annabel Patterson, *Censorship and Interpretation: The Conditions of Writing and Reading in Early Modern England* (Madison: University of Wisconsin Press, 1984), 17. See also Richard Dutton, *Mastering the Revels: The Regulation and Censorship of English Renaissance Drama* (Iowa City: University of Iowa Press, 1991), 89, 178; Blair Worden, "Literature and Political Censorship in Early Modern England," in *Too Mighty to Be Free: Censorship and the Press in Britain and the Netherlands*, ed. A. C. Duke and C. A. Tamse (Zutphen: De Walburg, 1987), 45–62.

3. Thomas Fuller, *Selections*, ed. E. K. Broadus (Oxford: Clarendon Press, 1928), 59.

4. Quoted in Michael McKeon, *The Origins of the English Novel, 1600–1740* (Baltimore: Johns Hopkins University Press, 1987), 49.

5. Quoted in Worden, "Literature and Political Censorship," 47. See also the complaint of Bayle, who was certainly no conservative, regarding the French *chroniques scandaleuses:* the "works are a mixture of fictions and truths, half romance, and half history," deliberately written in such a way as to make it extremely difficult "to distinguish fiction from true matter of fact." Hence, Bayle concludes, "I believe the civil powers will at last be forced to give these new romancers the option: either to write pure history, or pure romance; or at least to use crotchets to separate the one from the other, truth from fiction" (quoted in McKeon, *Origins of the English Novel,* 55).

6. *Tudor Royal Proclamations,* 3 vols., ed. Paul Hughes and James Larkin (New Haven: Yale University Press, 1969), 2:160–61. . On the political significance of such rumors, see Ethan Shagan, *Popular Politics and the English Reformation* (Cambridge: Cambridge University Press, 2003); G. R. Elton, *Policy and Police: The Enforcement of the Reformation in the Age of Thomas Cromwell* (Cambridge: Cambridge University Press, 1972), 68–70, 78–81.

7. *Tudor Royal Proclamations,* 2:445–49.

8. Ibid., 2:376–79, 3:13–17.

9. Philip Hamburger, "The Development of the Law of Seditious Libel and the Control of the Press," *Stanford Law Review* 37 (1985): 671.

10. Coke defines a scandalous libel (i.e., criminal defamation) as *"famosus libellus, seu infamatoria scriptura"* and a libeller as a *"famosus defamator"* (*The Reports of Sir Edward Coke,* 7 vols., ed. and trans. George Wilson [London, 1776–77], 3:125r). The modern distinction between libel and slander is post-Restoration; before 1660, the terms seem to be used interchangeably. See Hamburger, "Development of the Law," 661–766; W. S. Holdsworth, *A History of English Law,* 16 vols. (Boston: Little, Brown, 1922–38), 5:205–12, 8:333–78; J. H. Baker, *An Introduction to English Legal History,* 3rd ed. (London: Butterworths, 1990), 495–508.

11. Sir George Buc, *The History of King Richard the Third (1619),* ed. Arthur Kincaid (Gloucester: Alan Sutton, 1979), 166.

12. Janet Clare, *"Art Made Tongue-Tied by Authority": Elizabethan and Jacobean Dramatic Censorship* (Manchester: Manchester University Press, 1990), 84.

13. Patrick Collinson, *The Elizabethan Puritan Movement* (Berkeley: University of California Press, 1967), 314.

14. Philip Massinger, *The Roman Actor,* in vol. 3 of *The Plays and Poems of Philip Massinger,* ed. Philip Edwards and Colin Gibson (Oxford: Clarendon Press, 1976), 1.3.106–7. See also Chapman, *All Fools,* ed. Frank Manley (London, 1968), "Prologus," lines 13–19 (quoted in Clare, *Art Made Tongue-Tied,* 89).

15. Ben Jonson, *Poetaster,* ed. Tom Cairn (Manchester: Manchester University Press, 1995), 3.5.127–34, 5.3.137–44.

16. Mervyn James, *Family, Lineage, and Civil Society: A Study of Society, Politics, and Mentality in the Durham Region, 1500–1640* (Oxford: Clarendon Press, 1974),184–85.

17. Coke, *Reports,* 3:126v.

18. J. A. Sharpe, *Defamation and Sexual Slander in Early Modern England: The Church Courts at York,* Borthwick Papers 58 (York: University of York Press, n.d.), 3; Anthony Fletcher, "Honour, Reputation and Local Officeholding in Elizabethan and Stuart England," in *Order and Disorder in Early Modern England,* ed. Anthony Fletcher and John Stevenson (Cambridge: Cambridge University Press, 1985), 92, 115; Holdsworth, *History of English Law,* 5:207.

19. Coke, *Reports,* 125r; Holdsworth, *History of English Law,* 5:209.

20. Robert Darnton, *Literary Underground of the Old Regime* (Cambridge, MA: Harvard University Press, 1982), 203–5, quoted in *Leicester's Commonwealth* (1584), ed. D. C. Peck (Athens: Ohio University Press, 1985), 45.

21. Quoted in Matthias Shaaber, *Some Forerunners of the Newspaper in England, 1476–1622* (Philadelphia: University of Pennsylvania Press, 1929), 241.

22. Frederick Siebert, *Freedom of the Press in England, 1476–1776: The Rise and Decline of Government Controls* (Urbana: University of Illinois Press, 1952), 91; see also Castanien, "Censorship and Historiography," 54, 78.

23. *John Stubbs's "Gaping Gulf,"* ed. Lloyd Berry, Folger Documents of Tudor and Stuart Civilization (Charlottesville: University Press of Virginia, 1968), 3, 71, 80–81.

24. Mark Pattison, *Essays by the Late Mark Pattison,* 2 vols. (Oxford: Clarendon Press, 1880), 1:189–91, and *Isaac Casaubon, 1559–1614* (London: Longmans, 1875), 244.

25. Richard Baxter, *The Autobiography of Richard Baxter, Being the "Reliquiae Baxterianae" Abridged from the Folio (1696),* ed. J. M. Lloyd Thomas (London: Dent, 1925), 129.

26. Frederick Chamberlain, *Private Character of Queen Elizabeth* (London: John Lane, 1921), 185–87.

27. Peck thinks it more likely either that she committed suicide or that her spine collapsed—a result of her spreading cancer—causing the fall (*Leicester's Commonwealth,* 81, 265–67).

28. Ibid., 50–51.

29. The work is often attributed to Gasparo Scioppius, a feared and prolific polemicist, best known for savaging the reputations of Joseph Scaliger and Isaac Casaubon, but Winfried Schleiner has raised serious doubts about the validity of this ascription. See his "'A plott to have his nose and eares cutt of': Schoppe as Seen by the Archbishop of Canterbury," *Renaissance and Reformation* 26 (1990): 48–57.

30. Is. Causauboni *Corona regia* (London [i.e., Louvain], 1615), 35–36. "Concedas ipse, non sanguine; sed pietate originem Regum aestimandam esse. Volunt igitur qui te a natalibus norunt, non humanitus, sed diuinitus Regem esse.... Nam quasi Maria Scotiae Regina, quae mater tua perhibetur, indigna esset, quae Regem ederet, delusam esse aiunt. In grauidae vtero necari infans a Puritanis non potuit: natus mutari potuit, supponique, qui e Ministro Verbi Diuini procreatus, paternam indolem quandoque sceptro iungeret; qui pius, doctus, & pro Ecclesia Dei solicitus foret. Remoto igitur Mariae filio, & velut a Deo repudiato, in regias fascias cunasque tu locaris, felicissime Rex, & filius esse Mariae coepisti, ex qua non prodieras: vt negligere, odisse, atque etiam occidere, si opus, posses, cui te nullum naturae ius, nullumque vinculum obstrinxerat."

31. Schleiner, "'A plott,'" 18, 21.

32. Although other factions did their part: in the wake of the collapse of the Spanish match, Spanish diplomats thus spread rumors that Charles was impotent and informed James that Buckingham was plotting against him. See Thomas Cogswell, *The Blessed Revolution: English Politics and the Coming of War, 1621–1624* (Cambridge: Cambridge University Press, 1989), 106, 251.

33. Between 1603 and 1619 there had been only two royal proclamations dealing with censorship—one condemning Cowell's *Interpreter* (March 25, 1610), the other prohibiting reports of duels (October 15, 1613). By contrast, between 1620 and 1624—that is, the period immediately following the outbreak of the Thirty Years' War—James issued four separate proclamations condemning seditious and slanderous books (*Stuart Royal Proclamations*, vol. 1, *Royal Proclamations of King James, 1603–1625*, ed. James Larkin and Paul Hughes [Oxford: Clarendon Press, 1973], nos. 208, 218, 247, 256).

34. Alastair Bellany, "'Raylinge Rymes and Vaunting Verse': Libellous Politics in Early Stuart England, 1603–1628," in *Culture and Politics in Early Stuart England*, ed. Kevin Sharpe and Peter Lake (London: Macmillan, 1994), 303.

35. Bellany, "'Raylinge Rymes,'" 287; Cogwell, *Blessed Revolution*, 46–47.

36. Richard Cust, "News and Politics in Early Seventeenth-Century England," *Past and Present* 112 (1986): 73–74, 80, 83.

37. Robin Clifton, "Fear of Popery," in *The Origins of the English Civil War*, ed. Conrad Russell (London: Macmillan, 1973), 157–60, 165; Cogswell, *Blessed Revolution*, 24, 31, 35; Siebert, *Freedom of the Press*, 154.

38. Charles Carter, "Gondomar: Ambassador to James I," *Historical Journal* 7 (1964): 191–92.

39. *The Autobiography and Correspondence of Sir Simonds D'Ewes*, 2 vols., ed. James Halliwell (London, 1845), 1:158–60. On the reception of Scott's tracts, see Margot Heinemann, *Puritanism and Theatre: Thomas Middleton and Opposition Drama under the Early Stuarts*, Past and Present Publications (Cambridge: Cambridge University Press, 1980), 156; Shaaber, *Some Forerunners*, 72; Louis Wright, "Propaganda against James I's 'Appeasement' of Spain," *Huntington Library Quarterly* 6 (1943): 152–53.

40. Heinemann, *Puritanism and Theatre*, 151, 170; Albert Tricomi, *Anticourt Drama in England, 1603–1642* (Charlottesville: University of Virginia Press, 1989), 147–49.

41. Thomas Middleton, *A Game at Chess*, ed. T. H. Howard-Hill (Manchester: Manchester University Press, 1993), 3.1.85–88.

42. Robert Zaller, *The Parliament of 1621: A Study in Constitutional Conflict* (Berkeley: University of California Press, 1971), 15.

43. A. R. Braunmuller, "'To the Globe I rowed': John Holles Sees *A Game at Chess*," *English Literary Renaissance* 20 (1990): 353.

44. Middleton, *Game at Chess*, 3.1.256–62.

45. G. P. V. Akrigg, *Jacobean Pageant or The Court of King James I* (London: Hamish Hamilton, 1962), 382; Tricomi, *Anticourt Drama*, 148; Thomas Heywood, *An Apology for Actors* (London, 1612), G4v.

46. Dutton, *Mastering the Revels*, 212.
47. *The Tragedy of Sir John van Olden Barnavelt*, ed. Wilhemina Frijlinck (Amsterdam: H. G. van Dorssen, 1922), cxxxi–cxxxii.
48. Buc, *Richard the Third*, 6, 120–21.
49. Ibid., 45.
50. Ibid., 6, 45, 121, 125, 193.
51. Anthony Fletcher, *The Outbreak of the English Civil War* (London: Edward Arnold, 1981); Kevin Sharpe, *The Personal Rule of Charles I* (New Haven: Yale University Press, 1992), 911, 939; Clifton, "Fear of Popery," 161; Bellany, "'Raylinge Rymes.'"
52. Peter Lake, "Anti-Popery: The Structure of a Prejudice," in *Conflict in Early Stuart England: Studies in Religion and Politics, 1603–1642*, ed. Richard Cust and Ann Hughes (London: Longman, 1989), 73.
53. Baxter, *Autobiography*, 32.
54. K. Sharpe, *Personal Rule*, 939, 910; J. S. Morrill and J. D. Walter, "Order and Disorder in the English Revolution," in Fletcher and Stevenson, *Order and Disorder*, 147–48; Lucy Hutchinson, *Memoirs of the Life of Colonel Hutchinson*, ed. James Sutherland (London: Oxford University Press, 1973), 52; Clifton, "Fear of Popery," 144–45, 162.
55. Worden, "Literature and Political Censorship," 47.
56. Sharon Achinstein, *Milton and the Revolutionary Reader* (Princeton: Princeton University Press, 1994), 9: Andrew McRae, *Literature, Satire and the Early Stuart State* (Cambridge: Cambridge University Press, 2004), 13–14, 112.
57. Cited in Peck, *Leicester's Commonwealth*, 45.
58. Royal favorites changed their names often, Robert Carr being the same person as the Viscount Rochester and, after November of 1613, the Earl of Somerset. Correspondingly, Francis Howard, Lady Essex, and the Countess of Somerset have a single referent. I shall use their Christian names to avoid confusion.
59. Arthur Wilson, *The Life and Reign of King James I*, reprinted in vol. 2 of *The Complete History of England*, 3 vols., ed. White Kennett (London, 1706), 2:684–702, 790. Another libel accused Buckingham of poisoning a substantial number of noblemen; Sir Henry Wotton thus reports that he was commissioned "to examine a lady about a certain filthy accusation, grounded upon nothing but a few names taken up by a footman in a kennel, and straight baptised. It was a list of such as the duke had appointed to be poisoned at home, himself being then in Spain. I found it to be the most malicious and frantic surmise, and the most contrary to his nature, that I think had ever been brewed from the beginning of the world" (quoted in John Jesse, *Memoirs of the Court of England*, 6 vols. [Boston: L. C. Page, 1901], 1:139).
60. D'Ewes, *Autobiography*, 91, 263; Hutchinson, *Memoirs*, 47. I wrote this section before having had a chance to consult Alastair Bellany's splendid account of the Overbury murder and its aftermath in *The Politics of Court Scandal in Early Modern England: News, Culture and the Overbury Affair, 1603–1660* (Cambridge: Cambridge University Press, 2002).
61. Peter Heylyn, *Examen historicum: Or a Discovery and Examination of the Mistakes, Falsities, and Defects in some Modern Histories* (London, 1659), A4(v).

62. *Ben Jonson*, 11 vols., ed. C. H. Herford and Percy Simpson (Oxford: Clarendon Press, 1925–52), 4:352–53.

63. Wilson, *Life and Reign*, 792.

64. Fuller, *Selections*, 59–60.

65. Samuel Clarke, *A Collection of the Lives of Ten Eminent Divines* (London, 1662), A3(r).

66. *Tudor Royal Proclamations*, 2:128. Melanchthon suggests the potential implications for political critique: "tribuunt christiani sapientiam et iustitiam magistratui. . . . Deinde huc pertinet etiam errata legum et magistratuum tegere, excusare et mitigare. Haec *epieikeia*, cum in privata conversatione necessaria sit, multo magis necessaria est in publica societate erga magistratus, sicut scriptum est: 'Dilectio omnia perfert'. . . item: 'Omnia delicta tegit dilectio'" (*Commentarii in Epistolam Pauli ad Romanos* [1532], in vol. 5 of *Melanchthons Werke*, ed. Gerhard Ebeling and Rolf Schaefer [Tübingen: Gütersloher, 1965], 324–25).

67. Quoted in J. A. Sharpe, *Defamation and Sexual Slander*, 2. Coke invokes similarly religious language in his statement of the English law of criminal libel, which asserts that "libelling and calumniation is an offence against the law of God," citing "Leviticus 17. *Non facias calumniam proximo*. Exod 22. ver. 28. *Principi populi tui non maledices*" (*Reports* 3:126v).

68. Martin Ingram, *Church Courts, Sex and Marriage in England, 1570–1640* (Cambridge: Cambridge University Press, 1987), 294–95.

69. Baxter, *Autobiography*, 131 (emphasis added).

70. Samuel Daniel, *The Complete Works in Verse and Prose*, 5 vols., ed. Alexander Grosart (London, 1885–96), 1:184; Fulke Greville, "An Inquisition upon Fame and Honour," stanza 24, in *Certaine Learned and Elegant Works (1633)*, introd. A. D. Cosins (Delmar, NY: Scholars' Facsimiles, 1990), 37.

71. W. S. Holdsworth, "Defamation in the Sixteenth and Seventeenth Centuries," *Law Quarterly Review* 40 (1924): 407 n., quoting from Coke's report on Cromwell's case.

72. Ibid., 404–7; Baker, *Introduction*, 501–3; Thomas Aquinas, *Summa theologiae*, 2.2.60.4.

73. Jonson, *Poetaster*, 5.3.137–44. A seventeenth-century jurist uses similar terms to characterize the majority of actions for defamation facing the courts: they serve largely to "vent the spleen of private jars and discontents among men" (Holdsworth, "Defamation," 404 n.).

74. Daniel, "Epistle Dedicatory" to *The Collection of the History of England* (1626), in *Complete Works*, 4:78.

75. Daniel, "Funerall Poem," in *Complete Works*, 1:173 n.

76 Ibid., 1:184–85.

77. Robert Naunton (d. 1635), *Fragmenta Regalia, or Observations on Queen Elizabeth, Her Times and Favorites*, ed. John Cerovski (Washington, DC: Folger Shakespeare Library, 1985), 86.

78. Patterson, *Censorship and Interpretation*, 7, 11–15.

79. Richard Hooker, *Of the Laws of Ecclesiastical Polity*, in *The Works of Mr. Richard Hooker*, ed. John Keble, R. W. Church, and F. Paget, 3 vols., 7th ed. (London, 1888; reprint, New York: Burt Franklin, 1970), 5.49.2, 3.1.2.

80. Robert Fabyan, *The New Chronicles of England and France* (1516), ed. Henry Ellis (London, 1811), 417, 431.

81. Raphael Holinshed, *Holinshed's Chronicles of England, Scotland, and Ireland* (1587), 6 vols. (London: J. Johnson, 1807–8), 3:447.

82. Buc, *Richard the Third*, 193–94.

83. Quoted in Castanien, "Censorship and Historiography," 198.

84. *The Mirror for Magistrates*, ed. Lily B. Campbell (New York: Barnes and Noble, 1960), 198; Patterson, *Reading Holinshed's Chronicles*, 265.

85. Patterson, *Reading Holinshed's Chronicles*, 15.

86. Quoted in A. R. Braunmuller, "*King John* and Historiography," *English Literary History* 55 (1988): 316.

87. Ibid., 321.

88. George Herbert, "The H. Communion," line 22, in *George Herbert and Henry Vaughan*, ed. Louis Martz (Oxford: Oxford University Press, 1986), 45.

89. To be sure, the frequent use of defamatory tactics in both private and political quarrels indicates that such norms were regularly violated, but people often break rules that they, or at least their culture, nevertheless considers just; were this not the case, law would be either unnecessary or futile.

90. Gaius Suetonius Tranquillus, "Tiberius" 57, "Gaius (Caligula)" 11, "Domitian" 3, in *The Twelve Caesars*, trans. Robert Graves, introd. Michael Grant (London: Penguin Books, 1989).

91. Malcolm Smuts, "Court-Centered Politics and the Uses of Roman Historians, c. 1590–1630," in K. Sharpe and Lake, *Culture and Politics*, 36–37.

92. *The Works of Sir Walter Ralegh*, 8 vols., ed. William Oldys and Thomas Birch (London, 1829; reprint, New York: Burt Franklin, 1964), 8:539.

93. Louis Montrose, *The Purpose of Playing: Shakespeare and the Cultural Politics of the Elizabethan Theatre* (Chicago: University of Chicago Press, 1996), 91–93.

94. Ibid., 105.

95. See, for example, Margot Heinemann, "Political Drama," in *The Cambridge Companion to English Renaissance Drama*, ed. A. R. Braunmuller and Michael Hattaway (Cambridge: Cambridge University Press, 1990), 178.

96. Gary Taylor, "Forms of Opposition: Shakespeare and Middleton," *English Literary Renaissance* 24 (1994): 312; see also Franco Moretti, "'A Huge Eclipse': Tragic Form and the Deconsecration of Sovereignty," trans. D. A. Miller, in *The Forms of Power and the Power of Forms in the Renaissance*, ed. Stephen Greenblatt, *Genre* Special Topics 7 (Norman: University of Oklahoma Press, 1982), 7–8.

97. Logan Pearsall Smith, ed., *The Life and Letters of Sir Henry Wotton*, 2 vols. (Oxford: Clarendon Press, 1907), 2:32–33.

98. Shakespeare, *Henry VIII*, 5.5.48. Even *A Game at Chess*, while bitterly unjust to Cranfield and no reliable guide to Jacobean diplomacy, nevertheless depicts the English king and his family with respectful decorum. The play obviously outraged the Spanish ambassador, but since it was licensed for publication only two years later, the authorities cannot have found it particularly objectionable.

99. Michel Foucault, "What Is an Author?" in *The Foucault Reader*, ed. Paul Rabinow (New York: Pantheon Books, 1984), 108.

100. Edmund Spenser, *The Faerie Queene*, 5.9.25, in *Complete Poetical Works of Spenser*, ed. R. E. Neil Dodge (Boston: Houghton Mifflin, 1908). Further references to this work will be given parenthetically in the text.

101. Sir Philip Sidney, *An Apology for Poetry*, ed. Forrest Robinson, Library of Liberal Arts (New York: Macmillan, 1970), 13–14, 56–58.

102. Jean Howard, "The New Historicism in Renaissance Studies," *English Literary Renaissance* 16 (1986): 25, 27; Heinemann, "Political Drama," 177.

103. Jonathan Goldberg, "The Politics of Renaissance Literature: A Review Essay," *English Literary History* 49 (1982): 537–38; see Stephen Greenblatt, "Introduction," in Greenblatt, *Forms of Power*, 6.

104. Stephen Greenblatt, *Renaissance Self-Fashioning from More to Shakespeare* (Chicago: University of Chicago Press, 1980), 13.

105. The same holds true for legal fictions—perhaps the most important mechanism for change in early modern English law—which require all the parties involved to act as though they did in fact take patent falsehoods for literal truth.

106. John Nalson, *An Impartiall Collection of the Great Affairs of State* (London: S. Mearne, 1682), 2:809.

107. Robert Darnton, *The Forbidden Best-Sellers of Pre-Revolutionary France* (New York: Norton, 1995), 244; see also Georges Lefebvre, *La Grande Peur de 1789* (Paris, 1932).

108. Milton, *Paradise Lost*, 9.753–55.

EIGHT

"So Many Books, So Many Rolls of Ancient Time"
The Inns of Court and *Gorboduc*

Karen J. Cunningham

Michel Foucault's generalization that power acts by concealing itself, and that one of its historically persistent masks is the law, has contributed to a tendency in one strain of literary studies to identify early modern legal practices with the interests of court-centered power and political absolutism.[1] In emphasizing court-centered authority, however, these accounts overlook two things: the influence and activities of the Inns of Court and the central pedagogical process—mooting—through which law was taught. Yet in their own day the Inns were perceived as influential sites where law, though not made, was shaped, and where the sway of a monarch might be challenged by the inclinations of subjects. According to the legal historian J. H. Baker, "[T]he law ... was not confined to pronouncements in court, but was what common lawyers in general believed it to be."[2] This pattern of influence was sufficient to cause Henry VIII to complain about the Inns and to prompt Elizabeth to try to shut them down. Under Elizabeth, judges, who had often considered moot cases in making decisions, acquired increased autonomy from the opinions born in law schools, until "by 1573 the judges had the last word."[3] What the history of the Inns tells us is that relations between their speculative legal work and court-centered pronouncements had long been characterized by competition and conflict.

One side of the competition was represented by the central pedagogical practice—mooting or reading—through which law was taught, not as a self-interpreting code or as a reaction to real events, but as an evocation of the imagination and as a ritual performance.[4] What I mean to argue is that moots are unstable verbal and performance environments that provide an important model for analyzing the volatile discursive relations among the Crown, English subjects, and those who wrote for the theater in early modern England. Like legal discourses more generally, moots were widely circulated and consumed among all levels of society, and in them, such elusive and troublesome categories as "woman," "stranger," and "country" were continuously reformulated and redefined. As a preliminary foray into the study of relations between mooting and drama, I then glance briefly at the work of two men with strong ties to the Inns of Court: *Gorboduc*, by Thomas Sackville and Thomas Norton. The play's connections with Tudor political history are familiar: its authors had resided at the Inns; it was presented as a command performance for the relatively new Queen Elizabeth; and it took up the charged theme of uncertain succession. Rather than approaching this "maxim-hurling" play as a treatise on good government, I place it next to the speculative genre of mooting in order to interrogate its representations of legitimate proprietors of and threats to "Britain land" (5.2.182).[5]

I

Introduced into the law schools during the second quarter of the twelfth century, moot cases focused on "a specific problem with hypothetical facts—upon which a question would be framed."[6] The avowed purpose of mooting was "to preserve and elaborate the common learning concerning real property,"[7] and aspiring benchers were called upon to display their developing skills and qualifications by acting out conjectural cases. In this association between learning law and transmitting property, mooting ritualized and emphasized the issue of proprietorship. Certainly these law performances promulgated official monarchical views. Yet moots were constructed in ways that also admitted other, less constrained interpretations, opening out the conceptual borders of the land to a range of possible meanings. As law teachers conveyed legal principles through extensive discussions of cases that were "sometimes real, sometimes, imaginary,"[8] the purpose of judicial playing became calling to mind exceptions to traditional frames of reference. In the estimation of Francis Bacon, himself a resident of the Inns during the sixteenth century, the most visible effect of these legal fictions by the late Tudor era had become to cloud rather than shed light on legal principles. Contrasting what he imagines to be the superior, objective, ancient practice with that of his own day, Bacon determined

> to revive and recontinue the ancient form of [mooting], . . . being of less ostentation and more fruit than the manner lately accustomed; for the use then was substantially to expound the statutes by grounds and diversities; as you shall find the [mooting] still to run upon case of like law, and contrary law; whereof the one includes the learning of a ground, the other the learning of a difference; and not to stir concise and subtle doubts, or to contrive a multitude of tedious and intricate cases, whereof all, saving one, are buried, and the greater part of that one case, which is taken, is commonly nothing to the matter in hand; but my labour shall be in the ancient course, to open the law upon doubts, and not to open doubts upon the law.[9]

For Bacon, the practice of mooting had shifted from an early noble end of illuminating the "grounds and diversities" of a reliable, self-evident law to a later ignoble end of obscuring and undermining that law. As Bacon frames it, serious consideration had been supplanted by quibbling and gratuitous displays of intellectual gymnastics, a view broadly dispersed throughout popular culture in parodies such as Shakespeare's Dogberry in *Much Ado about Nothing* or Touchstone in *As You Like It*.

What is striking about moot cases, however, is that before they settle their issues, these legal fictions, which Baker identifies as "fugitive forms of literature," require the disputants to deliberate a wide range of imaginary, anomalous events. On the one hand, the setting and conventions of the mooting performance accustom young men to the ways that senior benchers "think" the law. That accustoming, in turn, is understood as shaping subjects' behavior. Bacon speaks for the majority in recognizing the importance of these practices: "It is . . . custom and education," he writes, "rather than nature which are the crucial determinants of human behavior."[10] On the other hand, the content of these cases brings into being diverse notions of England and its inhabitants, imagining a wide range of subject positions and requiring a speculative play that is at odds with customary social order.

As cases are structured for performance, the degree of latitude is contained: mooters adopt or are assigned two positions from which to argue. The form itself suggests there may be only two legitimate ways to see the issues. As their content is developed, however, moots multiply imaginative possibilities and positions. The relative conformity achieved in the ritual performance is continuously eroded by the acts of improvisation demanded by that performance. In what we might call an ideology of legal reassurance, moots anticipate threats to the realm, process those threats through imaginative discourse, and redefine them as contained within laws. It would be a mistake, however, to take any part of the practice as total, for the imaginative practices introduce into circulation elusive ideas that cannot be totally returned to the discourse that elicited them. Something always escapes containment, though not necessarily in intentional or predictable ways.

It appears that members of the Inns made a deep connection between the study of the law and writing of all kinds, including the imaginative.[11] Tradition has it that both Chaucer and Gower were members, and whatever the facts (the claim is unsubstantiated), the tradition itself suggests the mythological power of perceived relations between court and writer. Philip Finkelpearl has shown that in the sixteenth and seventeenth centuries "an astonishing number of important writers" occupied the Inns at some point: More, Ascham, Turberville, Googe, Gascoigne, Sackville and Norton, Lodge, Fraunce, Raleigh, Harington, Campion, Donne, Bacon, Davies, Marston, Ford, Beaumont, Shirley, Davenant, William Browne, Wither, Denham, Quarles, Carew, Suckling, and Congreve, among others.[12] Although Sir Philip Sidney's disciplinary rules limited lawyers to saying "what men have determined," many writers of extralegal stories lived in the Inns and grew "in effect another nature."[13]

Writers at the Inns wrote, commissioned, and produced revels, poems, plays, and masques. In addition to Sackville and Norton's *Gorboduc* (1561–62), for example, another Senecan tragedy, *Gismonde of Salerne*, was penned by five young law students and performed before the queen in 1566; and another, *The Misfortunes of Arthur*, by Thomas Hughes and other students of Gray's Inn, was penned in 1588 and was performed "for the Queen with dumb-shows conceived by the young Francis Bacon." *The Comedy of Errors* was famously performed at Gray's Inn.[14] Members self-consciously produced translations of Seneca from 1558 to 1572 and turned out such guides to governing as the *Mirror for Magistrates*.[15] The Inns were influential parts of a culture that did not bracket off imaginative practices from each other, literary and intellectual centers, and members were both creators and consumers of literature who assumed an easy transit between the legal and the literary. In the 1616 dedication to his play *Every Man Out of His Humour* (first performed in 1599), Ben Jonson offered his paean: "To the Noblest Nourceries of Humanity, and Liberty, in the Kingdome: the Innes of Court."

II

Mooting emerged as an identifiable practice in the Inns late in the fourteenth century; it enjoyed its heyday during the decades from 1450 to 1550; and it slowly faded until its curtailment in 1642.[16] Attempts to revive the practice in 1660 failed, and it never recovered its former importance as a site where doctrine was performed, fabricated, and challenged.[17] At its end, "the age-old obligation to moot [had been] commuted to cash payment."[18] Intellectual currency had mutated into coin, and the bencher, whose very designation insisted that he have his bottom firmly planted on English oak, had become the paid advocate, whose affiliations might shift as readily as two pence changed hands—a metamorphosis bitterly dramatized in Jonson's *Volpone* by the advocate Voltore, a "mercenary tongue" who "For six sols more would plead against his Maker."[19]

The basic structure of moots included four parts: (1) the problem; (2) the question arising from the problem; (3) the disputation, arguments pro and contra; and (4) the solution, any authoritative answer or ruling given by the teacher.[20] In elaborating the questions arising from the problem, a student typically listed copious illustrative examples. The more, and the more comprehensive, the examples, the better. "It does not seem to have mattered too much whether they were examples ever likely to be met with in the real world," Baker concludes, "though of course the law teacher's most unlikely academic fantasies have a habit of coming true. The prime purpose seems to have been to exercise the mind, in showing how the principles worked in hypothetical situations, rather than to explore new doctrine, criticise old doctrine, or open up loopholes."[21]

Since mooting involved performance, the customary practice at Middle Temple, where the same rooms served as sites for reveling and for solemn legal disputation, provides a glimpse of its social and pedagogical themes.

> The new barristers . . . are, for their degree, to perform each of them two several assignments of moots; which exercises are done in the hall in the termtime only, every Tuesday and Thursday night immediately after supper. The case is framed with apt and proper pleadings unto it by the two utter barristers

who are to perform the assignment. These pleadings are recited by two gentlemen under the bar, one of which speaks for the plaintiff, the other for the defendant.... Immediately after supper the benchers assemble themselves in the bay window at the upper end of the hall; where standing in order according to their antiquity, there repair unto them two gentlemen under the bar whose turn it is to hear the pleadings. Who, after a low obeisance, demand whether it be their pleasure to hear a moot, and depart with an affirmative answer.... When it is agreed on who are to argue, all the benchers depart out of the hall, leaving the rest of the company there. The two arguers walk a turn in the court or garden until the hall be prepared and made ready for them; which being done, they return into the hall and stay at the cupboard, demanding if the mootmen be ready.... [A]ll parties being ready, the two benchers appointed to argue, together with the reader elect, take their places at the bench table, the ancient bencher sitting in the midst, the second on his right hand, and the reader-elect on his left. Then the mootmen also take their place, sitting on a form close to the cupboard and opposite to the benchers. On the one side of them sits one of the students that recites the pleading, and the other on the other side. The pleadings are first recited by the students, then the case put and argued by the barristers, and lastly by the reader-elect and benchers, in manner and form aforesaid.... The moot being ended, all parties return to the cupboard, where the mootmen present the benchers with a cup of beer and a slice of bread; and so the exercise for that night is ended.[22]

The scene is a model of ideal pedagogical form. Time is made regular, useful, and precise: "every Tuesday and Thursday night," "immediately after supper." Rank is vigilantly differentiated and observed in the distribution of tasks: "the new barristers," "two utter barristers," "two gentlemen under the bar." Space is apportioned to replicate wider cultural values: "in the bay window at the upper end of the hall"; "two benchers take their place at the bench table." And bodies are positioned to reproduce a hierarchy of class, seniority, and deference: "standing in order of their antiquity," "after a low obeisance."

In his work on proximity, anthropologist M. L. J. Abercrombie explains that "spatial relationships of the objects and furnishings... convey information about the roles of the people using them." In mooting, benchers are positioned above and below the bar, above and below the cupboard, at the upper end of the hall, or at the center of the table. "Conventions of this kind," Abercrombie finds, "not only demonstrate the roles to be played by people, but support the people in their roles and make it difficult for them to adopt alternative ones."[23] Place signifies status, and figures of higher rank occupy higher spaces, "as though the more important person needs more [rarified] air to breathe."[24] Further, the process of mooting offers its concluding ritual of fellowship—sharing a cup of beer and slice of bread—as its *achievement*, as though the entire ceremony that preceded it were necessary to reach this moment of community. That achieved community is an effect of repetition, of taking the self through the same physical and mental acts that previous generations of students enacted. The performance is engaged in the paradox of constructing a "natural" affiliation among new barristers, as well as among new barristers and those of the distant past, by repeating a ritual practice.

These performances represent a utopia of embodied status in which each member of the society becomes a potential relay point in a widely dispersed network of judging and normalizing.[25] The success of the strategy as a pedagogical model depends upon its use of simple instruments, invisible to us now because embodied then, including a raised eyebrow, a bemused frown, or an encouraging nod. It disciplines by means of observation, integrating the details of surveillance into the teaching relationship. It organizes the minds and bodies of the scholars and constitutes them as objects of political work. Their study is regular and measurable; it is orderly and constant; and it serves both the self and the nation. "Look at the aspiring bencher," the practice seems to say. "In his relation to himself, a relation of discipline and labor, he reveals his relation to the laws of the land and exemplifies yours as well."

As it is represented in these performances, the relation of the subject to the law is one of inserting the self into a vital, continuing tradition. Exercises are regulated and administered with a strong sense of history revived, performed always "by the ancient custom of the house."[26] The terms for positioning the agents of the arguments emphasize self-effacement or immersion in a group. They train the subject to discover and realize itself within aggregate designations: "Une gent dient"; "ascuns diont"; "semble a auters"; "moy semble." The effect of this anonymity is to cast the disputes themselves as what "some" and "others" say, normalizing the anonymous speaking subjects as voices of "gentlemen" in a collective mentality. "Our laws are not individual, but communal and positional," this anonymity suggests; "they do not see or make visible prejudices of nature, nurture, and politics." Understood as a pedagogy aimed at inserting individuals into a collective and monovocal version of law, the practice of mooting supports a conservative agenda. In it, to become an English man means to affiliate oneself with what a historically generated "some" continue to "say" about the nation as it is represented in legal tradition. To be able to reproduce certain readings means that one is in possession of a particular version of English national identity.

Against the conservatism, however, the speculative play that characterizes moot texts creates an ideological instability at the center of the practice. Thematically and theoretically readings were devoted to collective wisdom and "common learning," yet in practice mooters "were always testing by disputation the borders of that common learning."[27] Although the purpose of mooting was the preservation of the common learning concerning property, that preservation was predicated paradoxically on keeping doubts alive and raising questions. Mooters were encouraged to invent what Baker labels "mind-stretching remote contingenc[ies]" and extemporaneous exceptions to pleadings.[28]

In *Purity and Danger,* Mary Douglas reminds us that different cultures perceive different things as dangerous and react differently to those perceptions.[29] Both the perception of danger and its solution, according to Douglas, are effects of "cultural bias."[30] What is the "bias" of these legal tales? Like other fictions, specific moots advance plots, suggest character (conventionally in archetypal terms), arrange space, and develop imaginative landscapes. What do they perceive as the dangers to which laws must respond? Positioning mootmen as the proprietors of something called "this realm," what do moots perceive as potential sources of and solutions to jeopardy?

The substantial majority of moots focus on claims of parties seeking to recover land or debts or other forms of property. Men and women are dispossessed, enter leases for life by indenture, marry strangers, convert to friars and abbesses, renounce their religion, die without heirs or die with multiple heirs, in cases that are compendia of the multiple legal actions a subject might (or might not) perform. Each event in a moot becomes a prompt for argument, as competing legal customs or statutes are pitted against each other. Cases conclude with forms of the question (typically in law French) "Ceux que droit en ount sont a lour recoverie," or, as it is roughly translated by Baker, "The parties with the right wish to be advised how to go about their recovery."[31] We find cases beginning:

> Someone makes a bond to two women; one of them marries an outlaw; the day arrives; the husband dies; the escheator obtains the deed.

Or

> A man and a single woman carry off the goods of an abbot; the man marries the same woman; the abbot gives all his goods to the husband; the abbot commits a felony for which he is attainted, and another is elected.

Or

> Someone makes a bond to another man and a single woman in £20, on condition that if he pays £10 at a certain day the bond will be void; the person who made the bond marries the same woman; the man to whom the bond was made appoints his executors, enters into religion, and is professed.[32]

The first part of the mooting exercise was to choose a writ (that is, an action under law), the parties to the action, and names for the parties. Even here, the imaginative strategies of mooting were activated: in naming the parties, students sometimes chose the names of real people (whether the case had or had not been based on a real action), sometimes their own names, and sometimes fictional names for the agents in the legal story. Every phrase in the imaginary case was an occasion for discussion, as pleadings "designed to raise all the questions secreted in the moot problem" followed one another.[33] Each part of the case might evoke separate pleas; each plea could raise a different aspect of the question; exceptions often emerged to questionable pleadings, and these exceptions themselves could be fully argued. Even if a plea were ruled bad, the student could simply go on to plead something else. Final rulings were made by the teachers, the Inns' pedagogical representation of the court of Common Pleas.[34]

Two often-repeated, classic cases serve as my examples of the England imagined in moots. In each, a particular figure threatens to disturb the smooth transmission of property. To preserve the distinctive flavor of these imaginary cases, I quote one here at length:

> Two brothers, who are villeins, purchase jointly certain land to which an advowson is appendant; the lord enters and leases the same land with the appurtenances to the two of them to hold in villeinage; the elder brother dies, his wife being secretly pregnant; the lord marries the same woman, who is delivered of a son and dies; the lord takes another wife and dies, his wife being secretly pregnant; the younger brother marries the same woman, who has a son, and then the wife dies; he takes another wife, who is pregnant by him before the espousals; the husband dies; the woman is delivered of two twin sons, namely Jacob and Esau; the elder brother's son enters in one moiety, and the three sons in the other moiety, but the attendancy is made to the elder brother's son; the three sons enter and make partition among themselves; the [elder] twin son grants what belongs to him and what belongs to

his younger brother to an abbot, unto him and his successors; the lord's son brings a writ of right of advowson against him, and after the mise joined he is nonsuited; then the elder twin son enters into religion in the same abbey; the abbot is deposed, and he is elected abbot; then the church becomes vacant; the abbot presents; and he is hindered by the three. Etc. Discuss.[35]

Since my purpose is not to debate the legitimacy of the law, I want to set aside certain prominent features, in particular the unfamiliar (or defamiliarizing) legal terms and the details of statutes regarding conveyance of property, in order to focus on how the case images the nation. No matter where he intervenes, the mootman enters a long line of memorializing. There is in this representation, as Glenn Clark as written in another context, "no natural, nonsocialized geography with which to start."[36] Representing a privileged spatial practice, the moot ensures uninterrupted transmission of property by offering verbal sequence as temporal continuity. In this, moots as a genre resemble the popular chronicle histories contemporary with them. Phyllis Rackin has shown how chronicles, "[o]rganized by temporal sequence and divided into units that represented the reigns of successive kings, . . . told the histories of royal dynasties."[37] Also organized by temporal sequence and divided into units that represent the ownership of successive husband-fathers, moots tell the histories of the commonwealth in its analogous form of the family.

Yet the intellectual or imaginative properties foregrounded in moots are largely non sequiturs, and their themes are the precariousness of life, the vulnerability of marriage, the changeability of the self, and the mortality of humankind. In this series of threshold experiences, brothers die, wives bear children, husbands perish, ad infinitum in endless repetition. The repetition promises to continue beyond the bounds of the school-case, and there is no apparent closure within the case. It stops rather than concludes. It imagines a place in constant jeopardy from undisclosed pregnancies, from arbitrary deaths, from men suddenly struck by religion. The force of the repetition makes it seem that England will continue well after an individual's claims on it end.

The association of marriage and property in moots carries us to the issue of women and chastity. When the female first appears, she is already both married and pregnant: "the elder brother dies, his wife being secretly pregnant," "the lord takes another wife and dies, his wife being secretly pregnant," "he takes another wife, who is pregnant by him before the espousals." When she emerges into visibility, it is as a representative of the category "wife" and, more precisely, as "pregnant wife"; in two cases, she is "secretly pregnant wife." Why does the moot keep these pregnancies "secret"? To whom are they unknown? The husband? The village? In these patterns, the moot demonstrates the remarkable mobility of the law; it is never stagnant. Here it preserves land transmission, wards off the social consequences of adultery and cuckoldry, and sustains the subject's honor and authority. It is as though the imaginative process had taken the legal concept of *femme covert* and enlivened it, and we witness an endlessly repeatable process of covering or subsuming a wife. Visible primarily as she is subsumed into a husband in marriage, the woman is always already an element in a teleology of matrimony that not only privileges heterosexuality but also equates it with reproduction.

While the representation of woman-as-wife-mother may be obvious given the topic of the linear conveyance of land, it also enforces an idea already in place in the culture about one role of the female: her position in an order of generation.[38] The moot sees certain possible disruptions—caused by secretly pregnant wives—to linear conveyance of property; it sees those potential disruptions as threatening to erode the legitimacy of the family name from within; and it resolves those questions of legitimacy by including both the pregnancy and its secrecy within the modes of legal succession. If a patriarchal culture fears female adultery because it can "make a mockery of the whole story of patriarchal succession,"[39] the moot is curiously tranquil: what counts is not the specter of an adulteress but the sequence of spouses and children. Linked in moots to the ideology of uninterrupted land succession, women are represented as "honest" by their links to clear kinship relations and to marriage.

In my second classic case, certain conventional themes recur, especially those associated with bloodline and legitimate transmission of property: "the son of the whole blood," that is, the son of the husband and wife with whom the case begins, claims property; "the brother of the half blood" also contends for the land; and "the son of the second issue enters" a case.

Added to the dynamic of imaging England in this moot, however, is another figure: the stranger. The case begins when a man holding land "marries a wife, they have issue two daughters, and die"; the daughters arrange "partition" so that each holds a portion of the land:

> [T]he elder marries; she and her husband have issue a son and a daughter; the husband dies; she marries another husband and they have issue a son and die; the issue by the first marriage leases the same land to a woman for life upon condition that if he grants the reversion to anyone else she shall

have fee; he then grants the reversion to a stranger; the tenant for life by his lease recovers; the person to whom the reversion was granted enters upon the woman; she brings an assize and recovers.[40]

Not all blood is created equal ("whole" and "half" characterizing the strength of a relationship to the land), yet the case allows figures of "half blood" to enter claims. These designations ensure the smooth transmission of property, but the logic of social legitimacy also works in reverse: bloodline legitimates the son's possession, but his legal possession also implies that he participates in the legitimate bloodline, whatever the biological facts might be. What fascinates me, however, is the stranger. He is a recurring type in moots, and he typically enters late in the story: *after* a landholder has committed a felony, lost his land, had daughters, and died, "the second grantee grants his services to a stranger for the term of his life"; *after* a villein has purchased land, had three daughters, bequeathed land, purchased more, married, had a son, and died, "the son aliens to a stranger." The stranger's story is a tale of belatedness, of deferring to an England that precedes and succeeds him; he always arrives a little too late to possess the realm.

Unlike women, however, the stranger is typically associated with danger of a specifically Calvinist slant: "What will remain safe in human society," Calvin had asked, "if license be given to bring in by stealth the offspring of a stranger? to steal a name which may be given to spurious offspring? and to transfer to them property taken from lawful heirs?"[41] As the moot positions him, the stranger begins as a figure unrelated to recognizable kinship bonds—"he then grants the reversion to a stranger"—and his function is to be suspended there unless (or until) he can be anchored in the soil or in sexual fertility. Were he able either to purchase or marry into the land, the stranger would be domesticated and made familiar by his ability to associate with the earth in terms the moot found acceptable. Here, however, the moot repels the stranger—"the person [stranger] to whom the reversion was granted enters upon the woman; she brings an assize and recovers"—preserving the family's orientation to each other and to the land at issue. Demonstrating the law's capacity to accommodate what it finds disorienting, the representation does significant cultural work: before expelling the stranger, it repositions him from potential threat to potential ally and from intruder to property owner, a figure whose legitimacy might be subsequently ensured by his right to transmit property. Before the stranger loses the case, the idea of land ownership temporarily eases his foreignness.

The imaginary worlds represented in moots are ordered by the recurrence of transience. It is not only the student's psyche or the English law that comes to seem mobile but the land itself, as it is verbally transported from claimant to claimant. This is the universe at its most Faustian, in which allegorical figures and archetypes appear willy-nilly, impinging on the idea of the stability of place. On one hand, moots involve a process of transforming the remote into the familiar and the improbable into the likely. On the other hand, they involve a complementary counterprocess, that of making the familiar strange and uncertain by calling down into the quotidian world curses, tragedies, and disasters. In this, moots are akin to the genre of romance, which accommodates the marvelous and unnatural to its morality. Moots can also be said to evoke a need for the vigilance they demand: they produce as problems (or perceive as dangers) events they also exist to resolve. (We might also note that in this logic preserving the legitimate transmission of the land is formally coterminous with preserving the Inns.) They accustom mootmen to a view of history in which the nation is always on the brink of dissolution, its continued existence threatened by events that might go unforeseen were it not for the custodial eyes of the members of the Inns of Court.

The practice of mooting provides one arena for exploring what lies latent in particular conceptions of "place." The England organized in these cases is eternal yet precariously situated; its soil is perpetually in jeopardy of masterlessness, misappropriation, or reversion to wilderness; and its residents are fickle, transient, mortal. Embedded in a pedagogy of fellowship, what moots most fear—and most often dramatize—is the potential for English soil quite suddenly to become what Douglas calls "matter out of order"—that is, dirt, with all its moral connotations.[42] What holds the soil in place, what "Englishes" it, are some of the least interrogated foundations of legal storytelling: acts of imagination.

III

Whether John Gassner is right in saying that Thomas Sackville and Thomas Norton, both of whom became members of Queen Elizabeth's first Parliament, "thought of themselves chiefly as statesmen enforcing a warning against divided rule in the kingdom rather than as professional playwrights," what is certain is that these authors of *Gorboduc* practiced both politics and playwrighting: Sackville, who was a barrister of the Inner Temple, later the Earl of Dorset, and Lord High Treasurer of England, and Norton, who became a distinguished lawyer, collaborated to produce the Senecan tragedy.[43] The drama premiered in the Hall of the Inner Temple, where both authors were students, and it was repeated before Queen Elizabeth in a command performance.[44]

Focused on challenges to succession, *Gorboduc* entertains a series of questions about divided kingdoms and the transmission of the monarchy before it resolves them at play's end firmly on the side of a single, native-born ruler. In his impressive reading, Franco Moretti argues that early scenes between Gorboduc and his counselors signal the beginnings of a sustained "deconsecration of kingship" in English drama throughout the sixteenth century. According to Moretti, in advising Gorboduc about dividing his kingdom among his sons, the counselors offer "reason." Gorboduc responds, however, not with counter-reasons, but with "will." And although in an ideal world a ruler possesses both, in Sackville and Norton's play will begins to dominate. Still, Moretti argues, in contrast to a later play like *Measure for Measure*, *Gorboduc* believes that these attributes ought to go together: a king must operate with both, or the kingdom will be destroyed.[45]

In taking jeopardy to the country as its recurring imaginative pattern, *Gorboduc* also reveals its kinship with the thematic and ideological work of moots. Both the play and the legal ritual represent privileged spatial practices: they both make claims on "Britain land" through evocations of a country in jeopardy. Both are vehicles for evoking anticipation and fear of disaster: "I wish not this, O king, so to befall, / But fear the thing, that I do most abhor" (1.2.367–68); "Lo, here the peril that was erst foreseen, / When you, O king, did first divide your land" (3.1.135–36). In *Gorboduc*, as in moots, there is no natural, nonsocialized geography with which to start. It is less royal succession that interests me here, however, than the two figures who most often disturb the world characterized in moots: the woman and the stranger, both of whom return in Sackville and Norton's play, where they retain their associations with disrupting social order.

We saw earlier that the woman enters moots as an element in a teleology of marriage, heterosexuality, and childbearing. The moot envisions certain possible disruptions, such as secretly pregnant wives, to linear conveyance of property; it perceives those as threatening to erode the legitimacy of the family name; and it solves questions of legitimacy by including the pregnancy and its secrecy within modes of legal paternal succession.

What is latent in the moot—that the female *could* disturb the line—is mined as the central issue in Sackville and Norton's work, announced when Videna revises the meaning of paternity: "A father? no: / In kind a father, not in kindliness" (1.1.17–18), she tells Ferrex. Videna is both guarantor of hereditary kinship *and* destroyer of emotional kinship. Where there ought to be a father, head of household and kingdom, there is instead a jealous spouse competing with his son for his wife's attentions:

> For, knowing well, my son, the tender love
> That I have ever borne, and bear to thee;
> He grieved thereat, is not content alone
> To spoil thee of my sight, my chiefest joy,
> But thee, of thy birth-right and heritage,
> Causeless, unkindly, and in wrongful wise,
> Against all law and right, he will bereave.
> (1.1.22–29)

What the moots struggle to secure, the smooth transmission of property through women, *Gorboduc* takes as its center of conflict, and although Ferrex evokes a hereditary assurance—"Their [the counselors'] ancestors from race to race have borne / True faith to my forefathers and their seed; / I trust they eke will bear the like to me" (1.1.51–53)—Videna anticipates disaster: "when lords and trusted rulers under kings, / To please the present fancy of the prince, / With wrong transpose the course of governance," Jove "roots their names and kindred from the earth" (1.1.59–67). The implied conveyance of the country through generations into an unexpressed infinity that characterizes moots becomes here a deliberately disrupted conveyance in which the woman, who typically authorizes sequence and succession, is displaced by the ruler, who himself disturbs the "natural" course of events: it is Gorboduc who chooses to divide his kingdom and bestow equal portions on both his sons.

As we saw earlier, moots emphasize individual ownership of property—possession is imagined as successive rather than contemporary. One effect of these representations is to divide men from each other as potential owners: forms of ownership or governance that might include collaboration or collective rule are excluded, made invisible. Yet what the moots make invisible *Gorboduc* makes visible, only to show co-ownership precipitating disaster. Videna speaks for the conservative view: traditional sequence and primogeniture should continue their authority. By replacing the traditional view with the invisible one, Gorboduc abdicates not only his crown but his claims to emotional paternity.

Videna's role as an insert into linear transmission of property is interrogated and made emotionally crucial in her soliloquy following Ferrex's death. She imagines Porrex as a murderous villain, and she imagines herself mother to only one son, Ferrex: "O my beloved son! O my sweet child! / My dear Ferrex, my joy, my life's delight!" (4.1.23–24). When she does recall her other son, Porrex, it is in order to articulate her separation from him: "Traitor to kin and kind, to sire and me, / To thine own flesh, and traitor to thyself" (4.1.31–32). Yet in a corresponding fit of imagination she emphasizes her bodily relationship to both her sons. Cursing what she identifies as Porrex's blood lust, she mourns "he who in the self-same womb was wrapp'd, / Where thou in dismal hour received'st life" (4.1.51–52), and she wishes away her role as the link among the men: "if needs, needs thy hand must slaughter make, / Mightest thou not have reach'd a mortal wound, / And with thy sword have pierc'd this cursed womb / That the accursed Porrex brought to light" (4.1.53–55). Videna's body becomes the center of the kinship and kindliness she refutes:

> Shall I still think that from this womb thou sprung?
> That I thee bare? or take thee for my son?
> No, traitor, no; I thee refuse for mine:
> Murderer, I thee renounce; thou are not mine.
> Never, O wretch, this womb conceived thee;
> Nor never bode I painful throws for thee.
> Changeling to me thou art, and not my child.
> (4.1.63–69)

Refused the birthright he shared with Ferrex, the Porrex Videna imagines is an uncivilized spawn of the land, denied both maternity and paternity: "wild and desert woods bred thee to life" (4.1.76). In Videna, all the links that moot cases evoke are undone. It is as though Sackville and Norton were interrogating the figure of the woman in moots, the silent female whose body is testimony to the legitimate paternity that assures land ownership, and finding in her other ways to comprehend succession and land transmission. When courtiers report that "the people . . . have slain their sovereign lord and queen" (5.1.5–7), it is specifically Videna who is culpable: the people "falsely charge / The guiltless king, without desert at all; / And traitorously have murder'd him therefore, / And eke the queen" (5.1.14–17). The play represents the consequences of woman's deliberate breach of succession as cosmic disaster: Videna murders Porrex and produces, in Marcella's terms, a "world / Drowned in blood, and sunk in cruelty" (4.2.250–51).

As he does in moots, in *Gorboduc* the stranger also becomes prominent, associated again with the homeland's vulnerability to possession by an outsider. And although in moots the stranger simply arrives and is inserted into a line of land transmission, in Sackville and Norton's work the stranger takes advantage of a political vacuum, entering a country already conditioned for enforced possession: "Lo Britain realm is left an open prey" (5.2.353). Disruptions to succession are figured as producing a vacuum in leadership that makes the realm vulnerable to a stranger's secret ambitions:

> The realm is reft both of their king and queen,
> The offspring of the prince is slain and dead,
> No issue now remains, the heir unknown,
> The people are in arms and mutinies,
> The nobles, they are busy how to cease
> These great rebellions, tumults and uproars;
> And Britain land, now desert left alone
> Amid these broils uncertain where to rest,
> Offers herself to that noble heart
> That will or dare pursue to bear her crown.
> (5.1.126–35)

Forging a conceptual link between the alien and servitude, the play imagines Albany's possession of Britain not as leadership but as enslavement *because* he is a foreigner. Against Albany's desires, Arostus praises the lords who agree "to save your realm, and in this realm yourselves, / From foreign thraldom of so proud a prince" (5.2.281–82); he emphasizes that "the proud attempts of this Albanian prince . . . threatens thraldom to your native land" (5.2.299–300).

In a dynamic of rhetorical and conceptual "othering," Britain here is imagined as a superior place and society preferable to a less civilized "other." Contemporary early modern discourses make clear an even stronger sense of a conceptual link between a man and his birthplace. A firm link to a particular birthplace was understood as enabling one to predict a man's character; birthplace anticipated behavior. In his *Arte of Rhetorique*, for example, Thomas Wilson makes it clear that theories of place are significant modes of explanation in early modern culture. "The country," he writes, "declares [a man's] natural inclinations." Wilson offers an especially useful version of the available meanings compressed into a theory of locale in 1560: "The Realme declares the nature of the people. So that some Countrey bringeth more honor with it, then an other doth. To be a French man, descending there of a noble house, is more honor than to be an Irish man: to bee an English man borne, is much more honor than to bee a Scot, because by these men, worthie Prowesses have beene done, and greater affaires by them attempted, then have beene done by any other."[46] To ensure the continuity of the values and honors originating in a particular place, the figures in *Gorboduc* are warned to choose a ruler from their homeland:

> ... let be your chosen king,
> Such one so born within your native land;
> Such one prefer, and in no wise admit
> The heavy yoke of foreign governance:
> Let foreign titles yield to public wealth.
> (5.2.331–35)

and "keep out also / Unnatural thraldom of a stranger's reign; / Ne suffer you, against the rules of kind, / Your mother land to serve a foreign prince" (5.2.338–41). As the stranger crosses from moots into the drama, he remains demonized and beyond domestication. Rather than the land naturalizing him, he makes it foreign, thereby converting it into a wasteland: "The wasted soil shall yield forth no fruit, / But dearth and famine shall possess the land" (5.2.387–88). Only a ruler with a relation to a "native line / Or ... some former law," one "born within your native land," can ward off possession by a stranger: "Such a one prefer, and in no wise admit / The heavy yoke of foreign governance" (5.2.328–35). Forging an affiliation between a "native born" man and "Britain land," *Gorboduc* returns the country to a legitimate ruler by verbally constructing a "natural" affinity between governor and governed. The true proprietor of the country is a natural-born English man.

IV

Near the end of *Gorboduc*, Eubulus in soliloquy eulogizes a lost Britain and laments that "though so many books, so many rolls / Of Ancient time" report the bloody consequences of rebellion and dissent, men "forget" the lessons of their history. Taking its cue from the practice of mooting, Sackville and Norton's play aims to remind men of those lessons. Unabashedly didactic and conservative, both moots and the play urge the English man to perceive himself as the "natural" proprietor of the realm, to be wary of the woman and the stranger, and to insert himself into a sustained tradition of envisioning "Britain land." Like the England organized in moots, *Gorboduc*'s homeland is represented as eternal yet precariously situated; its soil, too, is in perpetual jeopardy of masterlessness, misappropriation, or reversion to wilderness; it residents, too, are fickle, transient, mortal. Representing fictive struggles to anticipate and avoid "the unnatural thraldom of a stranger's reign" (5.2.339), both the Inns of Court and Sackville and Norton's theater secure the realm in acts of imagination.

NOTES

Portions of this essay dealing with mooting practices are reprinted from Karen Cunningham's *Imaginary Betrayals: Subjectivity and the Discourses of Treason in Early Modern England* (Philadelphia: University of Pennsylvania Press, 2002) and appear here by permission of the press.

1. Michel Foucault, *Discipline and Punish: On the Birth of the Prison*, trans. Alan Sheridan (New York: Vintage Books, 1979), 106. For one of his most extensive definitions of "power," which he perceives as dispersed and disunified, see 26–27. On court-centered power, see, for example, Jonathan Goldberg, *James I and the Politics of Literature* (Baltimore: Johns Hopkins University Press, 1983); Stephen Greenblatt, *Shakespearean Negotiations: The Circulation of Social Energy in Renaissance England* (Berkeley: University of California Press, 1988); Stephen Greenblatt, ed., *The Forms of Power and the Power of Forms in the Renaissance* (Norman: University of Oklahoma Press, 1982); and Leonard Tennenhouse, *Power on Display: The Politics of Shakespeare's Genres* (New York: Methuen, 1986).

2. J. H. Baker, "The Inns of Court and Legal Doctrine," in *Lawyers and Laymen*, ed. T. M. Charles-Edwards et al. (Cardiff: University of Wales Press, 1986), 283. Although they did not make law in the sense of establishing statutes, readers of moots did contribute to the consolidation and explanation of unwritten principles, establishing a tradition as to what was received learning and what was dubious. The influence of law schools, though unofficial, was deep. "Indeed, Littleton himself offered to 'prove' a proposition in the *Tenures* by saying he had often heard it in the readings on Westminster II, c. 3. It will be noted that the reference is not to a specific reader, but to a repeated assertion" (Baker, "Inns of Court," 278).

3. Ibid., 283.

4. In this essay I use the more general term *mooting* to describe all instances of speculative, theoretical study, including the related practice of *reading*, which described cases put without pleadings. See the descriptions in J. H. Baker, *Readings and Moots at the Inns of Court in the Fifteenth Century*, vol. 2, *Moots and Readers' Cases*, ed. Samuel E. Thorne and J. H. Baker (London: Seldon Society, 1990), xxiii–xxxiii and lxiv–lxv; and Philip Smith, *A History of Education for the English Bar* (London: Butterworth's, 1860), 21–40.

5. *Gorboduc*, ed. John Gassner, in *Medieval and Tudor Drama* (New York: Applause, 1983), 403–53. Subsequent references to the play are to this edition. For important studies of the *in utramque partem* tradition in rhetoric, see Joel Altman, *The Tudor Play of Mind* (Berkeley: University of California Press, 1978), and Victoria Kahn, *Rhetoric, Prudence, and Skepticism in the Renaissance* (Ithaca: Cornell University Press, 1985).

6. Baker, *Readings and Moots*, xvi.

7. Baker, "Inns of Court," 278. Although questions of real property dominated moots, topics did sometimes also extend to criminal law: Baker lists a series of questions about homicide, for example, that formed part of the "readings." Although readers could not lecture on the common law as such, there were pretexts for doing so under the guise of statutory interpretation (279–80).

8. Baker, *Readings and Moots*, xv.

9. Quoted in Smith, *History of Education*, 31–32.

10. Quoted in Jonathan Dollimore, *Radical Tragedy: Religion, Ideology and Power in the Drama of Shakespeare and His Contemporaries* (Brighton: Harvester Press, 1984), 17.

11. L. W. Abbott finds that the Inns were "the clearing-houses for much of the legal literature produced." L. W. Abbott, *Law Reporting in England, 1485–1585* (London: Athlone Press, 1973), 31.

12. Philip Finkelpearl, *John Marston of the Middle Temple* (Cambridge, MA: Harvard University Press, 1969), 19. For a discussion of the literary movement in the Inns at this time, see also 20–31.

13. Sir Philip Sidney, "An Apology for Poetry," in *Critical Theory since Plato*, rev. ed., ed. Hazard Adams (New York: Harcourt, 1992), 155.

14. Gassner, *Medieval and Tudor Drama*, 404.

15. Finkelpearl, *John Marston*, 21–26 and 78.

16. Baker, *Readings and Moots*, xxviii.

17. Baker, "Inns of Court," 281.

18. Baker, *Readings and Moots*, lxxvi.

19. Ben Jonson, *Volpone, or the Fox*, ed. Jonas Barish (Arlington Heights, IL: AHM Press, 1958), 4.2.122–27. For the historical process of paid attorneys distinguishing themselves from benchers, see Wilfrid R. Prest, *The Inns of Court under Elizabeth I and the Early Stuarts, 1590–1640* (London: Longman, 1972).

20. Baker, *Readings and Moots*, xvii. See also Altman, *Tudor Play of Mind*, 229.

21. Baker, "Inns of Court," 276.

22. Quoted in Baker, *Readings and Moots*, lxi. See also Smith, *History of Education*, 14–41.

23. M. L. J. Abercrombie, "Face to Face: Proximity and Distance," in *Rules and Meanings: The Anthropology of Everyday Knowledge*, ed. Mary Douglas (Baltimore: Penguin Books, 1973), 92.

24. Ibid., 92.

25. For ideas on disciplinary gestures that shape this paragraph, see Foucault, *Discipline and Punish*, 156, 170, and 175.

26. Smith, *History of Education*, 29.

27. Baker, "Inns of Court," 278.

28. Ibid., 280. See also Smith, *History of Education*, 21–22.

29. Douglas, *Purity and Danger: An Analysis of Concepts of Pollution and Taboo* (New York: Frederick Praeger, 1966).

30. Mary Douglas, *Cultural Bias* (London: Royal Anthropological Institute of Great Britain and Ireland, 1978).

31. Baker, *Readings and Moots*, xlvi.

32. The Snavernake Manuscript, cases 29, 21, and 15, respectively; in Baker, *Readings and Moots*, 9, 7, 5. For a historical account of the development of legal learning exercises in England, which included lecture and disputation, early teacher-driven forms of mooting, and moots with full student participation, see Baker, *Readings and Moots*, xvi–xxv and xxx–xxxiii. An overview of collections of mootable cases and moot books is in Baker, *Readings and Moots*, xxxiii–xlv.

33. Ibid., xlviii.

34. Ibid.

35. The Muschamp manuscript, case 5a, in Baker, *Readings and Moots*, 17–18.

36. Glenn Clark, "The 'Strange' Geographies of *Cymbeline*," in *Playing the Globe: Genre and Geography in English Renaissance Drama*, ed. John Gillies and Virginia Mason Vaughan (Madison, NJ: Fairleigh Dickinson University Press, 1998), 234.

37. Phyllis Rackin, *Stages of History: Shakespeare's English Chronicles* (Ithaca: Cornell University Press, 1990), 24.

38. See Michel Foucault, *The History of Sexuality*, trans. Robert Hurley (New York: Vintage Books, 1980), 4.

39. Rackin, *Stages of History*, 160.

40. Muschamp manuscript, case 4a; in Baker, *Readings and Moots*, 16–17.

41. Quoted in Mark Breitenberg, *Anxious Masculinity in Early Modern England* (Cambridge: Cambridge University Press, 1996), 70. On the idea that male relations are constructed through women, see also Eve Kosofsky Sedgwick, *Between Men: English Literature and Male Homosocial Desire* (New York: Columbia University Press, 1985). For a convenient overview of critical positions regarding representations of "self-Other," see R. S. Khare, "The Other's Double—The Anthropologist's Bracketed Self: Notes on Cultural Representation and Privileged Discourse," *New Literary History* 23 (Winter 1992): 1–23; Edward Said, *Orientalism* (New York: Vintage Books, 1978); and Clifford Geertz, *Local Knowledge: Further Essays in Interpretive Anthropology* (New York: Basic Books, 1983).

42. Douglas, *Purity and Danger*, 1.

43. Gassner, *Medieval and Tudor Drama*, 405.

44. Ibid., 404.

45. Franco Moretti, "'A Huge Eclipse': Tragic Form and the Deconsecration of Sovereignty," in Greenblatt, *Forms of Power*, 7–40.

46. Thomas Wilson, *Wilson's Arte of Rhetorique, 1560*, ed. G. H. Mair (Oxford: Clarendon Press, 1919), 12–13.

NINE

The Rich Cabinet
Bacon, Chapman, and the Culture of Corruption

Luke Wilson

Sixteenth- and seventeenth-century common-law reasoning about bribery was strikingly undeveloped. Its conceptual underpinnings were rarely enunciated explicitly, and its legislative and case histories aroused comparatively little interest. In his discussion of the term in *Third Institutes,* Coke cites mostly cases under Richard II or earlier, and he is primarily concerned with demonstrating that bribery should not be considered a felony rather than with the features of the crime itself; he mentions the recent case of Francis Bacon, of course, but his account gives scarcely a hint of contemporary interest in bribery and corruption, even though the second decade of the seventeenth century saw a sharp rise in their prosecution.[1] To name only the most prominent figures, within the space of seven years, Lord Treasurer Suffolk (Thomas Howard) and his wife in 1619, Lord Chancellor Bacon and Canterbury prerogative judge John Bennett, both in 1621, Lord Treasurer Cranfield in 1624, and Buckingham himself in 1626 were ruined by charges of bribery, extortion, and other forms of corruption.[2] The Crown had begun launching investigations of corruption in 1603, and Parliament in 1610, 1614, and 1621 aggressively investigated corrupt practices including monopolies, sale of offices, and bribery, passing several new pieces of legislation on bribery and sale of office and reviving the process of impeachment, last used in 1459.[3]

Not only did public and judicial scrutiny of corruption rise to new heights during the period, but the actual level of corruption, never of course absent from English government, did as well. Increasing undercompensation of government officials had at least since the 1550s forced officeholders to adopt questionable practices to meet the lifestyles demanded under a regime of conspicuous consumption; and since the accession of James the Crown's similar appetite for money had resulted in widespread sales of offices and honors (the introduction of the title of baronet) as well as customs farming and the sale of monopolies. These practices in turn provoked parliamentary demands for reform, which made things worse by hindering the free granting of money to the Crown and at the same time lighting a fire under James to sacrifice those most culpable for the abuses that his own financial needs had brought into being. By the 1630s, levels of corruption appear to have subsided, and the fact that Parliament did not meet between 1629 and 1640 meant the elimination of the court where the prosecution of the most prominent officeholders would have occurred.

The archive for an account of bribery and corruption from 1603 to 1644 is therefore rich. The case of Francis Bacon, whose political career was ended abruptly by accusations of bribery brought before the Parliament of 1621, is especially well documented. Drawing on both legal ideas of property and established protocols of gift exchange, the accounts of bribery transactions offered in testimony to Parliament, and in particular Bacon's own narratives about these transactions, offer a detailed picture of how licit and illicit exchanges were understood.[4] But bribery discourse extended beyond strictly political and legal contexts. It was a conceptually inevitable point of reference in both theological debates about man's agency in relation to God (God, of course, cannot be bribed; but if he is responsive to prayer, how exactly are specific appeals to God *not* bribes?), and in sermons focused on moral correction (the corrupt judge was routinely identified as among the most vile of misbehaving Christians).[5] Both these concerns, in turn, find expression in Jacobean drama, as when in *Measure for Measure* Isabella tells Angelo she'll bribe him, "not with fond sickles of the tested gold ... but with true prayers" (2.2.149–51). Indeed, the drama of Shakespeare, Webster, Chapman, and others shows more than a passing interest in corruption, especially as it is associated with the politics of the Jacobean court. Chapman's *Tragedy of Chabot* is especially germane to the case of Bacon, whether or not the play is, as has been suggested, a political allegory of Bacon's role in Somerset's trial in the Overbury affair and his own subsequent fall, for it provides a complex exploration of the relation between corruption in public office and the troubled nexus of generosity and dependence that both binds king and subject and thrusts them apart.⁶ Perhaps the most familiar theatrical metaphor for courtly corruption is the fountain that represents royal bounty but that, tainted by evil counsel, circulates poison throughout the land, as in Antonio's remark, at the beginning of *The Duchess of Malfi*, that

> a prince's court
> Is like a common fountain, whence should flow
> Pure silver drops in general; but, if 't chance
> Some curs'd example poison it near the head,
> Death and disease through the whole land spread.
> (1.1.11–15)

Webster's metaphor must have appealed to contemporaries because it distinguishes strategically between the source of value (the king, James for example) and the source of corruption (the evil counselor, Salisbury or Somerset for example), while preserving in displaced form the king's own liability for wrongs he himself has licensed in allowing his favorite free rein. Perhaps it seems so apt to us because its logic reveals corruption as *systemic*, with value originating in the king's bounty but nevertheless moving beyond his control, subject to a continual circulation in which value is added or lost with every subsequent transaction, every gesture of giving or taking, so that poison introduced anywhere may infect the whole. In light of modern historiography that seeks historical causation in systemic conditions, especially politico-economic conditions, rather than in individuals, and especially in the light of anthropological studies of gift exchange since Mauss's *Essai sur le don* (1923–24), which stressed the misrecognition of obligation upon which such exchange was understood to depend, up through Derrida's *Donner le temps* (1991), which follows through by insisting that since no "gift" is unmotivated, the gift as such is categorically impossible, scholars of early modern literature and politics quite rightly resist thinking of specific exchanges as ever perfectly self-aware or self-explanatory.⁷ Axiomatically, persons engaged in acts of exchange cannot reliably report what they are doing or why.

Yet, of course, sometimes they have a pretty good idea, and even when they are wrong they are wrong in interesting ways. If the metaphor of the fountain stresses systemic causes that seem to be identifiable and eradicable but often are not (as is suggested by the morally ambiguous endings of many early Stuart plays, where corruption seems to have metastasized beyond the point of surgical remedy), corrupt exchanges were also represented through equally traditional and equally powerful conceits in which the exchange nexus was singled out as conceptually, even corporeally, distinct. This is the case with *Chabot*. Similarly, although as I have already suggested Bacon's troubles in 1621 can be read persuasively in terms of systemic problems such as that of underpaid bureaucrats wielding unprecedented political and economic power (Bacon had no choice, and anyway everyone was doing it), or even in terms of mere political expediency and personal animosities (Bacon was framed), these explanations are unlikely to reveal much about what Bacon thought he was doing when he accepted what were later called bribes. Without losing sight of systemic explanations, what follows attempts to reconstruct the conceptual exercises through which individuals tried to make their acts of exchange meaningful to themselves and to give others an account of them.

In a modern taxonomy, if one were to measure the comparative legal standing of different varieties of exchange, the gift would occupy an uncertain middle between the contract and the bribe, which would be situated at either extreme (if a contract is a contract, it is enforceable; if a bribe is a bribe, it is illegal). The law has greater respect for a contract than for a gift, and for a gift than for a bribe: contract ⟶ gift ⟶ bribe. But on a line measuring not legal standing but a collective misrecognition, the enabling failure to understand that makes some practices possible, it is the bribe that occupies the uncertain middle ground in a sequence of increasing misrecognition: contract ⟶ bribe ⟶ gift. If the quantitative logic of reciprocity is in theory wholly transparent, wholly theorized and explicit, in the case of the contract, and at least sufficiently repressed and misrecognized in the case of the gift, the bribe combines these features in an unstable compounding of the unspoken and the spoken, the tacit and the explicit, the secret and the manifest. To sustain the illusion that the gift is free, the systematic repression of compulsory reciprocity must be collective, extending to all members of a community; to do its work, the bribe must be recognized as such by both the giver and the recipient but not by others. All gifts are perhaps bribes in the sense and to the extent that they extort a return gift; but the partners in a bribery transaction are not obliged to misrecognize this relation as noncoercive. On the contrary, for a bribe to function successfully, those involved must understand it to create an obligation. Bribery, in other words, calls for selective, rather than collective, misrecognition.

An early modern taxonomy would look rather different.[8] Although the notion of the pure, disinterested gift certainly existed, in practice most gift giving was understood as aimed at establishing reciprocal obligation; the notion that gifts were not normally free, that they did establish such obligation, cannot have seemed especially scandalous.[9] As the exchanges of the marketplace encroached ever further into the domains of other forms of exchange, the interested gift came to seem less benign; and a second consequence was that the need to assert the possibility of the disinterested gift eventually became more urgent.[10] The result has been a curious reversal. Where for a modern gift economy to function properly misrecognition of gifts as free must be collective, in sixteenth- and seventeenth-century patron-client relationships, to which gift giving, used to secure reciprocal obligation, was essential, the pretense of magnanimity, of gifts given freely and without any expectation of return, was upheld only in communication between giver and recipient, while outside that communication everyone spoke of such transactions in the language of quid pro quo.[11] Even within it, it was possible to incorporate, if facetiously, the legal language of contract, as when Henry Howard, Earl of Northampton, wrote to reassure his client Charles Cornwallis, ambassador to Spain, that their relationship remained sound. After comforting professions of support phrased in the language of the love, grace, favor, and trust between them, Northampton concluded that "therefore the condition of the contract standing still in force you need fear no forfeitures," even though there was no contract but rather a continuing reciprocal obligation.[12] Thinking through one form of exchange by means of others became in fact a characteristic of early-seventeenth-century thought.[13]

Bribery in early modern England is best understood, then, in the context of other closely related kinds of exchange, especially, as I have suggested, the contract and the gift, but also theft, loss, bailment, even witchcraft and sodomy; and in its jumbling of the markers distinguishing these from one another it presents distinctive conceptual complexities. It may be specious to claim that that any particular culture or historical period was more interested in the idea of exchange than any other. Yet there is much evidence to suggest that sixteenth- and early-seventeenth-century English men and women were newly conscious of certain forms of exchange and interested in grasping their structure and mastering their social meaning: historically momentous developments occurring in the law of contract; the complex social and economic issues involved in the practice of wardship, which gained an institutional presence with the establishment of the Court of Wards in 1540 but stood out as a particular sore point for seventeenth-century parliaments until its abolishment in 1660; the novel application of contractual language to negotiations between king and Parliament in the failed Great Contract of 1610; increased sales of monopolies by the Crown increasingly resisted by the Commons; innovations in economic theory by the likes of Misselden and Malynes; the expanded use of such financial instruments as insurance; the insertion for the first time in England of the language of the demonic pact into the 1604 witchcraft statute; a renewed interest in classical theories of gift giving (reflected in translations of Seneca's *De beneficiis*) and the ethics of public office (translations of Cicero's *De officiis*); the economic preoccupations of literary works like Shakespeare's *Sonnets* and the contractual language of such plays as Jonson's *Bartholomew Fair*; and so on. A wide range of conceptual experimentation responded to pervasive uncertainties. With traditional categories of exchange extending into new aspects of social life and thus acquiring new meanings, did the old taxonomic map need redrawing? Did exchanges bring people together or drive them apart? Could the relation between an audience and a playwright be described as contractual? Were classical accounts of gift exchange and patronage relations appropriate to a transformed political and economic order? Were witches guilty because they did harm or because they had made a quid pro quo pact with the devil? And was a public official guilty of bribery in accepting bribes even if he did not reciprocate by perverting justice?

He was. On January 30, 1621, Parliament met for the first time since the "addled Parliament" of 1614, called by the king because he needed money for himself and for an army to defend Protestant interests in the Palatinate. The House of Commons was ready to cooperate, provided its members got something in return, and what they wanted was an investigation into the royal monopolies on the pretext that these were being abused but fundamentally because they were disliked in themselves. The king himself could not conveniently be blamed, but in awarding the monopolies he had relied on the recommendations of certain "referees" who had been responsible for seeing that particular monopolies were steered to appropriate patentees. These referees were vulnerable, and Bacon was among them. Though he may have been the primary target of the investigation, he managed to escape serious trouble until new and, as it turned out, more lethal charges were brought against him. Beginning on March 14 with a petition to the Commons by Christopher Awbry, a discontented suitor who claimed to have given Bacon money to expedite his case in Chancery and not received satisfaction, a series of allegations that Bacon had accepted bribes, mostly in his office as Lord Chancellor, was brought before the Commons; these were forwarded to the House of Lords, which eventually assembled a list of twenty-eight articles against him. After some resistance, Bacon made a full confession on April 30. He lost his office, was briefly imprisoned, and was heavily fined and forbidden forever to come within the verge or hold office. His imprisonment lasted only a few days, and his banishment from the centers of power was eventually remitted. But his political life, at least in any official capacity, was over.[14]

The charges involved accusations of bribery, that is, of accepting money from persons whose suits were pending in Chancery. At least since Spedding and Gardiner, scholars have pointed out that the distinctions between bribes, fees, gratuities, and gifts—which have always been difficult to separate in practice—were particularly susceptible to confusion in the legal bureaucracy of early-seventeenth-century London. Given the structure of government financing, and in particular the absence of an established system of taxation, no government bureaucrat was salaried at anything like a sufficient wage;[15] Bacon's salary as Chancellor was £918, but his actual annual income from all sources during the same period has been estimated at from £9,000 to over £16,000.[16] Buckingham said he had heard that Bacon received over £100,000 in gifts during the four years he was Chancellor.[17] Twenty-five thousand pounds a year is probably an exaggeration, but perhaps not much of one.

Most bureaucrats in fact seem to have lived, and been all but required to live, well beyond their official salaries. The necessity of supplementing one's income in the ways Bacon did was thus built into the system; and the argument that the case against him was essentially political, and involved bribery only opportunistically, has some plausibility. One of Bacon's recent defenders proposes that while a fatal ambiguity in the practice among public officials of accepting supplementary income in the form of gifts made it possible for Parliament to use the charges against Bacon as a "political weapon," ultimately Bacon fell because the king permitted him to.[18] Like Robert Cecil, Earl of Salisbury, had he not died conveniently in 1610; like Robert Carr in 1615; like Thomas Howard, Earl of Suffolk, in 1618; like Lord Treasurer Cranfield in 1624, Bacon's number was in. He had many enemies, most formidably in Edward Coke, who from the first played a leading role in encouraging the Commons's interest in the case and who must have been delighted to see Bacon fall; and it is easy to imagine the king calculating the profit in letting Parliament have its way in this matter despite the loss it would entail of an effective and loyal servant.

Yet to leave the matter there would be to miss the work of thought that went into Bacon's attempts, as well as those of his adversaries, to conceptualize what he had done. As has been widely recognized at least since Spedding, no evidence emerged to suggest that Bacon had ever judged otherwise than fairly in cases where he was alleged to have accepted bribes; those clients who came forward to incriminate him were annoyed not that he took bribes but that he did not fulfill his part of the bargain.[19] The record of the proceedings against Bacon shows that there was little interest in establishing a causal connection between gifts and judicial rulings. But this does not necessarily mean, as is sometimes supposed, that his prosecution was political in any simple sense. It is certainly true that bribery was understood as a structurally contractual act intended by the payer to result in a perversion of justice. Yet Coke's definition of the term makes no mention of consequences, only of the acceptance by a magistrate of a gift presented by one having business before that magistrate.[20] And in a single sentence Bacon himself both denies that he took rewards to pervert justice and acknowledges that he "may be frail, and partake of the abuse of the times."[21] Most commentators on this passage have focused on how Bacon attempts to separate the faults of the man from the faults of the times. More striking is how he understands that he may be guilty of bribery and yet not guilty of wresting judgment. In other words, for him bribery is defined formally (acceptance, under certain circumstances, of what is offered as a bribe) rather than as a matter of consequence.[22] In fact, neither legal nor popular disapproval of bribery was limited to or even relied much on a consequentialist rationale. An implicitly apotropaic argument for the prohibition against bribery seems to have operated more powerfully: bribery might damage the body politic or infringe the rights of individuals by producing unjust rulings or policy, but whether it did or not it was filthy, corrupting, and evil.[23] Where the gift economy remained so large a part of public life it is perhaps not surprising that the illegality of bribery was not described in consequentialist terms. Since virtually all gifts were understood to be interested, given in order to influence the recipient's actions, to condemn bribes on those grounds was a less obvious basis for criminality than it might otherwise have been.

In this respect prohibitions against bribery resemble laws against witchcraft and against illicit sexual behavior. Early modern bribery was analogized to both. John Downame in 1613, for example, suggested that the distinction between good and bad witches and the distinction between those who accept money to do justice and those who accept it to pervert justice are equally specious. Downame explains that the judge who accepts payment to do justice will be inclined also to accept it to do injustice; but the analogy suggests that like the witch whose crime is not in doing evil directly to others but in contracting with the devil for the power to do so, all those accepting bribes err simply by the fact of the transaction. Similarly, "it cannot be but great prejudice to the vprightnesse of a Iudge, and a shrewed presumption of his corruption, when he receiveth gifts of those who haue suites depending before him; for as a wife or maide would incurre the danger of iust suspition, of hauing an vncleane heart, who being solicited by a fornicator to commit whoredome, should receive his gifts, although she should deny his suite: for howsoeuer in word she refuse his wicked motion, yet indeed she receiued pledges of his love."[24] The woman makes herself unclean merely by virtue of receiving the fornicator's gifts and regardless of whether he gets what he wants. In his comprehensive history of the bribe John Noonan remarks that witchcraft and bribery have long been regarded as pollutants threatening the integrity of the social structure in a very nonspecific sense; and both are "socially disapproved ways of influencing the accomplishment of a result the practitioner desires and believes he cannot accomplish openly by legal means or by force."[25] Because in the nonconsequentialist rationale bribery was already culpable without reference to any negative consequences it might or might not have—because it was intrinsically culpable before it was contingently culpable—it could function as a form of conceptual experimentation. Moral laws in general, of course, tend to erase their consequentialist origins in asserting themselves as incontrovertible, and prohibitions against bribery are no exception. But in an era in which the apotropaic origins of such prohibitions had begun to be subjected to skeptical examination, the persistence of nonconsequentialist rationales suggests that concepts like bribery and witchcraft worked as social allegories of human agency itself, ways of concretizing in a specific practice far more diffuse anxieties about both what one finds one can do and what one finds one cannot, by rendering the exercise of influence or power intransitive, as if to get a better look at it in isolation.

In analogizing witchcraft and bribery, Noonan is thinking of the English model of witchcraft, in which the culpable act is the *maleficium* of the witch, rather than, as on the Continent, the demonic pact; but new witchcraft legislation in 1604 conjoined the two crimes, so that *maleficium* was understood to come about by means of the pact.[26] This legislative innovation underscores the analogy between the two practices. Keith Thomas does not discern a distinct shift to the continental model in English witchcraft prosecutions after 1604; but in the letter of the law, at least, the pact was replaced by the *maleficium* as the basis of liability, and the focus of proof became ambiguously the evidence of injury (the withered arm or barren cow) and testimony of witnesses of or principals in the supposed contract with the devil.[27] The significance of the statute extends beyond its limited application in practice, for the legislators of 1604 and those of 1610 who attempted to draw up a contract with the king, or those of 1621 who made it their business to prosecute bribery, shared many assumptions and concerns. For these men, a successful prosecution for bribery did not need to demonstrate direct damage (bad rulings), only that a gift was received under certain conditions, an agreement or contract to perform being inferred. The 1604 legislation similarly provided that the witch had only to make the pact to be judged guilty.

The statutory contractualization of witchcraft resonates with one explanation of witch-hunting hysteria in the sixteenth and seventeenth centuries, that it was linked to a shift, from personal to communal (or governmental) responsibility for taking care of those less fortunate, that produced an uncertainty about the propriety of refusing direct requests for aid: the typical witch in this view was a woman denied by a neighbor the kinds of help once customary, the neighbor's sense of guilt producing a fantasy of supernatural harm.[28] Like the gift/bribe ambiguity among the bureaucratic elite under James, a sense that economic responsibilities are shifting seems to result in attempts to disambiguate certain classes of transactions by criminalizing them or by insisting that laws against them be enforced.[29] In theory, gifts become bribes when they create personal obligations in the recipient incompatible with the obligations he holds as a protector of the communal interest; bribery is prosecuted when the perceived disjunction between the two obligations is acute, as when communal interests appear to be threatened. In the case of witchcraft, the accuser's belief projects his own sense that he has violated an obligation to charitable giving. He resists the obligation (the returns on charity can be hard to identify), but he might have given anyway except that his resistance has been sanctioned by the notion that such obligations should be borne by the state. Witchcraft prosecutions, then, indirectly sanction the development of a central government with an expanded role by systematically relieving a lingering sense that the individual remains obligated. The foregrounding of the pact suggests that the witch has taken her business elsewhere. King James remarked that his judges should be paid only once—by him. Just as a corrupt justice should have avoided entering into obligations to others, the crime of the accused witch was that, refused individual acts of charity, she had appealed to the wrong source of assistance: she had contracted with the devil rather than with the state.[30]

Because allegations of bribery had no need to concern themselves with any specific effects once the bare possibility of those effects had been established, even as the model for the successful bribery transaction remained contractual, narratives of such transactions are often oddly lopsided, consisting of a *quid* and a *pro*, but no *quo*. Just as there was very little interest in how Bacon had decided particular cases—and, again, little if any evidence suggests he favored those who gave him gifts—the guilt of the other parties to the transaction, or what they may have gotten in return, was not of much concern.[31] The dismissal of the consequentialist argument and the substitution of the receipt of the bribe alone meant that it was enough to found the guilt of the one who had profited on the fact that he had profited; it also meant that the claim that Bacon had not wrested judgment according to the briber's desires was not only no defense but if anything further inculpatory (if he was going to take a bribe he might at least have done what he implicitly undertook to do). The formula of receipt independent of reciprocation, moreover, fits bribery neatly into Marcel Mauss's suggestion that the Latin word *reus* (guilty, as in the legal term *mens rea* or guilty mind), derives from *res*, thing, for the reason that one in possession of the thing (or as it were of one thing too many) has failed to reciprocate the gift or otherwise perpetuate the flow of exchange by passing the given thing back into circulation, and is therefore at fault, guilty, *reus*.[32] Particularly in a cultural context like that of early-seventeenth-century England, where movable possessions were more than ever a sign of status, and where the rapid rise of favorites and bureaucrats and monopolists was widely resented, such a link between *res* and *reus* is not implausible.[33]

Bribes, then, like contracts in their emphasis on voluntary undertaking and like witchcraft in the paradoxically intransitive nature of this undertaking, are unlike these, and like gifts, in their tendency to inculpate coercively by linking fault and obligation. Both bribes and gifts are potentially aggressive gestures and are likely to originate unilaterally; a proposed bribe amounts to a threat when suggested by the bribe taker (the only way you'll get what you want is to grease my palm) but also perhaps by the bribe giver (I am offering a bribe; you are already complicit; you must do as I ask or risk exposure). Straddling the line between licit and illicit exchange, presenting itself to others (if at all) as merely a gift, and to the parties to the transaction as contractual, bribes appear to have two faces. Yet in Bacon's case, at least, the distinction is not so clear. Not even those witnesses who testified to providing Bacon with what they understood to be bribes reported verbal exchanges that acknowledged this: the language that accompanied these transactions (at least as reported by the participants, even the payers, who do not seem to have considered themselves culpable or to have feared prosecution) seems almost always to have been allusive and elliptical, as if the parties themselves wished not to recognize the contractual nature of the bribe, or as if Bacon himself really did not grasp the purpose behind the gift.[34] In this respect bribery transactions often probably resembled noncontractual exchanges that similarly mingle the frank and free with the tacit and obligatory, as for example one documented in a letter sent by William Lambarde to his friend Ralph Rokeby in 1577, acknowledging receipt of a horse the latter had sent him.

> Albeit I see not (good m[aste]r Rokeby) with what face I may take this youre bonny beast, eyther in respect of my things heartofore proceeded fro[m] me (whereof nevertheless it pleaseth you to make an overlong enumeration) or in hope of my good pleasure, that (by my hope) may hereafter come towardes you by my meanes: yet synce it hathe not only pleased you to make so earnest offer of the same at our last being together, but now also (after the manne[r] of your invincible courtasie) to send your servant with him, I can not but (thus conquered by you) receave him, if not as myne of youre guift yet as youre owne in my custodie, least eyther you shold thinke me disdainfull in refusing youre great kindnesse, or daungerous and squaymishe to become hearby so much the more indebted to youe. You knowe right wel (good m[aste]r Rokeby) and I to my great comforte have felt, and may never without manifest note of ingratitude forget, how sundrie wayes I haue been gratified by youe, in regard whereof I am (or ought) not only to owe youe all dueties during my life, but also to stand therby so firmely persuaded of your fauoure, as I neede no new pledges therof: And, I would to god that you also would aswel acknowledge, as you knowe, it: for then would you limitte this youre overliberal bountie, and no[t] so throwe ye satchel of your freindlie actions behynd you, and thus continually heape your freindes with infinite fauours.... In summe, youe, so loade me (good m[aste]r Rokeby) with good turnes, that theare is as litle hope that I should requite theim, as theare is great cause that I should remember theim: and therfore, as mynd not to content that waye, so I pray god that I may thanke you, and thinke of theim, as it becommeth: besides w[hi]ch, theare is nothing within the [*illegible:* compass?] of my smalle power th[a]t may testifie [my] good harte towardes youe.[35]

For a variety of reasons, Rokeby is unlikely to have offered the gelding as a bribe in any legal definition of the term, especially since Lambarde had not yet assumed judicial office.[36] The letter's language resembles instead the rhetoric of patron-client relationships; the insistence that the gift is unmerited, the claim that one is accepting reluctantly, and only under compulsion, because the giver might otherwise suspect disdain or an unwillingness to increase an already overwhelming indebtedness, the protestation that one is unable to reciprocate adequately—these are common and even formulaic sentiments in early modern patronage relationships and gift exchange. In this rhetoric, the pleasure of receiving the gift is tempered by the knowledge that acceptance places the giver in the superior position; having the *res*, the beneficiary is *reus*, "loaded" and "heaped" with favors he cannot, he says, possibly requite. Whether the letter shows Lambarde genuinely uncomfortable with being in receipt of the gift or playing with the idea of being so, he contrives to accept without accepting, a feat he accomplishes by wittily suggesting that while the horse will remain in his custody, it may nevertheless continue to belong to Rokeby: he receives it "if not as myne of youre guift yet as youre owne in my custodie." Lambarde's "if" raises the question of whether Lambarde is accepting as a gift the horse or only the "custodie" of the horse. This uncertainty is preserved in the closing: "I truste that wee shal haue youre companie this christmas heare, for w[hi]ch, bothe I and my father and mother be desirous suitors to youe; Only let me knowe your daye by youre l[ett]res, and I will bring this your nag and an other for your man with me to grenewiche, or to Londo[n], for youe."[37] "[T]his *your* nag" suggests that ownership of the horse has not even changed hands and that the proposed transaction involves the return of possession ("custody") and use to Rokeby, ownership having remained with him all along. And yet the "for youe" with which the letter ends resists disambiguation: to be returned, as your property, into your possession? To be bestowed on you as a return gift? For your use only? And is the second horse "for your man" promised as a gift outright, or merely a gift of use? It would appear that Lambarde is merely offering to come pick Rokeby up (either in London or nearby in Greenwich) and bring him home with him for the Christmas holidays. Yet the horse that was "youre bonny beast" at the beginning, before Lambarde set about accepting it, remains "your nag" at the end.

While the distinction between use and ownership in the letter is in some sense inconsequential, the introduction of a conceptual separation of the two terms was fundamental to the development of English land law. Since ownership was not of lands themselves (which belonged only to the king) but of estates in land, ownershiplike rights to land had to be founded in estates that did not grant ownership. And gifts of land that were not gifts outright, but conditional gifts from which the conditions could not be detached, and not estates in fee simple, were perfected in Westminster II (1285), the statute *De donis conditionalibus*, which permitted donors to entail gifts of land in perpetuity, so that these lands were to be inherited by (for example) successive male heirs of the donor's body.[38] What *De donis* did for real property in 1285, however, was never extended to chattel (or movable) property. As Baker puts it, "[T]he common law did not allow future estates to be created in chattels. A gift of a chattel for an hour was a gift forever."[39]

If the entail allowed gifts in land from which the intent of the donor never released its hold, the law regarding chattels did not at first permit anything other than a gift outright. The medieval concept of property *(proprietas)*, applied to chattels, seems to have conflated ownership and possession, so that if I lend you my horse we both have property in it, only mine is of a higher degree than yours: you can defend your property in the horse against any claimant except me. But a case of 1459 established that property in a chattel could be distinguished from its use or possession: not two degrees of property but a right in the thing distinct from ownership of it. Handing over a thing to someone else without relinquishing ownership in it came to be called bailment, a concept essential, obviously, to mercantile exchange, and one that gave rise to an important series of cases concerning the liability (for loss or damage) of the bailee.[40] Similarly, and on the analogy of entailed estates in land, a conditional gift could be made of the use of the chattel but not of the chattel itself. Heirlooms (chattels entailed to successive heirs) thus became possible, though a current possessor could always destroy the heirloom (he just couldn't sell it or give it away).[41]

Lambarde isn't playing directly on the analogy with real property; but he is thinking about gifts of chattel property and the difference between the gift of a thing and a gift of the use of the thing. In distinguishing between ownership and use, Lambarde is able first to accept without accepting, to interpret the gift as a gift of use, as if at once to avoid the insult of refusal while diminishing the extent of his obligation, and then to reciprocate by offering what is in effect the use of a use. In this elaborately structured fiction, which must have been more in game than in earnest, Lambarde sets up the use he claims Rokeby gave him, and the use of the use he offers in return, as sufficiently different to avoid refusing the gift or, what comes to the same thing, giving in return the same gift or an identical one.

The story of an acceptance that is also a refusal is, in fact, conventional, especially where, as in cases of proposed bribery, the recipient may really feel uncomfortable with the gift, either because its acceptance exposes him to the charge of bribery or because he does not wish to be obligated in the way that a bribe would require. Perhaps the best-known instances of this conventional narrative occur in William Roper's *Life of Sir Thomas More*. In the first of these, More is presented with "a fair gilt cup for a bribe" by the wife of one Vaughan, a litigant whose suit is pending in Chancery; More fills the cup with wine, drinks a toast to the woman, and returns it to her.[42] In another case, "[O]ne Master Gresham . . . having at the same time a cause depending in the Chancery before him [viz., More], sent him for a New Year's gift a fair gilted cup, the fashion whereof he very well liking, caused one of his own (though not in his fantasy of so good a fashion, yet better in value) to be brought him out of his chamber, which he willed the messenger in recompense to deliver to his master. And under other condition would he in no wise receive it."[43] Roper's purpose, presumably, is to document at once More's exceptional probity and his ability nevertheless to preserve social decorum while scolding the suitors for their presumption; this combination of imperatives necessitates a refusal-in-acceptance as opposed to outright refusal. In distinguishing between the market values of the two cups and the values More assigns them ("value" and "fashion" respectively), Roper suggests that More is able to profit blamelessly, and outside the realm of monetary value, even though the constructive refusal is in both cases obvious.

Bacon himself had heard a version of the More anecdote and had recorded it as Apophthegm #23: "Sir Thomas Moore had sent him by a suitor in the chancery two silver flagons. When they were presented by the gentleman's servant, he said to one of his men; *Have him to the cellar, and let him have of my best wine.* And turning to the servant, said, *Tell thy master, friend, if he like it, let him not spare it.*"[44] The implication is that More has the flagons filled with wine and then returned to the giver, since the anecdote would have little point if More simply accepted the flagons and reciprocated with a gift of wine.[45] Where in the second of Roper's anecdotes it is the immediacy of the return as well as the very close similarity between gift and return gift that negates the transaction *qua* bribe (or for that matter *qua* gift), in the anecdote about Vaughan's wife and in Apophthegm #23 it is the insertion of a symbolic interval of use that makes these refusals merely constructive and not outright. In the early seventeenth century, the story of More's graceful negotiation of the conflict between personal and official obligations would have seemed (as it may have to Bacon himself) an example of the Tudor probity to which some observers called for a return. But between More and Lambarde, at least, less has changed than has remained the same. The real difference is that the anecdote associated with the former recounts the refusal (almost) of a bribe and the Lambarde letter the acceptance (almost) of a gift. More doesn't play on uses of chattels as a legal concept in the way that Lambarde seems to (though the concept of the use of chattels was already established), but the bribe is negated *qua* bribe in both Roper's and Bacon's versions of the story of Vaughan in a way similar to Lambarde's management of the gift horse, through the insertion of an interval of use that substitutes for an acceptance understood to imply a transfer of ownership. Like the aesthetic economy implied in More's preference for the less valuable cup, use here gestures beyond, even as it also only complicates, quantitative exchange. The result in Lambarde is a retention of the gift that is not exactly equivalent to its acceptance, and in More a return of the gift that is not quite a refusal.

It is noteworthy that the Vaughan anecdote appealed to Bacon, since among the "dozen of buttons," suits of hangings, diamond rings, tasters of gold, ambergrease, and sums of money he acknowledged receiving from suitors, he describes a transaction that falls perhaps somewhere in between Lambarde and More, though his management of it was hardly so adroit. Article 9, one of the twelve charges against Bacon that Gardiner felt could not be extenuated, alleges that the Lord Chancellor received from a man named Kennedy, whose suit was pending in Chancery, the gift of "a rich cabinet . . . prized at eight hundred pounds."

> I confess and declare, [Bacon responded,] That such a cabinet was brought to my house, though nothing near half the value; and that I said to him that brought it, that I came to view it, and not to receive it; and gave commandment that it should be carried back, and was offended when I heard it was not: and some year and an half after, as I remember, Sir John Kennedy having all that time refused to take it away, as I am told by my servants, I was petitioned by one Pinckney that it might be delivered to him, for that he stood engaged for the money that Sir John Kennedy paid for it. And thereupon Sir John Kennedy wrote a letter to my servant Shereborne, with his own hand, desiring I would not do him that disgrace as to return that gift back, much less to put it into a wrong hand: and so it remains yet ready to be returned to whom your Lordships shall appoint.[46]

This bizarre narrative raises several questions. Why, when he readily admits to the Lords that he accepted gifts, does he go out of his way to insist that he did not accept this one? And why, if he did not accept it, does he insist on its being worth less than the article alleges? What did he mean by saying he "came to view it, and not to receive it"? To whom did he "give commandment that it should be carried back"? If to his own servants, why was his order not carried out? If not to them, why not? And why, if he was so anxious to be rid of it, did he not, in defiance of Kennedy's request, have it delivered to Pinckney?[47]

In response to no other specific charge did Bacon insist that he had refused a gift; yet, given that the cabinet undeniably remained in his house, this seems an unlikely gift to make such a claim about. The story's substantial detail suggests that it must have some factual basis, but these details also convey an impression of overall improbability. Let us suppose Bacon is telling the truth. He admits possession but not ownership or even, apparently, use. Would it be more accurate to say then that in this account he accepted the gift or that he refused it? Bacon puts himself in a strangely passive position, as if he were powerless to resist: "What could I do?" he seems to say. It would take a lawyer, in fact, to figure out, on this evidence, to whom the cabinet belonged. Bacon admits it remained at his house for at least a year and a half; and a cabinet valued at £800, or for that matter £400, must have been of fairly substantial size; where exactly had it been all this time?

An exculpatory appeal to use, along the lines of More or Lambarde, appears impossible here. Use based on an interval of possession greater than the symbolic drinking of a health constitutes a valuable benefit, and the bribe remains a bribe, though one that Bacon might have made look a little better by claiming that the cabinet had only been lent to him, as he insisted that certain sums paid to him had been loans to be repaid. That strategy, of course, would be undermined, as it was in the case of the "loans," by his continued possession. In fact, Bacon seems to choose to emphasize the opposite. Instead of a use that would weave the cabinet into the flow of social life, of friendship and free generosity and shared resources, Bacon's account produces a sort of social isolation of both himself and the cabinet. Where More and Lambarde sought to redeem the transaction by inserting the thing into use, making it somehow not a thing but a relation between people, Bacon's impulse seems to be in the other direction, toward social disconnection. It is the taking it *out* of use that is supposed to negate the suspicion of bribery. His relation to the cabinet is insistently detached, distant, antisocial: he "came to view it not receive it." It remains in his house, but the account gives the impression that despite its presence there it is inert, lifeless, unused. It is as if Bacon wanted his judges to imagine the cabinet set down and abandoned in the middle of the entry hall at York House on the Strand, where he was born and where as Lord Keeper he had lived since 1617, so that he would have to step around it every time he left home or returned, an alien object inexplicably in his path.[48] And Bacon represents himself as similarly passive and disengaged. His servants don't do what he says. He relies on them to communicate with the other interested parties, to whom he feels no connection. He finds himself caught up unwillingly in the middle of a debt dispute that has nothing to do with him. He doesn't know why any of this is happening. He is offended by the cabinet's presence, but apparently not enough to do anything about it.

Why is it this gift in particular that has occasioned so problematic an account? It is impossible to say. Its first distinction is that it is one of only six gifts (out of the twenty-five alleged) that were not, explicitly at least, in cash. The others were the buttons, hangings, diamond ring, gold tasters, and ambergrease already mentioned. A small quantity of ambergris was worth a lot of money, and assuming that the buttons were of gold, the cabinet (along with the hangings) was the least moneylike, the least negotiable, the least portable, of the gifts in question, and for these reasons least like a bribe, despite its great value. So at least its description makes it seem. Given that cabinets were at least as much repositories for valuables as they were valuable in themselves (*OED* 5: "a case for the safe custody of jewels, or other valuables, letters or documents"), however, it is possible that the one presented to Bacon was "rich" in the sense that it contained something valuable: money or jewels. If so, the substitution of cabinet for contents—alternatively metonymic and synecdochic—raises other questions that makes this seem even less like a cash transaction.[49]

At the same time, the cabinet's uses are less personal, less associated with the body, than those of buttons, rings, or tasters, and it is less of an object of display than the hangings (which Bacon seeks to naturalize as one among many gifts he received when furnishing his house).[50] It is thus presented not only as less like a bribe than the others but also as less like a gift.[51] Because of what it was *called*, moreover, it may be considered a symbol of Bacon's practice of accepting bribes and of his own resistance to that practice, for, conveniently enough, the use of the word cabinet in a political sense, to designate an assembly of close advisors, seems to have emerged at around this time, having evolved from the word's meaning as "a small chamber or room, a private apartment, boudoir" (OED 1–3), a meaning parallel to the probable sense of the word in the passage above. The OED's first recorded use of the expression cabinet counsel as designating secret or private counsel is in Bacon's "Of Counsel," where Bacon remarks that getting good counsel, while essential to proper kingship, involves certain inconveniences, including breaches in confidentiality, weakened authority, and the possibility of being "unfaithfully counselled." "For which inconveniences, the doctrine of Italy and practice of France, in some kings' times, hath introduced cabinet councils, a remedy worse than the disease."[52] By 1644, says the OED, the word cabinet could stand alone as a substantive referring to the body of persons meeting in private to advise the king.[53] The word has related meanings as well, in all of which secrecy was centrally important. It could be a secret treasure room as well as a piece of furniture, and it was used as a substitute for *tabernacle* as a metaphor for the container of the body in which the soul was imprisoned (*OED* 1.b).

The association of Bacon's gift cabinet with an enclosed space of secret political advice, a place to keep valuables away from prying eyes, and with the body as an opaque container of the soul is especially suggestive here; given the word's uneasy superimposition of politics and secrecy, of the public and the personal, it is a fitting vehicle to import the meaning of the offered but only equivocally accepted bribe, since bribery may be said to exist where the distinctions between private and public come under stress in certain specific ways. As Sitta von Reden puts it in talking about exchange in ancient Greece, "[B]ribery presupposes the disjunction, but not the complete separation, of two transactional orders. These orders may be distinguished as public or private, sacred or profane, tribal or governmental, ritual or juridical. The idea of corrupted exchange arises at the moments when individuals have to fill roles in both these orders but mix their respective ties of obligation." Gabriel Herman's account of the gift/bribe ambiguity in the ancient Greek city-states suggests an at least superficial similarity to the early seventeenth century. As von Reden explains Herman's argument,

> the shifting meaning of *dora* was related to a shift of power from *basileis* with quasi-divine power to the constitutional government of the *polis*. A gift merged into a bribe when it came into conflict with the idea that the community, rather than a monarch, held supreme power. The communal interest as the *raison d'etre* of political organisation was the only background against which gift-giving could appear as bad. Outside the communal sphere, as for example in the exchange with gods, or with foreigners, a gift was implicitly good and bribery unknown.[54]

In making an analogy to early-seventeenth-century England it would be incorrect, of course, simply to say that the king and the political ideology he insisted on sanctioned the gift and bribe transactions, or that the House of Commons was motivated by some simply opposed ideology of public and representational authority. Even so, as we have seen, one of the standard explanations for Bacon's prosecution is that it was brought about by a developing ambiguity in the system by which public office was remunerated. Without a secure tax base the Crown was dependent on a supposedly free "gift" from Parliament; the alternative, to accentuate the contractual, quid pro quo nature of the relationship, had failed miserably in the Great Contract attempted during the 1610 Parliament. And reciprocally, because the king could not afford to compensate his servants adequately, they were virtually compelled to seek gifts that under certain circumstances could be confused with—could be—bribes.

The key point here is Hermann's remark that gifts to those outside the community could not be bribes. In early modern England that community excluded only God and the king, and soon enough people weren't going to be so sure about the king. Christian theology and the politics of the early modern court complicated both exclusions in ways that do not apply in the classical context. For Bacon had something like the same problem with the king that troubled the Christian's relationship with God: these figures of authority and judgment both must and must not be subject to bribery. Both must at once judge impartially (align themselves with justice) and be merciful, responsive to prayer or petition or offer of service.[55] As for the king, both court protocol and James's theory of sovereignty dictated that Bacon address him in terms not unlike those in which the Christian addressed God. Bacon ended his March 25 letter to James: "I have ever been your man, and counted myself but an usufructuary of myself, the property being yours; and now making myself an oblation to do with me as may best conduce to the honour of your justice, the honour of your mercy, and the use of your service, resting as clay in your Majesty's gracious hands."[56] Bacon's self-presentation here is complex. Like the Christian who belongs to God, whose life on earth is merely lent him for a time, Bacon confesses himself owned by the king. But in civil law, about which Bacon was especially knowledgeable, the usufructuary, the owner of a usufruct, had as such a right to enjoy the fruits of property vested in another.[57] Bacon's submission, in other words, also implies an assertion of legal right: you own me, yes, but in return I deserve to profit from my own use. His expression, however, is circular. If "myself" = x and the usufructuary function is $f(x)$, then x counts as $f(x)$. If the only way to know what x is is as a function of its usufruct, the equation (the "counting") is unsolvable for x. Bacon's self, only definable as a function of that self, is the missing value. Expressed algebraically, there is a series of equivalent functions that can go on indefinitely but will never get any closer to x: $x = f(x) = f(f(x)) = f(f(f(x)))$.... The series is also an extended metalepsis, where the vehicle of the first metaphor becomes the tenor of the second, and so on. The assertion of the right to use only piles layers of indirection on the absence of any self to which that right might accrue.

Debates over the law of uses and the continuing impact on it of the Statute of Uses (27 Henry VIII [1536]), while far more technical than Bacon's playful remark, centered on precisely what kind of right a beneficiary (the *cestui que use*) had in the assets held to his use. Bacon had made the statute the subject of his inaugural course of lectures as Double Reader at Gray's Inn in 1600.[58] How his professional interests bear on his choice of metaphor may be impossible to say precisely; and that Bacon thinks here of the usufruct of the person, a notion legally meaningful in Roman law pertaining to slaves but in an early modern English context more theologically than legally resonant, only complicates things. People are different from the crops that a piece of arable land produces or the fish a stream yields, for the reason that a person's labor and the products of that labor are not so easily distinguished from the person himself. Bacon's metaphor puts him in the place of the usufructuary; but when he goes on to speak of himself as an "oblation" presented to the king it seems clear that he also imagines himself as a use held to the king, rather than the other way around; both he and the king are by turns the *cestui que use*. Bacon claims both that he belongs to the king and that he has something of himself that he can present to him as a gift. The usufruct he offers as an oblation must be his own to give; one cannot, the passage implies, make a gift of what already belongs to the recipient.[59] Bacon seems to analogize the self to estate in land as it is opposed to mere use. But uses were, in a sense, all there were. As in Bacon's analogy so in land law: no x except x = king. The structure of Bacon's usufruct equation is the structure of land tenure generally, where title of ownership finally resides elsewhere (viz. in the king).

On April 21, the day before his first, very general confession, Bacon wrote again to the king, again hoping for royal intercession but well aware that he had lost, at least, his office as Keeper of the Great Seal. He again struggles with the same problem of use and the usufruct of the person, this time through a facetious reference to the charges against him: "But because he that hath taken bribes is apt to give bribes, I will go furder, and present your Majesty with a bribe. For if your Majesty give me peace and leisure, and God give me life, I will present your Majesty with a good history of England, and a better digest of your laws."[60] Bacon speaks jestingly, of course, though it is also true that the offer was genuinely intended as an inducement to the king to intercede in the parliamentary proceedings. The mercy of the king was going to cost more than that, however. Although James was determined to let the impeachment run its course, he informed Bacon through Buckingham that he would be pardoned afterwards, awarded a pension, and assisted with his debts.[61] Buckingham arranged for Bacon to pay his £40,000 fine not to the king but to trustees who would hold it for his own use; Bacon, in other words, was permitted to pay the fine to himself.[62] And by October 1621, James had signed a pardon (though, at first delayed until after the dissolution of Parliament, it never took effect).[63] Bacon himself probably drafted both documents. But these benefits only came at a price, and what Buckingham wanted was York House, of which Bacon insisted that "no money or value would make me part with it," offering his country house at Gorhambury instead.[64] But he was in no position to deal; the house went to Buckingham for £1,300, and in exchange Bacon received as well permission to come within the verge. It was business as usual in the court of King James.

In 1618 George Chapman dedicated his *Georgicks of Hesiod* to Bacon, who had just been elevated to the office of Lord Chancellor. Chapman dedicated no further works to Bacon, nor ever mentioned his name in print again, and it is impossible to say how, if at all, Bacon may have reciprocated.[65] Because an author could dedicate a book without presenting a copy to the dedicatee, and because dedications often sought to establish a patronage relation that did not yet exist, they ran the risk of ending up like the cabinet in Bacon's account, run aground in transit between giver and intended recipient, considered given by the giver but never quite accepted by the recipient, belonging then to no one. To make matters worse, since the gift of a dedication was strictly immaterial (not the book but the tribute paid in it to the potential patron), the only sign of acceptance was reciprocation, which was almost certain to be delayed and which could take many often indirect forms, some of them only ambiguously proof of acknowledgment. All gifts were subject to similar, if typically less acute, uncertainties about reciprocation. But at least with the gift of a material thing one could be sure of receipt, which, even if not quite equivalent to acceptance, as the story of the rich cabinet shows, founds at least a good probability. The dedicator had nothing comparable to go on.

It seems likely that what Chapman sought in exchange for dedicating his *Georgicks* to Bacon was the latter's intercession on behalf of the poet's erstwhile patron, Robert Carr, imprisoned since his conviction in the Overbury affair in 1616; Bacon himself had led the prosecution and by doing so must have angered Chapman; but now, newly installed as Lord Chancellor, he was in a position to help.[66] Chapman was notoriously unlucky in his choice of patrons, having cultivated Prince Henry in several dedications only to have him die in 1612; then Carr and his father-in-law Thomas Howard, the first convicted of murder in 1616, the second of corruption in 1618; and then Lionel Cranfield, destroyed like Bacon on charges of bribery in 1624.[67] Carr was not released from prison until 1622 and was not pardoned until just before James's death in 1625, when Bacon's influence over the king was not what it used to be.[68] Moreover, from the start of prosecutions in the Overbury matter Bacon's instructions from the king had been to convict Carr in such a way as to make a later pardon seem justified.[69] If Bacon did later pursue a pardon or release from prison, it seems unlikely that Chapman's dedication influenced him to do so. Carr was neither released nor pardoned until after Bacon's fall, and, especially since Bacon was in the habit of accepting favors without bothering to reciprocate, it seems probable that his response to the dedication was to ignore it. As a second source of resentment against Bacon, this adds plausibility to the argument that Chapman's *Tragedy of Chabot* was meant as an allegory of Bacon's part in the Somerset prosecution in 1616 and his subsequent fall five years later, in which Somerset is figured in Chabot and Bacon in Chancellor Poyet.[70] Chapman was so prone to getting into trouble through the topicality of his plays and poems that it is not hard to credit an allusion to contemporary events in the case of *Chabot*.[71]

Gifts of books and their dedications worked according to the exchange protocols of patronage relationships rather than those of bribery. Bacon's facetious recategorization shows both that such gifts were not normally considered bribes and that they nevertheless could be. Chapman, preoccupied more than other dramatists with the patronage system because he was so inept at playing it to his benefit, also returned again and again in his plays to corruption in the world of the court. Whether or not we accept that *Chabot* refers to Bacon, the play can be read as reflecting upon issues for which Bacon's case provides an example. The Admiral's rigged conviction in act 3 may allude to Somerset, whom Chapman loyally believed to have been condemned unjustly; and (assuming a late date for composition or revision) it is hard to disregard the similarity between Lord Chancellor Bacon and Lord Chancellor Poyet, especially in the trial of the latter in act 5. Yet the topical web of reference is fine enough that Chabot himself is caught up in associations with Bacon, even though the two appear in many ways opposites. Chabot's rejection of corruption, I suggest, resembled Bacon's embrace of it; and although Chabot refused the king's pardon where Bacon actively sought it, trial and conviction confronted the two with problems to which they responded in similar ways. In the end the difference between the two is the difference that the theater makes.

Bribery was one part of a more general discourse of political and judicial corruption. Both Bacon and Chapman acknowledged a tradition that distinguished between two forms of corrupt influence: respecting persons and accepting bribes. In *The Advancement of Learning* Bacon quotes Proverbs 28:21 in the vulgate—*Qui cognoscit in judicio faciem, non bene facit; iste et pro bucella panis deseret veritatem* (rendered in the King James version as "To have respect of persons *is* not good: for for a piece of bread *that* man will transgress")—and glosses, "Here is noted, that a judge were better be a briber than a respecter of persons; for the corrupt judge offendeth not so lightly as the facile."[72] Bacon distinguishes between two species of corrupted judgment, one performed in exchange for a payment and another in response to the judge's recognition of the individuality of one party to the cause. Thus he apparently reads the verse as referring to two separate offenses—

respecting persons and accepting a bribe (bread)—and as suggesting that any man who respects persons is likely also to take even a minimal bribe.

In the Greek New Testament the term *prosopolempsia* (face-noticing) is used in insisting that God is not subject to bribery, as for example in Romans 2:11, "For there is no respect of persons with God"; Augustine uses the expression *acceptio personarum* (the taking up of persons) in cases where "he who judges, leaving the merit of the case about which he judges, patronizes one against the other because he finds something in his person worthy of honor or mercy."[73] In translating John 7:24 ("Judge not according to the appearance, but judge righteous judgment"), the Latin Vulgate renders *kata hupsin* (by appearance) as *secundem faciem* (according to the face).[74]

Chapman alludes to the same distinction in *The Widow's Tears* (1604) when he has the incompetent Governor, called in to resolve the plot entanglements at the end of the play, declare his incorruptibility in the following equivocal terms: "I know no persons. If a Court favorite write to me in a case of justice: I will pocket his letter, and proceed. If a suitor in a case of justice thrusts a bribe into my hand, I will pocket his bribe and proceed" (5.5.193–96).[75] The court favorite requesting special treatment is an invitation to the Governor to "have respect of persons." Chapman's image of the receiving hand in the latter scenario is a regular feature of accounts of bribery; the hand's passivity, emphasized here for satirical purposes, suggests its own opposite, an active grasping after gain. In "A Paraenesis to Prince Henry," Sir William Alexander refers to a supposed pictorial tradition in which the just magistrate was depicted as without hands (by analogy with the more familiar figure of blind justice), indicating that he was honest and would not, could not accept a bribe.

> O! not without great cause all th'ancients did
> Paint Magistrates plac'd to explane the laws,
> Not having hands, so bribery to forbid,
> Which them from doing right, too oft with-draws;
> And with a veile the Iudges eyes were hid,
> Who should not see the partie, but the cause:
> Gods Deputies, which his Tribunall reare,
> Should have a patent, not a partiall eare.[76]

As in the case of the Governor in Chapman's play, the passage distinguishes between respecting faces and accepting bribes; only the latter is associated with the hand. Thus too, again in *The Widow's Tears*, Tharsalio offers a bribe "to keep thy hand supple," as though accepting were an activity in which the action of grasping was crucial and required regular lubrication.⁷⁷ The trope in which the hand that receives a bribe is a grasping hand, at once passively receiving and actively taking, appears clearly in a passage from John of Salisbury's *Policraticus* that distinguishes between the armed and unarmed hands of the republic, the soldier and the justice respectively, both of which require strict control to prevent their corruption. "And surely the unarmed hand is to be curbed more closely because while the armed hand is commanded to abstain from exactions and rapine, the unarmed hand is also prohibited presents."⁷⁸ The acceptance of gifts by justices is understood here to involve at least as much agency, as much hand-work, as the war crimes the soldier is likely to commit. This organization of agency is directly opposite modern usage, in which the giver of the bribe is the one who bribes, while the receiver is not a briber but a bribe taker, a difference reflected in the etymological vagaries of the terms. The vulgate's rendering of the phrase *bucella panis* (morsel of bread) in Proverbs 28:21 seems linked to Old French *bribe*, (piece of bread, frustum [bit, piece, morsel], panis); the medieval Latin *briba* had the same meaning. Old French *briber*, to be a mendicant or strolling beggar, was thus to be one who begged his bread. In English this produced *bribe* as a substantive meaning "theft, plunder, or spoil," the agent-noun *briber* coming to mean, successively, beggar, vagabond, thief, robber, extortionist, exactor of blackmail, and finally one who offered a bribe (*OED* s.v. "bribe"). Although subtle distinctions between licit and illicit (corrupt) gifts have been made since Old Testament times, no unambiguous word for the latter existed in Hebrew, Egyptian, Greek, or Latin.⁷⁹ Only in English did that word emerge; in Chaucer *bribe* suggests extortion more than it does something freely offered; but in early-sixteenth-century Reformation writings and translations of Scripture the word comes into its own.⁸⁰ This derivation initially makes an agent of the one who receives the bribe rather than the one who gives it—an attribution of agency directly opposite that in the modern sense of the word. The *OED* comments, "The sudden and startling change from the Baconian 'briber', who received douceurs, to the modern 'briber' who gives them, can be explained only by taking the latter as a separate derivation of the verb in its latest sense" (s.v. "bribe")—even if *to bribe* seems early on to have shifted its meaning from "to steal" to "to corrupt by offering a bribe to."

It is noteworthy that Bacon considers that "a judge were better be a briber than a respecter of persons" on the grounds that the latter is "lighter," more easily swayed from justice than the briber, who in contrast seems to set the sale of justice at a (higher) price. The respecter of persons is to be feared and loathed because he is a poor businessman; he is a poor businessman, for Bacon, because he sells justice for something unquantifiable, a social relationship the value of which is deferred, inexplicit, intangible. Respecting persons means wresting judgment on the basis of social or personal interests and connections; unlike bribery per se it is not contractual and does not involve a clear quid pro quo; compensation does not come in the form of a specific promise (to pay money, to perform some service)—that would be bribery. Value gained is the value of the relationship; there can be no promise, since in promising some performance the promiser marks off his liability as distinct from himself; that would be respecting a thing and not a person or a relationship. Respecting persons, moreover, need not involve a request or offer; the emphasis on vision implies there need be no interaction between the parties; the act arises upon the sight of the friend, ally, or acquaintance and can be entirely unilateral.[81] Bribery takes (at least) two. Yet respecting persons is the more socially engaged, and more complex, transaction, since it depends upon a history of connection (or the prospect of such a history). Since the money is what does the talking, bribery can—prefers to—function in a social vacuum: while the hands take care of business, the faces look away and the eyes do not meet. In a respecting of persons corruption can reside wholly in the sense of affection or obligation in the official who wrests judgment, and not in the person for whom judgment is wrested. The bribing hand gives, the respected face is just, passively, "respected."

Bacon's apparent approval of the preference for bribers over respecters of persons expressed in Proverbs 28:21 is thus consistent with his narrative management of the rich cabinet transaction, as well as with the fact that he was never charged with practicing favoritism in his judgments. Each instance suggests a refusal of the social embrace, a preference for the impersonal transaction performed by the hands (or by servants, or the hands of servants) while the eyes look elsewhere. There is perhaps as well a sense in which Bacon's habit of failing to reciprocate stems from the same refusal of obligation or connection. His predicament upon putting his case for mercy before James, of course, was that he had to rely on the latter's willingness to be a respecter of persons rather than a briber. As we have seen, that plea lost itself in his attempt to search out a foundation on which the transaction might seem more bribelike by distinguishing between himself and something he was able to offer.

Chapman's *Chabot* similarly engages the contrast between bribery and respecting persons. The play has been read as staging the conflict between royal prerogative and the rule of law and as a meditation on the disassociation of justice from the will of the king. The Admiral's tragedy is in his insistence that the two are inseparable, when the play shows us just how partial and confused the king's judgments are.[82] At the same time, Chabot rejects the premise that the king stands outside the exchange economy, that exchanges with him escape the principle of commensurability; he refuses, in other words, the analogy with God upon which divine right depends. When the king confronts Chabot after he has refused to sign a bill he considers unjust, Chabot rejects first the argument of political expediency and then the king's suggestion that he (the king) has the power to judge what is just. No, says Chabot, you've ceded that right to me; you look after the "general charge" while I judge particulars.[83] And then the king makes the incommensurability argument, though incoherently.

> Well Sir, grant
> Your force in this, my odds in benefits
> Paid for your paines, put in the other scale,
> And any equall holder of the balance
> Will shew my merits hoist up yours to aire
> In rule of any doubt or deed betwixt us.
> (2.3.88–93)[84]

To which the Admiral responds:

> You merit not of me for benefits
> More than my selfe of you for services.
> (2.3.94–95)

The king argues that the quantitative superiority of the benefits he has paid to Chabot will be proven at law. His faith in the law is not, however, that it will ferret out what is just but rather that it will confirm his own will. So the assumption is of incommensurability, even while the king looks to the law to affirm that incommensurability by performing a measurement. Chabot's resistance leads him to a complex expression of the relation between himself and the king.

> No Sir, tis plaine, and rude
> But true, and spotlesse, and where you object
> My hearty, and grosse vulgar love of riches,

> Titles, and honours, I did never seeke them
> For any love to them, but to that justice
> You ought to use in their due gift to merits,
> To shew you royall, and most open handed,
> Not using for hands talons, pincers, grapples;
> In whose gripes, and upon-whose gord point,
> Deserts hang sprawling out their vertuous limbs.
> (2.3.160–69)

The royal hand is "open," but it is not the hand of bounty, for merits' gifts are "due"; accordingly the royal pincers represent, first of all, inadequately rewarded merit. Their violence also suggests unjust punishment, which is what the king is threatening, and Chabot is fusing a justification of the material benefits of his office with a demand that the king respect his judgments in that office. But the substitution of talons, pincers, or grapples for hands also refers to the potentially corrupt instrumentality of officeholders and favorites, whom the king uses *for* (instead of) his hands to dispense justice, favors, and so on. Thus earlier in the play Chabot's father-in-law reproaches him for his new reconciliation with the Constable Montmorency, "that no suite may passe / One of the graples of your eithers rape" (1.2.27–28).[85] This technological transformation of the hand, which in effect doubles and tropes its instrumentality in relation to both body and mind, is also the point at which it is detached from either Chabot or the king: if it is the king's hand it is also Chabot himself in the sense that he is an instrument of the king's power; and if it is Chabot's hand it is also the king *him*self, in the sense that Chabot—as Bacon put it—is merely a usufructuary of the king, and his agency, like the labor that manifests it, is finally not his but the king's.

Chabot actively resists this condition of dependence. In the Admiral's rival Montmorency Chapman seems to have embodied, not the grasping inclination expressed in bribery, but rather the naive yet pernicious "respecting of persons" with which bribery proper is, as we have seen, often paired. He is thus a foil to Chabot's probity precisely in his openness to others; he is characterred by Allegre at the opening of the play

> As just, and well inclin'd when hee's himselfe,
> (Not wrought on with the counsells, and opinions
> Of other men) and the maine difference is,
> The Admirall is not flexible nor wonne

> To move one scruple, when he comprehends
> The honest tract and justnesse of a cause,
> The Constable explores not so sincerely
> The course hee runnes, but takes the minde of others
> (By name Iudiciall) for what his owne
> Iudgement, and knowledge should conclude.
>
> (1.1.83–92)

Asall in response agrees that this is

> A fault
> In my apprehension, anothers knowledge
> Applied to my instruction, cannot equall
> My owne soules knowledge, how to inform Acts.
>
> (1.1.92–95)

and illustrates his point with the Platonic analogy of light at successive removes from the source. As it is expressed here, Chabot's stoic individualism consists in a radical self-isolation in which *any* external influence on the faculty of judgment, whether in the form of respecting persons, pocketing bribes, or anything else, is perverse in preferring an inferior degree of reason. The analogy reveals a key assumption: others are not themselves individuals endowed with sovereign reason of their own (though this possibility is held out at 1.2.78–81) but pale reflections of Chabot's own reason. It is not that others' counsel threatens the integrity of judgment by its heterogeneity of interest but rather that Chabot and these others are always situated in a pathological relation of instrumentality to one another. In this strict accounting, even the act of respecting persons, which at least seems to offer an exit from the solipsism of stoic integrity, turns out to be merely a perversion of one's own reasoning faculty in the formation of an instrumental relation with oneself.

And it is with a collapse into the respecting of persons that the play concludes. As critics have remarked, it would be a mistake to see in the play a simple endorsement of Chabot's stoic isolationism.[86] The latter part of the play challenges not only the efficacy but the very coherence of this position. Following the king's realization that Chabot has been unjustly convicted, Chabot's health suddenly and mysteriously declines; and as it does so his resistance to corruption changes into a sentimental embrace of the practice of respecting persons, precisely what he refused to do when he tore the unjust bill in 1.2. These are, I suggest, related developments; both encode generic imperatives specific to the theater. When the king recognizes his mistake and offers Chabot a pardon, the latter refuses: he has done nothing wrong, he says, and therefore cannot be pardoned (4.1.234–39), adding that if he *were* guilty, to pardon him would be as great a sin as his own (4.1.268–71). Later, once proceedings against Poyet are under way, Chabot inquires pityingly of him and suggests he desires no revenge, having enough to cure his wounds in the example of the mercy of the king (5.3.72–84); in act 5 he repeatedly invokes the king's mercy in language at times approaching a parody of God's.[87] When the king asks him to decide on Poyet's sentence, Chabot predictably requests that the king show mercy (5.3.150; 5.3.192–97). Of course, Chabot here disregards Poyet's manifest guilt, as well as his own assertion that misapplied mercy is a sin; and he offers no reason why mercy should be shown in this case besides his own sentimental satisfaction: "I have no comfort else" (3.5.192). Chabot chooses to read the king's delegated power to judge as a personal favor to him (which in fact it is); and he judges accordingly, to satisfy himself rather than justice. To make matters worse, he makes sure that his faithful secretary Allegre, whom Poyet has had tortured almost to death, is appointed secretary to the king (5.3.120–35). Chabot, in short, wallows in a sentimental respecting of persons.

Respecting persons, Augustine argues, is akin to false mercy, mercy as corruption.[88] Augustine's context is Christian mercy, or *epieikeia;* but this theological principle was closely linked to the nevertheless distinct legal principle of equity. Theologians wrestled, as we have seen, with the uncomfortable similarities between mercy and respecting persons, for God was not, it is emphasized in Scripture, a respecter of persons.[89] By the Admiral's own principles, both of the king's acts of mercy—not only the attempted pardon of Chabot but also the accomplished pardon of Poyet—are false mercy and thus unjust. The secular exercise of the royal conscience in acts of mercy (in the form of pardons), together with its institutional expression in the courts of equity, above all the Chancery, is marked out in *Chabot* as suspect. As in Augustine, I suggest, in the play respecting persons resembles equity as a legal principle, which was described as involving a deep familiarity with the circumstances of the parties to a lawsuit (or, in the equitable interpretation of statutes, of the legislator) in part in order to understand the bearing on the case of their motives, intentions, constraints, usually with an eye toward a more favorable treatment of an accused, or of one party over another. Similarly, the judge who respects persons rules in favor of one of the parties on the basis of his prior knowledge of and acquaintance with that party. The analogy, however, is a distortion. In respecting persons the judge's interests are ambiguously in the parties and in himself, his relation to them. He judges for himself in the sense that he judges on the basis of *his* relationship with the person. Equitable judgment should look nothing like this; yet its lack of formal rules and its reliance on an entirely subjective measure, the Chancellor's conscience, suggested increasingly to the Chancery's seventeenth-century critics that it was no more reliable.[90] If respecting of persons is the perversion of equity, bribery, in its emphasis on impersonality, its blind adherence to a set of rules that disregard the social embeddedness of the particular case, is perhaps a perversion, or even a version, of law itself.

Whether or not Chapman (or Shirley) meant for *Chabot* to reflect on Lord Chancellor Bacon in its depiction of Chancellor Poyet, its critique of equity may extend to Chancery practice and to the theoretical understanding of Chancery equity as the expression of the conscience of the king through the conscience of the Chancellor. Certainly the prosecution of Bacon was closely linked in the 1621 Parliament to complaints about many aspects of the Chancery practice. Reform of Chancery procedure and fees, and limitation of its jurisdiction, were the subject of draft legislation and extensive debate. Christopher Neville made the link between attacks on the institution and attacks on the individual explicit when he suggested that in sending forward Bacon's case to the Lords for judgment they ought also to "note the luxuriant authority of that court [viz., Chancery], and how it is an inextricable labyrinth, wherein resideth such a Minotaur, as gormandizeth the liberty of all subjects whatsoever."[91] That Poyet is the beneficiary of a royal pardon just as Bacon was (though despite being signed by the king, Bacon's never went into effect) shows each benefiting unjustly from the royal prerogative institutionalized in the court of which Bacon was the head. But that in each case the pardon could be linked both to the king and to his favorite (James and Buckingham; Francis I and Chabot himself) makes the play both more and less than an indictment of the institution.

Critics find the play's conclusion, especially the Admiral's death, unsatisfactory; it is as if, as the play's 1908 editor put it, *Chabot* were really a comedy wrenched without justification into tragedy by an inadequately motivated turn of events.[92] But this discordant effect is part of *Chabot*'s design, which encodes in the Admiral's questionable appeal to the king's mercy, and his own delegated exercise of that mercy, a suspicion of equitable judgment. Such gestures—the dying man's plea for mercy on his rival, his looking out for the interests of a faithful servant—are conventional, especially in the drama; *Hamlet* is the most obvious example. Were

Chabot not on his deathbed, his behavior would not be acceptable. It is permitted only because he is dying; and reciprocally, because it is permitted, he must die.[93] The historical Chabot did in fact die shortly after his reconciliation with Francis I, as Chapman's source, Etienne Pasquier's *Les recherche de la France* (1611; another edition 1621) records. The necessity of the death is less a matter of adherence to the source, however, than of an apparent need to evoke, as in the Bussy and Biron plays, a tragic pathos, even though the material here is more resistant. The request that the actions the play has presented be judged with an intimate understanding of all the circumstances, with a familiarity with the inner life of those involved, is an aspect of the close alignment between equity and early modern theatrical representation. If drama's structure is fundamentally forensic (what happened and why, what are the consequences, what would justice consist in, and how, if at all, can it be achieved?), it pursues these questions through an epistemology *(enargeia)* and a methodology that are both equitable. But the theater's relation to equity can be more complicated, and even more adversarial, than this account suggests. *Chabot*, in particular, challenges this identification, as may Chapman's work more generally.[94] The play self-consciously declines into the false mercy of respecting persons, and this is associated both with the false pathos of Chabot's inadequately motivated death and with the generic readjustment from comedy to tragedy. It is also a concession to the theater as such; the false mercy of respecting persons is also a false equity associated, for Chapman as for forensic rhetoric generally, with theatrical perspicuity and the mode of proof it is supposed to ensure. Both Chabot's death and Poyet's pardon are associated with a sentimentalized equity; both also occupy the space of the personal, and both thus belie Chabot's investment in a justice founded on impersonal quantitation. Rather than the latter being rehabilitated through its similarity to equity, in this play it is equity, and with it the expectations of an equitable drama, that are vitiated when identified as an equivalent to the respecting of persons.

If Chabot's resistance to corruption and Bacon's practice of it place them in the same untenable position, Bacon also, and more directly, resembles Lord Chancellor Poyet. The queen mentions among Chabot's crimes his briberies (3.1.84), but this charge does not appear among those assembled against him at his trial. It is rather his tormentor, Poyet, who is charged with bribery, among other corruptions; and in her reading of the play as political allegory it is Poyet whom Norma Solve identifies as a figure for Bacon, first as presiding over the trial of Chabot/Somerset, and then as himself brought down, like Bacon, on charges of corruption.[95] Such identifications, while suggestive, are less to the point here than the ways in which the play conceptualizes bribery and other forms of corruption. When the Prosecutor opens his case against Chabot he begins by praising Poyet, claiming that his name "deriveth from the Greeke his Etymology *Poyeni*, which is to make, to create, to invent matter that was never extant in nature, from whence also is the name and dignitie of *Poeta*, which I will not insist upon, in this place, although I am confident his Lordshippe wanteth no facultie in making of Verses" (3.2.11–17). Later, in his case against Poyet, the same Prosecutor (now the Advocate)[96] claims that "Omnia ex lite fiant, we are all made by Law" (5.123–24) and goes on to interpret this maxim as meaning that the destruction of one person by law results in the creation of another, a claim he supports with a submerged biological metaphor. "The corruption of one must conclude the generation of another," he states but then adds,

> Not alwayes in the same profession; the corruption of an Apothecary, may be the generation of a Doctor of Physicke; the corruption of a Citizen may beget a Courtier, & a Courtier may very well beget an Alderman, the corruption of an Alderman may be the generation of a Country Iustice, whose corrupt ignorance easily may beget a tumult, a tumult may beget a Captaine, and the corruption of a Captaine may beget a Gentleman-Vsher, and a Gentleman-Vsher may beget a Lord, whose wit may beget a Poet, and a Poet may get a thousand pound a yeare, but nothing without corruption. (5.129–39)

In these sometimes mysterious transactions, "corruption" resists unambiguous definition, suggesting primarily the legal prosecution of such corruption (corruption as terminal, as consumption), whereby one man's fortune is made through another's fall, but also the corrupt practices by which a person betters himself. Resistance to a corrupt justice may result in a riot, and that riot will give a soldier the opportunity to rise to a captain; the justice may fall but the captain thrives as a result. But whether the captain becomes himself a gentleman usher through some corrupt dealing or his fall makes another's career as a gentleman usher is less clear. Similarly, does the witty (but also corrupt) lord become a poet himself, or does he have the wit to patronize, and thus to beget, a poet? The final transformation, in which the poet "may get a thousand pound a year," heads off the ambiguity, reducing begetting to getting, social or professional transformations to their monetary entailments: the subject of such transactions both becomes his own money and is alienated from it.

The passage presents, then, two models of corruption: one in which it enriches those who practice it, to the exclusion of others; and another in which it enriches others, especially (but not exclusively) when the capital accumulated through its means is freed up through legal prosecution. It is in the latter account that "corruption" is rehabilitated; there it is generative in two senses—because it is a way of doing business in which surplus value is produced (where the system's total value is increased because of it) and because, when the corrupt man falls, others rise at his expense, with a consequent increase in value. Each of the passage's "corrupt" transactions marks a move upward in social status, with an implied increase in value; and while there may be losers there is never an aggregate loss: a restricted economy, one in which excess registers as gain rather than loss. This is a model for social exchange and redistribution of wealth that is neither contractual nor sentimental. Corruption, etymologically a rupturing or breaking apart (from Latin *rumpere*, to break in pieces), is also what links individuals socially: a reduction of the social fabric to corrupted exchange that expresses, as if from opposite points of view, the assumptions of both the Advocate and Chabot himself. The difference is that for Chabot the social produces corruption, while for the Advocate corruption produces the social.

This is seemingly satire of a familiar kind. Yet the placement of the poet at the top of the chain of advancement through corruption is both the satirical thrust of a poet who believed himself too honest to be earning anything like a thousand pounds a year and a more complicated *alignment* of corruption and the poetic, of Poyet and Poet, signaled as well in the passage's intermixing of wit and corruption as only begetters of the poet, and preserving while inverting the praise of Poyet's fecundity earlier in Chabot's trial. When *poet* is read as *Poyet*, the thousand pounds a year is what someone like the Advocate may "get" by means of the Chancellor's downfall. At the same time, this is about what a hypothetical poet might hope to earn through productive participation in patronage relationships.

Chapman's poor success in recruiting secure patrons has already been noted. From 1614 to 1619 he was hiding from creditors at the family home in Hitchin, and he remained in want up to his death in 1634. He was certainly not getting a thousand pounds a year, and the application of the Advocate's chain of corruption may be that if Poyet thrived on corruption until it did him in, *this* poet ended up with "nothing" because he was, in contrast, "without corruption."

Yet if he would have described himself as uncorrupted, despite his disappointments he remained entirely committed to patronage as the path to financial security, patronage that in the final link of the chain—the lord whose wit (discernment) may beget a poet—is presented as productive corruption. The ambiguity that runs through the passage—does one man's corruption benefit himself only or does it also advance others and add value to the system at large?—here seems to run toward an uneasy insistence that patronage is productive corruption of the latter kind and that—even though out of office a patron cannot technically be corrupt at all—it more closely resembles respecting persons than bribery.

But can the Advocate's craven arguments, seemingly extemporized as he tries to save himself by prosecuting his former employer, really be read as escaping their broad satirical thrust and hitting on a logic Chapman in some sense takes seriously? I believe they can. Indeed, their appearing in this form, as the self-serving arguments of an unprincipled man, instructs us to read them as an allegory of the predicament of the poetic per se. Just as the defense of poetry is engaged in extracting legitimate benefit—an ethical utility—from its own mimesis of men behaving badly, to "prosecute the poet" is to rationalize him as productively corrupt. As itself an example of productive corruption, the Advocate's argument bootstraps itself into respectability.

The more shameless the Advocate's claims, the more they call out for a hermeneutic that will rehabilitate them. As he descends to ever more hyperbolic vilification of Poyet (Poyet "was borne with teeth in his head, by an affidavit of his Midwife, to note his devouring, and hath one toe on his left foote crooked, and in the forme of an Eagles talon, to foretell his rapacity" [5.151–55]), the Treasurer remarks his change of heart since his extravagant praise offered at the Chabot trial. The Advocate explains this change in such a way as to suggest the productivity not only of the exposure of corruption but also of that which is exposed.

> Your Lordship hath most aptly interpos'd, and with a word I shall easily satisfie all your judgements; He was then a Judge, and in Cathedra, in which he could not erre; it may be your Lordships cases, out of the chaire and seate of Iustice, he hath his frailties, is loos'ed and expos'd to the conditions of other humane natures; so every Iudge, your Lordships are not ignorant hath a kinde of priviledge while he is in his state, office and being, and although hee may quoad se, internally and privately be guilty of bribery of Iustice, yet quoad nos, and in publike he is an upright and innocent Iudge, we are to take no notice, nay, we deserved to suffer, if wee should detect or staine him. (5.170–77)

Two arguments merge here. Most obvious is the claim that a conventional infallibility attaches to the judge in his official capacity. But this convention is predicated here on the assumption not of probity but of its opposite. Perverting a technical distinction drawn from Aristotle and Aquinas, the Advocate distinguishes between guilt *quoad se* (in respect of himself) and innocence *quoad nos* (in respect of us), between internal and social truths: the same state of affairs that when viewed as internal to the magistrate denotes his guilt becomes, when understood as a social practice, not only innocent but a positive, productive good:

> [Every judge] may and ought to flourish in his greatnesse, and breake any mans necke, with as much facilitie as a jeast, but the case being altered, and hee downe, every subject shall be heard, a Wolfe may be appareld in a Lambskinne; and if every man should be afraid to speake truth, nay and more than truth, if the good of the subject which are clients sometime require it, there would be no remove of Officers, if no remove no motions, if no motion in Court no heate, and by consequence but cold Termes; take away this moving, this removing of Iudges, the Law may bury it selfe in Buckram, and the kingdome suffer for want of a due execution; and now I hope your Lordships are satisfied. (5.190–98)

The rapacity of the judge in office is consistent with the fury with which he is hunted down once he is out. As in the Advocate's earlier exploitation of the ambiguity of *corruption*, this account fuses the legal, social, and physical values of key terms *(removal, motion, cold, moving)* as if to describe social dynamics as determined by the laws governing the material world. Without "removal" the social world (beginning with the legal profession) comes to a standstill; and removal is predicated on corruption.

The Advocate's theory of corruption and its prosecution as the production of new social relations through capital transfers resembles, but should not be confused with, the apparently kindred claim by economic historians that, early in a nation's capitalist development, bribery arising under governmental policies that encourage rent-seeking behavior (attempts to purchase from the government privileges, for example commercial monopolies, that will render greater income than the purchase price), whether in Stuart England or in developing Third World countries in the twentieth century, assisted in economic diversification and industrial innovation by concentrating wealth in the hands of those individuals able to pay the highest bribes.[97] The Advocate's view is both less sanguine and more sanguinary.

Probably the central image of the play is Chabot's tearing of the bill. This violence and the retributive violence that follows from it are linked; as Allegre remarks, speaking generally (and prophetically), at the outset: "he [Chabot] tears the [unjust] Bill, / And would doe, were he for't to be torne to peeces" (1.45–46); ultimately, Chabot finds himself "tane a peeces" (5.461) by the king's unkindness, while Poyet, discovered in his plot to bring down the Admiral, says, "I fall in peeces" (4.340).[98] Everywhere bodies and social identities tend toward fragmentation and disarticulation; yet from the point of view of the Advocate this rupturing, associated so closely with corruption in all its forms, is constantly working to generate new social and economic relations among persons. Chabot's own atomizing individualism simply repeats this gesture in shattering social interdependency; his refusal to respect persons, and his consequent decline and death, are distinctly generative, producing new opportunities, associations, and allegiances. But it is hardly the case that the play endorses corruption. The Advocate's theory of generative corruption works as a critique both of Chabot's pose of stoic individualism and of the corruption against which that individualism defines itself; neither yields its social payoff except in exposure and destruction.

For Chabot, that destruction comes in the form of a surrender to what is for Chapman a suspect and sentimentalized respecting of persons. The descent into corruption coincides with its punishment, *its* corruption. His case is thus more consistent with the Advocate's theory of generative corruption than Poyet's, whose punishment is remitted at Chabot's intercession and who is required to make restitution out of his ill-gotten gains for all the harms he has caused (5.3.19–22), a restitution that from the perverse perspective of the Advocate would be considered retrograde, a restoration of the status quo ante rather than a productive redistribution of wealth.

Bacon's fall was almost as retrograde. Although there was some distribution of his assets—especially Buckingham's acquisition of York House for a fraction of its market value—for the most part he retained his gains. Like Poyet, he obtained the king's pardon and moreover with Buckingham's help evaded the crushing fine imposed on him by contriving to pay it to himself; unlike Poyet he made no restitution to any of those who had paid him money, even where he had ruled against them or had taken from both parties.[99] In this sense his fall was consistent with his career as a briber, where nonreciprocation was the rule. In neither the career nor the fall would Bacon have scored high on the Advocate's test for productive corruption.

But the career of Francis Bacon after 1621 offers a more complex lesson. If *Chabot* ends with a descent into a suspect theatricality corresponding to Chabot's suspect respecting of persons—with Chapman "prosecuting the poet" in both senses of the phrase—Bacon's disgrace was also productive, enabling him "to retire from the stage of civil action and betake [himself] to letters," or rather to present himself as doing so.[100] In fact he was busy during the remainder of his life in creating both the persona and the writings that established him for posterity as a major figure in intellectual history. Broken in pieces, he assembled himself into a coherence he might never have achieved had he continued in his political engagements. Just as Bacon arranged to pay his fine to himself, he managed also to profit professionally from his fall, just "not . . . in the same profession." It would be inaccurate to say that the bribery scandal produced the father of empiricism. If he spent his last years perfecting most of the works for which he came to be especially esteemed, these had been begun long before; Bacon himself, along with his literary executor, William Rawley, created the myth of an absolute separation between the careerist and the philosopher.[101] Yet the endurance of that myth, founded on the image of a broken Bacon, testifies to the productive power both of bribery and of its prohibition.

NOTES

1. Edward Coke, *Third Part of the Institutes of the Laws of England* (1628), 145–48. Exceptions include Coke's mention of Wolsey (21 Henry VIII), and Trever's Case (1611).

2. On the charges against Suffolk and Buckingham, see Linda Levi Peck, *Court Patronage and Corruption in Early Stuart England* (London: Routledge, 1990), 181–84, 190–96. On Lionel Cranfield's impeachment and fall as a result of numerous serious charges of corruption, including the acceptance of bribes from customs farmers, see Menna Prestwich, *Cranfield: Politics and Profits under the Early Stuarts* (Oxford: Clarendon Press, 1966), 423–68; and Conrad Russell, *Parliaments and English Parliaments, 1621–1629* (Oxford: Clarendon Press, 1979), 198–202.

3. Peck, *Court Patronage*, 5, 221; David L. Smith, *The Stuart Parliaments, 1603–1689* (London: Arnold, 1999), 35.

4. The broad context is best established by Peck, *Court Patronage*, esp. 185–207.

5. Assize sermons, delivered before the king's justices as they prepared to ride circuit, were especially likely to address the issue of judicial corruption. See J. S. Cockburn, *A History of English Assizes, 1558–1714* (Cambridge: Cambridge University Press, 1972), 65–66.

6. For the allegorical reading of *Chabot*, see Norma Dobie Solve, *Stuart Politics in Chapman's "Tragedy of Chabot"* (Ann Arbor: University of Michigan Press, 1929).

7. Marcel Mauss, *The Gift: The Form and Reason of Exchange in Archaic Societies*, trans. W. D. Halls (New York: Norton, 1990); Marshall Sahlins, "The Spirit of the Gift," in *Stone Age Economics* (Chicago: Aldine–Atherton, 1972), 149–83; Pierre Bourdieu, *Outline of a Theory of Practice*, trans. Richard Nice (Cambridge: Cambridge University Press, 1977);

Jacques Derrida, *Given Time I: Counterfeit Money*, trans. Peggy Kamuf (Chicago: University of Chicago Press, 1992).

   8. In the early modern period gifts often remained beyond the notice of the law, as is also the case today; but then as now in particular cases the law wants to have its say, sometimes because a statutory limit has been exceeded (as in U.S. tax law, which provides that gifts over a certain amount are taxable as income), sometimes because of the kind of gift they are (as in the law of testamentary gifts), and sometimes because the gifts are illegal (as in the law of fraudulent conveyance). On fraudulent conveyance, see J. H. Baker, *An Introduction to English Legal History*, 4th ed. (London: Butterworths, 2002), 249, 291.

   9. In law, a gift is a voluntary transfer of property or money from one person to another without either compensation or any obligation in the form of an agreement or contract.

   10. See Peck, *Court Patronage*, esp. 18–20; Natalie Zemon Davis, *The Gift in Sixteenth-Century France* (Madison: University of Wisconsin Press, 2000), 3–10.

   11. "Crucial to the success of court patronage was its disguise. While contemporaries were frank with one another about their desire for court office and titles, the rhetoric between patron and client drew on another language, one which stressed the free gift of royal patronage, the magnanimity of the patron, and the dependence of the client" (Peck, *Court Patronage*, 18).

   12. Quoted in ibid., 16–17. In the passage in full Northampton's rhetoric suggests that he is mocking his client both for being concerned that Northampton has abandoned him and for his vulnerability to just such an abandonment: he exaggerates his efforts on Cornwallis's behalf in a series of parodic parallelisms and then abruptly descends into the language of contract as if to puncture the elaborate pretense of the patron-client relationship.

   13. Thus Thomas Adams describes bribery as theft in his sermon *The white deuil, or The hypocrite vncased* (1613), sig. Gv. Or consider how in Jonson's *Bartholomew Fair* theft is repeatedly described as a form of buying and selling; see Luke Wilson, *Theaters of Intention* (Stanford: Stanford University Press, 1999), 116–17.

   14. The story of Bacon's fall has been told numerous times. See especially Samuel R. Gardiner, *History of England*, 10 vols. (London: Longmans, Green 1883), 4:56–107; James Spedding, ed., *The Letters and the Life of Francis Bacon* (London: Longmans, Green, Reader and Dyer, 1874), 7:209–348; Nieves Mathews, *Francis Bacon: The History of a Character Assassination* (New Haven: Yale University Press, 1996); Lisa Jardine and Alan Stewart, *Hostage to Fortune: The Troubled Life of Francis Bacon* (London: Victor Gollancz, 1998), 442–69; John T. Noonan Jr., *Bribes* (Berkeley: University of California Press, 1984), 339–65.

   15. Joel Hurstfield, *Freedom, Corruption and Government in Elizabethan England* (London: Jonathan Cape, 1973), 141–44.

   16. Mathews, *Francis Bacon*, 152.

   17. Noonan, *Bribes*, 360.

   18. Mathews, *Francis Bacon*, 153.

   19. Spedding, *Letters and the Life*, 7:266. Recent iterations of this point include Jardine and Stewart, *Hostage to Fortune*, 462; Stewart, "Bribery," 130. In fact, of the twenty-

one cases in which he was charged with bribery, in five of them Bacon took money from both sides, and in at least three others he ruled against the payer's interests (Noonan, *Bribes*, 354–57).

20. Coke, *Third Part of the Institutes*, 145: "Bribery is a great misprision, when any man in Judiciall place takes any Fee or Pension, Robe, or Livery, Gift, Reward, or Brocage of any person, that hath to do before him any way, for doing his office, or by colour of his office, but of the King only, unlesse it be of meat and drink, and that of small value, upon divers, and grievous punishments."

21. Spedding, *Letters and the Life*, 4:226.

22. One important formal criterion was acceptance of a gift from a party to a case currently pending. Even this, however, proved an unreliable indicator, since, as Noonan (*Bribes*, 358) points out, where receipt had occurred after cases were concluded there was evidence that Bacon's servants had arranged a prior agreement, and in any case Chancery practice was such that Chancery decrees were never enforceable without further proceedings.

23. See Noonan, *Bribes*, xix and passim.

24. John Downame, *Four Treatises, tending to diswade all Christians from foure no lesse hainous then common sinnes; namely, the abuses of Swearing, Drunkennesse, Whoredom, and Bribery* (London, 1613), sigs. Gg2–Gg2v.

25. Noonan, *Bribes*, xviii.

26. 1 Jac. 1, c. 12; reproduced in Barbara Rosen, ed., *Witchcraft in England, 1558–1618* (Amherst: University of Massachusetts Press, 1991), 58.

27. Keith Thomas, *Religion and the Decline of Magic: Studies in Popular Beliefs in Sixteenth and Seventeenth Century England* (New York: Oxford University Press, 1971), 442–45.

28. See, for example, Keith Thomas, "The Relevance of Social Anthropology to the Historical Study of English Witchcraft," in *Witchcraft Confessions and Accusations*, ed. Mary Douglas (London: Tavistock, 1970), 47–79; A. D. J. Macfarlane, "Witchcraft in Tudor and Stuart Essex," in *Crime in England, 1550–1800*, ed. J. S. Cockburn (Princeton: Princeton University Press, 1977), 72–89. It should be stressed that the economic explanation of witch hunting is only partial and cannot account for all instances; see Robin Briggs, "'Many Reasons Why': Witchcraft and the Problem of Multiple Explanation," in *Witchcraft in Early Modern Europe: Studies in Culture and Belief*, ed. Jonathan Barry, Marianne Hester, and Gareth Roberts (Cambridge: Cambridge University Press, 1996), 49–63.

29. "It could be speculated that the prosecution of Bacon was a reflection at the highest level of society about gifts analogous to the village phenomenon [of witchcraft hysteria]" (Noonan, *Bribes*, 755 n. 109).

30. Or, more exactly, rather than giving herself unconditionally to the state in order (paradoxically) to receive support. On Althusser's suggestion that the social contract is predicated on a prior and total gift of the self for which no compensation is possible, and therefore on "total alienation" rather than on a reciprocal contract, see Jean-Joseph Goux, *Symbolic Economies: After Marx and Freud*, trans. Jennifer Curtiss Gage (Ithaca: Cornell University Press, 1990), 55. Despite the requirement of submission without compensation, the transaction remains structurally an exchange.

31. It was just as illegal to offer a bribe as to accept one; see Coke, *Third Part of the Institutes*, 147. In Bacon's case, however, the Lords in effect granted immunity from prosecution to anyone who testified that he had presented Bacon with a bribe (Noonan, *Bribes*, 349). See also Thomas Adams's exculpation of the briber as a victim of theft in his sermon *The white deuil* (1613): "If there be any officer, that walkes with vnwashen hands, I meane, with the fowle fingers of briberie, he is a theefe.... Theft? who is robbed? the giuer? doth not the freedome of his will transfer a right of the gift to the receiuer? no; for it is voluntarie or willing will: but as a man giues his purse to the ouer-mastring theefe, rather than ventures his life; so this his bribe, rather than indanger his cause."

32. Mauss, *Gift*, 51–52.

33. On the increased prevalence and cultural valuation of movable property that distinguishes early modern from medieval culture, see Martha C. Howell, "The Language of Property in Early Modern Europe," in *The Culture of Capital: Properties, Cities, and Knowledge in Early Modern England*, ed. Henry S. Turner (New York: Routledge, 2002), 17–25.

34. That he just didn't understand that those paying him had a specific consideration in mind seems incredible, but it would help explain his habit of taking from both sides and his frequent failure to perform on behalf of those paying him. See n. 19.

35. The letter is preserved in the Folger Shakespeare Library (shelf mark X.d. 121(1)).

36. Lambarde (1536–1601) was not to become a justice of the peace until two years after the date of the letter and would not become a Master in Chancery until 1592. Rokeby, who was a Master of the Court of Requests at this time, could probably have done more for Lambarde than Lambarde could for him. We know that Lambarde wrote to him in 1588 (Folger MS X.d. 121 (2)) requesting that he intercede at the Court of Requests on behalf of some poor folk with whom he had sent his letter; see Wilbur Dunkel, *William Lambarde, Elizabethan Jurist, 1536–1601* (New Brunswick, NJ: Rutgers University Press, 1965), 101. Rokeby and Lambarde had met while at Lincoln's Inn. Apparently good friends, they interacted in legal matters of various kinds until Rokeby died in 1596. Thereafter, Lambarde and Sir Thomas Egerton were named in Rokeby's will as executors of his estate. See Retha M. Warnicke, *William Lambarde: Elizabethan Antiquary, 1536–1601* (London: Phillimore, 1973), 50–52. In some of these dealings Rokeby seems to have played the role of patron—bequeathing money in support of Lambarde's own college for the poor in Greenwich, recommending him to the Privy Council for interrogating recusants in Maidstone (Dunkel, *William Lambarde*, 92), for example—but as Lambarde's reputation caught up with him the two seem to have assumed rough professional parity.

37. Lambarde's reference to "my father and mother" is puzzling, since, assuming the letter's date of 1577 is correct, his parents were long since dead, his mother having died in 1540 and his father in 1554. He cannot be referring to the parents of either of his wives because his first wife, Jane Multon, died in 1573, and he did not marry the second, Sylvestre Dean Dalison, until 1583. For all dates (except that of the letter), I rely on Warnicke, *William Lambarde*, xiv–xv.

38. Baker, *Introduction*, 273–74.

39. Ibid., 389.

40. See Oliver Wendell Holmes, *The Common Law* (1881), ed. Mark DeWolfe Howe (Boston: Little, Brown, 1963), 130–62.

41. Baker, *Introduction*, 390.

42. William Roper, "The Life of Sir Thomas More," in *Two Early Tudor Lives*, ed. Richard S. Sylvester and Davis P. Harding (New Haven: Yale University Press, 1962), 231. See also the very similar and apparently derivative account of these anecdotes illustrating More's probity in the anonymous manuscript *Sir Thomas More* (c. 1599), in Christopher Wordsworth, ed., *Ecclesiastical Biography*, 4th ed., 4 vols. (London: Francis and John Rivington, 1853), 2:80–81.

43. Roper, "Life of Sir Thomas More," 232.

44. Francis Bacon, *Works*, ed. James Spedding, Robert Leslie Ellis, and Douglas Denon Heath (Boston: Brown and Taggard, 1860), 13:334.

45. Mathews (*Francis Bacon*, 153) thus suggests the anecdote may be a conflation of the two incidents reported in Roper, "Life of Sir Thomas More."

46. Spedding, *Letters and the Life*, 7:255.

47. It is not entirely clear from Bacon's account whether Kennedy simply owed Pinckney an amount equivalent to the value of the cabinet or whether he owed Pinckney this amount because Pinckney had himself provided him with the cabinet.

48. On Bacon's occupancy of York house, see Jardine and Stewart, *Hostage to Fortune*, 28, 416.

49. If Bacon had reason to be euphemistic in this way, his accusers did not; why would they have identified the gift as the cabinet rather than anything it might have contained? Moreover, since Bacon could have emptied the cabinet of its contents beforehand, might he be quibbling when he says in self-defense that he demanded it be taken back?

50. Spedding, *Letters and the Life*, 7:254–55.

51. Ibid. The cabinet shares some of the characteristics by which noncash gifts are considered more meaningful than cash gifts—anticipate the recipient's tastes and needs; they posses specific suitability; they can't be given by just anyone (they reflect the giver's tastes as well as his familiarity with recipient). These give it something of the aura of a gift and gesture toward its disqualification as a bribe, though only weakly. At the other end of the spectrum of thing-gifts from diamonds and gold was food, for which special rules applied in both England and France. Early legislation prohibited judges riding circuit in England from accepting any gifts besides food and drink. Similarly, in sixteenth-century France, early laws excepted food and drink from gifts judges were not allowed to receive; but two successive laws, in 1561 and 1579, eliminated this exception (Davis, *Gift in Sixteenth-Century France*, 85–87). The rationale for the exception, presumably, was that consumables were of relatively slight value, perishable, and not easily converted into cash. But see ibid., 88, on how these limitations were overcome by litigants and judges. Food is, indeed, a very special category of thing, a money equivalent but in most cases both unstable and difficulty to transport (certain spices being significant exceptions).

52. Francis Bacon, *A Selection of His Works*, ed. Sidney Warhaft (Indianapolis: Bobbs-Merrill, 1965), 99.

53. John Webster puns on the two uses of the word in his character of a Jesuit (*Characters*, in *Complete Works*, ed. F. L. Lucas, 4 vols. (London: Chatto and Windus, 1927): "Hee is a false Key to open Princes Cabinets, and pry into their Counsels" (4:42). In "Bribery, Buggery, and the Fall of Lord Chancellor Bacon," in *Rhetoric and Law in Early Modern Europe*, ed. Victoria Kahn and Lorna Hutson (New Haven: Yale University Press, 2001), 125–42, Alan Stewart argues that in Bacon's case charges of bribery and buggery were linked through Bacon's mismanagement of his servants, who functioned prominently in contemporary accounts of both allegations, and more generally through his failure to separate the domestic and the professional. On the early modern closet more generally, see Alan Stewart, *Close Readers: Humanism and Sodomy in Early Modern England* (Princeton: Princeton University Press, 1997). Stewart emphasizes those instances where Bacon's servants used the authority derived from their proximity to Bacon to exact bribes for themselves; yet officials who accept bribes typically operate through the intermediary of a bagman, and the suggestion that his servants were in business for themselves rather than on his behalf may have been an exculpatory exaggeration. Bacon may have been a better household manager than Stewart's argument suggests.

54. Sitta von Reden, *Exchange in Ancient Greece* (London: Duckworth, 1995), 94. Compare the similar confusion of public and domestic space noted in Stewart's account of Bacon's fall in "Bribery and Buggery."

55. On bribery as a theological problem, see Noonan, *Bribes*; and Noonan, "Agency, Bribery and Redemption in Thomas Aquinas," *Recherche de Théologie Ancienne et Médiévale* 49 (1982): 159–73.

56. Spedding, *Letters and the Life*, 7:226.

57. See Barry Nicholas, *An Introduction to Roman Law* (Oxford: Clarendon Press, 1972), 144–48. The usufructuary in Roman law resembles the *cestui que use* in English common law, the person enjoying the benefit or use of assets held in trust for him or her by a feofee for uses; see A. W. B. Simpson, *A History of the Land Law*, 2nd ed. (Oxford: Clarendon Press, 1986), 173–74.

58. Jonathan Marwil, *The Trials of Counsel: Francis Bacon in 1621* (Detroit: Wayne State University Press, 1976), 98–99; Catherine Drinker Bowen, *Francis Bacon: The Temper of a Man* (Boston: Little, Brown, 1963), 92–93. Bacon's reading was first published as *The learned reading of Sir Francis Bacon, one of Her Majesties learned counsell at law, upon the statute of uses* (1642). Bacon praised the statute lavishly but also considered its interpretation especially vexed: "I have chosen to read upon the Statute of Uses . . . a law whereupon the inheritances of this realm are tossed at this day, as upon a sea, in such sort that it is hard to say which bark will sink, and which will get to the haven: that is to say what assurances will stand good, and what will not" (*Works*, 7.416). Essentially, the statute "transferred the seisin and legal estate to the *cestui que use*"; but this raised complex problems (Simpson, *History of the Land Law*, 187). In Baker's words, it reunited the legal estate with

the use (*Introduction*, 256). It also affirmed the common-law interpretation of the use against that of the Chancery. Basically, the statute made possible the transition from feudal relations to early modern property relations by turning the right of the feudal tenant to the fruits of the land into the right to the land, that is, into an estate in the land.

59. In the context of Bacon's allusions to the civil law, it is significant that, in addition to its theological meanings, *oblation* meant, in Roman law, "an amount due" *(OED)*.

60. Spedding, *Letters and the Life*, 7:241–42.

61. Noonan, *Bribes*, 361.

62. Ibid., 362.

63. Jardine and Stewart, *Hostage to Fortune*, 478–79. Neither this nor a royal warrant for a pardon issued several years later ever resulted in an actual pardon being enrolled (496–97).

64. Noonan, *Bribes*, 362.

65. George Chapman, *The Georgicks of Hesiod*, Sig. A2–A3. See also A. R. Braunmuller, *Natural Fictions: George Chapman's Major Tragedies* (Newark: University of Delaware Press, 1992), 139.

66. See Solve, *Stuart Politics*, 30–31.

67. Thomas Howard, Earl of Suffolk, was father of Carr's wife, Frances; he and Carr dominated James's court between 1614 and 1616, but in 1618 he was charged in Star Chamber with embezzlement and fraud in his office as Lord Treasurer; the conviction of both his daughter and Carr three years earlier in the Overbury murder made his own conviction (along with his wife and an associate) in 1619 possible (Peck, *Court Patronage*, 181–82).

68. David Lindley, *The Trials of Frances Howard: Fact and Fiction in the Court of King James* (London: Routledge, 1993), 150.

69. Jardine and Stewart, *Hostage to Fortune*, 373.

70. How persuasive such a reading is depends in part on the dating of the play, a question complicated by its having been revised by James Shirley some time before its publication for the first time in 1639. This was the theory advanced by Solve, *Stuart Politics* in 1929, who accordingly argued for a date of composition of 1621, much later than the 1611–14 proposed by Thomas Marc Parrot, *The Plays and Poems of George Chapman*, 2 vols. (1910; reprint, London: Routledge, 1961), 1:631–37. The earlier dating is argued as correct by Albert H. Tricomi, "The Dates of the Plays of George Chapman," *English Literary Renaissance* 12 (1982): 261–65; but others remain persuaded by Solve's dating, if not by the details of her theory of topical allegory: see, among others, G. E. Bentley, *The Jacobean and Caroline Stage*, 7 vols. (Oxford: Clarendon Press, 1941–68), 5:1088–91, and more recently G. Blakemore Evans's textual introduction in *The Plays of George Chapman: The Tragedies with Sir Gyles Goosecappe*, ed. Allan Holaday (Bury St. Edmunds: St Edmundsbury Press, 1987), 617–25, which provides a good summary of the debate.

71. Chapman was in trouble with the authorities for topical references beginning with his part in the ill-fated *Eastward Ho!* (1605) and continuing with his *Byron* (1608) and with *Andromeda Liberata* (1614).

72. Francis Bacon, *The Advancement of Learning*, ed. G. W. Kitchin (London: Dent, 1973), 2.23.6 (183–84).

73. Quoted in Noonan, *Bribes*, 68.

74. See generally ibid., 55–82, to which this paragraph is heavily indebted.

75. *The Plays of George Chapman: The Comedies*, ed. Alan Holaday (Urbana: University of Illinois Press, 1970).

76. *The Poetical Works of Sir William Alexander: Earl of Stirling*, ed. L. E. Kastner and H. B. Charlton, 2 vols. (Edinburgh: Scottish Text Society, 1921–1929), 2:396.

77. George Chapman, *The Widow's Tears*, 2.4.13–14. Compare the expression "to grease someone's palm." John Webster in his *Characters* says of "A mere Petifogger": "Only with this, I wil pitch him o're the Barre, & leave him; That his fingers itch after a Bribe, ever since his first practicing at Courthand" (Webster, *Complete Works*, 4.35). Here the work of bribery is associated with that of writing, with almost a suggestion that *courthand* may be used as a cant term for bribery. See also Webster's character of "A Reverend Judge" (38).

78. Quoted in Katherine Rowe, "'God's Handy Worke': Divine Complicity and the Anatomist's Touch," in *The Body in Parts: Fantasies of Corporeality in Early Modern Europe*, ed. David Hillman and Carla Mazzio (New York: Routledge, 1997), 286.

79. Noonan, *Bribes*, 313.

80. Ibid., 314–17.

81. For these reasons, the criminality of respecting persons was even less clearly defined than the criminality of bribery per se. In the wake of Bacon's impeachment and a consequent investigation of sale of offices among the Masters of Chancery, it occurred to the Commons to initiate a bill prohibiting both bribery "of reward" and "of affection," the latter being parliamentary idiom for respecting persons; see *Commons Debates, 1621*, ed. Wallace Notestein, Frances Helen Relf, and Hartley Simpson, 7 vols. (New Haven: Yale University Press, 1935), 3:100; 5:104. The bill received one reading but was never sent up to the Lords (*Commons Debates* 7:306).

82. Robert Ornstein, *The Moral Vision of Jacobean Tragedy* (Madison: University of Wisconsin Press, 1960), 78; Braunmuller, *Natural Fictions*, 139.

83. Coke, similarly, argued in 1608 that the English monarchy had exhausted its powers of adjudication in the act of establishing the central courts; the delegation of the power to judge had been permanent and complete and could not be reversed (Baker, *Introduction*, 98).

84. All references to the text of *The Tragedie of Chabot* are to Holaday, *Plays of George Chapman: The Tragedies*.

85. The graphic quality of the image is accentuated by "rape," suggesting not only seizure by force but also "rasping, scratching or scraping" *(OED)*. *Chabot*'s preoccupation with hands (the word itself occurs thirty times in the play) is linked not only to an underlying interest in the bribery relationship but also to the play's many references to anatomical dissection, a practice closely associated with the agency of the hand (see 1.1.26, 4.1.355–58, 5.3.98–105); the term *dissection* is used figuratively but in close relation to images of vi-

olence against the body. See Rowe, "'God's Handy Worke.'" Like the image of the king's hands as cruel pincers, the dissection images, which link torture and execution with anatomical procedure and the epistemologies it implies (as they were generally linked both conceptually and in material practice), pathologize instrumental agency. To imagine the king's hands as pincers is to combine concern for the potential corruption both of royal giving and of the king's officers with imagery from the torture chamber; one cause of Chabot's eventually fatal suffering is the frequently mentioned racking of his faithful servant Allegre (see 3.1.45–53, 5.211–18, 5.2.125–30, 5.3.35, 5.3.124).

86. See Braunmuller, *Natural Fictions*, 132.

87. See, for example, 5.3.76–84, where Chabot makes his relation to the king both that of the sinner condemned by law and redeemed by God's mercy and that of God's sacrifice of what he loved most.

88. Noonan, *Bribes*, 71.

89. See Noonan, "Agency."

90. Baker, *Introduction*, 109–10. Chancery jurisdiction survived as long as it did in part because it shifted away from "conscience" to formal rules of equity; this shift, under way by the early sixteenth century, was not enough, however, to quell growing resistance to equitable jurisdiction (106).

91. *Commons Debates*, 2.240.

92. George Chapman and James Shirley, *The Tragedie of Chabot Admirall of France*, ed. Ezra Lehman (Philadelphia: University of Pennsylvania Press, 1906), 34–35.

93. One must wonder about the appropriateness of this outcome if Chapman really did write the play as a comment upon Somerset's mistreatment and a plea for his release from prison, as Solve claims in *Stuart Politics*. If Chabot dies *despite* being reconciled to the king, one might ask what kind of incentive that would be for his release, which, by analogy, wouldn't make any difference.

94. Chapman's understanding of *enargeia*, for example, departs from standard rhetorical accounts like that of Quintilian and is distinctly untheatrical. See John Huntington, "Virtues Obscured: George Chapman's Social Strategy," *Criticism* 39 (1997): 165–66.

95. See Solve, *Stuart Politics*, esp. 128–33.

96. The Prosecutor of 3.2 is identified in the speech prefixes of 5.2 as Advocate; but 5.2.59–71 makes clear that these two are one and the same.

97. Peck, *Court Patronage*, 134–60. Peck argues that in the case of Stuart England, at least, the argument that bribery promoted economic growth is mostly unfounded.

98. See also 2.0 (s.d.), 2.3.35, 3.2.80–87, 4.1.4–9, 4.1.274, 4.1.356, 5.2.169–70, 5.3.48.

99. Noonan, *Bribes*, 364.

100. Quoted in Jardine and Stewart, *Hostage to Fortune*, 474.

101. Ibid., 475–76.

Epilogue
The True Image of Authority

Deak Nabers

This volume is about the relationship between law and literature, but the two disciplines are hardly equally represented in its contents. Its contributors are all literary, rather than legal, scholars, and by and large they act like literary scholars. The payoff for most of the essays here comes in literary currency. We get new readings of classic literary works and new accounts of the function of literature in the Renaissance. What we do not get, with only a few exceptions (most obviously Luke Wilson's essay on the idea of the bribe and Debora Shuger's essay on censorship), are new accounts of either the nature of the law or the meaning of its history. This is not to say that legal theory and legal history are unimportant in these essays; it is just to say that, unlike more literary matters, they are approached from a distance, frequently through the lens of other scholars, rather than confronted directly.

    This epilogue will not exactly balance the volume's emphasis on the literary. Like all the other contributors, I come to the volume from an English department rather than a law school. But it will attempt to measure and present the contributions of these essays to the questions of legal, rather than literary, inquiry. And it will suggest that though these legal questions frequently lie beyond the explicit concerns of the contributors, their essays nevertheless ultimately present an in-

Epilogue

sightful and suggestive account of what constitutes the idea of law—an account that usefully resonates with a long line of Anglo-American efforts to say what exactly the law is and how it might differ from other forms of interpersonal coercion. I will begin by laying out the legal issues I think the volume usefully glosses, and I will then proceed to show how in glossing these issues it differs from some other recent efforts in the field of law and literature. From there I will examine in detail the way in which several of the essays take up the idea of the law with a view toward revealing their utility in making sense of several more explicitly theoretical legal projects, namely Foucault's efforts to distinguish sovereignty from governmentality and Blackstone's efforts to specify the relationship between custom and the law. Before I conclude I hope to make clear that the domain of literature, especially the domain of drama, is hardly as remote from the domain of the law as we might expect, and that in presenting their various accounts of the law's impact on literary materials these essays also present accounts of what the law is in the first instance. In laying out these claims, I will not provide summaries of each of the essays in this volume, nor will I address each of the essays in equal detail. Rather, I will focus on a core set of concerns that make regular, if not exactly systematic, appearances throughout the volume, and I will address these concerns chiefly in terms of their appearances in those essays in which they play their largest roles. My goal is less a listing of the topics engaged in the essays in the volume than an analysis of the legal theory that emerges, often implicitly, from the way in which they engage those topics.

> LEAR. What, art mad? A man may see how this world goes with no eyes. Look with thine ears. See how yond justice rails upon yond simple thief. Hark in thine ear: change places and handy-dandy, which is the justice, which is the thief? Thou hast seen a farmer's dog bark at a beggar?
> GLOUCESTER. Ay, sir.
> LEAR. And the creature run from the cur. There thou mightst behold the great image of authority—a dog's obeyed in office. (4.6.148–56)

In this famous sequence Lear raises the problem that has in many ways structured Anglo-American accounts of the nature of the law: What is the relationship between physical force and a legal command? The question emerges here because it is unclear in Lear's example whether the dog's authority stems from his position ("in office") or from his capacity to arouse fear. Lear himself, of course, derives a message about the nature of "offices" from the beggar's flight. But he has produced an account of that flight that makes it seem at best only tenuously related to the office to which he connects it. On the face of it, it is odd to think of a farmer's dog as occupying any "office": not only do dogs not seem self-evidently plausible candidates for offices, but the dog's activity here—scaring a beggar, one who is not even said to be trespassing, away from a piece of property—does not really look like the activity of those figures, dog and nondog alike, who hold offices. We might think that the dog is merely performing the office of protecting the farmer's property from the beggar's trespass, but Lear doesn't exactly press this scenario upon us. He initially stresses the dog's active power rather than its status: it becomes a "cur" in the account before it assumes an office. The issue of offices is a late arrival on a scene to which it looks somewhat alien, and its entry, coming as it does after a dash, is marked as much as a break with the parable it is said to gloss as the inevitable conclusion of it.

From this perspective we might even say that Lear does not merely present two different accounts of the nature of "authority" so much as two incompatible accounts of it. For the dog's use of force would actually seem to compromise our sense that it occupies an office: it is hard to think that the beggar actually *obeys* the dog here rather than simply responding to its threat. But does it make sense to posit this distinction between obedience and obligation? For many legal theorists in the Anglo-American tradition, the dog's acts of force are precisely what provides him with his office. As H. L. A. Hart explains in his seminal *The Concept of Law* (1961),[1]

> The gunman orders his victim to hand over his purse and threatens to shoot if he refuses; if the victim complies we refer to the way in which he was forced to do so by saying that he was *obliged* to do so. To some it has seemed clear that in this situation where one person gives another an order backed by threats, and, in this sense of "oblige," obliges him to comply, we have the essence of law, or at least "the key to the science of jurisprudence" [quoting John Austin]. (6)

For Hart this scenario does not provide "the essence of the law," though, and it does not provide the law's essence for exactly the reasons that it does not exactly quite count as "the great image of authority" for Lear. Hart and Lear are both as interested in the status of the order backed by force as they are with the fact that the order is backed by force in the first instance. Hart's name for what Lear calls an "office" is "rule," and what he means by a rule is a structure that establishes a person who makes a threat backed by force as one who has the authority to make such a threat. He makes this point through an example not far removed from the domain of *King Lear*'s concerns—the question of how one source of authority might succeed another. Hart acknowledges that a person whose "general orders are habitually obeyed" (to whom he gives the name "Rex") might look a legal authority, but he is unwilling to admit that the fact that his orders are obeyed in and of itself constitutes his legal authority. And he thinks this point emerges most clearly at the moment in which Rex's successor (call him Rex II) begins to make orders that are habitually obeyed: for what makes Rex II's orders authoritative cannot be the authority of Rex I: "Even if we conclude that a person such as Rex, whose general orders are habitually obeyed, may be called a legislator and his orders laws, habits of obedience to each of a succession of such legislators are not enough to account for the *right* of a successor to succeed and for the consequent continuity in legislative power" (59). The horror of Lear's "image" from this perspective is not simply that it makes the forces that provide what he calls the "authority" and Hart calls "the right" of one to rule seem entirely arbitrary but rather that in making the origin of this authority seem arbitrary it makes the authority look like a function of, rather than an alternative to, the law's violence. Hart's notion of the rule and the rights it confers on a legislator is designed to separate the legislator from the gunman. Lear's parable makes even the rights of the legislator a result of his use of a gun.

Lear's account does not fuse the two alternatives that Hart wishes to distinguish so much as expose the ways in which Hart's apparatus for effecting this distinction—the idea of the rule—is not quite up to the task. Lear's image of authority reveals that, even on Hart's account, all that stands between Rex's successors and the gunman is the attribution of such a right—the fact that such a right is, as Hart famously articulated the point, "recognized" (94) or "accepted" (100). And whether this acceptance can be distinguished from the acceptance we perform in response to the gunman is a famously difficult matter. What endows a rule giver with the "*right*" to give rules? Hart wishes to attribute that right to a formal structure: he has that right because he occupies the position of the rule giver. But Lear's example makes this claim look either circular (he has that right because he takes it) or sociological (he has that right because people attribute it to him), and in either case the effect is to disconnect whatever authority Rex might have from the idea of his "right." The concept of the rule provides an account of the necessary structural groundings for a legal order: there must be what Hart calls primary and secondary rules; there must be both rules that regulate conduct and rules about who gets to make them. But it does not provide an account of what confers authority upon those structures.

Hart emphatically rejects one obvious source for that authority—morality. "[T]here are no necessary conceptual connections between the content of law and morality," he insists; "and hence morally iniquitous provisions may be valid as legal rules or principles" (268). But the most thoroughly elaborated extension of Hart's accounts of the nature of the law has actually taken morality up and located it within the legal structures from which Hart would like to exclude it; it has, indeed, placed morality in the position in relation to the notion of the rule that Hart places in relation to acts of force. This extension lies in Ronald Dworkin's *Law's Empire* (1985),[2] which, though it presents itself as a critique of Hart and his positivism (and indeed is a critique of Hart's *positivism*), ultimately redeploys the structural principles that Hart placed at the center of his definition of the law. In *Law's Empire* Hart's primary and secondary rules emerge as moral and formal features of the law, and the "rights" of the lawgivers are grounded not in a purely formal structure of interlacing rules but rather in a structure of interlacing rules and values. Just as Hart's structure does not devolve either into the authority of the lawgiver or into the authority of the system that endows him with that power, Dworkin's law does not devolve either into ethics or into positivism but rather is the name for their mutual interpenetration: "Present law," the purely positive and formal law of the realm, "contains another law," he explains, "which marks out its ambitions for itself; the purer law is defined by pure integrity" (406–7). Lear's image of authority is powered by the sense that the law lacks this integrity and that it lacks it because, while it has acts of power and rules of recognition, it does not "contain" any other "purer" law according to which its ambitions might be measured.

I begin with this long effort to locate Lear's concerns in the context of the tradition of Anglo-American answers to the question "What is law?" because it seems to me that the essays in this volume, though they do not all take the subject up explicitly, largely revolve around this question.[3] They repeatedly engage and reveal the necessary structural complexity of the law, the ways in which the law requires both offices and force, rights to rule and acts of ruling. And in so doing they represent something of a departure of what has usually marched under the banner of the so-called law and literature movement. That movement, at least on most recent accounts of it, has been largely concerned with the study of the appearance of legal themes in literary works and with the rhetorical underpinnings of legal writings. "Literature has been seen," Barbara Johnson has recently claimed, "as a locus of plots and situations that parallel legal cases or problems, either to shed light on complexities not always acknowledged by the ordinary practice of legal discourse or to shed light on cultural crises and debates that historically underlie and inform literary texts."[4] Shoshana Felman makes essentially the same point:

> The dialogue between the disciplines of law and literature has so far been primarily thematic (that is, essentially conservative of the integrity and of the stable epistemological boundaries of the two fields): when not borrowing the tools of literature to analyze (rhetorically) legal opinions, scholars in the field of law and literature most often deal with the explicit, thematized reflection (or "representation") of the institutions of the law in works of the imagination, focusing on the analysis of fictional trials in a literary plot and/or on the psychology or the sociology of literary characters whose fate or whose profession ties them to the law (lawyers, judges, or accused).[5]

To be sure, there are essays in this volume that are interested in the appearance of legal thematics in literary works, essays that devote themselves to the "parallel" between literary and legal "cases" and "problems." But in these essays the law is seldom simply a "thematic," and the relevant parallels are seldom "explicit." Indeed, the presence of the law in these arguments is often so subtle as to make Felman's conflation of the "reflective" and the "representational" seem somewhat peculiar. Take, for instance, Heather Dubrow's reading of *King Lear* in terms of the questions of legal authority and property ownership that emerge in the passage with which I began. For Dubrow, "Contemporary tensions about property ownership lie behind the anxieties about housing and displacement that run throughout" *King Lear,* but they hardly count as the play's explicit content. Indeed, their presence is for her a "flicker" of "'Dreamwork'" rather than an open topic of discussion: "The relationship of land law to the lawless world of *King Lear* is . . . as subterranean as it is significant." The force of her reading is thus to "activate" "a social and legal history," and what this process of activation entails is not the compiling of references to the relevant social and legal history so much as the chronicling of that history's eruption into the midst of what look like references to other things. Dubrow sometimes evinces a frustration with the ease with which land law may be disinterred from the "lawless world of *King Lear.*" The play is deeply devoted to articulating the terms on which one might be said to hold property, but her interest lies as much in refashioning our understanding of moments throughout the Renaissance that have tended to be interpreted in terms of what she calls "national politics" as it does in registering the relatively less spectral presence of anxieties about property in *King Lear*: "Arguably such anxieties about deceptive Spaniards, dark-skinned women, and disloyal priests intensified, figured, and were figured by fears of invasion by one's own neighbors in the course of a land dispute." If this "spectral" presence pushes Dubrow's argument into the realm of speculation (it is only "arguably" the case, and the way she follows this speculative claim with a claim of its logical consequences thus only underscores, rather than mutes, the suggestiveness of her claim), it certainly ensures that she will not be giving us a straightforward or simple reading of the thematic of law in Shakespeare.

It is possible to conclude, though, that Dubrow still does little more than "shed light on" a "cultural crisis," albeit one that has not tended to "underlie or inform" our sense of the literary texts with which she associates it. Johnson thinks that we should instead wonder about "the relations between the laws of genre and the laws of state," precisely the topic taken up in a number of the essays here, most prominently in Matthew's Greenfield's account of the War of the Poets. At first glance, Greenfield's essay might look like another instance of the "use of the tools of literature to analyze" legal documents. Greenfield is interested, for instance, in locating a level of anxiety within seemingly straightforward legal claims: since on his account legal narratives require descriptions of an agent's motives, and since those descriptions almost always entail what he calls a "reliance on inference," "legal narratives [are] epistemologically anxious in a way that satire, for example, is not." But Greenfield's primary interest lies less in the unmasking of legal presuppositions (what Johnson might call "complexities not always acknowledged by the ordinary practice of legal discourse") than in detailing the functional power of those presuppositions when they enter a generic field—namely satire—to which they are seemingly alien. To put the argument in Johnson's terms, the rules of state require that accusations be cast in terms of what Greenfield calls "not only the actions but the intentions of [the] defendants"; the rules of genre require that accusations strip their targets of agency "by representing their degeneration into beasts, automata, or allegorical figures." But Johnson's terms are slightly less radical than Greenfield's here, for in Greenfield's essay the rules of state themselves constitute a "genre," not an alternative to the generic: to call a document an "arraignment," as Jonson calls *Poetaster* (1601), is to provide it with a "generic label." And thus if *Poetaster* stands as an "unstable . . . hybrid" the source of both its hybridity and its instability is "generic," which is to say that it results from a competition between genres rather than competition between genre and its other. The stability of what Felman calls "the stable epistemological boundaries of the two fields" is precisely what is challenged in Greenfield's reading of *Poetaster*. Felman imagines that the new studies of law and literature should expose the "structure and process" (739) of legal narratives in relation to literature. This would seem to be precisely what Greenfield does.

Even as Greenfield explores the hybridity of *Poetaster*, he allows the legal and literary epistemologies he confronts to remain fairly stable: indeed, on his account, the hybridity of *Poetaster* is actually a result of the presence of two stable epistemologies within it, epistemologies that are juxtaposed, but never wholly combined or synthesized, throughout the work. The law becomes generic, but its emergence as a genre does not wholly erode its difference from other, more literary, genres. For recent students of the relationship between law and literature, the difference between law and literature has constituted a subject as engaging as the question of exactly what happens to the two discourses when they are juxtaposed, and a large number of critics have recently insisted that the real value of the comparative study of law and literature lies precisely in its ability to highlight what is distinctive about each of the two fields, not its capacity to subsume both of them in the same generality. It is possible to configure almost the totality of recent law and literature scholarship in these terms. The notion that study of the relationship between law and literature should focus on the necessary differences between legal and literary activities lies at the core, to take only a few examples, of Martha Nussbaum's notion of "poetic justice,"[6] Wai Chee Dimock's interest in the "incommensurate,"[7] Brook Thomas's effort to specify what "role" "imaginative visions" might play in "political criticism,"[8] and even Johnson's interest in the relationship between "personification" and the legal subject.

But if there is nothing particularly unusual in Greenfield's finding an interest, both legal and literary, in the juxtaposition of literature and law, there is something unusual about the relative value he assigns each of the two. Though he calls law and literature "two representational modes and two definitions of the human," Greenfield ultimately casts the satirical "representational mode" in terms that make it look as if it entailed an assault on the human rather than an account of it: satire hinges on the "degeneration" of persons "into beasts, automata, or allegorical figures." The general tendency in recent law and literature work has been precisely in the opposite direction. For figures like Nussbaum, it is precisely the point of the juxtaposition of law and literature to return the law from its formalism to a more specifically human (Johnson might call it "inferential") account of the subject. Literature stands as the domain of persons, and bringing the law into contact with it can only help us repair the breach between the law and the subjects it governs. What is remarkable about Greenfield's essay, from this perspective, is that it renders the law a reflection of personhood, if not the actual origin of it, and that it suggests that the law reflects or generates personhood in the face of the dehumanizing forces of literature.

Greenfield is not alone in this volume in suggesting that legal conceptions of the subject are actually central to our sense of the human and that their centrality to our sense of the human is in part a function of their capacity to correct for distortions that arise from literature. Debora Shuger's essay takes an almost identical position. Shuger's general interest is in turn-of-the-seventeenth-century censorship laws, or, more particularly, in both the absence of contemporary objections to those laws and the unusual forms in which the rationale for them was articulated. On Shuger's account, "[V]irtually all modern accounts of censorship have built on anachronistic premises." If we tend to understand censorship in terms of individual liberty, "principled dissent," and "uncomfortable truths," at the turn of the seventeenth century the issues surrounding licensing tended to revolve around "the circulation of falsehood" rather than the suppression of debate. And, consequently, censorship was seen less as a way of protecting the state against alien and potentially subversive political movements than as a way of protecting individuals within the state from assaults on their dignity—assaults that, as Shuger notes, were not nonpolitical so much as nonideological. Censorship laws were thus largely efforts to prevent defamation, and their goals lay in the preservation of normative standards of what Shuger calls "decency" and defines as "the mutual trust and forbearance that make community possible" rather than in the protection of the ideological authority of particular political institutions.

Shuger's distinction between the civility-based regime of the Renaissance and the rights-based regime of the present may not be entirely coherent,[9] but whether we inhabit a legal domain in which "civil harmony" is less important than individual expression is less important than the way in which Shuger joins Greenfield in making the law—here censorship law no less—look like the custodian of human status rather than a power arrayed against it. For both of them the law vouchsafes the human rather than compromising it; and for both of them what it vouchsafes the human against are the workings of at least one kind of literature. Shuger's confidence that the law might serve this function, though, is hardly absolute. She repeatedly reveals the social value of early modern censorship laws, but she is quick to say that she would not advocate a return to them: "I am not defending early modern censorship." Monitoring "our commitment to subversive critique" so as to resist "sympathy" for slander, we might retain the value of calling men "to charity" without persecuting them. The hope here seems to be that there might be some way to derive the benefits of the law without ever having to deploy its force, and that hope is routinely denied in other recent readings of the relationship between Renaissance theater and the law. The most significant of these readings comes in the form of Jonathan Goldberg's *Shakespeare's Hand* (2002). What Shuger sees as expressions of respect for the "communal bonds of truth and community," for instance, are what Goldberg calls "calling out the law," and for him this activity, rather than standing in need of some nonpersecutory performance, actually is itself a form of persecution.[10]

Goldberg makes this point in part by stressing the extent to which the law does not have to assume a "sovereign repressive" (91) form to do its work. His essay begins with the claim that "[i]t is most often the law that fastens on the body of the sodomite and most often its embrace is annihilative. The strictures of sodomy represent the will to make disappear, and absolute repression" (79). But Goldberg is as interested in what does not happen "most often" as he is in this "annihilative" thrust. His essay is in large part devoted to leading us to "recogniz[e] that the model of the sovereign repressive law was not, in fact, the only model to operate in the identification of sodomites, as has hitherto been assumed" (91). This claim takes two forms. On the one hand, certain legal institutions, like the Office of the Night in quattrocento Florence, operated, at least on Goldberg's account, more along the model of Foucault's "governmentality" (95) than the model of the "singular" "sovereignty of the law" (95). On the other hand, legal institutions, no matter what model on which they might operate, can never count as the entirety of the domain of the social. Goldberg insists upon the possibility of social behavior beyond, not within and not against, the law; and he imagines that attentiveness to such behavior will lead us to view the historical in an entirely new light. In the place of a historical practice that might simply reproduce the law's "annihilative" thrust by imagining that the totality of social experience could be abstracted in legal categories, he seeks a way, as he puts the point by way of Jacques Ranciere, "to capture the possibilities that still inhere in history, rather than to freeze history into a determinative narrative, tethered wherever it may be" (87) or "to open[] history and leave[] history open" (87).

Calling men to charity requires that we subject their behavior to norms of civil decency; opening history requires that we search for behavior wholly alien to such norms. In *Solon and Thespis* this historical practice finds its most powerful, and its most unexpected, articulation in Paul Cantor's examination of the free-market principles operating in Jonson's drama. Cantor seems as opposed to left-wing pathos as Goldberg is enraptured by it, but he shares Goldberg's radical legal skepticism—the sense that the law is merely a form of power like any other ("Far from providing an alternative to the venality of the market, the law seems to operate according to the same principles"), and shares with him the sense that its imposition of external norms might profitably be replaced by organic developments within social formations ("not by regulations imposed from above by an outside authority but by self-regulating principles generated from within"). Of course, the basis for the "new futures" that interest Cantor is "the market," not the sexualized body; and this difference might seem to matter a great deal. The "self-regulating principles" that interest Cantor are precisely what constitute the ground for the annihilative homophobic activity against which Goldberg means to position himself—both in the sense of constituting a reason for the oppression and in the sense of making the oppression look like something other than oppression. The category of "natural human desires" on which Cantor wants the state to rely for its more organic rules is the same category Goldberg thinks the state has deployed in its imposition of "regulations . . . from above by an outside authority." But the difference here is perhaps less stark than it first appears. Though Goldberg might have reservations about the very term *natural*, his alternative to the law also ultimately relies on something like "human desire" in its unregulated mode; it relies, that is, on human desire before it has been "translat[ed]" (83) into the state's "spheres of . . . discursivity" (83).

At this point, we would seem to have moved far afield from the more quotidian legal world of Dubrow. Figures like Cantor and Goldberg are more concerned with specifying what it means that we have laws than unpacking what the various laws we have had might mean. Whether a stance so external to the actual operations of the law can provide much in the way of an account of the meaning of the law has itself been a fairly controversial issue in recent accounts of the relationship between law and literature. If literary critics are more likely to care about the law as such than its internal dynamics, are they all that likely to tell legal scholars anything about the law they might find interesting? Ronald Dworkin thinks not. Acknowledging that some have argued that "[a] proper understanding of law as a social phenomenon demands . . . a more scientific or sociological or historical approach that pays no or little attention to jurisprudential puzzles over the correct characterization of legal argument" (12), he nonetheless insists that "[t]heories that ignore the structure of legal argument for supposedly larger questions of history and society" are "perverse" because "they ignore questions about the internal character of legal argument" (14). But it is not entirely clear that the "internal character of legal argument" is wholly absent or invisible in arguments in literature's broader relationship to legal discourse. Indeed, it seems to me that, far from obscuring the structure that gives legal argument its complicated and complicated "internal character," these arguments actually present that character in a highly legible form.

We can begin to register the force of this point by noting that Cantor does not just happen to take up an external stance in relation to the law: he is instead *committed* to such an external stance, committed to dwelling, insofar as it is possible, in a place to which it will be hard to "call out the law." Cantor calls this place the "free market," and he locates its coordinates in literature, whose cognitive structure perfectly approximates the paradoxical legal premises of the market ("the play obeys Jonson's cherished law of the unities, while appearing to be wholly free and above and beyond any formal law"). Where Shuger invokes the law to tame literature's antisocial powers, Cantor instead joins figures like Nussbaum in imagining that literature might serve as a model for justice, a model that the law ignores at its peril. But is this domain he associates with literature entirely "beyond" or "outside" or even different from the legal world to which he opposes it? Cantor essentially concurs with Lear's thinking about the "great image of authority": in his hands the law is nothing more than the repressive acts of an agent authorized to engage in repression. But we may well wonder, as both Hart and Dworkin wonder and as Lear makes us wonder, how such an agent receives such authority. And if we think about the law as a formal structure that requires that such an agent have *some* authority (Hart) and imagine that a formal structure, as such, might not ever count as an adequate ground for his or her authority (Dworkin), we may quickly find ourselves locating the concerns Cantor places in literature in the midst of the law, indeed, at the very core of the law's legality.

Here Goldberg's account of the law as being defined by a "will" to "make" certain things "disappear" becomes suggestive (79). On the face of it, of course, this is a highly unusual account of what the law does. We might think of the law as establishing a set of norms, of encouraging certain conduct, or of seeking to abolish certain activities. It is hard to see, though, how any of these projects is exactly the project of making something disappear (which would seem to entail that the thing or activity exist—as Goldberg puts it, "the phenomenon of sex with women was known" [80]—and that it be concealed). It is hard to see, that is, exactly why making things disappear would count as a value that anyone would want to use the law to achieve. But it is possible to see why the law itself, as a regime of social control and knowledge, might seek to make things disappear. For "phenomena" like the "phenomenon of sex between women," at least as someone like Goldberg would have it, constantly undermine the law's capacity to present itself as what Traub calls the "arbiter of social fact" (87). They mark the extent to which the law must "allow to appear or attempt to deny" (90) practices whose meaning and content lies outside its regime rather than deploying its "productive ability" to generate, prohibit, or regulate such practices. The problem here, though, is that in the passage I just cited Goldberg actually argues that the law does have something on the order of this "productive ability" insofar as we should be wary of the idea of a "preexistent sexuality" (90) beyond it. The law, that is, stands both as the ultimate "arbiter" of social fact and as something whose "productive ability" must be stifled by the radical historiographer.

In summoning this tension between the law's positivist and substantive interests, Goldberg is rehearsing one of the oldest difficulties in the history of legal philosophy, a difficulty on spectacular display in an essay that plays a prominent, if somewhat implicit, role in the legal theory underwriting *Shakespeare's Hand* as well as many of the essays in *Solon and Thespis*: Foucault's "Governmentality."[11] On Foucault's account, sovereignty is essentially a self-reflective operation, a project of the law's repeatedly establishing itself as the law. The "end of sovereignty," he insists, "is internal to itself and possesses its own intrinsic instruments in the shape of its laws" (95), by which he means that "what characterizes the end of sovereignty ... is in sum nothing other than submission to sovereignty" (95). And consequently "the end of sovereignty is circular: the end of sovereignty is the exercise of sovereignty" (95). This would seem to be the world of Goldberg's "make disappear" regime. But just as Goldberg's law does something other than simply operate, just as it operates for and is authorized to operate by a purpose, so too does Foucault's sovereignty ultimately look less circular than his most categorical claims might suggest. The point becomes clear in his comments about Machiavelli, who stands in "Governmentality" as the preeminent theorist of the sovereign:

> For Machiavelli, it was alleged, the prince stood in a relation of singularity and externality, and thus of transcendence, to his principality. The prince acquires his principality by inheritance or conquest, but in any case he does not form part of it, he remains external to it. The link that binds him to his principality may have been established through violence, through family heritage or by treaty, with the complicity or the alliance of other princes;

this makes no difference, the link in any event remains a purely synthetic one and there is fundamental, essential, natural and juridical connection between the prince and his principality.... [This] principle and its corollary [that because his subjects "have no *a priori* reason to accept his rule" the prince's control of them is "fragile" and "continually under threat"] lead to a conclusion, deduced as an imperative: that the objective of the exercise of power is to reinforce, strengthen, and protect the principality, but with this last understood to mean not the objective ensemble of its subjects and the territory, but rather the prince's relationship with what he owns, with the territory he has inherited or acquired, and with his subjects. (90)

This passage's immense complexity flows from the ambiguity surrounding Foucault's claim that the sovereign prince's chief "objective" is to "protect the principality," a phrase that certainly on its face would seem to suggest precisely the opposite of what Foucault wants to suggest by it. What he means by "principality," of course, is the prince's *hold* on the principality, not the realm's actual conditions. But the phrase "reinforce, strengthen, and protect the principality" certainly strongly hints at, if it does not out and out refer to, something else— namely the welfare of the civic entity the prince controls (or what Foucault calls "the objective ensemble of its subjects and the territory"): the prince is not present, even in the form of a possessive pronoun, in the principality he is given an "imperative" to protect. Foucault himself is obviously aware of the difficulty, for immediately after producing the phrase he feels a need to define it, to remove it from the set of associations with which it initially arrives. And these associations do not merely have the effect of undoing, or at least compromising, the claim Foucault wishes to make about the nature of the prince's actions. They also have the effect of undoing the claims Foucault makes about the nature of the prince's relationship to the "principality." For the moment in which his hold on the principality and the status of the "objective ensemble of its subjects and its territory" are aligned it becomes harder to imagine that the prince's relationship to the principality is so casual as Foucault makes it. The principality begins to look as if it belongs to the prince only so long as he protects it, and thus he begins to look less like a gunman than Hart's Rex, less like a person whose authority is "external" to the realm he controls than a person who is "linked" to the principality by a set of protocols to which he is a subject rather than a "transcendent" author.

We might be inclined to write off the rhetorical effects of Foucault's formulation here as mere rhetorical effects but for the way in which they are echoed in the trajectory of the essay as a whole. The tendency of Foucault's account of the sovereign to turn into an account of something slightly less self-absorbed than the sovereign is mirrored by the way in which the basic distinction around which "Governmentality" is organized repeatedly crumbles in Foucault's elaboration of it. That distinction is between sovereignty and governmentality, and it is grounded in the notion that, while sovereignty entails merely the maintenance of the sovereign as the source of authority, governmentality entails the proper organization of the "ensemble of [the] subjects and the territory" that constitute the state. But just as sovereignty is implicitly aligned with governmentality in Foucault's efforts to define it, so too does governmentality seem to take on sovereignty's form as Foucault begins to present it: "'[G]overnment is the right disposition of things, arranged so as to lead to a convenient end.' Government, that is to say, has a finality of its own. ... With government it is a question not of imposing laws on men, but of disposing things: that is to say, of employing tactics rather than laws, and even using laws themselves as tactics—to arrange things in such a way that, through a certain number of means, such and such ends may be achieved" (94–95).

"Convenience," of course, feels a lot like Foucault's gloss on "principality"; indeed, it looks more like a plausible concern for the wholly self-serving prince than the allegedly outwardly driven governor. And, along these same lines, it is strange that Foucault describes the seemingly end-driven government in terms of its having a "finality of its own"—again seemingly a more plausible account of the circular authority to which governmentality would be opposed than its putative vectored authority. These two equivocations prepare us for the final, and in some sense definitive, equivocation in the passage: the moment in which Foucault imagines that the governor might "use laws themselves as tactics." In "using laws themselves as tactics" how does the governor differ at all from his princely brother, who relates to the law only in terms of the tactical maintenance of his authority? The question would seem to be about what ends they seek with laws, not whether they seek them in the first place (a point that Foucault more or less admits slightly later on when he allows that if "[g]overnment ... has a finality of its own," the "the state ... has its own proper form of rationality" [97], albeit one of "a different sort" [97]); and, as we have already seen, the ends of the prince do not necessarily look all that different from the ends of the governor. What is interesting here is the way in which Foucault both opposes laws to "tactics" and makes laws a kind of tactic—or, to put it slightly differently, the way in which he both undermines the legality of the idea of law (in imagining that the law might merely be a tactic, be it either the governor's or the prince's—call this the Lear position) and persists in thinking that that legality is an essential feature of the law (in imagining that laws must transcend tactics—call this the Hart position).

Part of the interest in essays like Cantor's and Shuger's lies in their capacity to account for the ways in which Foucault's categories collapse into one another in "Governmentality." Their essays reveal the extent to which the governmental and the sovereign are actually two separate, and necessary, features of the law, the ways in which each category refers to a domain from which any act must proceed for it to be called the act of what Hart would call a "legislator." In this regard, they stand as a powerful, if unstated, gloss on what might be the central text in the history of Anglo-American jurisprudence, Blackstone's *Commentaries on the Common Law of England* (1765–69),[12] the text in which the legal puzzles opened up in Lear's claims about "authority" find their most rigorous exposition. Unlike Machiavelli, Blackstone is not interested in openly elaborating the grounds on which the law can retain its authority, but his account of the nature of that authority would seem, on its face at least, to be every bit as circular as Foucault suggests an account of legal sovereignty would be. He often seems to suggest that the law's authority lies merely in its status as law, in its being, as he might term it, "old law" (70). As Bentham explained in *A Fragment on Government* (1776), his critique of the *Commentaries,* Blackstone "will not suffer any one so as to imagine, that an old-established law could in any respect be a fit object of condemnation."[13] But even if Blackstone frequently makes the law's status as the law its only source of authority, he also suggests that the law has this authority in part because it is equal to any of the kinds of challenge Bentham might launch against it. This point emerges in Blackstone's account of how a judge might deal with a law worthy of such an attack. After explaining that the judge is bound to decide cases "not according to his own private judgment, but according to the known laws and customs of the land" (69), and that he is "not delegated to pronounce a new law, but to maintain and expound the old one" (69), Blackstone acknowledges that "this rule admits of exception" (69). The exception occurs "where the former determination [of what the old law is] is most evidently contrary to reason. But even in such cases the judges do not pretend to make new law, but to vindicate the old one from misrepresentation. For if it be found that the former decision is manifestly absurd or unjust, it is declared, not that such a sentence was *bad law,* but that it was *not law*" (70).

On this account, the law is good in principle. We cannot determine that a law is "absurd" or "unjust"; we can only determine that it is not law at all. To give a description of the law, then, is in some sense to give an apology for it, for as long as something counts as law it will also count as good law. And from this perspective Bentham's attack on Blackstone seems slightly misplaced. It is not as though Blackstone refused to allow any criticism of legal doctrine (we can still call some "sentences" "absurd" or "unjust"). But insofar as that criticism counts as just and fair criticism it cannot count as criticism of the law; it must instead count as a criticism of a doctrine for failing to be the law. "And hence it is," Blackstone concludes, "that our lawyers are with justice so copious in their enconiums on the reason of the common law; that they tell us, that the law is the perfection of reason, that it always intends to conform thereto, and that what is not reason is not law" (70). The law is not the perfection of reason so much in practice as in principle. That which "is not reason is not law" here not because all things called law in England are reasonable but because the common law is itself a principle of reasonableness. This is a circular universe, but its circularity does not preclude something like Foucault's account of "convenience" (of which, of course, Bentham was a leading theorist); it actually entails it. The world outside the law is rendered a necessary component of what the law is.

At this moment, though, the law does not simply *become* a commitment to the convenient. Were it to do so, of course, we would simply be in the world of governmentality, a world in which legal agents, rather than enacting laws, simply made the world a better place. Blackstone is committed to the idea that the law makes the world a better place, but he never allows that such an endeavor is the only requirement of it. His legal agents are always princes as much as governors. As remarkable as it might be that the law would be said to be good in principle, it is equally remarkable that it would be said to be old in principle. But this is precisely what Blackstone insists. Judges not only cannot make a bad law; they also cannot make a new one. Each new law will always be redescribed as "an old one" "vindicated" from "misrepresentation" by the very act that seems to produce it. And while this redescription in and of itself may not seem all that bizarre, it is slightly more bizarre to think that a judge could at one and the same time replace one legal custom (the bad nonlaw) with another (the good old law) and insist that the new custom stand, as Blackstone puts it, as "the established custom of the realm" (70). What is bizarre about this cycle, of course, is that insofar as the judge is discarding an old nonlaw, it would seem as though nothing more than his decision itself would "establish" the new custom as a custom. It could not have been in place, except in some highly theoretical way, prior to his decision.

Blackstone insists upon the importance of this highly theoretical realm, though, and he insists upon it largely because, as Hart's idea of the rule has already shown us, an essential feature of the law (a feature as essential to the law as its inherent and necessary goodness) is that it can never be said to be established by any particular agent. The remarks I have been tracking emerge in the context of a general discussion of the relationship between judges and law. Just a page before, Blackstone had raised the question "How are the[] customs and maxims" that make up the common law "to be known, and by whom is their validity determined?" (69). There is at least one easy answer to this question, of course, and Blackstone hits on it right away: "The answer is, by the judges in the several courts of justice" (69). But as judges become "the depositary of the laws; the living oracles" (69) and as "their judicial decisions" become "the principal and most authoritative evidence, that can be given, of the existence of such a custom as shall form part of the common law" (69), it begins to seem possible that we might think of the judges themselves, rather than custom and historical practice, as the origin of the law. Insofar, that is, as the chief value of the common law seems to lie in the way in which it "depends on custom" (74), the fact that it depends so much on judges might come look like a problem. To put the point in Hart's terms, we might have acts of force without rules of recognition. And as a result, no sooner does Blackstone raise the possibility that judges might stand as the "depositary of the laws," than he deposits the real authority of the law elsewhere, in those precedents ("known laws and customs of the land" [69]) that generate judicial decisions. And he is not content merely to say that these precedents *should* generate judicial decisions. He ultimately argues that they *must* do so, that any change in the law should actually count as a rediscovery of an "old one" rather than the production of a new one.

Hence, while the sequence begins by imagining that judges' opinions would count as the law, it ends by specifically separating off the law from what judges say: "So that *the law*, and the *opinion of the judge* are not always convertible terms, or one and the same thing; since it sometimes may happen that the judge may *mistake* the law" (71). In making it possible for the judge to "mistake the law," we might say, Blackstone makes it impossible for the judge to make any other mistake. For as the relevant question becomes the question of the relationship between the judge's judgment and what the law is, it becomes impossible to think of the judge as making a mistake about what the law *should* be. Blackstone's commitment to the oldness of the law, as it were, is ultimately a commitment to the idea that judges can only do interpretive work, to the idea that they "represent" the law but do not make it. To cast the point in the terms of this volume, judges will always count both as actors (repeating lines already written) and as persons (saying what they think is justice). The law's empire is a space in which persons can, and indeed must, perform both of these activities simultaneously. It is a space, to put the point in terms of the passage from *King Lear* with which I began, in which each act of authority will require an image of authority.

Judges are ultimately no different from any other legal actors in this scheme. The opening pages of the *Commentaries* are in some senses nothing more than an extended series of bait and switch maneuvers, in which a potential source of law is presented (what we might call Rex) and withdrawn (on behalf of the rule of recognition that gives Rex II the same authority). After the judges come the members of Parliament, who, though Blackstone "know[s] of no power which can control" them (91), nonetheless act less as the generators of the law than its analysts. They may be the "makers ... of English law" (9) but they are also its "interpreters" (9), and indeed they are ultimately more its interpreters than its makers. Their principal obligation is always to the "law itself" rather than the people they represent. "Statutes," Blackstone explains, "... are either *declaratory* of the common law, or *remedial* of some defects therein" (86): the object of legislative attention here will always be the law itself; the legislature will either declare what the law has always been or will remedy it. What it will not do is address the social as such, remedy a social problem.

It might make sense, of course, to immerse judges and legislators in the law, but Blackstone goes so far as to immerse even God himself within it. His accounts of God's supreme authority ultimately make God look as much like a judge or legislator as the creator of the law:

> Thus when the supreme being formed the universe, and created matter out of nothing, he impressed certain principles upon that matter, from which it can never depart, and without which it would cease to be. When he put that matter into motion, he established certain laws of motion, to which all movable bodies must conform. And, to descend from the greatest operations to the smallest, when a workman forms a clock, or other piece of mechanism, he establishes at his own pleasure certain arbitrary laws for its direction; as that the hand shall describe a given space in a given time; to which law as long as the work conforms, so long it continues in perfection, and answers the end of its formation. (38)

The mark of the supreme being's supremacy, on this account, is that his "arbitrary" whim becomes the necessary law of those dependent upon him. But it is odd to think of the watchmaker's relationship to his clock in exactly the same terms of God's relationship to the world. For while it may be the case that, like God, this "workman" "can establish" some of the relevant laws for his "watch" "at his own pleasure," the watch would seem always to be bound to another set of forces wholly outside the workman's control. The watch does not produce time, after all; it represents it. The workman here is as obliged by the object of his labor as that object is obliged by him. His supremacy is only partial.

But if this limitation on his authority would seem initially to mark his distance from the supreme being to which he is analogized, it ultimately stands as the way in which he is most like him. For it turns out that not even God has the authority to make a law that Blackstone will honor: "Considering the Creator only as a being of infinite *power*, he was able unquestionably to have prescribed whatever laws he pleased to his creature, man, however unjust or severe. But as he is also a being of infinite *wisdom*, he has laid down such laws as were founded in those relations of justice, that existed in the nature of things antecedent to any positive precept. These are the eternal, immutable laws of good and evil, to which to the creator himself in all his dispensations conforms" (40). Here we can witness a stunning emergence of a set of criteria by which God himself will be judged (fortunately he is wise enough to pass that test). From the perspective of God's "infinite power," we might imagine that justice would be nothing more than what he said it was. We might imagine, that is, that his infinite power entails the capacity to declare what is just. But Blackstone will allow nothing that kind of power. And while the results are somewhat baffling (it is hard to see exactly how there was "a nature of things" independent of the supreme being's will prior to the creation), they at least have the effect of ensuring that the law will not be, to return to the passage about the watch, "arbitrary." All laws, in the end, will be bound by something other than a particular agent's assertion. Each law Blackstone honors will have as its basis another law, not an act of sovereignty. Even God's laws must be old laws.

From this perspective, at every phase of its elaboration the law is always both substantive and formal. Each interpretation of the law is creation of it; each creation of it is an interpretation of it. The law is grounded in moral virtue, but it is also grounded in formal authority. It entails the deployment of force and involves only the application of a rule. Its categories produce values in the world, but they also respond to them. The law will always have its literary side—its side that is not governed by force and rules—but this side will always be only one of its sides. The perversity of the law lies in the way that a proper analysis of it entails an analysis of what seems to be exterior to it. Judith Butler suggests that the sources of the law's "historical variability and possibility" (66) might actually lie within the law: "If subversion is possible," she claims, "it will be subversion from within the law, through the possibilities that emerge when the law turns against itself and spawns unexpected permutations of itself" (93).[14] Blackstone helps us see the way in which the law will always "maintain," as Butler puts it, an "'outside' within itself" (106). But he also helps us see that the law's hybridity is not exactly a source of its subversion; it is instead the nature of its operation. "[U]nexpected permutations" are the method of the law's development, not an alternative to its regular workings. This is not to say that some "permutations" will not *look* subversive; obviously some will (Dubrow, for instance, is interested in some of these permutations). It is only to say that, at least from Blackstone's perspective, they will not actually *be* subversive: all of the laws will still be good and they will still be old.

"The law wishes to have a formal existence," insists Stanley Fish.[15] "This means, first of all that the law does not wish to be absorbed by, or declared subordinate to, some other—nonlegal—structure of concern; the law wishes, in a word, to be distinct" (141). But, from the perspective we can see emerging in this collection, the law does not "wish" to have a "formal existence" so much as it *must* have one. The claims of law require a particular kind of structure, one that entails Hart's rules as well as Fish's force. To put this point this way, though, is not to claim that the law has *only* a formal existence. For the law's formality must always be grounded in something that seems to transcend it. "Morality is something to which the law wishes to be related, but not too closely," Fish claims (141). Just as it is misleading to say that the law "wishes" to have a formal existence, so too is it misleading to say that it "wishes" to be "related" to something like morality. Instead, it must be related to something like it, and indeed "related" is not exactly the right word here (nor spatial imagery the right imagery), for the law is not required to be "close" to morality so much as it is partially composed of it. This, again, is not to say that the law is reducible to morality. Just as the law's formality does not require that the law be wholly formal, so too does the law's morality not require that it be wholly moral. The law is not reducible to morality, and not because such a reduction, as Fish puts it, would make the law "superfluous" (142), but rather because such a reduction compromises the formality that is necessarily implicit in any specifically legal claim we might make. In terms of our reading of Blackstone, the law will always be grounded both in the positivist systematicity of strong precedents and in the ethical liberation of moral command.

Acknowledging that the law is built around this duality has proved an enormously difficult task for legal theorists. Even those who come closest to accepting this insight frequently ultimately abandon it. Dworkin, for instance, produces an elaborate account of the duality; but, strangely, he casts this account as a lesson about how the law should work rather than a description of how, so long as it would remain law, it must work. He thinks that judges and other legal actors need to recognize the law's duality. But it would make more sense to say that by virtue of their operating in a legal system they have necessarily recognized it and have committed themselves to operating within the law's two orders. Fish gets this point. In *Doing What Comes Naturally: Change, Rhetoric, and the Practice of Theory in Literary and Legal Studies*, he argues that "[a]s an account of what legal actors do, 'law as persuasion' is powerful and persuasive; lawyers and judges do, in fact, see the law as 'structured by a set of coherent principles' which they feel obliged to take into account and extend. But, precisely because this is what they already do by virtue of their being judges and lawyers, it is pointless to enjoin them to do it" (368).[16]

But in his own accounts of what judges do Fish manages always to produce a setup in which such advice would not be pointless (or at least would not be pointless because it was already being followed). For though Fish sometimes claims that legal actors are "always in a forum of principle" (*Doing What Comes Naturally*, 369), he more frequently claims—especially in the works he has produced since his initial exchanges with Dworkin—that principle is precisely what the "forums" legal actors inhabit preclude. The point emerges most graphically in the moments when he claims that we should understand Dworkin as "a rhetorician rather than a theorist" (*Doing What Comes Naturally*, 390), a move that seems to gives Dworkin's work precisely the normative power Fish had once seemed eager to deny it. To be sure, Fish still does not think that Dworkin is giving the kind of advice he thinks that he is giving (Fish says that Dworkin explains how to justify decisions reached outside "forums of principle" rather than explaining that we should proceed within them). But Dworkin's argument nonetheless does become a kind of advice, and it becomes a kind of advice because Fish has, in effect, siphoned both the law's formalism and its morality from its force. He has made the legal activities of the law seem unrelated to its actual practice: Judges "know perfectly well what they are doing" when they write opinions. "They are engaging in the practice of self-presentation, that is, the practice of offering a persuasive account of why they have done what they have done—decide the case this way rather than that—which is not the same thing (why on earth should it be?) as offering an account of how they did it" (389). Here what Dworkin calls "law as persuasion" and what Blackstone calls "law" is not what judges and lawyers "already do by virtue of their being judges and lawyers"; it is what they say (or should say) that they have done. Blackstone's judge has become Lear's dog.

Both Dworkin and Fish confront a composite law; and they both render that composite law pure—Dworkin in the form of the judge who might follow only one of the law's two commands (might implement only old or good law), Fish in the form of a judge who simply issues commands rather than following them. The law's hybridity emerges far more clearly in *Solon and Thespis*, where the law emerges as both immensely rigid and miraculously supple. From the perspective I have been elaborating, the law will always be both too rigid (insofar as it retains a formal element, its interests will never be as supple as the ethical claims and social practices to which it responds), and too flexible (insofar as it is not simply its formal element, it will always be subject to the shaping influences of matters— social practice, ethical argument—that seem somewhat alien to it). The juxtaposition of these two claims emerges with admirable clarity in Cantor's essay:

> Jonson's criticism of the law is double-edged. On the one hand, the law appears to be too rigid; . . . But on the other hand, the law appears to be too flexible and arbitrary. . . . Ultimately in Jonson's portrayal the problem with the law is mindless legalism. The law tries to codify the fluidity of life into binding rules, but . . . once a legal document is written down, it can all too easily be rewritten and hence become fluid itself. As Jonson presents it, the law seems to alternate between defining the terms of human life too tightly and defining them too loosely. In either case, the law gives some human beings despotic power over others.

It might seem odd to claim that the problem with the law is its legalism—and if the problem with the law is its *mindless* legalism we might wonder why the problem lay in the law rather than the mindlessness around it. It is equally unclear, moreover, what Cantor means in his account of the law's providing some people with "despotic" power over others. Following Hart, we might well wonder how any power could avoid the tinge of despotism *without* the authority of the law. But the point here is not that Jonson's criticism of the law might need the idea of the law in order to proceed. It is instead that Jonson's criticism of the law is ultimately less a criticism of the law than an account of it, an account of not only its structural dependence upon both flexibility (which, from the other side, is simply its capacity to be arbitrary) and formality (which, from the other side, is simply its refusal to recognize any terms but its own) but also its functional dependence upon force (the law must be executed, which, from the other side, will mean that the law is necessarily tyrannical). And this is why it makes sense for Cantor to suggest that the "problem with the law" is its legalism; the problem with the law here is what it is. What I have tried to show is that this "problem with the law" is also, in Dworkin's terms, the "law's integrity" and that in their efforts to specify the "problem" the essays in this volume also, and necessarily, illuminate the "integrity." They reveal the ways in which it makes sense for one volume to have accounts of the law that locate it at the center of the human world (Greenfield and Shuger) sitting side by side with essays that locate it at the center of that world's "disappearance" (Cantor). The law's power, and the law's interest, lie precisely in the fact that it will always, and simultaneously, play both of these roles.

NOTES

1. All references to H. L. Hart, *The Concept of Law* (1961; Oxford: Oxford University Press, 1994), will appear in parentheses in the body of my essay.

2. All references to Ronald Dworkin, *Law's Empire* (Cambridge, MA: Harvard University Press, 1985), will appear in parentheses in the body of my essay.

3. I should acknowledge at the outset that I have no illusions that I have presented a complete account of this context. Such an account would address a great many figures who will remain aloof from these pages, figures like John Austin, Oliver Wendell Holmes, Roscoe Pound, Lon Fuller, Joseph Raz, Roberto Unger, and so forth. I mean only to present an account of one line along which this inquiry has developed, a line that is, I think, meaningfully illuminated by the essays in this volume.

4. Barbara Johnson, "Anthropomorphism in Lyric and Law," *Yale Journal of Law and the Humanities* 10 (1999): 549.

5. Shoshana Felman, "Forms of Judicial Blindness, or the Evidence of What Cannot Be Seen: Traumatic Narratives and Legal Repetitions in the O. J. Simpson Case and in Tolstoy's *The Kreutzer Sonata*," *Critical Inquiry* 23 (1997): 739.

6. Martha Nussbaum, *Poetic Justice: The Literary Imagination and Public Life* (Boston: Beacon, 1995).

7. Wai Chee Dimock, *Residues of Justice: Literature, Law, Philosophy* (Berkeley: University of California Press, 1996).

8. Brook Thomas, "*China Men, United States v. Wong Kim Ark*, and the Question of Citizenship," *American Quarterly* 50 (1998): 691.

9. As Robert Post, on whose work Shuger explicitly relies in developing her notion of the morality of language, has pointed out, even the protection of individual expressive rights ultimately entails the establishment of norms of behavior and license. "In the end," he explains, "there can be no final account of the boundaries of the domain of public discourse," by which he means that any set of relating to what he calls "public discourse" will "hegemonically establish[] authoritative cultural standards upon which persons can rely"

(Robert Post, *Constitutional Domains: Democracy, Community, Management* [Cambridge, MA: Harvard University Press, 1995], 177, 163).

10. All references to Jonathan Goldberg, "Calling Out the Law," in *Shakespeare's Hand* (Minneapolis: University of Minnesota Press, 2003), will appear in parentheses in the body of my essay.

11. All references to Michel Foucault, "Governmentality," in *The Foucault Effect: Studies in Governmentality*, ed. Graham Burchell, Colin Gordon, and Peter Miller (Chicago: University of Chicago Press, 1991), will appear in parentheses in the body of my essay.

12. All references to William Blackstone, *Commentaries on the Laws of England*, 4 vols. (1765–69; reprint, Chicago: University of Chicago Press, 1991), will be to the first volume and will appear in parentheses in the body of my essay.

13. Jeremy Bentham, *A Fragment on Government* (1776; reprint, Cambridge: Cambridge University Press, 1990), 9–10.

14. All references to Judith Butler, *Gender Trouble: Feminism and the Subversion of Identity* (New York: Routledge, 1990), will appear in parentheses in the body of my essay.

15. All references to Stanley Fish, "The Law Wishes to Have a Formal Existence," in *There's No Such Thing as Free Speech, and It's a Good Thing Too* (New York: Oxford University Press, 1994), will appear in parentheses in the body of my essay.

16. All references to Stanley Fish, *Doing What Comes Naturally: Change, Rhetoric, and the Practice of Theory in Literary and Legal Studies* (Durham: Duke University Press, 1989), will appear in parentheses in the body of my essay.

Contributors

PAUL CANTOR is Clifton Waller Barrett Professor of English at the University of Virginia. He is the author of *Shakespeare's Rome: Republic and Empire* and the *Hamlet* volume in the Cambridge Landmarks of World Literature series.

KAREN J. CUNNINGHAM, lecturer in Early English Literature at the University of California, Los Angeles, is the author of *Imaginary Betrayals: Subjectivity and the Discourses of Treason in Early Modern England* (2002) and coeditor of *The Law in Shakespeare* (2006). Her essays on Shakespeare, Marlowe, and early modern women have appeared in *PMLA, Shakespeare Quarterly, Renaissance Drama, Journal of Medieval and Renaissance Studies,* and elsewhere. Her current project is a book on women and law in Shakespeare.

HEATHER DUBROW, John Bascom Professor and Tighe-Evans Professor at the University of Wisconsin-Madison, is the author of five books on early modern literature and culture, most recently, *Shakespeare and Domestic Loss: Forms of Deprivation, Mourning, and Recuperation*. She has also just finished a book on lyric. Her other publications include two chapbooks of poetry and numerous articles on teaching.

ERNEST B. GILMAN is professor of English at New York University. He is the author of three books on Renaissance literary and visual culture, the most recent of which is *Recollecting the Arundel Circle*. He is currently completing a book on the literature of the plague in seventeenth-century England.

Contributors

MATTHEW GREENFIELD is associate professor of English at the City University of New York's College of Staten Island. With Jennifer Morrison, he coedited *Edmund Spenser: Essays on Culture and Allegory*, and his essays have appeared in several anthologies and in *Raritan*, *PMLA*, *Shakespeare Quarterly*, and *English Literary Renaissance*. He is completing a book on late Elizabethan satire.

DENNIS KEZAR is associate professor of English at Vanderbilt University. He is the author of *Guilty Creatures: Renaissance Poetry and the Ethics of Authorship*, and his essays on Shakespeare and Milton have appeared in *Critical Inquiry*, *ELH*, *Modern Language Quarterly*, and elsewhere. He is currently working on a book-length study of the conceptualization of addiction in the early modern period.

DEAK NABERS is assistant professor of English at Brown University and the author of *Victory of Law: The Fourteenth Amendment, the Civil War, and American Literature, 1852–1866*.

DEBORA SHUGER is professor of English at the University of California, Los Angeles. She is the author of *Censorship and Cultural Sensibility* (2006), *Political Theologies* (2001), *The Renaissance Bible* (1994), *Habits of Thought in the English Renaissance* (1990), and *Sacred Rhetoric* (1988), as well as articles on Spenser, Milton, Shakespeare, Sidney, Hooker, Jonson, et alia.

FRANCES TEAGUE is Josiah Meigs Professor of English at the University of Georgia. She has published several books and many articles on Renaissance drama, including *The Curious History of "Bartholomew Fair"* and *Shakespeare's Speaking Properties*; with John Velz, she edited the Crosby letters in *One Touch of Shakespeare*. Her book *Shakespeare and the American Popular Stage* is forthcoming from Cambridge. Her work on early women writers includes a biography, *Bathsua Makin, Woman of Learning*.

LUKE WILSON is associate professor of English at the Ohio State University. He is author of *Theaters of Intention: Drama and the Law in Early Modern England* (2000), and has published on a variety of literary and legal topics in *Representations*, *ELH*, *Renaissance Drama*, *Cardozo Studies in Law and Literature*, and elsewhere.

Index

Abercrombie, M. L. J., 202
Achinstein, Sharon, 193n56
Adelman, Janet, 152n7
Alexander, Sir William, 241
Altman, Joel, 215n5
antitheatricalism, 1, 10, 11
Austin, John, 287n3

Bacon, Francis, 24, 175, 199, 200, 218–65
bail, 231
Baker, J. H., 197, 230
Bakhtin, Mikail, 15n16
Barish, Jonas, 1, 3, 63n43, 89, 97n19
Barton, Anne, 35n2, 75n8
Bednarz, James, 35n2
Bellany, Alastair, 170, 192n34
Bentham, Jeremy, 279
Berger, Harry, 136, 153n13, 156n35
Blackstone, William, 265, 279–85, 288n12
Bourdieu, Pierre, 255n7
Bowen, Catherine Drinker, 260n58
Braunmuller, A. R., 192n43, 262n86
bribery, 219–65
Butler, Judith, 277–83, 288n14

Calvin, John, 208
Cantor, Paul, 10, 13, 274–75, 286

censorship, 10, 163–96, 272–74
Chapman, George, 218–65
charity, 179, 180–90, 247, 273
Charles I, 125, 151n1, 173, 185
Civil War, 113, 163–64, 174–90
Clark, Glenn, 206
Coke, Sir Edward, 23, 70, 175–78, 218–19, 224
Colie, Rosalie L., 89, 97n20, 98n28
Collinson, Patrick, 166, 190n13
colonialism, 99–123
contracts, 221–65
court of wards, 222
Cunningham, Karen J., 8, 11, 12

Daniel, Samuel, 178–79
Danson, Lawrence, 36n2
Davis, Natalie Zemon, 256n10
Dawson, Anthony, 136, 140–43, 156n32, 160n62
defamation. *See* slander
Dekker, Thomas, 19–39. *See also The Witch of Edmonton*
Delany, Paul, 89
Derrida, Jacques, 255n7
Dershowitz, Alan, 3, 6, 15nn6, 7
Doctor Faustus. See Marlowe, Christopher

Index

Dollimore, Jonathan, 216n10
Douglas, Mary, 204
Downame, John, 225–26
Dubrow, Heather, 10, 12, 269–71
Dutton, Richard, 36n2, 285–86, 287
Dworkin, Ronald, 7, 274–75

Eliot, T. S., 59n1
Elizabeth I, 197, 198, 209
Elton, William, 98n29
equity, 230–65
ethics, 23–30, 124–60, 223–65, 268, 284

Fawkes, Guy. *See* Gunpowder Plot
Felman, Shoshana, 5, 6, 16n18, 269, 287n5
Fish, Stanley, 81, 284–86
Fletcher, Anthony, 193n51
forgery, 171, 188
formalism, 4, 16n29, 172–78, 244
Foucault, Michel, 196n99, 197, 215, 265, 276, 278, 288n11
free market, 42–63

Gassner, John, 209
genre, 3, 9, 150, 270–72
  allegory, 22
  drama, 4–9
  hybridity, 19–39, 280–86
  lyric, 4–6
  narrative, 4–8
  polyvocality, 5–7, 15n16
  satire, 19–39, 251–65
  tragicomedy, 142–50, 157n41
gift, 221, 240–63
Gilman, Ernest B., 12
Goldberg, Jonathan, 196n103, 273–78
Gorboduc, 198, 200, 209–12, 214
Gray's Inn, 237
Green, Thomas, Andrew, 39n31, 153n14

Greenblatt, Stephen, 75n7, 97n21, 121n5, 125, 126–28, 144, 151n3, 153n12, 159n57, 215n1
Greenfield, Matthew, 6, 10, 270–72
Gunpowder Plot, 11, 65–75

Hamburger, Philip, 190n9
Hart, H. L. A., 266–68, 277, 280, 284
Hawley, William M., 15n10
Hayek, Friedrich, 43, 60nn10, 13
Heinamann, Margot, 171, 192n39, 195n95
Helgerson, Richard, 21
Henry VIII, 83, 197
Herman, Gabriel, 236
Hill, Christopher, 189n1
Hobbes, Thomas, 163–64
Holinshed, Raphael, 181–82
Hooker, Richard, 180–81
Horace, 25–39
Howard, Jean, 196n102
Huntington, John, 263n94
Hutson, Lorna, 7

Ingram, Martin, 194n68
Inns of Court, 197–217
intention, 20–21, 23, 218–63

James I (VI), 105, 106, 112, 131, 155n27, 177, 237–38
Jardine, Lisa, 256n14
Johnson, Barbara, 15n16, 268–69
Jonson, Ben, 8–9, 19–39, 64–80, 286–87
  The Alchemist, 40–43, 65, 68
  Bartholomew Fair, 10, 12, 40–63, 68
  Eastward Ho, 71
  Epicoene, 65, 68
  Every Man in His Humor, 65
  Every Man Out of His Humor, 201
  Poetaster, 71, 185, 270
  Underwood, 75
  Volpone, 9, 40, 42, 43, 64–77, 201

Index

Kahn, Paul, 14n4
Kahn, Victoria, 7, 215n5
Kaplan, Lindsay, 15n10, 35n2

Lake, Peter, 173, 193n52
Lambard, William, 229, 234
land law. *See* property
law
  English common law, 4, 11, 15n10, 40–98, 100–115, 116, 168–90, 190n10, 196n105, 197–217, 223–65, 282
  Roman law, 11, 237–39, 260n57, 261n59
"law and literature," 2–6, 9–10, 264–88
law and theater, 1–12
Levao, Ronald, 154n21
Liu, Alan, 16n29
Loewenstein, Joseph, 35n2

Machiavelli, Nicolo, 184–85, 276
Marcus, Leah, 62n34, 142–43
market economy, 1–3, 13, 40–63
Marlowe, Christopher, 146
Marston, John, 19–39
Marvell, Andrew, 99, 120
Marwili, Jonathan, 260n58
Maus, Katharine Eisaman, 37n13, 153n15
McKeon, Michael, 96n6, 190n4
mens rea, 228
Meron, Theodore, 14n4
metatheater, 13
Middleton, 54, 171. *See also The Witch of Edmonton*
Miles, Rosalind, 35n2
Milton, John, 163–64, 196n108
Montrose, Louis, 16n29, 109, 122, 184
mooting, 201–17
More, Thomas, 173, 231–32
Moretti, Franco, 210

Nabers, Deak, 14
Nalson, John, 188
Nashe, Thomas, 25–39
Nicholas, Barry, 260n57
Noonan, John, 226
Nussbaum, Martha, 3, 5, 6, 272, 287n6

Orgel, Stephen, 108–9, 114, 117
Ornstein, Robert, 262n82
Ovid, 25–39

Patterson, Annabel, 36n7, 189n2, 194n78
Peters, Julie Stone, 14n3
piracy, 172
Poetaster, 6, 27–28
Posner, Richard, 9, 16n28
Post, Robert, 287n9
Privy Council, 11
property, 81–98
Puritanism, 42–43, 50–55, 131, 137, 150, 163–67, 171–90

Rackin, Phyllis, 206, 217n37
Ralegh, Walter, 255
Rawley, William, 255
Roper, William, 231, 259n42

satire. *See* genre
Scot, Reginald, 124
Seneca, 25–26
Shaaber, Matthias, 191n21
Shakespeare
  As You Like It, 87, 199
  Comedy of Errors, 200
  Cymbeline, 87
  Hamlet, 119, 130, 248
  Henry IV, 119
  Henry VI, 110, 126
  King Lear, 12, 81–98, 265–70, 279
  Macbeth, 127–28
  Measure for Measure, 219

Shakespeare (cont.)
    Merchant of Venice, 148
    Midsummer Night's Dream, 129
    Much Ado about Nothing, 199
    Richard II, 7
    Tempest, 12, 87, 99–123, 139
    Winter's Tale, 86, 139
Shuger, Debora, 10, 264, 272–75, 287
Shwarz, Kathryn, 122n23, 152n5
Sidney, Sir Philip, 187
Skura, Meredith, 96n15
slander, 10, 30–34, 128, 163–96
Steggle, Matthew, 35n1
Sullivan, Garrett, 96n5

Tacitus, 173–90
Taylor, Gary, 185
Teague, Frances, 9, 11

Thomas, Brook, 287n8
Thomas, Keith, 226, 257n27
treason, 104–23

von Redden, Sitta, 236

War of Theaters (War of Poets), 6, 19–39
Weber, Max, 49
Webster, John, 219–20, 260n53
White, James Boyd, 7–8, 16n21
Wilson, Arthur, 154n22, 193n59
Wilson, Luke, 11, 36n9
Wilson, Thomas, 213
witchcraft, 104–23, 226–30
The Witch of Edmonton, 12, 13, 124–60
Worden, Blair, 189n2

Ziolkowski, Theodore, 4

www.ingramcontent.com/pod-product-compliance
Lightning Source LLC
Chambersburg PA
CBHW071403300426
44114CB00016B/2164